thinking allowed

thinking
allowed

The Best of Prospect
1995–2005

Edited and introduced by
David Goodhart

Prospect

Atlantic Books
London

First published in 2005 by
Atlantic Books.

Atlantic Books is an imprint of
Grove Atlantic Ltd.

10 9 8 7 6 5 4 3 2 1

A CIP record for this book is
available from the British Library.

ISBN 1 84354 481 4

Printed in Great Britain by
CPD, Ebbw Vale, Wales
Design by Lindsay Nash

Atlantic Books
An imprint of Grove Atlantic Ltd
Ormond House
26–27 Boswell Street
London WC1N 3JZ

The publishers and *Prospect* magazine
gratefully acknowledge permission
to reproduce the following extracts:
"Dominant minorities" by Amy
Chua, from *World on Fire* © Amy
Chua. Reprinted by permission of
Random House. "America's demon
in the cellar" by Anatol Lieven, from
*America Right or Wrong: An Anatomy of
American Nationalism* © Anatol Lieven.
Reprinted by permission of
HarperCollins Publishers. "Afghan in
the dock" by James Fergusson, from
Kandahar Cockney: A Tale of Two Worlds
© James Fergusson. Reprinted by
permission of HarperCollins
Publishers. "Searching for mother" by
Richard Hoggart, from *First and Last
Things* © Richard Hoggart. Reprinted
by permission of, Curtis Brown Ltd.

"After the revolution" by Ernest
Gellner is an edited version of an
essay that first appeared in the
Political Quarterly. "My Germany" by
Jens Reich is an edited version of a
talk delivered as part of the series
"Germany, my Germany" at the
Goethe Institute, London. "England
is a garden" by John Keegan is an
edited version of an essay that first
appeared in the *American Scholar*.

For Derek and Jennifer

Contents

BRITAIN

ARTS & LETTERS

IDEAS & POPULAR SCIENCE

LIFE

Acknowledgements

There are many people to thank, both for this book and for *Prospect* magazine itself. At the top of the list come Derek Coombs and his family. Derek backed us with his money and determination when nobody else believed in the idea. All the directors and the 70-plus investors, big and small, deserve thanks too, in particular Rudi Bogni, Marwan Assaf, Nick Draper, Bob Boas, the late Bob Johnson and the late Hans-Jürgen Schwepcke.

Over the past 10 years many dozens of people have worked at *Prospect* on the editorial and business side—almost all of them have been underpaid and overworked. On the business side special thanks to Charles Seaford, the founder-publisher, Stephen Brown, Hugh MacLeman, Polly Knewstub, Milan Shah, Helen (and Tom) Johnson, Jenny Shramenko, Rhiannon Williams, Andy Hawkins and the current publisher Nicholas Dale-Harris. On the editorial side a special thanks to my two deputies Valerie Monchi (1995 to 2000) and Alex Linklater (2001 to today) and to the current team of Susha Lee-Shothaman (who shares the *Prospect* long-service award with Jenny Shramenko), Tom Nuttall and Ayanna Prevatt-Goldstein. Other editorial stalwarts have included Ravi Mattu, Nadine Wojakovski, Anke Lueddecke and Lucy Roeber. We have been blessed with first-class proofreaders in the late Gay Firth, Annie Henry and our current proofreader Philippa Ingram, and two excellent designers in Susan Buchanan (1995 to 2000) and Stuart Brill (2000 to today).

Thanks to all our writers, especially the regulars, who have had to put up with ungenerous payment and interventionist editing. Thank you, too, to *Prospect*'s regular illustrators and cartoonists. I have also benefited from a large, shifting group of active advisers, among whom the following deserve special thanks: Don Berry, Bartle Bull, Kathleen Burk, Anthony Dworkin, Samantha Ellis, Charles Grant, AC Grayling, Lucy Heller, David Herman, Kate Kellaway, Michael Lind, John Lloyd, Mike Maclay, Jasper McMahon, Oliver Morton, Kamran Nazeer, Ben Rogers and Erik Tarloff.

The single best source of advice and ideas both on the editorial side and, more recently, on the business side too has been Toby Mundy. Toby, who is publisher of Atlantic Books, acts as a bridge between the magazine and the book. Others who have made the book possible include Alice Hunt and Clare Pierotti at Atlantic Books.

Finally, thanks to my mother and father and to the many Goodharts who have contributed to *Prospect* in one way or another. Above all, thanks to my wife Lucy Kellaway and our four children— Rosie, Maud, Art and Stan—for not minding too much about my absences in both body and mind fretting over that demanding fifth child, *Prospect*.

Introduction
Ten years of *Prospect*

Prospect magazine is ten years old, but its story really began on the evening of 9th November 1989 with the fall of the Berlin wall. I was in east Berlin that night—rather bizarrely I was attending a conference of rock music producers in my capacity as a *Financial Times* German correspondent—and I subsequently had a ringside seat as the unification drama unfolded. Covering such a world-historic event changed my life. It put me off the idea of returning to everyday office-life in London and made me believe that I should reach for something more journalistically and personally ambitious. *Prospect* magazine is the result and this volume collects together some of the highlights of our first ten years.

Prospect is also a child of the post-cold war era in another sense. It is not trying to save the world from anything, nor convert it to something (unlike one of our monthly predecessors, *Encounter*, which was saving us from communism, or another, *Marxism Today*, which was committed to socialist transformation). At *Prospect* we try to reflect and celebrate the messiness of our times. We are more liberal than conservative in political outlook but we have not tried to stand for much beyond good writing, independence of mind and an optimistic realism about human affairs.

After German unification I did return to London to work at the *FT* for another three years, but in 1994 I took a year's leave of absence to attempt to raise £350,000 to start the magazine (with the help of a friend and the first publisher of *Prospect*, Charles Seaford). Throughout the 1980s I had enjoyed a journalist's good fortune of often being in the right place at the right time. I was a labour reporter on the *FT* during the miners strike of 1984–85 then switched to writing about companies and the City when the takeover boom took off in 1986–87. (In between I was at the Heysel stadium on that terrible night in 1985 when 39 football fans died and I flew into Moscow as the Chernobyl disaster struck in 1986.)

My luck continued to hold with *Prospect*. For 1994–95 turned out to be a good time to be raising money for a politically liberal, internationally-minded magazine. The long Conservative hegemony in British politics was ending. Tony Blair had just become leader of the Labour party. There was a ferment of new thinking on the centre-left, and few outlets for it. There was also growing anxiety about "dumbing down" and insularity in the British media.

Such factors may have helped to make *Prospect* possible, but they did not make it easy. Nobody had heard of either me or Charles Seaford. I had no track record as an editor, neither did he as a publisher. But I had begun to think that creating this magazine was my destiny. And I did have some things going for me. After 12 years on the *FT* I had a fat contacts book full of names from the worlds of both serious journalism and business. And despite having three children under five, my family circumstances were also favourable: my wife, Lucy Kellaway, had a well-paid job on the *FT* and I was able to draw on the remains of a financial inheritance from the American side of my family to tide me over while there was no income coming in. It was entrepreneurship with a safety net. My biggest risk was making a fool of myself.

If American money helped to make it possible, it was also American magazines that provided the inspiration. In the 1980s and early 1990s I would read the *New York Review of Books* (and its *London Review* cousin), the *New Yorker*, the *Atlantic Monthly*, and others. These magazines were a showcase for the kind of essay, often on subjects in which I had no particular interest, that, if well written enough, would not only provide the pleasure of an absorbing read but also leave me at the end knowing more about the world. Why couldn't I produce a magazine that provided three or four such essays each month? I imagined a publication that was grounded in the world of politics, culture, literature and ideas, but was also in the intellectual entertainment business—providing clarity, rigour and good writing about the things that matter. A magazine infused with a didactic spirit, but without sermonising or championing a big cause.

There wasn't any one specific magazine or journal in Britain that was already doing it, although most of the individual ingredients could be found elsewhere. The weeklies (the *Spectator*, *New Statesman* and *Economist*) were news-led with pieces too short to do much more than assert a view. *Granta* was a genuine literary magazine. The *TLS* and the *LRB* were both book-review based and primarily literary too. The two earlier intellectual monthlies—*Encounter* and *Marxism Today*—had both expired at the end of the cold war. But there was no shortage of first-class British essayists—one only had to open some of the American publications mentioned above to enjoy their writing. *Prospect* intended to set them to work closer to home.

I had convinced myself that there was both a commercial and a cultural gap for a British magazine of essays, but could I convince anyone else? There was no problem finding writers committed to writing for it or members of the great and good happy to sign up to our editorial board (headed from the start by the indefatigably helpful AC Grayling). Finding investors who would at least pretend to believe in our business plan was harder. One of the first to bite was Bob Gavron, then still head of the big printing and publishing group St Ives. I knew him from having written about his company for the *FT* but I also knew that he was a generous backer of good causes. I had lunch with him and breathlessly described the plan. Gavron looked bored. He had heard such idealistic plans many times before and simply did not believe that there was a British market for such a magazine. He advised me not to sever my links with the *FT* but said he would put in £10,000 as a friendly gesture. This allowed us to boast to other potential backers that we had the backing of one of Britain's biggest publishers.

But the man who turned out to be our saviour was the ex-Tory MP turned businessman Derek Coombs. Derek, who abandoned his old party over its hostility to the EU, had been interested in investing in a political magazine for several years. His attempt to buy the *New Statesman* had been rebuffed in 1993 and he then started talking to various prominent journalists about starting a rival. Charles Seaford and I went to see him and persuaded him that an essay-based monthly could have just as much impact as a weekly. Derek is now our chairman, the largest single shareholder and the commercial driving force behind *Prospect*. But we also have another 70-plus investors of all sizes, among whom Rudi Bogni, the Schwepcke family and the late Bob Johnson deserve a special mention.

When it became clear that we were going to reach the £350,000 target laid down in the business plan we rather quickly needed a title, a design, some staff and an office. I had wanted to call the magazine *The Month* but the Catholic publication of that title was not happy to share its name. We eventually plumped for *Prospect*—inspired partly by the American New Democrat journal, *American Prospect*. The title was intended to signify the possibility of still seeing the big picture in what sometimes felt like an increasingly opaque world.

I was lucky to find a first deputy editor—Valerie Monchi—previously deputy foreign editor of the *Jewish Chronicle*, who became as obsessively committed to making *Prospect* work as I was. And after many depressing days trailing round potential offices in dowdy parts of London we found a surprisingly affordable attic in Bedford Square which became our home for the next eight years, and the place where we too often heard the dawn chorus on our deadline nights in those early months.

With the help of some generally friendly pre-publicity in the press (we launched at about the same time as *The Week*, which may have helped) and a big party organised by the fashionable PR company Hobsbawm Macaulay, our first issue was launched upon a somewhat indifferent world on 28th September 1995. We printed 50,000 copies of the first issue and sold about 11,000. In retrospect it doesn't seem a bad figure for a brand new, serious-minded magazine without much marketing behind it, but at the time I remember feeling disappointed that there might not be a reservoir of pent-up demand for a magazine of this type after all. Indeed, things got worse before they got better with circulation falling to a low point of about 5,000 after the fourth issue, before it started its long, slow climb.

Comparing that first issue with one from 2005 there are strong family resemblances. We maintain a hybrid of forms: the short opinion pieces and one-page columns that could appear in a newspaper or weekly; the 3,000 to 6,000 word (usually polemical) essays which certainly couldn't; more information-based *Economist*-style special reports and briefings; reportage; and so on. Amartya Sen's first-issue cover essay on the interconnection between economic growth and political freedom—with special focus on China and India—is the kind of ambitious, big picture, argument that we might easily run as a cover story today. There were plenty of stylish writers on display: Alan Ryan, Frederic Raphael and the then unknown comic writer Jeremy Clarke (who was poached a few years later by the *Spectator*). Andrew Adonis, now a junior minister in the education department, then a journalist on the *FT*, wrote a prescient piece urging Tony Blair to be his own secretary of state for education when he became prime minister. Adonis went on to become an education adviser to Blair and, some said, the agent through which Blair was, indeed, his own education secretary.

Apart from a big essay by Brian Glanville on sports journalism there was not much writing about culture. But since the arrival of Alex Linklater as my new deputy in 2001, culture and the arts have commanded more space (including regular columns on film, television, the visual arts and music) and there is more narrative journalism and interior life. Thanks to some financial assistance from the Arts Council of England, we also now run a short story in each issue. (*Prospect*'s fiction is soon to expand its reach as we launch a national short story prize, the biggest of its kind in the world, in partnership with Radio 4 and with sponsorship from Nesta, the

National Endowment for Science, Technology and the Arts.)

Today's magazine is printed on better paper, uses more colour and generally looks a far more grown-up product than the early issues, which had something of the smart student magazine about them. It also has more light and shade (cartoons did not feature for the first few years), and is more tightly edited. Looking back on those first issues I wince at some of the baggy, under-edited pieces.

But it was satisfying and motivating that few people, in the first year or two, gave us a chance of surviving. As relatively favourable comments began to flow in our confidence grew: the irritating phrase that was often pinned on us was "succès d'estime." We certainly weren't a commercial success. In fact it was dismaying in those early days how few people had heard of the magazine, so I took to handing out copies at parties. I became a *Prospect* obsessive. Consumed, like an addict, with one big thing: how to make each issue as good as time, slender resources and limited experience allowed. It also toughened me up. I learned how to sack staff and spike pieces by internationally celebrated authors.

Now that we sell nearly 24,000 copies a month, things are more solid beneath our feet. We remain a small outfit with only nine full-time staff, and if we can use our redesigned website to increase international sales (now around 4,000) we may even reach the sunlit uplands of financial stability in the next couple of years. Our readers are, in the main, highly educated, intellectually curious people but spread pretty widely across the professions. The biggest single group—people working in higher education—are only about 15 per cent of the total. And I still believe that if we continue improving the magazine and our marketing of it, we could double our circulation.

Prospect was based on an optimistic premise about the market for serious journalism in Britain. It was also born at a time of high hopes for rapid progress in human affairs. Many of those high hopes have been disappointed. It has been an action-packed and often dismaying ten years: the collapse of peace hopes in Israel/ Palestine; the continuing disintegration of Yugoslavia culminating in the bombing of Belgrade in 1999; the introduction of the euro; the election of

George W Bush; 9/11; war in Afghanistan and then Iraq; the rise and fall of the European constitution; the rise and rise of China and India and of the internet.

When we launched in September 1995, Yitzhak Rabin was still prime minister of Israel (he was shot two months later), Bill Clinton was heading towards re-election in the US and Tony Blair towards his first election in Britain. In the west, liberal baby-boomers were coming to power hoping to take advantage of the end of the cold war to reform domestic and international politics. Ten years on the new world order has given way to the war on terror, and in Britain—notwithstanding the many successes of New Labour—we have a third term Blair government that, especially after the London bombs, has had to focus on reassuring anxious citizens that the state can still protect them from the many demons that haunt them. Of course the world wasn't in marvellous shape in 1995. We had recently seen the genocide in Rwanda and ethnic cleansing in Bosnia (Aleksa Djilas reflected gloomily on the latter in our first issue). And it isn't that dreadful now: the west is more focused on global poverty, especially in Africa, than at any time in living memory and, who knows, perhaps a democratic Iraq will help to unblock some of the multiple failures of the Arab and Muslim world and spring a few more surprises in the middle east.

Flicking through the last ten years of *Prospect* provides an overview on these big events and the debates that they have spawned. One also gets an impression of just how rapidly intellectual fashions come and go. In our early days much of the domestic debate was focused on whether "stakeholding" was a sensible idea for Britain's political economy. That debate has almost completely disappeared (along with the attempt to forge a third way ideology), although in practice a distinctive Anglo-social model does seem to be emerging. We also plunged into the globalisation debate, which is, of course, still with us, albeit in a more nuanced form than in the mid-1990s. In culture, popular science writers were dominating the conversation. *Prospect* reflected this boom, especially the interest in genetics and neo-Darwinian evolutionary psychology. And in what must count as one of the oddest marketing stunts in publishing history we gave away a

CD-rom of the human genome (the first organisation in the world to do so) to mark our fifth anniversary in October 2000. The popular science boom has dimmed a bit since then but *Prospect* readers—perhaps seeking new intellectual anchors in a post-ideological age—still seem to have a big appetite for the latest guide to developments in everything from brain science to astrophysics.

The terrorist attacks of 9/11 transformed the intellectual agenda as well as the political one. The strike took place just 24 hours before our monthly deadline but Anatol Lieven managed to turn around a 5,000-word overview in that time even before it became clear who was responsible for the attacks. For a while the magazine became more focused on foreign policy, addressing themes such as Islam and democracy and the emerging tension between the US and Europe. (We have always been ready to re-run pieces published elsewhere if they are sufficiently interesting and we were the first European magazine to publish Robert Kagan's devastating neo-conservative analysis of that transatlantic tension, with its now famous soundbite: "Americans are from Mars and Europeans from Venus.") In our second most eye-catching marketing stunt we gave away a CD-rom of the Koran (plus a bluffer's guide to Islam) in our November 2001 issue.

Directly and indirectly as a result of 9/11, submerged political and cultural themes returned—religion, empire, the roots of democracy—and some themes closer to the surface were given a new impetus (above all the question of the gap between rich and poor countries). At *Prospect*, as at other serious magazines, we enjoyed an upturn in interest and circulation as big things seemed to be at stake once again in the realm of ideas and there was a more pressing need for good interpretation and analysis.

Throughout the last ten years we have thought of ourselves as a European, not merely a British, publication and we continue to run monthly columns from France and Brussels (and more occasionally from Berlin). We have also had plenty of continental European contributors and enjoy close links with the Swedish magazine *Axess*. But despite the best of intentions we seem to illustrate the fact that, culturally speaking, the channel remains wider than the English-speaking

Atlantic. It has been easier to attract the intellectual stars of North America—Francis Fukuyama, Jared Diamond, Steven Pinker, Michael Ignatieff and others—than their equivalents in France, Germany or Italy.

Perceptions, once established, are hard to shift. Many people who have heard of the magazine but never read it, regard *Prospect* as a "British policy magazine" (as the *New Yorker* once described us). It is true that in our early days we did write more about British policy debates than we do today. It is also true to say that we were then a more overtly political magazine, a forum for debate across much of the spectrum but very much focused within the centre-left. We closely followed the arguments about the shape of New Labour up until 1997 and then we charted the progress of the "project" in its first few years in office.

Around the time of the millennium the magazine began to shift its focus, partly because the broad contours of British politics seemed set for at least two or three more elections and partly because other things crowded in, including 9/11. We stopped worrying so much about the progress of, say, Britain's constitutional reform programme and began to explore the wider tensions within modern progressive thought itself. This led to my own essay, "Too diverse?", which was reprinted in the *Guardian* in February 2004 and provoked a big, sometimes acrimonious, debate about whether there is a tension between solidarity and diversity. *Prospect* has also been a forum for the debate within liberal baby-boom Britain about the legacy of the 1960s (see the debate between Melanie Phillips and Polly Toynbee on the family and Michael Elliott's "Rude Britannia" in the "Britain" section of this collection, plus the Hitchens brothers' exchange in the "Ideas and Popular Science" section).

Indeed, the clash of ideas—different points of view arguing it out within one magazine—has been a *Prospect* hallmark from the start. Several of our most striking letter exchange debates are included in this collection (although, alas, we could not find room for two of my favourites—Kathryn Hughes and Ben Rogers debating whether the *ER* television drama is art in summer 1999, or AC Grayling and Keith

Ward on God after the tsunami in early 2005). In the case of the "roundtables" (in which six or seven people debate a theme for a couple of hours, with their discussion then edited down to the highlights) we decided not to include any in the book, but it is worth recalling some of the best: the 1999 discussion on the global order in the 21st century with Francis Fukuyama, Eric Hobsbawm, Edward Luttwak, Timothy Garton Ash, Pierre Hassner and others; the 2000 debate on the meaning of the genetics revolution with James D Watson, Steve Jones, Robert Plomin and others; the November 2001 discussion on Islam and the west with Fred Halliday, Mai Yamani, Abdelwahab El-Affendi and others; and the roundtable on Britishness in early 2005 with Gordon Brown, Linda Colley, Kenan Malik, Roger Scruton and others.

George Orwell remains a guiding light to most people in Britain engaged in serious journalism and *Prospect* is no exception. Yet I often think that he would have found the world of contemporary British politics tame—no world wars, no clashing totalitarianisms of left and right, not enough at stake in our intellectual debates. It is instructive to recall, for example, the thunderous controversy which divided the British intelligentsia when it was discovered in 1967 that *Encounter* magazine had been receiving an annual grant from a body funded by the CIA. Many of *Encounter*'s liberal and left-wing writers refused to contribute ever again to the magazine. Such cold war passions would have made sense to Orwell but seem hard to understand only 35 years later. *Prospect*'s biggest brush with controversy—aside from my diversity essay—was probably our decision to choose only 12 women in our list of 100 Top British Public Intellectuals (to mark our 100th issue in July 2004). A vivid example of the culture wars eclipsing cold war geopolitics. And perhaps also an illustration of the big political truth, pointed out by Geoffrey Wheatcroft in his piece in this collection on 1997, that the story of the past 25 years in Britain and much of the west is that the right has won the economic argument while the left has won the cultural argument.

The *Encounter*/CIA story illustrates something else too. In much of the post-war period intellectual life in Britain was smaller and more clubbish than it is today—for 30 years after 1945 it was gathered together in a few high brow magazines, the *Observer* books pages, the Third Programme. (Sometimes the complaint about dumbing down seems to be an expression of regret that this club no longer exists.) Ideas today are discussed in a different way partly because of the profusion of outlets both electronic and print, partly because of the more diffuse character of the intellectual class—both the people who constitute it and the things they are interested in.

The almost complete disappearance of the serious left in either politics or intellectual life is another of the marked changes since the days of *Encounter*. Michael Jacobs, then head of the Fabian Society, regretted this in a *Prospect* essay in October 2002 when he complained that notwithstanding the achievements of New Labour's piecemeal social reform the spirit of transformative politics had been extinguished and that "politics has been disenchanted." After reading Jacobs's piece I remember thinking that it ought to be part of *Prospect*'s purpose to challenge this idea. Politics in a more technocratic age need not be dull and disenchanted—there can be eloquence in complexity and in value trade-offs and it is not as if our world is without its problems, even in "end of history" western Europe. Many people, of course, still yearn for political certainties which in Britain today they tend to find in international issues (consider the Iraq war and the politics of third world development). But our times are quite interesting enough not to require nostalgia for the cold war or the old absolutes of left and right.

Several people, particularly people on the political left, admonished me in the early days saying that *Prospect* could not be a magazine of ideas without a clear set of ideas of its own. I thought that in time we would find our own niche, and so we have in the dilemmas and unintended consequences of progressive politics. What we have not found so easily is a pithy one sentence description of the magazine—something I consider an editorial boast even if it is also a marketing headache. Current affairs monthly is a bit prosaic. Intellectual monthly is unnecessarily forbidding, especially in a country in which most of the cleverest and most interesting people would never dream of calling themselves intellectuals. Political and cultural monthly sounds a bit precious.

A brief word about the collection in front of you. It was an extremely hard job deciding on the final selection of pieces. We decided in the end not to try to cover all the big subject areas—so you will, for example, find very little here on China or Africa (or indeed the development debate in general) and nothing on brain science in the science section. This is not because we have not covered these things but because there was not a piece that seemed quite to fit between hard covers.

Similarly we have not included several pieces that started debates or attracted wide attention—such as David Marquand, Will Hutton and others responding to New Labour in office, John Lloyd's 2002 essay which triggered the latest media power debate and Rodric Braithwaite's establishment scepticism about the value of the Anglo-American "special relationship" after the Iraq war—because they seemed too much of their moment. Other notable absences include several essays by Timothy Garton Ash, Michael Lind and Robert Cooper on world affairs (although the latter two are represented in the collection); Tim King's essays on France; Jason Cowley's early literary portraits; John Kay on Oxford; Tristram Hunt on Prince Charles; Stella Tillyard on Germaine Greer; David Herman on Edward Said; Simon Blackburn on Richard Rorty; Adair Turner's polemics against John Gray and Bjorn Lomborg; some of the millennium "overview" pieces; our imagined interviews (particularly Bhikhu Parekh's debate between Gandhi and Bin Laden and Donald Sassoon talking to Karl Marx); Richard Jenkyns's piece on the state of the English language; Nick Crowe's pieces on the rock music industry; Ben Lewis's more recent pieces on the British art scene; and *Prospect*'s recidivist prisoner Peter Wayne.

I have had the good fortune not only to help found a magazine that will, with luck, remain a lasting feature of Britain's journalistic, political and intellectual life but also to appoint myself to the dream job of editing it. Ploughing through the back issues in preparation for this collection was perhaps not quite as pleasurable an experience as I had hoped, in part because I was painfully reminded of how perilous the magazine's journey has been. But here we are ten years later—a post-grand narrative magazine with, I hope you will agree, lots of grand stories to show from our first decade.

David Goodhart
Millook, North Cornwall, July 2005

WORLD

"Consider yourself conquered. We really have to move on"

After the revolution • Ernest Gellner

MAY 1996

The manner of the dismantling of the Russian revolution may come to be seen as a disaster comparable only with the revolution itself. I do not wish to be misunderstood. I write as a life-long anti-communist and anti-Marxist. For a person of my age and background, I belong to what sometimes felt like a small minority of people who never passed through a Marxist phase. As a schoolboy in wartime England I was powerfully influenced by Arthur Koestler and George Orwell; later, Karl Popper made the strongest impact on me in philosophy, and Raymond Aron in sociology. The toolbox of the halftrack I drove to Prague for the victory parade in May 1945 contained four books: Koestler's *Darkness at Noon,* Orwell's *Animal Farm,* the now forgotten but then widely discussed *Managerial Revolution* by James Burnham, and Cyril Connolly's *Unquiet Grave.*

Yet I deplore the disintegration of the Soviet Union; not because I ever sympathised with the ideology which had inspired it, but because of concerns about the need for continuity. Marxism had provided the societies under its sway with a moral order—a set of moral values which helped people to orient themselves. They knew what the rules, the idiom and the slogans were. These added up to a system you could understand and adjust to, whether or not you approved of it. An east European living under communism who confronted a person from the free world had a measure of dignity: deprived of many civil liberties, and a western standard of living, he nevertheless belonged to a rival civilisation—one which stood for something different. It had not been doing very well, by its own standards or by most others. But that had not always been obvious and no single individual had been personally dishonoured by the historic mistakes which had led to communism. Today, a typical east European is simply a very poor cousin. If he is an intellectual, his best prospect is temporary or permanent migration. East Europeans do not represent a failed, but important, alternative; they represent failure by the standard norms.

Meeting them, you feel a certain embarrassment—a bit like what you might feel in the presence of a person suffering from a disfiguring physical ailment. In the past, he could decently hide it by his clothing; but now, for some reason, he is obliged to lay it bare, and you are obliged to observe it—and he knows it. Imagine you were living in a Catholic country, without being a believer in any way. Over the years, as a matter of courtesy, you have developed a habit of referring with respect to your neighbours' beliefs and practices. In formal discussions, you do not hide the difference between your convictions and theirs; but in everyday life, "in front of the children," you subscribe to the polite convention of equality-in-difference. Then, one day, there is an internal crisis in the Vatican and the Holy Father declares that the Catholic faith must be abolished; it was based on an error. This is the predicament of former communists.

They had either believed, and now stand exposed as fools; or they had not, and are now revealed to have been opportunists, hypocrites, or cowards. The faith had permeated their lives to such a degree that it became part of their identity. What or who are they now? When talking to ex-communists, you fear to meet their gaze lest they read in your eyes the question: were you a fool or a coward? Institutionally imposed faiths confer an identity on their captive clientèle: if the faiths suddenly disestablish themselves, they betray their adepts, leaving them naked overnight. Not all faiths do this. (There ought to be a law against it.) But the Marxist church, in the manner of its sudden, total and unqualified surrender and dissolution, seems to have acquired yet another inglorious historic first.

I would have preferred a gradual ideological and institutional transition—one which would preserve the idiom and ritual of the past, but empty it of content, or make its content adjustable to taste and occasion. The red flag and the romanticism of the revolution would be retained (as, in fact, Lenin's statues *are*, at least in Russia), but the distribution of power would gradually change. Retaining the idiom would have the advantage of preserving the semblance of continuity, while providing some orientation in daily life. The CPSU (Soviet Communist party) would be, so to speak, anglicanised; it would concern itself with the fight against *enthusiasm*; ensure that no one took Marxism with undue seriousness.

Mikhail Gorbachev, however, seems to have been prey to two illusions: the Soviet illusion that the problem of nationalism had been solved; and the western laissez-faire illusion that liberalisation would promptly yield economic benefits. Boris Yeltsin had a better grasp of politics in the post-Soviet era: he used the dissolution of the union to rid himself of his rival (repeating Lenin's historic surrender of the Ukraine), and then later tried to recover what he could of the power of the Russian state.

The astonishing and unexpected collapse of communism has disoriented all of us. The opposition between liberal and Marxist industrial societies defined not only the political map of the world, but also its conceptual map. People became used to thinking in these terms; this liberal/Marxist divide characterised the European world—much in the same way that the Catholic/Protestant divide had done previously. Yalta and Potsdam were the Peace of Westphalia of the postwar system. We might have expected the two systems to become more routinised, more tolerant, more ecumenical; to communicate more and to excommunicate less. But history did not repeat itself. This time, one of the two opponents capitulated—to an unprecedented degree.

Is this a vindication of a laissez-faire vision of society? No. This model, too, is unworkable in industrial societies. Why? First, the enjoyment of industrial affluence depends only in part on individual possession of material goods; above all, it depends on a shared, weighty and indivisible infrastructure. Take a familiar example: the use of a car. It depends not only on the machine, but on the availability of a well-maintained and regulated road system, parking facilities, and so on. The enormous proportion of the national income which goes through the hands of politicians (between 30 and 50 per cent) is not due, as rightist ideologues would have it, to creeping socialism: it is inherent in the logic of industrialism. Decisions concerning our shared infrastructure cannot be left to "the market." They involve long term, complex considerations. They are necessarily political.

Second, the power of modern technology is so huge that, if left uncontrolled, its consequences for ecology and terrorism are horrifying. Early human societies could not be market societies because their technologies were too feeble: they could not leave social stability and security at the mercy of the vagaries of the interactive strategies of individuals freely operating in "the market." In poor and stagnant economies, there is no use for those famous signals which, according to Friedrich Hayek, indicate the best use of resources. These societies know but one signal: they must survive; and they can only do so by allocating resources in a way which perpetuates internal order and ensures external defence. Advanced societies cannot be laissez-faire either, but for the opposite reason: their economy is not too feeble, but too powerful.

Third, the moral legitimacy of a wealth-based social hierarchy made some sense during the period of the early industrial revolution, when individual producers were, so to speak, "face to face" with nature; those who returned with greater booty wrested from nature could claim legitimacy by virtue of their contribution to the general good. In modern societies, virtually no one is face to face with nature—except in the course of recreation. Innovation is carried out on the shoulders of the achievements of countless others; it is entirely dependent on a shared scientific/technological culture, to which many have contributed, and which is quite impossible to disaggregate. All trading is insider trading.

Fourth, and notoriously, modern societies are confronted with the problem of nationalism. This crisis is not rooted in some bizarre atavistic stirrings of the human heart, the call of blood and soil; it is an underlying condition of industrial life. On the one hand, the nature of industrial production requires and engenders cultural homogeneity: "work" is semantic, not physical; it entails communication with a large number of anonymous interlocutors; effective participation is possible only for those who master the shared literate culture of the society within which they operate. The dependency on a culture which we have mastered, and within which we are accepted, engenders the political identification known as nationalism. It is simply the political expression of a social order in which participation requires a shared codified culture. At the same time, however, the unevenness of economic development between different areas produces unstoppable labour migrations, so that even if a region has not inherited an ethnic patchwork from its past, it will become ethnically plural after industrialisation.

Finally, the free play of the market and the atomisation of family units, combined with labour migrations, engender a new form of inequality, with an underclass composed partly of handicapped, isolated individuals and partly of members of stigmatised subgroups caught in a vicious circle of discrimination and criminalisation. This form of destitution in the midst of plenty is not only morally obscene; it has social consequences which affect everyone. These problems cannot conceivably be solved by "the market"; they can only be handled politically.

Ironically, it was one of the most devious and trimming-addicted of Labour leaders who declared, moralistically, that the Labour movement was nothing if not a "crusade." The point about any new socialism is that it must not be a crusade. It must, as Stendhal said about his study of love, be dry—free of ardour. It must look at the boundary between private and communal economic power, not with faith and passion, but coldly, without messianic or crusading zeal. Political control of economic life is not the consummation of world history, the fulfilment of destiny, or the imposition of righteousness; it is a *painful* necessity. To those on the right, one has to say that it is a painful *necessity*. There is nothing inherently good about political inter-ference in economic life; the idea that it is a sufficient condition of virtue or of human fulfilment is absurd. But it is a condition of decency, just as its partial absence is a condition of liberty.

The liberal societies which have emerged as the victors of the cold war have had their institutions and quasi-ideologies (it is of their essence that they are held in a lukewarm, ambiguous, spirit) vindicat-ed, to some degree. But they are not vindicated in any firm, permanent or clear manner: history has not come to an end, as Francis Fukuyama proclaimed. If the end of the cold war has decisively eliminated one alternative, it has not established the other. What has been eliminated is the messianic manner of running an industrial society—one which treats power as the agency of righteousness rather than as a public convenience.

Industrial societies cannot be run by an absolute moral order—the final imposition of righteousness on earth. This was the essence of Marxism, and it envisaged a future which does not work. An absolute moral theory requires a firm and permanent vision of the nature of things. This is incompatible with science and technology, which operate within a fluctuating framework and a morally neutral ontology; these, if given free rein, end up eroding any faith. Moreover, an expanding economy requires autonomy and elbowroom for the constituent productive units—also a condition of freedom and the rule of law. A modern state must have the monopoly of legitimate force. (Office workers, unlike pastoral tribesmen, cannot simultane-ously attend to their work and their physical security; computer and fax users cannot, like shepherds and occasionally even peasants, be expected to shoot their way to work.) Pluralism, deprived of any base in the political system, finds its base in the economy.

The victors of the cold war have established various social-political cultures. All of them share a family resemblance: they have refrained from completing *doctrinally* the transition from the values and faith of an agrarian order to those of a scientific / industrial one. The old tran-scendent truth cannot be replaced by a new earthly revelation—only by doubt, irony and compromise. Given the interdependence of the world, our best hope is for an unholy alliance of consumerist non-believers, committed to government through bribery by growth, who do not take their own beliefs too seriously.

Liberal societies have worked out a whole range of suitable compromises, but they have had several centuries to do it in. The process was often bloody; it is only of late that the rival parties have settled down to amicable cohabitation. Our century saw not only the elimination of the Marxist alternative, but also the elimination, by a hot rather than cold war, of the attempt to run industrial societies through a return to a pagan version of the hierarchical, military, blood-and-soil values of an archaic social order. That struggle was more demanding than the cold war—it was a damn close run thing. The conversion to a liberal outlook only took place *after* the war, when the losers found industrial growth to be a more effective way to power and prosperity than striving for *Lebensraum* through valour.

The elimination of the messianic plan for industrial society does not mean, as has been suggested by Samuel Huntington, a switch to a "clash of civilisations," at least in the literal sense of competition with pre-industrial civilisations. It is too early to tell what will happen to the latter: it would be rash to assume that they will all be liberal. There is some evidence to suggest that a fundamentalist regime—one which seriously implements its own values rather than privatising virtue and salvation in the liberal manner—may be attempted within Islam. The thrust in this direction is very powerful, and the only (but very costly) cure seems to be to allow it its head for a period. This may be self-curing: there are signs of such a development in Iran, in the emergence of a new trend seeking to find an Islamic way to the separation of state and faith. But such a totalitarianism, when it exists, differs significantly from the Marxist form: it does not sacralise the economy (and so is not brought down by its failure), and is not inspired by the technological transformation of human life—though it seems to be compatible with it.

The stunningly sudden collapse of Bolshevism has presented the ex-communist world with the same problem—but virtually no time in which to solve it. In a moral and institutional vacuum, any strategy constitutes a shock therapy. Peter the Great may have chosen shock therapy to liberate Russia from its Byzantine past, but his successors are having shock therapy thrust upon them. The fact that they do not believe with any great conviction the theories underlying the shocks, makes their task even harder.

The problem of erecting a liberal, stable and prosperous society on the ruins of a totalitarian industrial ideocracy is absolutely new; no one knows what the answer is, or indeed whether there is one. Marx said, on no good evidence whatsoever, that mankind only sets itself such problems as it can solve. My own impression is that people often face problems set by their historical situation for which they lack solutions. The victorious version of industrial society is not without problems, options and uncertainties, as the end-of-history thesis would suggest. The moral vacuum in the east presents at once a serious problem and a new source of evidence for the understanding of our own predicament. In the west, liberalism emerged as a result of at least three elements: the remnants of the old honour ethic, a new individualist work ethic, and a reactive egalitarianism trying to correct the previous two. In Russia, the Bolsheviks made a fine job of destroying the past: individualism was never all that strong, and faith in the capacity of formally egalitarian socialism to correct injustices has received a powerful blow. What's left? Russia resembles the Weimar republic—inflation, humiliation, criminalisation, illegitimate new wealth—except for one element: in interwar Europe, the worst were full of passionate intensity, the best lacked all conviction. Now, fortunately, the worst lack all conviction too. We must wait and hope, and assist when we believe that our aid will be effective.

What is certain is that the pattern will not be the same in all the former communist countries. Those favoured by smallness, ethnic homogeneity and sound local traditions (or merely 40 rather than 70 years of Bolshevism) will probably be successful: there can be little doubt that the Czech Republic will succeed; the prospects in Hungary, Poland and the Baltic republics are not too bad; in the Balkans, the situation is varied; and the Yugoslav catastrophe has already taken place. The real question mark hangs over the eastern Slav states, the Muslim ex-Marxist world, and the Caucasus.

And what of Russia? A country which has great difficulty in conquering Chechnya seems unlikely to embark, for the time being, on a new drive to the river Elbe. The Russians have made their contribution to the exploration of dead ends for industrial society: messianic righteousness through total collectivisation has been conclusively shown to be unviable. The same is true, I believe, of total *laissez-faire*, unsustained by other moral and institutional support. Let us hope that we can spare the Russians the task of demonstrating this truth as well. For once, let someone else have a go.

Is military intervention in Kosovo justified?
• Robert Skidelsky vs Michael Ignatieff
JUNE 1999

3rd May 1999

Dear Michael,

I have been instinctively against Nato's bombing of Serbia from the day it started on 24th March. I was incredulous that Nato seemed to have no military strategy except to bomb Serbia to smithereens. I could not believe that bombing a defenceless country was the right way to wage "holy war." But above all I was alarmed by the thought that a new doctrine of international relations was being forged which would make the world a much more dangerous place.

This is what I want to discuss. Given that Nato's values are superior to Milosevic's values, is it right or prudent to try to force our values on him? Until recently, most of us have signed up to quite a different doctrine of international relations. The UN was founded on the principle of national sovereignty. States could and should be sanctioned for acts of aggression against other states, but within their borders they were free (with one large caveat) to do what they liked. You might say that this was a pretty minimal basis for a world order. But the UN was founded on prudential, not ethical, rules, and it was a great advance to get states to sign up to them.

Now to the caveat. Chapter seven of the UN Charter says that states can be sanctioned for actions which are a "threat to peace." This allows the UN to take into account the spillover effects of domestic policies—if, for example, they produce floods of refugees or destabilise other states. But human rights abuse *per se* is not a ground for intervention (Pinochet's Chile was never sanctioned). This is for the good reason that there is no international agreement on the standards to be upheld and the means to uphold them.

The old imperialism had its own way of overcoming this problem. Advanced states conquered "barbarous" ones and imposed "civilised standards" on them. But as even Churchill conceded, this process had become "contrary to the ethics of the 20th century." Not, apparently, to the ethics of Tony Blair. In his Chicago speech on 22nd April he advanced what he called "The Doctrine of International Community." Globalisation, he said, means: "We cannot turn our backs on the violation of human rights in other countries if we want to be secure." This fact required an "important qualification" to the principle of non-interference. The UN Charter should be amended to make this possible. And Blair was insistent that having made a commitment to intervene, "we cannot simply walk away once the fight is over: better to stay with a moderate number of troops than return for repeat performances."

Blair takes direct issue with the prudential tradition of diplomacy. "Bismarck," he remarked, "famously said that the Balkans were not worth the bones of a single Pomeranian grenadier." He added smugly: "Bismarck was wrong." Who would you have preferred to be in charge in 1914: Bismarck or Blair?

Blair wants international cooperation on the basis of agreed values and rules. But Nato did not agree on the values or rules with Russia, China or anyone else before it started bombing Serbia. Nor did it seek UN authorisation. Thank goodness Russia is doing what it can to find a compromise, but its official line is that the bombing of Serbia was an "act of aggression" which flouts the UN Charter and international law. Moreover, Foreign Minister Ivanov says Nato's attempt to "tear Kosovo out of Yugoslavia" threatens Russia's own relations with its Islamic minorities.

We stand at a fork in international affairs. Does the west have *carte blanche* to make its values prevail whenever it has the temporary power to do so? Or will it confine its ethical ambitions to limits acceptable to other great powers with different values and interests?

Let me end with four assertions and one question. First, there is no international consensus on the standards expected of states in dealing with their own subjects or on the sanctions appropriate to breaches of agreed standards. Second, Nato failed to seek UN authorisation for its attack on Serbia because it knew it would not get it. Third, the by-passing of the UN by Nato sends a clear message to all countries that force, not law, governs international affairs. Fourth, if membership of the UN no longer protects states from invasion, all governments which can, will acquire weapons of mass destruction to deter or repel foreign invasion. Now the question: do you really think that the west has the guts to fight its way into other countries and occupy them for indefinite periods of time?

Yours,

Robert Skidelsky

4th May 1999

Dear Robert,

I couldn't disagree with you more, but we need to clear away the areas of common ground in order to figure out exactly where our disagreement lies. I agree with you that there should be a general presumption in favour of state sovereignty in international affairs. Such a presumption provides alibis for dictators, but it also protects weak but democratic states from more powerful neighbours. Where states are democratic, their sovereignty is also an expression of their people's right to self-determination. So there are reasons of principle *not* to interfere in states whose internal affairs we find disagreeable. I also accept that human rights abuses, by themselves, do not legitimise military intervention. Other kinds of "soft" intervention—formal protests, assistance to persecuted groups, boycotts and sanctions—are preferable. Military intervention should always be an instrument of absolute last resort. So the question is to define when human rights abuses in another country justify that last resort. I believe that armed intervention can only be justified in two instances: first, when human rights abuses rise to the level of a systematic attempt to expel or exterminate large numbers of people who have no means of defending themselves; second, where these abuses threaten the peace and security of neighbouring states. Two further conditions should be added: first, all diplomatic alternatives must have been exhausted; second, force can only be justified when it stands a real chance of working. Force can't be justified simply to punish, avenge or signify moral outrage. It must be a credible way to stop abuses and restore peace.

Before we consider whether the Kosovo situation meets these criteria, we must clear away another matter. You maintain that there is "no international consensus on the standards expected of states in dealing with their own subjects." This is not the case. Since Nuremberg, since the Universal Declaration of Human Rights, there has been a set of international norms on the internal conduct of states which those who sign these conventions—and Yugoslavia is a signatory—are supposed to abide by. So the problem about intervention does not lie, as you suppose, in the relativity of international norms. Serbia's violation of these norms in Kosovo is not a matter of serious dispute. These norms exist; the problem is whether an international right of intervention should trump state sovereignty in the case of the Serb abuses in Kosovo.

In my view Kosovo does meet the strict criteria for a justified intervention. A defenceless people have been driven from their homes and their arrival in Albania and Macedonia is destabilising a strategically important region. Your position—to stay out and do nothing—is sustainable only on the assumption that Milosevic is telling the truth, and that the deportees were driven out by Nato bombing. Having just spent a week in the camps in Macedonia, talking to families evicted from Pristina, I am in no doubt that the ethnic cleansing was system-atically planned before the Nato bombing. Western intelligence confirms that Operation Horseshoe was already under way before the first Nato airstrikes.

You make a crucial concession: that Chapter seven of the UN Charter mandates interventions in cases where domestic policies "produce floods of refugees or destabilise other states." But this is precisely the case in Kosovo. Serbian policy has never been a strictly internal matter: in Kosovo, Milosevic decided to solve an "internal" human rights problem by exporting an entire nation to his impover-ished neighbours. His actions have bequeathed chaos to a whole region and guaranteed that there will be armed conflict until the Kosovars can rule themselves free of Serb repression.

In understanding why we have a right to intervene militarily, we also need to understand Milosevic's consistent attempt to deny the right of self-determination to anyone except his own Serbian people. He chose war, rather than peace, in 1991, when Slovenia and Croatia exercised their rights of self-determination. In 1992, he armed an insurrection against a UN recognised state, Bosnia, and since 1989 he has systematically withdrawn the limited rights of self-government enjoyed by the Kosovars under the Tito constitution of 1974. At any point, he could have chosen another path—peacefully to negotiate minority rights guarantees for the Serbian minority within the new republics. Instead, he chose war, and the result has been the death of up to 250,000 people and the displacement of 2m people. It is difficult to respect the territorial integrity and sovereignty of a state which has shown such disregard for the integrity and sovereignty of its neigh-bours. His regime has been a clear and present danger to the stability of an entire region of Europe for nine years.

The second area of disagreement between us is whether military intervention can be justified without explicit UN sanction and approval. In principle, member states should seek approval of the use of force from the Security Council. The veto system in the council can provide a useful break on imperialist misadventure. But the veto system has also prevented the UN from intervening when it should have done. Sticking only to the most recent and relevant instances, the UN security council's failure to prevent genocide in both Rwanda and Bosnia has made it essential that where a veto threatens to make the international community complicit in evil, coalitions of member states should be able to act on their own. I appreciate that this entails risks, but coalitions can exert restraints on their more excitable members. Nato is much condemned for waging war by committee, but it is precisely because 19 member states must be persuaded before military action can be undertaken, that such action has not become indiscriminate or disproportionate.

You say, finally, that Nato action will send a message that force, rather than law, governs international affairs. There are occasions, on the contrary, when if force is not used there is no future for law. Failure to reverse the most meticulous deportation of a civilian population since the second world war would have set a fatal precedent wherever authoritarian leaders believe that force should substitute for dialogue in their domestic affairs.

Yours,

Michael Ignatieff

6th May 1999

Dear Michael,

You define several fruitful areas of disagreement between us. The first concerns the importance to be attached to the principle of non-interference in the domestic affairs of states. You admit that there is a "general presumption" in favour of non-interference, but you qualify this so heavily as almost to turn it into its opposite. That is, you seem to believe that intervention is justified whenever human rights are violated, but must be proportional to the offence. Military force is reserved for two cases: genocide or mass expulsion; and when human rights abuses threaten the peace and security of neighbouring states. Since, as Tony Blair admits, there are "many regimes ... engaged in barbarous acts," the scope for intervention is in principle huge. Moreover, since Nato (or rather the US) has overwhelming air superiority almost everywhere, your prudential qualification, "only when force has a real chance of working," is less than it seems.

You also weaken the presumption of non-interference unduly by omitting the most compelling argument in its favour, namely that it offers the only secure basis for good (and peaceful) interstate relations in a world where values differ. This has been the conclusion of three centuries of European statecraft, first enunciated at the Treaty of Westphalia. Perhaps you rate justice higher than peace. If so, this is a disagreement between us.

This brings me to your contention that all UN members accept the same norms of domestic behaviour. You cite Nuremberg verdicts and the Universal Declaration of Human Rights. I accept that Nuremberg gave legal force to two universally accepted norms: that genocide and the planning and waging of aggressive war are wicked and should always be prevented or punished. The fact that we have not acted on the first since the second world war is a dreadful blot.

I doubt if there is genuine consensus on much else. You seem to believe that when states sign up to lists of rights they all think that they mean the same thing. This is a familiar western (particularly American) delusion and I'm surprised you fall for it. I'm talking about substantive agreement, not legal decoration.

Even assuming more agreement than is the case, the practical problems nearly always arise when norms conflict. The classic case is when two ethnic or religious groups have claims on the same territory and cannot work out a *modus vivendi*. In such a case, separation (which always involves some ethnic cleansing) may be the best solution. Yet this was never on the table at Rambouillet, despite the fact that there have been many relatively successful postwar examples, such as the separation of Jews and Arabs in Palestine, or of Greeks and Turks in Cyprus. Our inability to accept that large parts of the world do not work according to western rules has brought enormous troubles on us and those we succour.

You say that force should only be used when it is a "credible way to stop abuses and restore peace." But do you seriously believe that Nato bombing is a credible method of achieving these goals? There is nothing more immoral than making promises to endangered people and then leaving them to their fate.

Finally, you rather airily wave aside the objection that Nato is making war on a member of the UN without UN authorisation. The veto is not an inconvenient obstacle to humanitarian designs. It is there to ensure international consensus for UN intervention. Such a consensus does not exist in the security council—and most members of the UN are opposed to the Nato bombing.

This does *not* mean that "stay out and do nothing" is the only option; nor do I believe Milosevic's propaganda. Had Nato accepted from 1998 that force was ruled out without clear evidence of genocide or mass expulsion, the diplomacy would have been different. A joint approach would have been hammered out between the US, the EU and Russia as the basis of any demands on Serbia. At this stage, Nato should not have been involved at all. It was Nato's willingness to use force without achieving a Great Power consensus which is directly responsible for this tragic turn of events—from which we now rely on Russia to rescue us.

Yours,

Robert

7th May 1999

Dear Robert,

Our disagreement is wider than the issue of Kosovo. We have different views of the international system itself. This is a disagreement about facts as well as their implication. You are a Westphalian: for you the only relevant actors in the international system are states; their inviolability is all but absolute; and there are no agreed norms to regulate their conduct other than the obligation not to commit genocide or wage aggressive war. I am an internationalist: states have rights and immunities but so do individuals. When these rights are violated, individuals have recourse in law to human rights bodies in the UN system. When persecuted individuals or national groups have exhausted all remedies and stand defenceless before aggression in their home state, they have the right to appeal and to receive humanitarian and even military assistance. Contrary to what you say, I construe the grounds for military interventions narrowly: they should always be a last resort, when every other peaceful means of assisting a vulnerable population has been exhausted.

We also disagree about the cross-cultural validity of human rights norms. Unlike you, I believe there is a widening range of internationally agreed norms for the conduct of both international and domestic policy. We are not living in the culturally relative moral world that you describe. All nations formally accept that torture, rape, massacre and forcible expulsion are violations of international humanitarian law. There is no intercultural dispute as to whether such abuses have occurred in Kosovo or whether they violate international norms of conduct.

You dismiss this structure of international human rights law as nothing more than the homage which vice pays to virtue. I do not deny that states honour these obligations more in the breach than in the observance, but it seems incontrovertible that international rights norms do operate as a real constraint on the domestic behaviour of a growing number of states. If the conduct of states were as you describe, Serbia's behaviour in Kosovo would not be the exception which it is. There is simply no other state in Europe which commits such violations of internationally agreed norms.

You construe attempts by outsiders to monitor human rights in other states as a meddlesome post-imperial moralism, attempting to apply "western rules where these do not apply." But the mandate to intervene comes not just from "our" side but from "theirs." Our military intervention in the Balkans is not imposing moral standards on a people who do not accept their validity. On the contrary: Kosovar Albanians have been begging for our assistance in the face of more than 12 years of increasing Serbian repression.

As to the specifics of what you propose in relation to Kosovo. You suggest that the west should have negotiated with Milosevic on the basis of a joint approach hammered out between the US, EU and Russia. You seem to forget that this is exactly what happened: such an approach was agreed by the Contact Group, which included the Russians. It respected the territorial integrity of Yugoslavia, insisted that the KLA insurgents be disarmed and provided for explicit guarantees of Serb minority rights and protection of their holy places. Such a deal offered a credible solution to the Kosovo crisis because it respected the essential national interests of the Serbian people. Milosevic turned it down.

You maintain that the tragedy has occurred because the west resorted to force without first securing a Great Power consensus. On the contrary, the tragedy occurred because Milosevic thought that he could divide Russia and the west, and get away with a final solution of the Kosovo problem.

Your suggestion that the ethnic groups be separated logically implies partition—which in turn implies a substantial erosion of the sovereignty of Yugoslavia. If this *is* your position, it contradicts your support for non-interference. In any event, partition is impractical, because both communities are distributed throughout the province, as are their cultural and religious sites. This leaves either complete independence for Kosovo or a UN protectorate. If it is to be independence, the Serbs have to understand that it is entirely their conduct which has lost them the territory.

As for the UN, the secretary-general himself has said that the resort to force can be justified in Kosovo, because there is a threat to the peace and security of the region. You yourself concede that the deportation of an entire nation constitutes such a threat, yet you do not commit yourself to any practical action which would restore these people to their homes. Your objections are focused on the failure to secure UN approval. The western countries are not bypassing the UN: as the recent G7 negotiating position makes clear, the Russians are now prepared to approve a resolution in the security council mandating a deployment with Nato troops at its core. This would return the whole operation under a UN umbrella where it belongs. The real obstacle to a settlement remains Milosevic himself. It is disingenuous to claim that only one side in this dispute has failed to abide by the UN Charter: the list of UN resolutions which Milosevic has ignored or violated is exceedingly long.

As for the bombing, I framed my conditions for the use of military force in the belief that force can only be justified if it achieves precise military objectives. If Milosevic agrees to negotiate a settlement which allows for the refugees to return under international protection, then the bombing should cease at once. If he refuses to negotiate, the bombing should continue until Serb forces are sufficiently weakened to permit a ground invasion of Kosovo, whose aim would be to occupy the province, disarm Serb forces, return the refugees, rebuild the province, place it under UN administration and then exit as soon as a permanent ceasefire could be negotiated with the Serbs. A bombing campaign which is not geared to this objective, and which simply continues to destroy the infrastructure of Serbia and kill civilians, would have nobody's support in the long term. The bombing must be directed at military targets with the aim of introducing ground troops as soon as possible.

Yours,

Michael

8th May 1999

Dear Michael,

Evidently we disagree both about the nature of the international system and about the facts of the case. What you see as the actually existing international order, I see as a project to refashion it according to western norms. I believe strongly in these norms. But the attempt to conduct international relations as though all these states accepted them can only serve to make the world more war-prone. This is why I am, as you say, a Westphalian. One must always remember, though, that the system of "live and let live" did not exclude agreed action by the Great Powers if a domestic conflict threatened international peace.

This brings me to the facts. I am amazed that you continue to believe that Russia at any time supported the Nato solution. The bombing in particular has united all Russians, from liberals to communists, in opposition to Nato action. Yeltsin has ordered the development of new tactical nuclear missiles to counter a perceived increased threat from Nato. So much for Russia being "on side."

Historians will argue about when or whether Milosevic's savage reprisals against the KLA turned into a deliberate programme of ethnic cleansing. What is undeniable is that the mass exodus from Yugoslavia started after the bombing started. I would have expected more scepticism from you about Nato's claims. My main point, though, is that the Nato action has made the world a more dangerous place.

Yours,

Robert

10th May 1999

Dear Robert,

You can only maintain your position by misrepresenting the facts. Ethnic cleansing was under way in Kosovo ten months before the bombing began. The departure of the Kosovar Albanians was not an "exodus," but systematic deportation, using military units. You argue as if these facts were still in dispute: but the facts are plain. They constitute the worst political crime in Europe since 1945.

You cling to the fiction that diplomacy might have averted war, and argue that we didn't do enough to line up the Russians behind diplomatic pressure. What do you suppose was going on between May 1998 and March 1999? You forget that the Russians were at Rambouillet, that they did everything they could to get the Serbs to sign on to the deal. Even now, after weeks of bombing, the Russians and the G7 countries still maintain a common set of demands that the Serbs must meet. The fact which you do not wish to face is that every peaceful diplomatic alternative to war was tried and failed. Why? Because Milosevic gambled that we would fold. And you seem to wish that we had. The word for this is appeasement.

Yours,

Michael

The Israel lobby • Michael Lind

APRIL 2002

Until recently, America's middle east policy was a peripheral part of its global strategy, which focused on preventing the Soviet Union from intimidating US allies in western Europe and east Asia. Britain was the dominant western power in the middle east until the 1960s, and US influence was countered in much of the region by the Soviet Union until the end of the cold war. The indifference of much of the national security elite and the public to the region, in between crises, permitted US policy to be dominated by two US domestic lobbies, one ethnic and one economic—the Israel lobby and the oil industry (which occasionally clashed over issues like US weapons sales to Saudi Arabia).

Times have changed. Today the middle east is the centre of US foreign policy—a fact illustrated in the most shocking way by the al Qaeda attacks on New York and Washington. A debate within the US over the goals and methods of American policy in the middle east is long overdue. Unfortunately, an uninhibited debate is not taking place, because of the disproportionate influence of the Israel lobby.

Today the Israel lobby distorts US foreign policy in a number of ways. Israel's occupation of the West Bank and Gaza, enabled by US weapons and money, inflames anti-American attitudes in Arab and Muslim countries. The expansion of Israeli settlements on Palestinian land makes a mockery of the US commitment to self-determination for Kosovo, East Timor and Tibet. The US strategy of dual containment of Iraq and Iran pleases Israel, which is most threatened by them, but violates the logic of realpolitik and alienates most of America's other allies. Beyond the region, US policy on nuclear weapons proliferation is undermined by the double standard that has led it to ignore Israel's nuclear programme while condemning those of India and Pakistan.

The debate that is missing in the US is not one between Americans who want Israel to survive and those—a marginal minority—who want Israel to be destroyed. The US should support Israel's right to exist within internationally recognised borders and to defend itself against threats. What is needed is a debate between those who want to link US support for Israel to Israeli behaviour, in the light of America's own strategic goals and moral ideals, and those who want there to be no linkage. For the American Israel lobby, Tony Smith observes in his authoritative study, *Foreign Attachments: The Power of Ethnic Groups in the Making of American Foreign Policy* (Harvard), "to be a 'friend of Israel' or 'pro-Israel' apparently means something quite simple: that Israel alone should decide the terms of its relations with its Arab neighbours and that the US should endorse these terms, whatever they may be."

The Israel lobby is one special interest pressure group among many. It is a loose network of individuals and organisations, of which the most important are the American Israel Public Affairs Committee (AIPAC)—described by the *Detroit Jewish News* as "a veritable training camp for Capitol Hill staffers"—and the Conference of Presidents of Major American Jewish Organisations. The Israel lobby is not identical with the diverse Jewish-American community. Many Jewish-Americans are troubled by Israeli policies and some actively campaign against them, while some non-Jewish Americans—most of them members of the Protestant right—play a significant role in the lobby. Even pro-Israel groups differ on the question of Israeli policies. According to Matthew Dorf in the *Jewish Telegraphic Agency*: "The Zionist Organisation of America lobbies congress to slow the peace process. Their allies are mostly Republicans. At the same time, the Israel Policy Forum and Americans for Peace Now work to move the process along. Democrats are most sympathetic to their calls."

The Israel lobby is united not by a consensus about Israeli policies but by a consensus about US policies towards Israel. Most of the disparate elements of the pro-Israel coalition support two things. The first is massive US funding for Israel. In 1967 Israel's defence spending was less than half the combined defence expenditures of Egypt, Iraq, Jordan and Syria; today it is 30 per cent larger. Israel receives more of America's foreign aid budget than any other country—$3bn a year, two thirds in military grants (total aid since 1979 is over $70bn).

Along with aid, the Israel lobby demands unconditional US diplomatic protection of Israel in the UN and other forums. To a degree, this is justified; the US has been right to denounce the ritual "Zionism is racism" rhetoric of various kleptocracies and police states. The US, however, has been wrong to repeatedly block efforts by its major democratic allies in the UN security council to condemn Israeli repression and colonisation in the occupied territories.

It is difficult to prove direct cause and effect connections between the power of a lobby and America's foreign policy positions. But in the middle east, it is hard to explain America's failure to pressure Israel into a final land for peace settlement—particularly since the Oslo deal in 1993—without factoring in the Israel lobby. The influence of the lobby may be easier to detect in the way US positions have shifted on more specific totems of the conflict. For example, Israeli settlements in the occupied territories were regarded as illegal during the Carter administration. Under Reagan, they shifted to being an "obstacle" to peace and are now just a complicating factor.

Concern on the part of US citizens about the fate of members of their ethnic group or religion in foreign countries is nothing new. The Irish-American, Cuban-American and Greek-American lobbies have all significantly influenced US foreign policy. However, the Israel lobby is different in strategy and scale from other historic American ethnic lobbies. Most ethnic lobbies—of which the German and Irish diasporas were the most influential in the past—have based their power on votes, not money. (Most immigrant groups have been relatively poor at first, and have lost their ethnic identity on becoming more prosperous.) The influence of these lobbies has usually been confined to cities and states in which particular ethnic groups have been concentrated—Irish-American Boston, German-American Milwaukee, Cuban-American Miami. The emergent Latino lobby is similar in its geographic limitation. The small US Jewish population (about 2 per cent of the total) is highly concentrated in New York, Los Angeles, Miami and a few other areas.

The Israel lobby, however, is not primarily a traditional ethnic voter machine; it is an ethnic *donor* machine. Unique among ethno-political machines in the US, the Israel lobby has emulated the techniques of national lobbies based on economic interests (both industry groups and unions) or social issues (the National Rifle Association, pro and anti-abortion groups). The lobby uses nationwide campaign dona-tions, often funnelled through local "astroturf" (phony grassroots) organisations with names like Tennesseans for Better Government and the Walters Construction Management Political Committee of Colorado, to influence members of congress in areas where there are few Jewish voters.

Stephen Steinlight, in an essay for the Centre for Immigration Studies, describes how the Israel lobby uses donations to influence elected officials: "Unless and until the triumph of campaign finance reform is complete ... the great material wealth of the Jewish commu-nity will continue to give it significant advantages. We will continue to court and be courted by key figures in congress. That power is exerted within the political system from the local to national levels through soft money, and especially the provision of out of state funds to candi-dates sympathetic to Israel." Steinlight adds: "For perhaps another generation ... the Jewish community is thus in a position to divide and conquer and enter into selective coalitions that support our agendas." Steinlight is the recently retired director of national affairs at the American Jewish Committee.

As well as campaign contributions, the Israel lobby's power is exer-cised through influence on government appointments. Until recently, Democrats and Republicans differed in their attitude to the lobby but now both parties are significantly influenced by it, although in different ways.

Historically, Jewish-Americans have been part of the Democratic coalition and they remain the only white ethnic group which consis-tently votes overwhelmingly for Democrats. By contrast, between Eisenhower and the elder Bush, many Republicans shared the atti-tude attributed, perhaps apocryphally, to a former Republican secretary of state: "Fuck the Jews. They don't vote for us anyway." Influenced by big business and the oil industry in particular, Republicans often tilted towards the Arabs (Arab regimes, not voice-less Arab populations). Although Nixon, an antisemite in his personal attitudes, rescued Israel in the 1973 war, Eisenhower infuriated the Jewish-American community by thwarting the joint seizure of the Suez canal by Israel, Britain and France in 1956. Another Republican president, George Bush Sr, enraged the Israel lobby during the Gulf war by pressuring Israel not to respond to Iraq's missile attacks, choos-ing not to occupy Baghdad and promising America's Arab allies that the US would push Israel on the Palestinian issue. The elder Bush was the last president to criticise the lobby publicly, in September 1991, when he complained that "there are a thousand lobbyists up on the Hill today lobbying congress for loan guarantees for Israel and I'm one lonely little guy down here asking congress to delay its considera-tion of loan guarantees for 120 days."

The Democrats exploited this split between the Israel lobby and the first Bush administration. President Clinton went on to appoint Martin Indyk, a veteran of a pro-Israel think tank associated with AIPAC, as ambassador to Israel, only a few years after this Australian received his US citizenship papers. It is true that Clinton (and Indyk) took the Palestinian cause seriously and the US administration did push Israel further than it wanted to go on some issues prior to the Wye river agreement and in the failed Barak-Arafat negotiations. But the fact that so many US administration officials involved in those failed negotiations had ties to the Israel lobby raised troubling ques-tions about the ability of America to act as an honest broker.

Most Jewish-Americans are hostile to George W Bush, whose alliance with the Christian right disturbs them. Yet the younger Bush has, in practice, been influenced more by the Israel lobby than by the oil lobby. The state department of Colin Powell, who has called himself a "Rockefeller Republican" and supports a Palestinian state, has lost influence to the defence department, where a cadre of pro-Israel hawks allied with deputy secretary of defence Paul Wolfowitz has seized the initiative.

Richard Perle, chairman of Bush's defence policy board, co-authored a 1996 paper with Douglas J Feith for the Likud prime minister Binyamin Netanyahu. Entitled "A Clean Break: A New Strategy for Securing the Realm," it advised Netanyahu to make "a clean break from the peace process." Feith now holds one of the top positions in the Pentagon—undersecretary of defence for policy. He argued in the *National Interest* in fall 1993 that the League of Nations mandate granted Jews irrevocable settlement rights in the West Bank. In 1997, in "A Strategy for Israel," Feith called on Israel to re-occupy "the areas under Palestinian Authority control" even though "the price in blood would be high."

The radical Zionist right to which Perle and Feith belong is small in number but it has become a significant force in Republican policy-making circles. It is a recent phenomenon, dating back to the late 1970s and 1980s, when many formerly Democratic Jewish intellectuals joined the broad Reagan coalition. While many of these hawks speak in public about global crusades for democracy, the chief concern of many such "neoconservatives" is the power and reputation of Israel. William Kristol, editor of the right-wing *Weekly Standard*, explained the reason for the rhetoric about global democracy to the *Jerusalem Post* in July 2000: "I've always thought it was best for Israel for the US to be generally engaged and generally strong, and then the commitment to Israel follows from a general foreign policy."

The liberalism and Democratic partisanship of most Jewish-Americans forces the Zionist right to find its popular constituency not in the Jewish community itself, but in the Protestant evangelical right of Pat Robertson and others—many of whose members share the Christian Zionism of the early British patrons of Israel. In 1995, after I exposed the antisemitic sources of Pat Robertson's theories about a two-century-old Judaeo-Masonic conspiracy in an essay in the *New York Review of Books*, Norman Podhoretz, the editor of *Commentary*, denounced *me* rather than Robertson. Podhoretz conceded that Robertson's statements about Jewish conspiracies were antisemitic but argued that, in the light of Robertson's support for Israel, he should be excused according to the ancient rabbinical rule of *batel b'shishim*.

After campaign contributions and high-level appointments, media influence is the third major asset of the Israel lobby. The problem is not that Jews in the media censor the daily news; there are passionate Zionist publishers like Mort Zuckerman and Martin Peretz, but their very ardour tends to discredit them. The reporters of the *New York Times*, the *Washington Post*, the *Wall Street Journal* and the television networks are reasonably fair in their coverage of the middle east. The problem is that the Arab-Israeli conflict is presented in the absence of any historical or political context. For example, most Americans do not know that the Palestinian state offered by Barak consisted of several Bantustans, criss-crossed by Israeli roads with military checkpoints. Instead, most Americans have learned only that the Israelis made a generous offer which Arafat inexplicably rejected.

It is not in the news stories, but in the opinion pages and the journals of opinion—which ought to provide the missing context—that propaganda for Israel has free rein. There are several widely syndicated columnists and television pundits who are apologists for the Israeli right, like Safire, Cal Thomas, George Will and Charles Krauthammer. Others, like Anthony Lewis, Flora Lewis and Thomas Friedman, do criticise right-wing Israeli governments, but anything more than the mildest criticism of Israel is taboo in the mainstream media.

The taboo against anti-Arab bigotry, however, is weak. One of the saddest consequences of Israel's colonialism has been the moral coarsening of elements of the Jewish-American community. I grew up admiring Jewish civil rights activists for their sometimes heroic role in the fight to dismantle segregation in the US. But today I frequently hear Jewish acquaintances discuss Arabs in general, and Palestinians in particular, in terms as racist as those once used by southerners in public when discussing black people. "Israel should have given the Palestinians to Jordan after 1967," a Jewish editor recently said to me, in the same tone used by an elderly white southerner who once told me, "We should have left them all in Africa." The parallel can be extended. After 1830, the defence of slavery and later segregation in the old south led white southerners to abandon the liberal idealism of the founding era in favour of harsh racism and a siege mentality. Since 1967, the need to justify the rule of Israel over a conquered helot population has produced a similar shift from humane idealism to unapologetic tribalism in parts of the diaspora, as well as in Israel.

The restraint on robust debate about Israel in the political centre means that the most vocal critics of Israeli policy and the US Israel lobby are found on the far left and the far right. Critics on the left, like Edward Said and Noam Chomsky, are not taken seriously outside of left-wing academic circles because their condemnations of US and Israeli policy in the middle east are part of ritualised denunciations of all US foreign policy everywhere.

But the Israel lobby's influence on US policy and public opinion is challenged by some more credible groups ranging from the increasingly vocal Arab-American lobby and black Democrats (who tend to sympathise with the Palestinians), to career military and foreign service personnel and the Republican business establishment, particularly oil executives, who are more interested in the Persian Gulf than in the West Bank. In the long run, the relative diminution of the Jewish-American population, as a result of intermarriage and immigration-led population growth, will combine to attenuate the lobby's power.

At present, however, members of congress from all regions are still reluctant to offend a single-issue lobby that can and will subsidise their opponents; many journalists and policy experts say in private that they are afraid of being blacklisted by editors and publishers who are zealous Israel supporters; top jobs in the US national security apparatus routinely go to individuals with close personal and professional ties to Israel and its American lobby; and soldiers and career diplomats are sometimes smeared in whisper campaigns if they thwart the goals of Israeli governments. In these circumstances, how could US policy not be biased in favour of Israel?

The kind of informed, centrist criticism of Israel which can be found in Britain and the rest of Europe, a criticism that recognises Israel's right to exist and defend itself, while deploring its brutal occupation of Palestinian territory, is far less visible in the US. What is needed at this moment in American and world history is a responsible criticism of the US Israel lobby which, unlike the left critique, accepts the broad outlines of US grand strategy as legitimate and which, unlike the critique of the far right, is not motivated by an animus against either Jewish-Americans or the state of Israel as such.

In the past, the Israel lobby had one feature which distinguished it from, say, the Irish lobby: the country it supported was threatened with extinction by its neighbours. That is no longer the case. Moreover, most Americans would support Israel's right to exist and to defend itself against threats even if the Israel lobby did not exist. However, in the absence of the Israel lobby, America's elected representatives would surely have made aid to Israel conditional on Israeli withdrawal from the occupied territories. It is this largely *unconditional* nature of US support for Israel that compromises its middle east policy.

In the years ahead, we Americans must reform our political system to purge it of the corrupting influence, not only of corporations and unions, but also of ethnic lobbies—all of them, the Arab-American lobby as well as the Israel lobby. As the percentage of the US population made up of recent immigrants grows, so does the danger that foreign policy will be subcontracted to this or that ethnic diaspora encouraged—by the success of the Israel lobby—to believe that deep attachment to a foreign country is a normal and acceptable part of US citizenship.

The truth about America's Israel lobby is this: it is not all-powerful, but it is still far too powerful for the good of the US and its alliances in the middle east and elsewhere.

Nuclear calm in the subcontinent •
Pervez Hoodbhoy
JULY 2002

Nuclear tensions in the subcontinent are now down a couple of notches and some semblance of normalcy has returned. But, even at the peak of the crisis, few Indians or Pakistanis lost much sleep. Stock markets flickered, but there was no run on the banks or panic buying of necessities. Schools and colleges, which close at the first hint of a real crisis, functioned normally. We saw the crisis as more of the usual, with the rhetoric just a bit fiercer.

The outside world saw it in very different terms—as a potentially suicidal struggle between two nuclear armed states, inexperienced in the practice of nuclear brinkmanship. Foreign nationals streamed out of both countries. They may have been right to do so.

In a public debate in Islamabad on the eve of the Pakistani nuclear tests, the former chief of the Pakistan army General Mirza Aslam Beg said, "We can make a first strike, and a second strike or even a third." The prospect of nuclear war left him unmoved. "You can die crossing the street," he said, "or you could die in a nuclear war. You've got to die someday, anyway."

Across the border, India's Defence Minister George Fernandes, in an interview with the *Hindustan Times*, voiced similar sentiments: "We could take a strike, survive, and then hit back. Pakistan would be finished." Indian Defence Secretary Yogendra Narain took things a step further in an interview with *Outlook* magazine: "A surgical strike is the answer," he said. But if that failed to resolve things, he said, "We must be prepared for total mutual destruction." Brahma Chellaney, a hawk whose feathers caught fire during the Kargil war, demanded that India "call Pakistan's nuclear bluff."

Pakistan and India are making history in their own way. No nuclear states in the world have ever engaged in such rhetoric. The fear of mutual destruction has always put sharp limits on the tone and volume of nuclear shadow boxing. So, what accounts for this extraordinary difference between us—Pakistanis and Indians—and the rest of the world? What makes us such extraordinarily bold nuclear gamblers, playing close to the brink?

In part, the answer is that India and Pakistan are largely traditional societies, where the fundamental belief structure demands disempowerment and surrender to larger forces. A fatalistic Hindu belief that the stars above determine our destiny, or the equivalent Muslim belief in *qismet* certainly accounts for part of the problem. Conversations often end on the note "what will be, will be," after which people shrug their shoulders and move on to something else. Because they feel that they will be protected by larger, unseen forces, the level of risk-taking is extraordinary. The fact that people travel at all on the madly career-ing public buses of Karachi or Bombay, which routinely smash into and kill pedestrians, is good evidence.

But other reasons may be more important. Close government control of national television, especially in Pakistan, has ensured that critical discussion of nuclear weapons and nuclear war are not aired. Instead, in Pakistan's public squares and crossroads stand fibre-glass replicas of the nuclear test site. For the masses, they are symbols of national glory not death and horror.

Nuclear ignorance is almost total, extending to the educated. When asked, some students at the university in Islamabad where I teach said that a nuclear war would be the end of the world. Others thought of nukes as just bigger bombs. Many said it was not their concern, but the army's. Almost none knew about the possibility of a nuclear firestorm, about radioactivity, or damage to the gene pool.

Because nuclear war is considered a distant abstraction, civil defence in both countries is non-existent. India's Admiral Ramu Ramdas, now retired and a peace activist, caustically remarked recently, "There are no air raid shelters in this city of Delhi, because in this country people are considered expendable." Islamabad's civil defence budget is $40,000 and this year's allocation has yet to be disbursed. No serious contingency plans have been devised, plans that might save millions of lives by giving information about non-radio-active drinking water, escape routes and so on.

Ignorance and the consequent lack of fear make it easier for leaders to treat their people as pawns in a mad nuclear game. How can one explain Indian Prime Minister Atal Bihari Vajpayee's recent exhortations to his troops in Kashmir to prepare for "decisive victory?" His nuclear brinkmanship has been made possible by influential Indian experts seeking to trivialise Pakistan's nuclear capability. Such analysts have gained wide currency.

The reasoning of the "trivialisation school" goes as follows: Pakistan is a client state of the US and Pakistani nuclear weapons are under the control of the US. Hence, in an extreme crisis, the US would either prohibit their use by Pakistan or, if need be, destroy them. At a meeting in January in Dubai, I heard senior Indian analysts say that they are "bored" with Pakistan's nuclear threats and no longer believe them. K Subrahmanyam, an influential Indian hawk, believes that India can "sleep in peace."

Indian denial of Pakistani capabilities is not new. Two months before the May 1998 nuclear tests by India and Pakistan, as part of a delegation from Pugwash (an international organisation of scientists concerned about nuclear war), I met with Prime Minister Inder Kumar Gujral in Delhi. In response to my worries about a nuclear catastrophe on the subcontinent, he assured me—in public and privately—that Pakistan did not have the capability to make atomic bombs.

Pakistan proved the doubters wrong. Forced out of the closet by the Indian tests, Pakistan's nuclear weapons gave the country a false sense of confidence and security. This encouraged it to launch its secret war in the Kargil area of Kashmir. In fact, this war will be seen by historians as the first that was initiated by nuclear weapons. Although India wanted to respond, the existence of Pakistan's deterrence limited its options.

Then came 11th September. In a global climate deeply hostile to Islamic militancy, new possibilities opened up to India. Seeking to settle scores with Pakistan, India now began to consider strikes on militant camps on the Pakistani side of the line of control in Kashmir. To sell this to the Indian public, denying the potency of Pakistan's nuclear weapons was essential.

But to challenge a nuclear Pakistan requires a denial of reality. It is a big leap of faith to presume that the US has either the will—or power—to destroy Pakistani nukes. Tracking and destroying even a handful of mobile nuclear-armed missiles is not easy. During the Cuban missile crisis, the US Air Force could not ensure more than 90 per cent effectiveness in a surprise attack against the Soviet missiles on the island even though it had aerial photos of the missile locations and its planes were only minutes flying time away. More recently, in Iraq, US efforts to destroy Iraqi Scuds had limited success. There is no precedent for one country trying to destroy another's nuclear bombs. And 100 per cent success is required—one remaining nuke could unleash catastrophe.

Fight or flight? Biological evolution has programmed us for two elemental responses to external threats. Without fear there is no flight, just fight. But the brave are doomed. Ignorant and fearless, India and Pakistan could still add a frightening new chapter to the nuclear deterrence textbooks.

Marriage for a night in Iran • Wendell Steavenson

OCTOBER 2002

O n my first day in the Islamic Republic of Iran, all I could think about was my *hijab*, the Islamic covering which I was required to wear as a matter of law whenever I was in a public space. My headscarf itched under my chin; my coat felt tight under my arms. I worried about the inch of hair that was showing; I reached up constantly to adjust it, smoothing, checking. I felt oppressed. I saw how men walked and worked, wearing trousers and shirts just as they liked. Watching the women, I noted the variations of *hijab*: trousered legs and thigh-length jackets, sheer flowered headscarves, blue headcoverings with a hole for the face that came down to the breast bone, knee-length manteaus and black *chadors*—tents of sheer rayon that fell from the forehead in a mass of folds to the ankle. They seemed difficult to control. The women who wore them were constantly hitching a fold under an arm, grasping a hem with their fingers, drawing it close in around the eyebrows.

Then, after a few days, I got used to the headscarf. I stopped fidgeting and felt normal. As Iranian women often reminded me, "*Hijab!* It's nothing. In Iran, we have much more important battles to fight."

In Iran, two women are the equivalent to one man as witnesses in a court of law. A woman must have permission from her husband if she wants to leave the country. Men can take up to four wives, but a woman must have her father's permission to marry. Men are granted divorces relatively easily; a woman has to prove abandonment, addiction or impotence. After a divorce, women have custody of boys only until the age of two and girls until they are seven.

However, Iran is also a country where 62 per cent of university students are women, where women work in ministries, schools and hospitals, where they can run their own businesses, drive and vote. There are several female MPs and a female minister of the environment. Iran is a country where, professionally, women can do almost anything.

I was new and confused, a western woman trying to unravel law from religion from culture. I came up with a Venn diagram of three intersecting circles: one for the Islamic Republic and the laws of the mullahs, one for the Koran and its directives from the prophet Muhammad, and one for the culture of the Iranian people—customs and traditions that stretch back millennia, long before Islam came to Persia.

Iran is full of anomalies. In the Tehran bazaar I saw women covered in flapping black *chadors* shopping for short-sleeved, bare-shouldered white wedding dresses. Eminem is predictably outlawed and predictably popular. But Dariush, a banned Iranian singer who lives in LA and sings traditional Iranian songs backed with drum machines, is more popular. The 14th-century poet Hafiz, who praises women and wine, is so much a part of the national soul that even clerics recite him. At a party, my host offered me a glass of smuggled Australian Shiraz (the fabled Persian grape) and told me that he had paid off the police not to harass female guests for scant *hijab* and being seen with men who were not of their immediate family. Yet more than half of Iranian women choose to wear the unwieldy *chador*, even though a full length manteau is acceptable to the authorities.

In the midst of all of this, at the heart of my western questions about sex and freedom, religion and female independence, I found the strangest anomaly of all: the *sigheh*.

The *sigheh* is a form of temporary marriage peculiar to the Shia branch of Islam. In its fundamentals it is just like a regular marriage, a contract in which women are entitled to a *mehriyeh*—an amount of money—and in which any children born of the union are considered legitimate. The only difference is that the *sigheh* has a time limit that may be as long as many years or as short as a few hours.

This sounds like an excellent way to avoid the illegality of adultery and sex outside marriage, punishable by stoning (though this almost never happens), lashes and fines. In reality, the practice of *sigheh* is the ultimate oddity in Iran—a sexual freedom sanctioned by the religious establishment but taboo in society.

"In Iranian society, women do not like to admit to *sigheh*," Shirin Ebadi, a specialist in family law, explained. A married man may take as many women as *sigheh* as he likes. Married women, however, may not enter into a *sigheh*. A divorced woman may arrange a *sigheh* freely; an unmarried woman must have the permission of her father.

Ebadi has several certificates from foreign human rights organisations in her office as well as a green, flowery towel framed and hanging on her wall—a souvenir from her 25 days detained in prison for defending a group of students who had been assaulted by vigilantes after student unrest in 1999. She is as outspoken as any woman I spoke to in Iran. "Our problem is not religion, it is the ruling male chauvinist culture," she told me.

I was continually impressed in Iran by women who had stuck their heads above the parapet and suffered the consequences. One afternoon I met Manijeh Hekmat, a director who had recently finished a film entitled *Women's Prison*, in which the prison warden was characterised as a dictator, inmates were shown without *hijab* and there was a lesbian subplot. Unsurprisingly, the film was banned. Hekmat was tired of her failed efforts to get through the censor. "Prison conditions are the reflection of society," she said, planting her red Doc Martens squarely on the floor and pulling her long *hijab* coat over her knees.

Ebadi and Hekmat are at the forefront of feminist argument. The more conservative women I met attending Friday prayer were not so concerned with reform. These were the traditional women of south Tehran, wives and mothers of the workmen and small shopkeepers. When they learned that I was a journalist, they crowded around me.

One wanted me to know that her daughter was a doctor, but that she also knew the Koran by heart. A robust middle-aged woman told me she studied at a theocratic school, another that she had been illiterate before the revolution, "but now I have a high school diploma." "We go swimming twice a week," announced a younger woman.

This was the biggest surprise of all. Far from repressing women, the revolution freed them from the seclusion of their homes. Traditional families began to send their daughters to school and university—because they would be in *hijab*, and because in the Islamic Republic there were no discos, no alcohol.

In some respects, what Iranian women have gone through in the last 20 years is much the same as western women over the last 50. Education has brought women into the workforce and given them financial independence. The difference in Iran is the lack of an accompanying sexual revolution. Women are still not supposed to have sex outside marriage. Virginity is highly valued in a bride. Divorced or widowed women entering into *sigheh* are viewed as something between a prostitute and a mistress. For unmarried girls, *sigheh* is completely unacceptable.

"Men are obsessed with the blood. Our boys expect to see blood when they sleep with their wives for the first time," Massey Shiravi told me, pouring more tea, proffering another chocolate. She is a gynaecologist, sympathetic and practical. She sees women before the wedding and the day after, with parents and husbands. Always there is the question of blood. Often girls beg Shiravi to repair a hymen and, illegally, she does so. If there has been no blood on the wedding night the husband will be furious, the girl humiliated. Shiravi gives the girl a private consultation, takes a napkin, puts a spot of blood at its centre and shows it to the husband. "Men are really stupid. I make up all sorts of stories about a bruise or a blood blister, explaining why he could not produce the blood but I was able to. They believe it."

I asked her if things had changed over the 40 years she had been practising. She said no. She told me about 14 year olds beaten by their fathers because a government pathologist—the doctor who determines virginity—had found a damaged hymen; of husbands' families coming to her house in the middle of a wedding night screaming, "no blood!"; of incest cases thrown out of court…

"The trouble with Iran is that when you scratch the surface you find a lot of nasty tales," Pari told me me. Pari, a freelance journalist, had been educated in Britain and had returned to Tehran recently. She was my bridge between worlds. We were discussing things in a tea house in Tajrish. "So what do people do?" I asked, "What do girls and boys do?" "They play around," Pari said, at ease with western curiosity, "they play with it, but don't penetrate."

Sigheh is a Shia solution to a physical reality. It's a way of trying to organise sexual relations and the need for them within Sharia law. There are many women, for example, who hover around the religious shrines of Qom and Mashhad offering *sigheh* for a couple of hours to travelling clerics and pilgrims. During the war with Iraq, the government encouraged *sigheh* for war widows on the grounds that they could form relationships and receive some money to relieve their plight. More recently, elements in the government have even tried to suggest that *sigheh* could be a way for girls and boys to get to know each other before marriage. "It's a way of trying to control what is already happening," explained Parvin Ardalan, a journalist specialising in women's issues. "They used to arrest a boy and a girl found together. They might say that they were *Sigheh Mahram*, which meant they were legally engaged. They would then have to go before a judge. The girl's hymen would be checked and, if she was not a virgin, she could be lashed. Nowadays there is not so much of this harassment; there are new cafés opening all the time where boys and girls go together."

The Koran is like a handbook; its directives for how to live a good Islamic life are specific. It is not like the Bible, which is full of stories and allegories to interpret. In the holy city of Qom, the intellectual cradle of the revolution, the Grand Ayatollah Sanei explained to me, "Islam is a religion which comes as advice for the human being and there are laws which should be based upon those principles… The principles are of justice, equality and freedom and of easiness." Sex is a part of life and the Prophet is clearly in favour of it. "Islam is a very sexual religion," declared Parvin, as we sat in a kebab place one night, "it allows sexual relations for men in many cases, but the problem is women. Women are supposed to control and guard their sexuality."

Sigheh's tacit nod at sex—at women having sex—is at the nub of the ambivalence. Zahra Mostafavi is the head of the Women's Society of the Islamic Republic of Iran, an organisation which acts as a sort of think tank advising the government on women's issues. Mostafavi's conservative Islamic credentials are impeccable; she is the daughter of the late Ayatollah Khomeini. "It's a natural thing for both sexes to have sexual tendencies," she admits. For Mostafavi, and for other conservatives, *sigheh* is justified on two grounds: that men have these urges and they should have some legal outlet, and that women are, in fact, protected in a *sigheh* because they take on the rights of a real wife— albeit temporarily. "*Sigheh* is actually beneficial for women because it makes the man not take the relationships lightly," she says.

But for many in the clerical establishment, the reality of the arrangement remains distasteful. Grand Ayatollah Sanei is known for his liberal views on women; he talks openly about the need for reform on issues like unequal blood money, women as valid witnesses, and getting women on the national jurisprudence committee. "I believe *sigheh* is a spare tyre," he told me, "really it should only be used in cases of emergency. Problems cannot be solved by *sigheh*; it can in fact ruin lives."

I heard many different stories about *sigheh* situations. They were seldom happy tales of sexual freedom; mostly they were sordid extramarital complications. Pari told me about her neighbour who lived upstairs. A very traditional woman, she hardly left her apartment, and depended on her husband even to do the shopping. The woman could not have children, but her husband stayed with her anyway, perhaps because the apartment was in her name. One day she found a small repair in one of her husband's underpants; she knew it wasn't her repair. It turned out that he had had a *sigheh* with another woman for some time and had a daughter from the relationship. Pari's neighbour was distraught, but still she didn't throw him out of the house—not even when the daughter turned seven and came to live with them. "Effectively, she is bringing up this child who is not her own; it's a disaster for her," Pari said. "What about the daughter's natural mother?" I asked. "Apparently she has several other children, by other men she has had *sigheh* with—she was happy to have someone else bring up this child."

The emotional toll of *sigheh*, often just a sanctioned infidelity, is hidden. I found it almost impossible to find women who had had a *sigheh* to talk about it. I went to see a male notary. "Not so many *sighehs* are registered here," he told me. "They prefer to keep it quieter and go through a mullah. I register only about six or eight a month." There are many circumstances in which a couple might get a *sigheh*: young, liberal people who fancy each other, a divorcee trying to shore up her finances, or even people who work in the same office. But in practice, most *sighehs* occur between older men and divorced woman. "Usually the woman is having some kind of family problem," the notary told me. Legally, men must have permission from their first wife in order to get a *sigheh*, but we usually give it to them without this because in Sharia law it is not required."

I leafed through photocopies of *sigheh* registrations. There was definitely a norm: almost three quarters of the couples had stipulated a contract for one year and the price, the *mehriyeh* due to the woman, was 14 gold coins. One gold coin is worth about $80. "That's not bad money," I remarked.

Finally, on my last day in Tehran, I met a woman who had had a *sigheh* and was willing to talk about it. Feri was not what I expected. She decanted herself from a sheer black headscarf and a slinky black coat. She had a swathe of blonde hair, high-arched tweezered eyebrows and endless legs. She was 26. "I consider it a duty as a woman to explain these things," she said. Feri was divorced and had a baby son. She was not a typical Iranian woman, but she was at the vanguard of something, young and angry. "A girl in this country has no rights," she said. "She is either under the protection of her father or her husband. She just goes from one man to another."

After her divorce, Feri had a boyfriend of whom her father disapproved. Their *sigheh* had been an arrangement for legal purposes only ("it didn't change anything between us," she said) but it also served as a slap in the face for Feri's father. He was furious. "He didn't want me with any man," she told me, describing him as a "savage dictator" and saying that she thought he was a typical father. "But he has made *sigheh* a hundred times. My mother knows this quite well. But, no, it's not allowed for his daughter."

Such double standards are manifold. They are there in the shrines where mullahs preach family values but sign short-term *sighehs* for travelling colleagues. One young university professor I talked to said that he understood the theory about boys and girls and free relationships, but he admitted that when he applied it to his own possible future wife, he didn't like the idea at all.

The Koran, on the other hand, is in this respect without hypocrisy. Muhammad preached kindness and consideration to women. Some practices like polygamy may seem strange to westerners, but in the context of 7th century war-torn Arabia, it allowed war widows to be taken into a family. And it may seem unfair to a western mind that a sister only inherits half the amount her brother does, but it still grants financial independence to a woman and is far fairer than primogeniture. Famously, the *hijab* is not compulsory in the Koran; neither is the ban on alcohol. Many of the rules we see as discriminatory were progressive for their time. And if some of the laws seem a little unbalanced for a modern society in which women work and earn, the Shia religion allows for modifications.

The difficulty is that Iranians live according to the laws of the Islamic Republic and the prescriptions of the prevailing social culture. In Iran, prohibitions on satellite dishes, parties, alcohol, books, independent journalism, foreign movies, American pop—on ideas and culture contrary to the revolution—are quite freely flouted by much of the urban middle class. But the constraints on the relationships between men and women are much less flouted and no one ever makes light of them. It turns out to be easier to ignore the law than to contravene sexual convention. The final irony for the westerner is that sexual attitudes are the result of a kind of collective will; in short, they are the most democratic feature of the country.

Dominant minorities • Amy Chua

DECEMBER 2003

One morning in September 1994, I received a call from my mother in California. In a hushed voice, she told me that my Aunt Leona, my father's twin sister, had been murdered in her home in the Philippines, her throat slit by her chauffeur. My mother broke the news to me in our Hokkien Chinese dialect. But the word "murder" she said in English, as if to wall off the act from the family through language.

The murder of a relative is horrible for anyone, anywhere. My father's grief was impenetrable; to this day, he has not broken his silence on the subject. For the rest of the family, though, there was an added element of disgrace. For the Chinese, luck is a moral attribute, and a lucky person would never be murdered. Like having a birth defect, or marrying a Filipino, being murdered is shameful.

My three younger sisters and I were very fond of my Aunt Leona, who was petite and quirky and had never married. Like many wealthy Filipino Chinese she had multiple bank accounts, in Honolulu, San Francisco and Chicago. She visited us in the US regularly. Having no children of her own, she doted on her nieces and showered us with trinkets. As we grew older, the trinkets became treasures. On my tenth birthday she gave me ten small diamonds, wrapped in toilet paper. My aunt loved diamonds and bought them by the dozen, concealing them in empty Elizabeth Arden moisturiser jars. She liked accumulating things. When we ate at McDonald's, she stuffed her Gucci purse with free packets of ketchup.

According to the police report, my Aunt Leona, "a 58-year-old single woman," was killed in her living room with a "butcher's knife" at 8pm on 12th September 1994. Two of her maids were questioned, and they confessed that Nilo Abique, my aunt's chauffeur, had planned and executed the murder with their assistance. But Abique, the report went on to say, had "disappeared." The two maids were later released.

My relatives arranged a funeral for my aunt in the prestigious Chinese cemetery in Manila where many of my ancestors are buried.

After the funeral, I asked one of my uncles whether there had been any developments in the murder investigation. He replied tersely that the killer had not been found. His wife added that the police had essentially closed the case.

I could not understand my relatives' almost indifferent attitude. Why were they not more shocked that my aunt had been killed by people who worked for her, lived with her, saw her every day? Why were they not outraged that the maids had been released? When I pressed my uncle, he was short with me. "That's the way things are here," he said.

My uncle was not simply being callous. My aunt's death was part of a common pattern. Hundreds of Chinese are kidnapped or murdered every year by ethnic Filipinos. Nor is it unusual that my aunt's killer was never apprehended. The police in the Philippines, all poor ethnic Filipinos themselves, are notoriously unmotivated in these cases.

My family is part of the Philippines' tiny but economically powerful Chinese minority. Although they constitute 1 per cent of the population, Chinese Filipinos control about 60 per cent of the private economy, including the country's four airlines and almost all of the banks, hotels, shopping malls and big conglomerates. My own family runs a plastics conglomerate and owns swathes of prime real estate—and they are only "third-tier" Chinese tycoons. They also have safe deposit boxes full of gold bars, each one the size of a chocolate bar. I myself have such a gold bar. My Aunt Leona sent it to me as a law school graduation present a few years before she died.

Since my aunt's murder, one childhood memory keeps haunting me. I was eight, staying at my family's splendid hacienda-style house in Manila. It was before dawn, still dark. Wide awake, I decided to get a drink from the kitchen. I must have gone down an extra flight of stairs, because I stumbled on to six male bodies. I had found the male servants' quarters, where my family's houseboys, gardeners, and chauffeurs—I sometimes imagine that Nilo Abique was among them—were sleeping on mats on a dirt floor. The place stank of sweat and urine. I was horrified.

I mentioned the incident to my Aunt Leona, who laughed affectionately and explained that the Filipino servants were fortunate to be working for our family. If not for their positions, they would be living among rats and open sewers. A Filipino maid then walked in; she had a bowl of food for my aunt's Pekingese. My aunt took the bowl but kept talking as if the maid were not there. The Filipinos, she continued—in Chinese, but not caring whether the maid understood or not—were lazy and unintelligent. If they didn't like working for us, they were free to leave.

Nearly two thirds of the roughly 80m ethnic Filipinos in the Philippines live on less than $2 a day. But poverty by itself does not make people kill. To poverty must be added indignity, hopelessness and grievance. In the Philippines, millions of Filipinos work for Chinese; almost no Chinese work for Filipinos. The Chinese dominate industry and commerce at every level of society. Global markets intensify this dominance: when foreign investors do business in the Philippines, they deal almost exclusively with Chinese. Apart from a handful of corrupt politicians and a few aristocratic Spanish mestizo families, all of the Philippines' billionaires are of Chinese descent. My relatives live literally walled off from the Filipino masses, in a luxurious, all-Chinese residential enclave, on streets named Harvard and Princeton. The entry points are manned by armed guards.

My aunt's killing was just a pinprick in a violent world. But there is a connection between her murder and the Serbian concentration camps of the early 1990s, the murder of 800,000 Tutsis by ordinary Hutus in Rwanda in 1994, the mobs in Indonesia in 1998 which looted hundreds of Chinese properties leaving nearly 2,000 dead, and even the terror attacks of 11th September. The connection lies in the relationship among the three most powerful forces operating in the world today: markets, democracy and ethnic hatred. There exists today a phenomenon—pervasive outside the west yet rarely acknowledged, indeed often viewed as taboo—that turns free market democracy into an engine of ethnic conflagration. I am speaking of the phenomenon of market-dominant minorities: ethnic minorities who, for varying reasons, tend under market conditions to dominate economically, often to a startling extent, the indigenous majorities.

Market-dominant minorities can be found in every part of the world. The Chinese are a market-dominant minority throughout southeast Asia. In 1998, Chinese Indonesians, only 3 per cent of the population, controlled 70 per cent of the private economy, including all of the big conglomerates. In Myanmar, the Chinese dominate the economies of Mandalay and Rangoon. Whites are a market-dominant minority in South Africa—and, in a more complex sense, in Brazil and much of Latin America. Indians have historically been a market-dominant minority in east Africa, the Lebanese in west Africa and the Ibo in Nigeria. Croats were a market-dominant minority in Yugoslavia, as Jews are in post-communist Russia (six of the seven biggest "oligarchs" are of Jewish origin). India has no market-dominant minority at the national level but plenty at the state level.

Market-dominant minorities are the Achilles heel of free market democracy. In societies with such a minority, markets and democracy favour not just different people or different classes but different ethnic groups. Markets concentrate wealth, often spectacular wealth, in the hands of the market-dominant minority, while democracy increases the political power of the impoverished majority. In these circumstances, the pursuit of free market democracy becomes an engine of potentially catastrophic ethnonationalism, pitting a frustrated indigenous majority, easily aroused by opportunistic politicians, against a resented, wealthy ethnic minority. This conflict is playing out in country after country today, from Bolivia to Sierra Leone, from Indonesia to Zimbabwe, from Russia to the middle east.

Since 11th September, the conflict has been brought home to the US. Americans are not an ethnic minority. But Americans are perceived as the *world*'s market-dominant minority, wielding disproportionate economic power. As a result, they have become the object of the same kind of popular resentment that afflicts the Chinese of southeast Asia, the whites of Zimbabwe, and the Jews of Russia.

Global anti-Americanism has many causes. One of them is the US-promoted global spread of free markets and democracy. Throughout the world markets are perceived as reinforcing US wealth and dominance. At the same time, global populist and democratic movements give strength and voice to the impoverished masses.

For globalisation's enthusiasts, the cure for group hatred and ethnic violence around the world is more markets and more democracy. Together, markets and democracy will gradually transform states into a war-shunning, prosperous community, and individuals into liberal, civic-minded citizens and consumers. Ethnic hatred and religious zealotry will fade away.

I believe, rather, that in the numerous societies around the world that have a market-dominant minority, markets and democracy are *not* mutually reinforcing. Because markets and democracy benefit different ethnic groups in such societies, the pursuit of free market democracy produces highly combustible conditions. In absolute terms, the majority may or may not be better off—a dispute that much of the globalisation debate revolves around—but any sense of improvement is overwhelmed by its continuing poverty relative to the hated minority's economic success. More humiliating still, market-dominant minorities, along with their foreign investor partners, invariably come to control the crown jewels of the economy, which are often symbolic of the nation's patrimony and identity—oil in Russia and Venezuela, diamonds in South Africa, silver and tin in Bolivia, jade, teak and rubies in Myanmar.

Introducing democracy under such circumstances does not transform voters into open-minded co-citizens in a national community. As America celebrated the spread of democracy in the 1990s, the world's new political slogans were these: "Georgia for the Georgians," "Eritreans out of Ethiopia," "Kenya for Kenyans," "Kazakhstan for Kazakhs," "Serbia for Serbs," "Hutu Power," "Jews out of Russia."

The backlash against a market-dominant minority typically takes one of three forms. The first is a backlash against markets that seem skewed in favour of the market-dominant minority. The second is an attack on democracy by forces favourable to the market-dominant minority. And the third is violence, sometimes genocidal, against the market-dominant minority itself.

Zimbabwe illustrates the first kind of backlash—an ethnically targeted anti-market reaction. For many years, Robert Mugabe has encouraged the violent seizure of 10m acres of white-owned commercial farmland. As one Zimbabwean argued, "The land belongs to us. The foreigners should not own it. There is no black Zimbabwean who owns land in England." Mugabe has been more explicit: "Strike fear in the heart of the white man, our real enemy." Most of the country's whites are third-generation Zimbabweans. They are 1 per cent of the population, but they have for generations controlled 70 per cent of the best land, largely in the form of highly productive 3,000-acre tobacco and sugar farms.

Watching Zimbabwe's economy take a free fall as a result of the mass land grab, the US and Britain, together with dozens of human rights groups, urged Mugabe to step down and called for "free and fair elections." But the idea that democracy is the answer to Zimbabwe's problems is naive. Perhaps Mugabe would have lost the 2002 elections in the absence of foul play. But even if that is so, it is important to recall that Mugabe himself is a product of democracy. The hero of Zimbabwe's black liberation movement and a master manipulator of the masses, he swept to victory in the elections of 1980 by promising to expropriate white land. Repeating that promise has helped him win every election since. Moreover, Mugabe's land seizure campaign was another product of the democratic process. It was deftly timed in anticipation of the 2000 and 2002 elections, and calculated to mobilise popular support for the teetering regime.

In the contest between an economically powerful ethnic minority and a numerically powerful impoverished majority, the majority does not always prevail. Rather than a backlash against the market, in some cases there is a backlash against democracy. The world's most notorious cases of "crony capitalism" have all involved partnerships between a market-dominant ethnic minority and a co-operative autocrat. Ferdinand Marcos's dictatorship in the Philippines sheltered and profited from the country's wealthy Chinese before he was driven from office in 1986. In Kenya, former President Moi, who had once warned Africans to "beware of bad Asians," was sustained by a series of "business arrangements" with local Indian tycoons. And the bloody tragedy of Sierra Leone's recent history can be traced in significant part to the regime of President Siaka Stevens, who converted his elective office into a dictatorship during the early 1970s and formed an alliance with five of the country's Lebanese diamond dealers.

The third and most ferocious kind of backlash is majority-supported violence aimed at eliminating a market-dominant minority. Three recent examples are the ethnic cleansing of Croats in parts of the former Yugoslavia, the attacks on the Chinese minority in Indonesia and the Tutsi slaughter in Rwanda. In each case, democratisation released long-suppressed hatreds against a prosperous ethnic minority.

In the former Yugoslavia the Croats, along with the Slovenes, long enjoyed a strikingly higher standard of living than the Serbs and other ethnic groups. Croatia and Slovenia are largely Catholic, with strong links to western Europe, while the Eastern Orthodox Serbs inhabit the rugged south and lived for centuries under the Ottoman empire. By the 1990s, per capita income in northern Yugoslavia was three times that in the south. The sudden coming of electoral democracy helped to stir ancient enmities. In Serbia, Slobodan Milosevic swept to power in 1989. In a famous speech delivered in March 1991— including an allusion to Croat and Slovene market dominance —Milosevic declared: "If we must fight, then my God we will fight. And I hope they will not be so crazy as to fight against us. Because if we don't know how to work well or to do business, at least we know how to fight well!"

Critics of globalisation draw attention to the grotesque imbalances produced by free markets. Defenders of globalisation respond that the world's poor would be even worse off without global marketisation, and recent World Bank studies show that, with some exceptions, including most of Africa, globalisation's "trickle down" benefits the poor as well as the rich in developing countries. But both sides of the argument tend to see wealth and poverty in terms of class conflict, not ethnic conflict. This might make sense in the advanced western societies, but the ethnic realities of the developing world are different.

The anti-globalisation movement asks for more democracy. But unless democratisation means more than unrestrained majority rule it can be short-sighted, even dangerous. The fall of Suharto's Indonesian dictatorship in May 1998, for example, was accompanied by an eruption of anti-Chinese violence. For three days, Chinese shopkeepers huddled behind locked doors while Muslim mobs looted. In the end 2,000 people died and tens of billions of dollars—belonging to Chinese cronies of Suharto—left the country, plunging the economy into a crisis from which it has still not recovered. Moreover, little noticed in the west, the post-Suharto government has nationalised about $58bn of Chinese assets.

Markets, democracy and, especially, ethnicity are notoriously difficult concepts to define. Ethnic identity is not a static, scientifically determinable status but shifting and highly malleable. In Rwanda, for example, the 14 per cent Tutsi minority dominated the Hutu majority economically and politically for four centuries, as a kind of cattle-owning aristocracy. But for most of this period, the lines between Hutus and Tutsi were permeable. The two groups spoke the same language, intermarriage occurred, and successful Hutus could "become Tutsi." That ceased after the Belgians arrived and, steeped in specious theories of racial superiority, issued ethnic identity cards on the basis of nose length and cranial circumference. The resulting sharp ethnic divisions were later exploited by the leaders of the Hutu Power movement, especially after US and French pressure to democratise in the early 1990s. Along similar lines, all over Latin America today—where it is often said that there are no "ethnic divisions" because everyone has "mixed" blood—large numbers of impoverished Bolivians, Chileans and Peruvians are suddenly being told that they are Aymaras, Incas, or just *indios*, whatever identity best resonates and mobilises.

Ethnic identity is rarely constructed out of thin air. Subjective perceptions of identity often depend on more objective traits assigned to individuals based on physical features, language differences, or ancestry. If you tell black and white Zimbabweans that "ethnicity is a social construct" you will not be taken seriously. Moreover, there is zero intermarriage between blacks and whites in Zimbabwe, just as there is almost no intermarriage between Chinese and Malays or Arabs and Israelis. Ethnicity can be both palpably real and an artefact of the imagination rooted in the recesses of history—fluid and manipulable, yet real enough to kill for. This is what makes ethnic conflict so hard to understand and contain.

I do not propose a universal theory applicable to every developing country. There are certainly developing countries without market-dominant minorities: China and Argentina are two major examples. Nor do I argue that ethnic conflict arises only in the presence of a market-dominant minority. There are countless instances of ethnic hatred directed at economically oppressed groups. And I am emphatically not suggesting that free market democracy is more likely to lead to ethnic conflict than authoritarianism or communism.

The point, rather, is this: in the many countries that have pervasive poverty and a market-dominant minority, democracy and markets—at least in the raw forms in which they are now being promoted—can proceed only in deep tension with each other.

Where does this leave us? What are the implications of market-dominant minorities for national and international policy-making? Commentators such as Fareed Zakaria and Robert D Kaplan have suggested holding back on democracy until free markets produce enough economic and social development to make democracy sustainable.

The best economic hope for developing and post-communist countries does lie in some form of market-generated growth combined with some form of democracy, with constitutional constraints, tailored to local realities. But if global free market democracy is to succeed, the problem of market-dominant minorities must be confronted.

The most obvious step is to try, in consensual ways, to dilute the market dominance of certain groups. In South Africa or Latin

America, for example, educational and other opportunities for the indigenous majority should be strongly backed by the international community. Yet research suggests that spending on education, if not accompanied by major socioeconomic reforms, produces few benefits.

To level the playing field in developing societies will thus be a painfully slow process, taking generations if it is possible at all. Western-style redistributive programmes—progressive taxation, social security, unemployment insurance—should be encouraged, but, at least in the short run, have limited potential. There simply is not enough to tax, nor a reliable transfer mechanism. Other possibilities include the idea of Peruvian economist Hernando de Soto (in *The Mystery of Capital*) to give the poor in the developing world formal, legally defensible property rights to the land they occupy but to which they very often lack legal title. This would make it easier for them to join the market system.

A more controversial strategy consists of direct government intervention in the market designed to "correct" ethnic wealth imbalances. The leading example of such an effort is Malaysia's New Economic Policy (NEP), a programme established after violent riots in 1969 by indigenous Malays angry over the economic dominance of foreign investors and the country's Chinese minority. The Malaysian government adopted sweeping ethnic quotas on corporate ownership, university admissions and jobs.

In many respects, the results have been impressive. While the NEP has not lifted the great majority of Malays out of poverty, it has helped to create a substantial Malay middle class—between 1970 and 1992 the percentage of Malays occupying the country's most lucrative professional positions went from 6 per cent to 32 per cent. The former prime minister, Mahathir Mohamad, defended the policy in these terms: "With the existence of the few rich Malays at least the poor can say their fate is not entirely to serve rich non-Malays. From the point of view of racial ego, and this ego is still strong, the unseemly existence of Malay tycoons is essential."

But few countries enjoy the prosperity to make NEP-type programmes feasible. Affirmative action in favour of disadvantaged *majorities*—rather than *minorities* as in the west—also risks alienating the wealthy educated minority who may abandon the country, taking their skills and assets. Moreover, such programmes can exacerbate ethnic tensions rather than relieve them, especially when politicians are themselves ethnic partisans. In his own mind, Slobodan Milosevic was conducting a form of affirmative action on behalf of a long-exploited majority.

For better or worse, the best hope for global free market democracy lies with market-dominant minorities themselves. Or at least they are in the best position to address today's most pressing challenges. To begin with, it must be recognised that some market-dominant minorities engage in practices—bribery, discriminatory lending, labour exploitation—that reinforce ethnic stereotypes and besmirch the image of free market democracy. In Indonesia, Suharto's "crony capitalism" depended on a handful of Chinese magnates and fuelled huge resentment of the Chinese community generally.

More positively, if free market democracy is to prosper, the world's market-dominant minorities must begin making significant and visible contributions to the local economies in which they are thriving. There are some famous models here. The University of Nairobi, for example, owes its existence to wealthy Indians in Kenya. The Madhvani family, owners of the largest industrial group in east Africa, provide education, healthcare and housing for their African employees, and also employ Africans in top management. In Russia, there is the unusual case of the Jewish billionaire Roman Abramovich, whose philanthropy won him election as governor of the poverty-stricken Chukotka region in the Russian far east. More typically, however, building ethnic goodwill requires collective action through ethnic chambers of commerce, clan associations, and so on.

The argument of this essay is about unintended consequences, not about apportioning blame. My own view, for example, is that the results of democratisation in Indonesia have been a disaster. But if forced to place the blame somewhere, I would point to 30 years of autocracy and crony capitalism under Suharto. Similarly, in Iraq, with its complex mix of religious and ethnic groups, popular democracy might produce undesirable results. But that is not the fault of democracy. If anything, the blame rests with Saddam Hussein's regime which fostered divisions of various kinds. This does not, however, alter the fact that given the conditions that exist in many postcolonial countries—created by history, colonialism, divide and rule policies, corruption, autocracy—the combination of laissez-faire capitalism and unrestrained majority rule can have catastrophic consequences.

Europe without illusions • Andrew Moravcsik
JULY 2005

The people of France and the Netherlands have spoken. The constitution is dead, Turkish membership is too, and progress in areas from services deregulation to Balkan enlargement will now be hard. Yet for the chattering classes the result was an opportunity to repolish long-held positions. In the face of implacable opposition to Turkish membership, the ever liberal *Economist* blithely interprets the referendums as evidence that Europe has gone too far, too fast—except, of course, on enlargement. Timothy Garton Ash, perennial optimist about the reconciliation of Britain's transatlantic and European vocations, spies another promising moment for Blairite diplomacy. The court philosopher of continental social democracy, Jürgen Habermas, calls on European leaders (read: his former student Joschka Fischer) to recapture the "idealism of 1968" by leading a leftist movement against neoliberal US hegemony. With quintessentially French misanthropy, Serge July of *Libération* accuses French politicians of opportunism and French voters of racism. Across the Atlantic, neocon kingpin Bill Kristol, undeterred by the massive protest vote against economic reform, calls for rejection of the welfare state, open borders to immigration and an embrace of America.

It is time to view Europe as it really is. Far from demonstrating that the EU is in decline or disarray, the crisis demonstrates its essential stability and legitimacy. The central error of the European constitutional framers was one of style and symbolism rather than substance. The constitution contained a set of modest reforms, very much in line with European popular preferences. Yet European leaders upset the emerging pragmatic settlement by dressing up the reforms as a grand scheme for constitutional revision and popular democratisation of the EU.

Looking back in 50 years, historians will not see the referendums as the end of the EU —not even as the beginning of the end. The union remains the most successful experiment in political institution-building since the second world war. Historians will see instead the last gasp of idealistic European federalism born in the mid-1940s, symbolised by the phrase "ever closer union," and aimed at establishing a United States of Europe. It is time to recognise that the EU can neither aspire to replace nation states nor seek democratic legitimacy in the same way nations do. The current EU constitutional settlement, which has defined a stable balance between Brussels and national capitals and democratic legitimacy through indirect accountability and extensive checks and balances, is here to stay. To see why this is so, we must understand the nature of the current constitutional compromise, the reasons why European leaders called it into question, and the deeper lessons this teaches us about the limits of European integration.

Voting patterns in the recent referendums were a reflection of three related motivations that have dominated every EU election in history. First is ideological extremism. The centre supported Europe, while the extreme right and left, which now account for almost one third of the French and Dutch electorates, voted "no." Second is protest voting against unpopular governments. Third, and most important, is a reaction against the insecurity felt by poorer Europeans. Whereas business, the educated elite and wealthier Europeans favoured the constitution, those fearful of unemployment, labour market reform, globalisation, privatisation and the consolidation of the welfare state opposed it. Today these concerns dovetail with the perceived economic and cultural threat posed by Muslim immigration.

This type of disaffection is the primary political problem for European governments today, since it is directed both against poor economic performance and against reform measures designed to improve it. As Fareed Zakaria observes, the tragedy is that "Europe needs more of what's producing populist paranoia: economic reform to survive in an era of economic competition, young immigrants to sustain its social market, and a more strategic relationship with the Muslim world, which would be dramatically enhanced by Turkish membership in the EU."

Forgotten in the electoral chaos was the document itself. The constitution is, after all, a conservative text containing incremental improvements which consolidate EU developments of the past 20 years. The "no" campaigns conceded the desirability of the modest reforms from the start—including the foreign minister, stronger anti-crime policy and streamlining of voting procedures. Such changes are popular, not least in France, which proposed most of them. One is forced to conclude that this document became controversial not because its content was objectionable, but because its content was so innocuous that citizens saw a chance to cast an inexpensive protest vote.

What were they protesting against? Here, too, the referendums cannot be viewed as plebiscites directed at the EU's policies. Though the EU is associated, via its advisory "Lisbon process," with labour market and welfare reform, these matters remain firmly within the competence of the member states. The EU's activities as a whole, while they include oversight of state subsidies and trade policy, may just as reasonably be seen as part of a European effort to *manage* globalisation rather than promote it. Opponents made occasional mention of EU policies not contained in the constitution, such as the recent enlargement to 25, the introduction of the euro, the deregulation of electricity and Turkish accession. Yet only the last of these seems to have swayed many voters, and they seem to have been unaware that free migration has been ruled even before negotiations begin.

So what lesson should the EU take away? The relative lack of direct criticism of the constitution, the lack of fundamental objections to EU policies and, above all, the stunning lack of positive proposals for reform are striking evidence of the underlying stability of the EU system. The 15 years since the fall of the Berlin wall has been, after all, the most successful period in EU history. The single market, the euro and a nascent European foreign and defence policy came into being. EU enlargement was carried out with surprisingly little disruption in existing member states, and proved the most cost-effective western instrument for advancing global democracy and security. In sum, the EU appears to have quietly reached a stable constitutional settlement.

What is that settlement? The EU is now pre-eminent in trade, agriculture, fishing, eurozone monetary policy and some business regulation, and helps to co-ordinate co-operation in foreign policy. Contrary to statistics one often reads, this amounts to only about 20 per cent of European regulation and legislation. Most areas of greatest public concern—taxes, health, pensions, education, crime, infrastructure, defence and immigration—remain firmly national. With a tax base a fiftieth the size of the member states, an administration smaller than that of a small city, no police force or army and a narrow legal mandate, the EU will never encompass these fiscally and administratively demanding tasks.

There is no new *grand projet*, akin to the single market of the 1980s or the single currency of the 1990s, to justify change. In 18 months of deliberation, the constitutional convention devoted only two days to the expansion of EU competences. European health, pension, fiscal and education policies have little support, while a US-style military build-up exceeds Europe's means and insults its "civilian power" ideals.

Consider European social policy, of which we heard so much in referendum campaigns. What concrete EU policies should this imply? Blocking sensible efforts to reform the welfare state for long-term sustainability is short-sighted. While many studies show that a division of labour between the new and old members of the EU will generate growth, there is little evidence of a regulatory or fiscal "race to the bottom" driven by the EU, and there remains plenty of room for social policy at national level. The neoliberal "Anglo-Saxon" threat is a myth. Britain is building up its welfare state faster than any of its

partners, based partly on a Scandinavian model that tops international competitiveness rankings. Indeed, with continental liberalisation
and British social democratisation, Europe's social systems are con-
verging—through the pressure of national politics, not as the result of
some EU social policy pipe dream.

A similar constitutional compromise has emerged with regard to
institutions. Though Anglo-American Eurosceptics have sought to
resurrect the bogeyman of a Brussels superstate headed by the
European commission, treaty changes since 1970 have consistently
moved Europe in the opposite direction. They have increased the
power of the council of ministers (favoured by France and Britain,
particularly for matters outside the economic core) and the directly
elected European parliament (favoured by Germany) at the expense
of the technocratic commission.

The proposed constitution sought to marginally improve the EU's
efficiency and transparency, while retaining its basic structure. All of
this is the sensible stuff policy wonks love and publics generally
support: European parliamentary co-decision was expanded, national
parliaments gained an advisory and gatekeeping role, the rotating
presidency was abolished, voting weights were adjusted to represent
large countries more fairly, foreign policy co-ordination was centralised in a foreign minister and so on. The result was a multinational
constitutional compromise that attended to the interests of large and
small countries, left and right parties and Europhile and Eurosceptic
tendencies. The reforms enjoyed broad support among member
states, and none met a serious challenge in the referendum debates.
The biggest change—creation of a European foreign minister
empowered to recommend, though not impose, a more co-ordinated
foreign policy—enjoys 70 per cent approval across Europe. And
recognising the EU as it is, the constitution struck the classic idealist
phrase "ever closer union" from the treaty of Rome, and substituted
the more balanced "unity in diversity."

So it was not the substance of the emerging constitutional settlement that triggered opposition. The objectionable aspect was its form:
an idealistic constitution. Since the 1970s, lawyers have regarded the

treaty of Rome as a de facto constitution. The new document was an unnecessary public relations exercise based on the seemingly intuitive, but in fact peculiar, notion that democratisation and the European ideal could legitimate the EU. In the wake of the Nice and Amsterdam treaties, Euro-enthusiast scholars, politicians and commentators argued that the EU is unpopular primarily because it is secretive, complex, unaccountable and distant from the public—in sum, because it suffers from a "democratic deficit." Joschka Fischer, the German foreign minister, gave the idea of constitutional legitimation a big push with his celebrated lecture on the end point of integration at Humboldt University in 2000. But like the other European leaders who jumped on his bandwagon, Fischer, while ostensibly transcending a narrow, national discourse, was in fact framing the argument in a familiar domestic manner: in his case 1968er German anti-nationalism.

The idea was to legitimate the EU not through trade, economic growth and useful regulation, as had been the case for 50 years, but by politicising and democratising it. This was to be done via a constitutional convention. Enthused by the prospect of a re-enactment of Philadelphia 1787, millions of web-savvy Europeans were supposed to deliberate the meaning of Europe. More pragmatic voices simply hoped to combat cynicism by simplifying the treaty and delineating EU prerogatives. To justify the need for change, reformers also seized on the perception that the EU would need a radical overhaul to avoid gridlock with 25 rather than 15 members—a fear that now seems unjustified, both because the new states are proving constructive and because the EU is not moving as far or fast as it once did.

Of course, the constitutional deliberation did not mobilise Europeans. Few citizens were aware of the 200 *conventionnels'* deliberations. When testimony from civil society was requested, professors turned up. When a youth conference was called, would-be Eurocrats attended. When those who did attend came to consider democracy, they found that the arrangement Europe currently has is appropriate to a diverse polity in which member states insist on checks and balances at every level. There was little popular or elite support for democratic reform beyond the modest increases in scrutiny by national and European parliaments the constitution contains.

This is as it should be, for there is no "democratic deficit" in the EU —or not much of one. Once we set aside ideal notions of democracy and look to real-world standards, we see that the EU is as transparent, responsive, accountable and honest as its member states. The relative lack of centralised financial or administrative discretion all but eliminates corruption. The EU's areas of autonomous authority—trade policy, constitutional adjudication and central banking—are the same as those in most democracies, where these functions are politically insulated for sound reasons. The notion of imposing democratic control through multiple checks and balances, rather than through elections to a single sovereign parliament, is more American than European—but it is no less legitimate for that. Everyone gets a say in a system in which a European directive needs approval from a technocratic commission, a supermajority of democratic national governments and a directly elected parliament, and must then be implemented by national regulators. Studies show that EU legislation is both consensual and relatively responsive to shifts in partisan and popular opinion.

Enthusiasts for democracy fail to grasp its limits. Engaging European citizens will not necessarily create rational—let alone supportive—debate, because those with intense preferences about the EU tend to be its opponents. Average citizens and political parties keep only a few issues—usually those involving heavy tax and spending—in their mind at any one time, and thus respond only to highly salient ideals and issues. The pull of Europe remains weak, while the bread and butter policies citizens care about most, including the welfare and identity issues that dominated referendum debates, remain almost exclusively in national hands. The failure of European elections to generate high turnouts or focus on EU issues over the years suggests that citizens fail to participate in EU politics not because they are blocked from doing so, but because they have insufficient incentive.

Some democratic enthusiasts propose jump-starting EU democracy by incorporating hot-button issues like social policy and immigration, despite the lack of popular support for doing so. This is, in essence, Habermas's vision. Yet anyone except a philosopher can see that this is the sort of extreme cure that will kill the patient. There is little that could lead the European public to decisively reject an institution as deeply embedded as the EU, but transferring controversial issues like social policy to it without justification might just do it.

More sober voices propose to empower national parliaments, which the constitution sought to do in a modest way. Yet this reveals a final fallacy of the democratisers. For there is little reason to believe that turning policy over to a legislature makes it more legitimate. In western democracies, popularity is inversely correlated with direct electoral accountability. The most popular institutions are courts, police forces and the military. Parliaments are generally disliked. Whatever the source of Europe's declining popularity—a general decline in political trust, unfamiliarity with institutions, xenophobia, discontent with economic performance—it has little to do with its democratic mandate.

Forcing an unstructured debate about an institution that handles matters like telecommunications standardisation, the composition of the Bosnia stabilisation force and the privatisation of electricity pro-duction inexorably drove debate to the lowest common denominator. When pro-European political elites found themselves defending a constitution with modest content, they felt they had no alternative but to oversell it using inflated notions of what the EU does and rhetoric drawn from 1950s European idealism. Small wonder they were out-gunned by grumpy populists with stronger symbols rooted in class, nation and race (and even more inflated views of what the EU does). Publics became confused and alarmed by the scare tactics of both sides. The referendums came to inhabit a strange twilight zone of symbolic politics, in which claims about the EU bore little relationship to reality, and support and opposition for a status quo constitution became a potent symbol for the myriad hopes and fears of modern electorates.

In the wake of this debacle, European politicians must find a constructive path forward. They should start with a collective mea culpa. The document itself must be renounced. Then over the next few years, the EU should return to its successful tradition of quiet and pragmatic reform. Europeans consistently support incremental advances in the union's foreign, internal security and economic policies along the lines set forth in the constitution. Turkish membership is off the agenda, as it probably would have been even without the referendums. Politicians need to concede this, and concede it loud and clear, in order to preserve continued EU enlargement in the Balkans. Yet a halfway arrangement acceptable to both EU and Turkish publics remains a realistic goal over the next 20 years and may be better for Turkey than the limited type of EU membership that is currently on offer. No other European policy could contribute as much to global peace and security.

Above all, European politicians need to acknowledge explicitly the existence of a stable European constitutional settlement. The unique genius of the EU is that it locks in policy co-ordination while respecting the powerful rhetoric and symbols that still attach to national identity. Publics will be reassured if it is portrayed as stable and successful. There is no shameful compromise with grand principles here. On the contrary, a constitutional order that preserves national democratic politics for the issues most salient to citizens, but delegates to more indirect democratic forms those issues that are of less concern, or on which there is an administrative, technical or legal consensus, is highly appealing. The EU's distinctive system of multi-level governance is the only new form of state organisation to emerge and prosper since the rise of the welfare state at the turn of the 20th century. Now it is a mature constitutional order, one that no longer needs to move forward to legitimate its past and present successes. Left behind must be the European centralisers and democratisers for whom "ever closer union" remains an end in itself. They will insist that the answer to failed democracy is more democracy and the answer to a failed constitution is another constitution. But Europe has moved beyond them. Disowning this well-meaning, even admirable, band of idealists may seem harsh, but it is both necessary and just. On this basis, Europeans can develop a new discourse of national interest, pragmatic co-operation and constitutional stability—a discourse that sees Europe as it is. The constitution is dead, long live the constitution!

Letter from New York • Ben Cheever

OCTOBER 2001

My wife and I invited five guests and their dogs to watch the tragedy on the 6.30pm evening news. The dogs were kept outside, as were the smokers. I stood behind my house with the food editor and the distinguished journalist. We peered through the windows into my living room.

"We're nicotine negroes," the distinguished journalist told me. "Not a bad line," he said. "You can use it in one of your novels."

The footage of the airplanes hitting the towers was extraordinary. More so than the much-touted battle scenes from *Pearl Harbor*. Did any of you Brits see *Pearl Harbor*? It's the movie in which I learned that the Battle of Britain was won by a few resolute and devilishly good-looking Americans.

Enough of movies. Back to television. We'd been watching reality television all day. But there was starting to be too much reality in it.

Ordinarily, in America, we'll do anything to be on television. But on the morning the Twin Towers fell something elemental changed. Police and fire officials were turning away from the camera. It wasn't a toy anymore.

As the day wore on, though, we returned to form. You could hear the newscasters squabbling with each other. Then we learned that Tom Clancy had already written this in a novel. Thanks Tom. There are many things wrong with this country, but none of them would be solved by a more careful reading of the Clancy oeuvre.

We don't know if President Bush has studied Clancy. We know he's studied Ronald Reagan. He probably remembers the joke that got

Reagan in: "What's flat and glows in the dark? Iran after Ronald Reagan takes office."

So our president came out swinging. "Terrorism against America will not stand," he said. The television anchorman told us what a great nation we are, mighty and innocent. "Innocent?"

Nobody we know intimately had been killed, though I have friends in Manhattan I still haven't spoken to. The lawyer knows the manager of Windows on the World, which was on the top of the World Trade Center. But Glen was on the ground when the first plane hit.

The architect had been in Manhattan. She'd seen the Towers pluming smoke. The psychiatrist's daughter had phoned her mother to say she'd seen the World Trade Towers collapse. "I didn't believe her until I switched on the television," said the psychiatrist.

If a friend has died, everything will change. But for now it's like a blizzard, a sinister adrenal rush, and something to talk with strangers about. My 12-year-old hopes he'll get out of school tomorrow. "A day of national mourning," he explained. Today they had a special assembly, complete with a speech in which FDR was invoked and the word "infamy" recalled.

I got three e-mails asking if I was all right. One was from London, another from Kansas. The one from California was titled "WAR." (They know how to push the envelope in California.) My mother phoned from Ossining, New York, which is about five miles away.

She started on about how she hoped we wouldn't hurt those lovely Palestinians. I told my mother: "right now I'm not having good thoughts about Palestinians." The networks had been showing pictures of Palestinians chanting "God is great" and celebrating in the West Bank city of Nablus. But the clips showed the same children over and over again. They didn't even look particularly happy. The networks are thrusting the celebrations in our faces.

NBC anchorman Tom Brokaw has dubbed the Americans who fought Hitler "The Greatest Generation." His book was a bestseller. I'm a baby boomer and so a member of the worst generation. We refused to go to Vietnam. We wouldn't even wear a necktie. We still won't go to war. We'll watch one on television though. Or in the movies. Ronald Reagan wasn't the only American to confuse war movies with the real thing. I went to see an afternoon show of *Dances With Wolves* during the Gulf war, but left early, because I didn't want to miss the evening news.

Why do we so badly, and repeatedly, need to watch the news? I remember Challenger going up in smoke. Jack Ruby shooting Lee Harvey Oswald. There are many important events in American history. Then there are the ones that got filmed.

News organisations are savvy about this. Two thousand people die in Burma. A house trailer is destroyed in Coral Gables, Florida. We see the house trailer. Why? No pictures from Burma.

Our guests stayed all the way through the news. After the news the president was going to address the nation. The guests all left. My wife and I watched the president alone.

This was a war between good and evil, Bush told us. "Make no mistake, the United States will hunt down and pursue those responsible for these cowardly actions." A stirring call to arms. So why had his audience faded away. Bad politics? Possibly. Bad television? Definitely.

How do you square it with the fact that those pictures of the towers collapsing were thrilling? If Bush's people had projected them onto the background while he spoke he might have doubled his audience. There's no reason to deny the president of the US props that even local newscasters insist on.

When I went to bed, the adrenaline was wearing off.

The next empire • Robert Cooper

OCTOBER 2001

Imperialism, empire, imperial: at worst these words have become a form of abuse; at best they sound merely old fashioned, historical curiosities. Empire, it seems, is history. The empires have gone, leaving behind some ruins, some laws, some coins and the occasional road.

Empire is indeed history. Almost all that we know of history, from Sumeria through Babylon, Egypt, the Assyrian empire, through Persia, Greece, Rome, Byzantium, through the Chinese dynasties, the Carolingian empire, the Holy Roman Empire, the Mongol empire, the Mogul empire, the Habsburg empire, the Spanish, Portuguese, British, French, Dutch and German empires to the Soviet empire, plus many that we have forgotten, all of this suggests that the history of the world is the history of empire.

Or should we say "was"? One of the most remarkable changes in a remarkable century is the almost total disappearance of empires. The world began the 20th century covered in great empires and ended without a single one. With their defeat in the first world war, the Austro-Hungarian, German, Russian and Ottoman empires broke up. Kemal Atatürk embraced the end of the Ottoman empire as a chance to create a modern, national (and European) Turkish state. So, earlier, had the foundation of nation states in Italy, Norway and, up to a point, Germany, been seen as the path of modernisation. Atatürk imposed the reading of the Koran in Turkish, echoing the events of centuries earlier when Luther's Bible had begun the awakening of a German national consciousness.

Not only did the first world war destroy two European empires but, with Woodrow Wilson's 14 points, it established the principle of national self-determination and created a band of nation states in central Europe out of the German, Russian, Austro-Hungarian and Ottoman empires. Most of them turned out to be weak and poorly governed. Following the war, the Irish Free State was established, ending centuries of British rule, and in the 1930s the US applied the principle of self-determination to itself and gave independence to the Philippines.

The next great burst of decolonisation came with the second world war where the defeats of Britain, France and the Netherlands by Japan removed the aura of western superiority—already badly shaken in India by Gandhi—which had sustained their eastern empires. The French, who had acquired their empire by arms, fought for it; the British, who had acquired theirs partly by accident, got out.

The result was, in the end, the same. African decolonisation followed as self-determination caught on abroad and the costs of empire grew at home. In 1974, the Portuguese revolution—which grew out of the costs of colonial wars—led to the end of that empire. And finally, in 1989, the end of the cold war brought the collapse of the Soviet Union's external empire, followed shortly thereafter by the end of Russia's internal empire.

Decolonisation was a last act of imperialism. At the heart of imperialism is the imposition of alien laws and systems of administration. Decolonisation left former colonies with nation state structures that were, in many cases, quite foreign to their traditions. Some peoples and parts of the world have long histories of alien rule: for them at least decolonisation may have been more profoundly imperialist than empire—a last legacy from the last imperial masters.

Have we seen the last of empire? It is hard to tell. Sometimes one can only identify something as an empire after it has broken up. Now that it has separated we can identify British rule in Ireland as imperialist; but had Gladstone's campaign for home rule succeeded, Ireland might be a part of a rather different Britain instead of a former colony. How China, India and Indonesia are seen in future will depend on how they are governed and what happens to them.

The world of empires, which dates back as far as we can remember and which was thriving in 1900, has, 100 years later, become a world of nation states. Compared with empire, the nation state is a new concept; the small state began to emerge with the Renaissance and the nation became a major political factor only in the 19th century. For most of the period since, the nation state has been confined to a limited part of the globe. Not by accident, this has also been the most dynamic part. The non-existence of empire, however, is historically without precedent. The question is whether this can last.

There are both theoretical and practical reasons for thinking that it won't. The nation state has proved a powerful engine for growth and modernisation, but that does not make it a good basis on which to organise the entire world. The theoretical reason is that there is no clear definition of the nation. If nations were fixed, like geographical features, we could draw a map of the world which neatly divided people up into nation states, just as the dynastic monarchs of Europe once hoped to contain their territorial states within natural frontiers. Unfortunately, nations are not like that: "Now we have created Italy," said Cavour after he had driven the Austrians out, "next we must create Italians" (at the time only 2 per cent of the population spoke modern-day Italian). The Yoruba language—and in a sense the Yoruba people —was the creation of the missionaries who standardised local dialects in a translation of the Bible (just as Luther had done in Germany). Nigeria itself is, of course, a creation of the European powers at the Congress of Berlin. Had it been better governed, Yugoslavia might still be a nation and Serbo-Croat might be one language instead of two (or three since the Bosnians are working on their own version).

Are the Irish one nation or two? One could ask the same of the Welsh. Are the Bretons and the Basques, the Catalans, the Cockneys, nations? Are the Arab people a nation? How many nations are there in South Africa? Even the Japanese, who have a powerful national myth and identity, might have broken up if the Meiji restoration had turned out differently. The examples are endless but the conclusion is clear: the nation is often the creation of the state (and especially of the ministry of education).

If the nation is created by the state—even some of the time—then we cannot say that states should be defined by nations. The consequences of this circularity are beginning to become apparent as more and more groups decide that they would like to break away and form new states. Who is to tell them that they cannot? On top of this is the practical problem that ethnic and linguistic groups do not always exist in neat geographical packages. Nation states almost always contain minorities. A state which is based on nationality and national identity has a natural tendency to exclude minorities. Taken to its hideous conclusion, it will try to eliminate them. Why should the minorities not be granted self-determination, since by its self-proclaimed definition the nation state makes clear that they do not really belong to it?

Today's world frowns on repressive measures against groups seeking self-determination. There will often be a good market for their views. Most people, quite naturally, dislike governments; it may not therefore be difficult to convince them that they would be better off with a different government in a different state—something closer to them and to their ethnic identity. As for the politicians promoting this cause, they have everything to gain: a chance to go down in history as fathers of the nation (however small), the prospect of running things for themselves and perhaps the wonderful opportunities for corruption which arise when you run your own state. Internationally, you can pose on the world stage; and at the UN you are—in theory at least—the equal of the US. What is there to stop the creation of an ever greater number of ever smaller states?

Paradoxically, growing economic integration makes political disintegration easier. In the days of national economies and protective tariffs, it was important to be big; but in a borderless world, what difference does it make? Being small does have costs: administration is more expensive and security is less certain. But the first is not always easily visible and the second may not be a convincing argument either to people who live in a peaceful part of the world or to those who, as minorities, feel insecure even in their own state. In the last 50 years, the number of states has increased dramatically: 51 signed the UN Charter in 1945; today it has 189 members. It will be surprising if we do not see more in the next 50 years.

The practical problem with a world of nation states is that many of the post-colonial states have weak national identities, weak political institutions and weak economies. Some of these states—especially in Africa—are near collapse. Others in central Asia, southeast Asia or the south Pacific do not look healthy. In many cases one would have to say that self-government and self-determination have failed. What should we do? In the past, the solution would have been colonisation. But today there are no colonial powers willing to take on the job. In some respects the need for outside authority is even greater today than it was in, say, the 19th century. Then the peoples of Africa and Asia were organised in a reasonably stable manner in traditional societies based on family and tribe. Those bonds were irreparably damaged by western traders and missionaries; whatever was left has now been destroyed by education, ideology and television. There is no going back. But going forward is not easy either: collapsing states are awash with guns, law and order breaks down and government begins to resemble organised crime. Some writers refer to "the new middle ages." With the breakdown of order, the possibility of attracting foreign investment falls to zero.

Those who can get themselves into the global economy do well—prosperity helps stability and stability attracts investment. Those who are left out fall into a vicious circle: economic failure undermines government; weak government means disorder and that means falling investment. In the 1950s, South Korea had a lower GNP per head than Zambia: the one has achieved membership of the global economy, the other has not. Is it a surprise then that the top 20 per cent of the world now earns 86 per cent of world income and the bottom 20 per cent gets only 1 per cent? In 1820, when the 19th century colonial expansion began, the top 20 per cent were earning only three times the income of the bottom 20 per cent. We should probably expect that this gap will widen.

The weak states of the post-imperial world are disastrous for those who live in them and are bad for the rest of us. There is no need to dwell here on the mutilations in Sierra Leone, the oppression of women and many others in Afghanistan, the genocidal violence in the Balkans or the daily insecurity and injustice in many other countries. Such conditions make life a terrifying experience for those who live under them. For those who are outside, there are risks too: risks for investors and risks for neighbours. The risks for neighbours are especially important. The domino theory was false for communism, but it may be true for chaos. Sierra Leone destabilises Liberia (and vice-versa), Afghanistan helps destabilise central Asia.

All the conditions seem to be there for a new imperialism. There are countries which need an outside force to create stability (recently in Sierra Leone a rally called for the return of British rule). There are metropolitan countries which want stability so that they can trade. And though there are fewer missionaries today there is a new class of imperial auxiliaries in the form of NGOs trying to help people who need it and preaching human rights—the secular religion of today's world.

If the rich took over the world when they were only three times richer than the poor, why do they not do so again when they are 86 times richer? The answer is that the very ideas that have made them rich—the ideas of free exchange, free speech and the rule of law—are anti-imperialist. (To reverse the remark by Macbeth's porter on drink, bourgeois values promote the performance but take away the desire.) The bourgeois values of Deng Xiaoping: "It is glorious to be rich," define success in terms of purchasing power, not subjecting people.

Nor do today's poor wish to be colonised, except perhaps briefly under extreme circumstances. In the 19th century, a number of countries offered themselves up to imperial powers. Since then the spread of western ideas—liberty, equality and fraternity—has disrupted traditional societies so they have difficulty in governing themselves, and has also made them unwilling to accept foreign domination. Both the supply and the demand for imperialism has dried up.

And yet a system in which the strong protect the weak, in which the efficient and well governed export stability and liberty, in which the world is open for investment and growth—all of these seem eminently desirable. If empire has not often been like that, it has frequently been better than the chaos and barbarism that it replaced. There have even been times and places—the Roman and Athenian empires are distant enough for us to see things in perspective—where it has helped the spread of civilisation.

But in a world of human rights and bourgeois values, a new imperialism will in any case have to be very different from the old. Perhaps we can begin to discern its outlines. It has two forms: the imperialism of globalisation and the imperialism of neighbours. Both, in keeping with the times, are voluntary.

Empire is about control. It involves control above all over domestic affairs (academic writers contrast this with hegemony, which consists of control of foreign affairs only). That is why interference in domestic affairs is so resented—it represents a taint on independence that reeks of imperialism. And yet it is precisely domestic affairs that need guidance if countries in trouble are to find their way back into the global economy, attract investment and return to prosperity. The conditions which the IMF sets for its loans are almost all about domestic economic and political management. In return for accepting these conditions, states which are in danger of falling behind and dropping out of the global economy receive help, not just from the IMF but from the governments of the rich and from Wall Street. These days, aid programmes are less often about dams and roads. It is generally recognised instead that having a good government and administration is essential to development. Many programmes are, therefore, about the way in which the country is organised and governed—so called good governance provisions.

How different is this from what Lord Cromer and others did in Egypt? From 1875, a representative of British bondholders controlled the revenue of the Egyptian government, while representatives of the French government controlled expenditure. Foreign debt funding was overseen by an international committee, who effectively decided how much foreign exchange the government should be allowed. Does this not sound remarkably like a rather strict IMF programme? Perhaps, but there is one vital difference: when a new Egyptian government threatened to ignore the programme, Britain did not renegotiate the programme or even cancel the external financial support, as the IMF might do today. Instead it sent General Wolseley and 31,000 troops to restore government, order and, of course, financial discipline.

Today's voluntary imperialism may place advisers in key ministries as Cromer did in Egypt. But there is no violence, only money. No one has to accept these programmes. Those who do may well benefit. Today's imperial intervention is also limited in time and in extent. Since it is voluntary, perhaps it is wrong to call it imperialism at all. It represents not so much a loss of sovereignty, but a temporary loan of sovereignty. Nevertheless, the relationships are similar to those of empire: it is a relationship between strong and weak; and it is about the organisation of domestic affairs.

The classic writers on imperialism—Lenin, Schumpeter, Hobson—associated it with economic interests. Either trade followed the flag or the flag followed trade, or both. So it is no surprise that in a global economy there are global institutions—anonymous and objective as such institutions tend to be—which make the world safe for investment. And since we live in a post-imperial age, the control which they exercise is light, temporary and voluntary.

The second form of the new imperialism is that of neighbours. Mismanagement and instability in places where your companies wish to invest money is inconvenient. Instability in your neighbourhood can have much more serious consequences. The remarkable thing in today's world is that the US, in spite of a position of dominance—military, political, commercial, cultural—unequalled since Rome, is not the world's leading imperial power. Having few neighbours, the US is interested primarily in the lighter form of the new imperialism—assistance through multilateral organisations. Mexico is doing well and Nafta may help it do better. There are worries in the Caribbean and Colombia, but for now the US, in spite of its enormous wealth and power, can afford not to take the risks or pay the costs of some form of imperial enterprise—though it is possible that an American free trade area could develop in this direction.

With Europe it is different. On the EU's eastern borders are a large number of recently decolonised states. Many are making progress, but anyone who wants to see the risk of weak states has only to look at the Balkans. Here, for the last ten years, we have seen a mixture of misgovernment, ethnic violence and crime (the three often being indistinguishable) which not only offends the conscience of the rich but also brings costs for the stable parts of Europe. The Balkans are on the transit route for drugs and a centre for smuggling. Smuggling people, in particular, is a major new industry: the Chinese who were found dead in the docks at Dover, arrived there via Belgrade. Violence reached its extremity in Bosnia and Kosovo, both of which are now effectively UN protectorates. In each case, there is a UN High Representative who has more or less plenipotentiary powers. It is no surprise that both the High Representatives are Europeans. Europe provides most of the aid that keeps Bosnia and Kosovo running and most of the soldiers (though the US presence is an indispensable stabilising factor). In a further unprecedented move, the EU has offered unilateral free market access to the countries of the former Yugoslavia for all products including most agricultural produce.

It is not just soldiers that come from the international community, it is police, judges, prison officers, central bankers and others. A whole team of European officials is creating a Bosnian customs administration. Elections are organised and monitored by the Organisation for Security and Co-operation in Europe (OSCE). Local police are financed by the UN. As auxiliaries to this effort—in many areas indispensable to it—are over a hundred NGOs.

The Balkans is an extreme case, but it illustrates the costs of instability turning into real conflict. In the rest of the area to its east, the EU is engaged in a programme which will eventually lead to massive enlargement. From Stettin on the Baltic to Tirana on (or near) the Adriatic, every country between Vienna and Moscow wants to join the EU and Nato. To do this they are rewriting their laws and constitutions and reorganising their military. Some have hardly begun and may not yet understand what is required to join; but others have made good progress. The EU negotiations cover agriculture, industry, transport, environment, competition policy, monetary policy, foreign affairs and much else. In the past, empires have imposed their laws and systems of government. In this case, no one is imposing anything but a voluntary movement of self-imposition is taking place. The countries concerned are not unstable, but without the objective of EU membership and the support they have received from the EU, some of them might have been at risk. It is probably good, on balance, that a set of western rules and norms is available off the peg. While you are a candidate for EU membership you have to accept what is given—as subject countries once did. But the prize is that once you are inside you will have a voice in the commonwealth. If the process is a kind of voluntary imperialism, the end state might be described as co-operative empire. "Commonwealth" might not be a bad name.

Many parts of Europe have lived longer and perhaps more happily in an imperial framework than as nation states. The Balkans with its patchwork of ethnicities has known little else. Belgium, Germany and Italy all flourished under one form or another of imperial suzerainty—in the case of Germany this came close to being a co-operative empire. Admittedly the imperial periods were associated with decayed and rigid aristocratic regimes; and the nation states that swept them away brought modernisation, dynamism and democracy. But the clarity and vigour of the nation state also brought bloodshed—both in wars among themselves and in the way they handled their minorities. Armenians, Albanians and Kurds lived more safely in the Ottoman empire than in its more modern successors. In those times, the empire could sometimes function as a third party, above the ethnic groups and keeping the peace between them. Today that role too belongs to the international community, which is invited in, in the form of monitors or peacekeeping forces.

In his classic work on empires, Michael Doyle argues that the successful empires were those which created an imperial bureaucracy that governed for the empire as a whole and not just for the metropole (Rome did this; the British empire did not).

A persistent empire presupposes imperial bureaucratic coordination and transnational integration in the political, economic and cultural spheres. This integration can merge the metropole and the periphery, as Caracalla legally integrated the two in the Roman empire in 212. At this point the empire no longer exists and the many peoples have become one. In the case of Rome the many were assimilated into a common despotism, but the continuing attraction of the otherwise reprehensible international domination of empire lies in the possibility that all might be assimilated to a common liberty. Empires continue to attract as a road to peace, but imperialism holds a double tragedy. First, modern empires, resting upon a metropolitan, ethnic nationalism, may not be able to travel the whole way to integration.

Second, any extensive empire, to survive long enough for integration to occur must cross the Augustan threshold to imperial bureaucratic rule—and bureaucratising the metropole destroys participatory government. Liberty and empire emerge, both analytically and historically, as opposites, for the periphery from the beginning and for the metropole in the end.

The attraction of the EU is that, if we can get it right, it might just offer a way out of this dilemma. Conceived as a state, the EU is not merely unattractive—it is unworkable. But as a co-operative empire, a commonwealth, in which each has a share in the government in which no single country dominates and in which the governing principles are not ethnic but legal; conceived in these terms it might just work. The lightest of touches will be required from the centre; the "imperial bureaucracy" must be under control, accountable and the servant, not the master of the commonwealth. Such an institution must be as dedicated to liberty and democracy as its constituent parts. Like Rome, this Europe would provide its citizens with some laws, some coins and the occasional road. None of this will be easy but perhaps it is possible to imagine a future Europe, with 30 or so members, as a modernised, democratic, co-operative empire offering both a road to peace and the possibility of assimilation in a common liberty. It is, at the least, a noble dream.

My Germany • Jens Reich

NOVEMBER 2000

Throughout my life I have dreamed of leaving Germany. And yet now, as I grow old, I have a feeling of resignation, even of mild satisfaction at the idea of ending my days here in Berlin, where I'm writing these words. I have been reconciled to my Germanness and can reflect on it in a calm mood.

Strictly speaking, I am only half-German and for most of my adult life I have been a political dissenter (albeit a quiet one) against the German state in which I lived. My mother was not German in a 20th century sense: She was born in the Habsburg empire, to an ethnically German family, and became a citizen of Czechoslovakia as a child, after the first world war. She became German against her will after the occupation of northern Bohemia—the result of the Munich conference in 1938. She had been against her fellow Austrian Adolf Hitler from the start, although inactively and then powerlessly so. One of my earliest memories comes from the war years. We lay in our beds while mother crouched under hers, trying to listen to the news from the BBC, with its unmistakeable signal of the first bars of Beethoven's Fifth Symphony. I will never forget the feeling of anxiety and excitement mingled. Listening to London could result in denunciation to the Gestapo. But mother wanted to know the truth, especially about the eastern front, where my father was serving as a medical officer. My mother's behaviour was a lesson for us children in silent dissent; how one could withhold legitimacy from a tyranny in a very private manner.

My mother and we children spent the war years in the house of my grandfather, a chemist who owned a textile factory in Warnsdorf, close to the border between Germany and Bohemia. In Warnsdorf we were beyond the reach of the Allied bombs. Life was quiet there, and I was brought up in a German environment with that admixture of Czech servants, housemaids, chauffeurs and workmen which was so characteristic of bourgeois German life in Habsburg Bohemia. It made a deep impression on me to discover that there were two different languages to say the same thing. For the same reason, it was no big shock to later learn the opposite—that one may say fundamentally different things in exactly the same words, using double-speak. I have also retained from these years a lifelong attachment to the Slavic idiom.

Towards the end of the war we were expelled, and fled to Germany. We then had to escape from Plauen, Dresden and Halberstadt, one after the other, as each was bombed. I was then six. There were corpses in the streets. A town full of flames is a dramatic thing, unforgettable to a child. I remember standing on the staircase of a house which had been hit by a bomb. My mother was crying: "Jump! I'll catch you in my arms!" Behind me the house was burning and cracking, and in front of me was a bomb crater, going right down to the basement. I was afraid of falling into it, not daring to jump. Finally a man picked me up and jumped over the hole with me in his arms.

Another scene etched into my memory is of being attacked in a field by a low-flying Allied aircraft, as we fled from Halberstadt to the nearby mountains. The pilot amused himself by strafing the refugees with his machine gun. Flying over us, shooting, turning, coming back, attacking again, while we crouched in the roadside ditch.

Later on, life became quieter. Our family settled in Halberstadt, which was in East Germany, but close to the border with what became the Federal Republic. In fact, it was occupied first by the US army and later on handed over, to our lifelong regret, to the Soviet army. My father was a doctor of internal medicine who worked in the municipal hospital. My mother stayed at home and stubbornly defended her bourgeois origins, surrounded by what remained of the old furniture, paintings and books. We had hung on to these things because grand-father had been allowed by the Czech authorities to serve as technical director in his own factory, after 1945, until a Czech engineer got to know the ropes. He was exiled in 1948, with a furniture van containing some of his belongings.

Mother ensured, with dogged persistence, that we became "contras" in the GDR. "Contra" was not only a political stance, it meant opposition to the whole petty-bourgeois/proletarian culture of the early GDR. Mother saw to it that we were instructed as Catholics, which was a clear disadvantage at school and university at the time. Father did not interfere much in family education. He was a bit pink; he had some socialist ideals. Our family attitude may be best described as one of "internal resistance" without open opposition. We thought that the system could not last for long, but that we had to endure it as a punishment for Nazism, Hitler, mass murder, the war, and all that.

As I grew up, literature added to the influence of my family experiences. Somebody lent me Koestler's *Darkness at Noon*, with its theme of idealism perverted by dictatorship. I also read accounts of Hitler and why he was never overthrown. I remember a fierce argument with my father after reading John Wheeler-Bennett's *The Nemesis of Power*, which condemned the hesitant high-ranking German army officers. Father defended the honour of his army. Generational conflicts of this type were fought and settled in our family in the 1950s, so we felt that West Germany was catching up with *us* when the 1968 movement fought the same battles. Even now the Goldhagen debate about German anti-semitism—innate or not—seems to me to be oddly out of date.

I often asked my parents why they did not emigrate before the war, and how all those atrocities could happen in a civilised country. Mother's answer was: "How? With father a doctor and only a few high school words of English and French?" And later on they were simply scared of the Gestapo. One may denounce all this, but it is a natural reaction of self-protection in a cruel system. At any rate, I adopted the same attitude of internal resistance in the GDR. I learned to live a split life. At school we had to memorise the dogma of Marxism-Leninism; at home mother denounced it. My decision to become a doctor and, later on, a scientist, was an attempt to find a non-political niche in this environment. It was a sort of camouflage. Given a free choice, I would have preferred to pursue the liberal arts or literature, but they were pervaded by the ideology of Marxism-Leninism. My father advised me: "Go into science or medicine. This is where you can survive as an independent-minded person." So I studied medicine at Berlin's Humboldt University. It was a happy time; we students spent much of our leisure in west Berlin and led a life between the two superpowers. The option to go west remained open. But I was attached to my family, to my friends, to the homeland where I lived, so that I did not decide before 1961, and afterwards the Berlin wall made up my mind for me.

After 1961, behind the wall, we were very, very depressed. I vividly remember seeing (during my first conference visit to Prague) a film about the Californian student movement in 1969: I watched it with

envy. I thought that here, locked up in East Germany, we were condemned to live in the dullest period in history. Nearly every
conversation ended up lamenting our situation. Men used to wait
eagerly to become 65, women 60, the age when passports for travel
were first issued to all those who did not belong to the nomenklatura.

But we also realised that in spite of all our complaints we had to
make something out of life. By now I was married with children. We
found new friends with young children. We all suffered from the same
claustrophobic feeling about life in the GDR, and tried to help our
children cope with their fractured lives—complying with the official
doctrine at school, while living with different beliefs at home. Our
"counter-life" took place during the weekends in a tiny peasant's
house 30 miles from Berlin. Here the children could do whatever they
wanted, while the adults convened a more formal intellectual life. In
our circle were people of many professions and views, which compensated for the limited access to knowledge outside one's own work. We
formed a kind of secret university, called the "Friday evening club,"
with lectures, seminars, and even performances.

During the 1970s we remained strictly private and silent, with no
intention of leaving our closed circle. We hoped that conditions would
become better with political liberalisation, which to a limited extent
they did. But towards the end of the 1970s, under Erich Honecker, the
reins were pulled in, and we lost hope again. This time we did not stay
inactive. Some people went into open opposition and suffered perse-
cution, others began to work actively for emigration, still others tried
to join the system in order to change it. I remember being advised
often by friends from the west to do the latter. Luckily I did not take
their advice—after 1990 the same people would have stoned me for
collaboration with the system. All these contradictory attitudes
produced tension among us. Legal emigration became possible after
the Helsinki convention of 1975, although only after a period of discrimination, unemployment and sometimes arrest which, in the case
of one friend, lasted seven years. Illegal emigration over the mined
border zone or via some western "tugboat" organisation was dangerous and could end in prison or even death. We were particularly

concerned for our children, because quite naturally young people preferred the quick and dangerous way to the agonising wait.

My "coming out" into open political dissent came in the late 1970s, and was triggered neither by the material hardship of everyday life (which, compared to the Soviet Union, was still tolerable) nor by the block in my professional career (I had not joined the communist party and was therefore ineligible for the top posts). My motivation had two sources. One was the fear of leading the same secluded silent life as my parents, in circumstances much less harsh than theirs. They feared the Gestapo and concentration camps, whereas we were afraid of being discriminated against and at worst being driven out of the country into the Federal Republic. The second reason in my case was observation and experience: I had spent, together with my wife and children, several long-term working stays in the Soviet Union; far from Moscow, in a research institute in the back of beyond. The material conditions were harsh, but it provided us with experience of everyday life in another country. It was also a source of anxiety. The Soviet Union was the master country of the communist bloc and hence the model for the social and political trends of the future. These trends were ominous. We lived in Russia, in a country with a talented and decent population, which nevertheless was clearly heading for political disaster—a disaster which could end in world war. In those pre-Gorbachev days we could not imagine a peaceful transition from decaying socialism to a better society. We were convinced that the elite would defend their position to the end, as almost every ruling class had done in history.

By the 1980s, the Friday circle was no longer sufficient. Some of us joined church-based groups and began circulating forbidden literature. I contributed to the samizdat literature with articles on the Soviet Union and Poland, and translations from their clandestine literature. There were consequences. I lost my position as a scientific group leader. My house was bugged. Our flat was searched. I was summoned by the police on the pretext of a security leak in our institute. We received open and coded threats. All this was clear at the time, but we received full confirmation in 1993 when the Stasi files became available.

Our Friday club finally joined the open opposition when the New Forum movement was founded in September 1989. Many of us became activists in the autumn movement which toppled the regime. I was elected to the first and last freely elected parliament of the GDR and served as an MP from March to October 1990. With reunification, I resigned and returned to my job. There was a short interlude in 1994 when I was persuaded to run for the presidency of the unified country as an independent candidate, but this was largely symbolic. I continued to work and did not fight a real campaign.

I have described my political life in order to explain my ambiguous position towards "my" country. German is the culture and language that I understand to the roots. My command of Russian is good, that of English and French not bad, yet I am a stranger in these realms. I am German if nothing else. And yet I lived in the eastern half of the country for 45 years and longed to escape. My country, East Germany, made me homesick for a better one.

Unlike, say, the Estonians or Lithuanians, there was no simple national struggle against a former ruler for us. Gradually I began to understand that my task was not just to exist in my Germany, but to build it up, to make it better, to contribute to a reform that would make it acceptable to our children. This led to my political activism of the 1980s and produced a paradoxical outcome: I became a convinced citizen and active supporter of my country, the GDR, during its very last year of existence. With the implementation of the political goals of the American and French revolutions, I felt obliged to participate in the reconstruction of a society that had experienced two dictatorships over three generations. I did not imagine the future in terms of a unified Germany, although all my life I had considered the divided Germany as a scandal and personal offence. But reunifying Germany appeared both unnecessary and impossible. I could not believe that the Soviet Union would be prepared to give up its east European empire. And it was not clear that a united Germany would create a more stable Europe. In a more positive vein, I thought that a second democratic Germany could make a contribution to unifying Europe.

We know now that this was an illusion. The Russians ceded the Tehran/Yalta/Potsdam/Helsinki construction that they had defended so stubbornly over decades. I still do not really understand why this happened when passive resistance to change would have sufficed to stop it—I guess it was lucky that Gorbachev's rule lasted just long enough to confirm the peaceful ending of postwar Europe.

Another paradox was that my commitment to our post-communist reform state met with the opposition of the overwhelming majority of the people. They made it clear that they wanted unification at once, not reform experiments with unclear results. In 1990, they withdrew support from the autumn movement. We faced the choice between battling against the popular will and withdrawal from politics.

I chose not to fight for three reasons. One was that in 1990 there was a unique opportunity to end the division of Germany. The second factor was that life would become easier after unification. My salary is now paid in a hard currency. I can order any book from England, America or France at a cost affordable to me. After decades spent like a bird in a cage, I can travel to almost any country. I longed for this. A third factor was my frustration with my role as a politician. In 1989, when it required some courage to speak up publicly, you felt the support and solidarity of normal, decent people. But in 1990, when many careerists rushed into office, the population began quickly to become cynical about politicians and their attendance allowances. The only role our own people would grant us was to agree to an immediate merger of the two countries and then quit the stage for the doers from the west. At that time the west German politicians enjoyed full confidence, although this trust was to dissolve quickly in the post-unification depression.

To this day I cannot disentangle whether it was profane consumerism or national idealism which contributed most to the surge of pressure in 1990 from east Germans for immediate unification. Helmut Kohl had tears in his eyes when the people of Dresden cheered him with German flags, while Otto Schily (now interior minister) raised a banana into the flashlights of television cameras in order to reveal what he considered to be the true motive. I admit: I had both aspirations. A visit to the Tate Gallery in London (my preferred object of consumption) is not inherently different to a visit to the Costa del Sol (preferred by more of my compatriots).

The new unified Germany is now 10 years old. It has been a much less powerful force than hoped for by some and feared by others. Germany did not become the superpower that Bismarck's Germany became after the 1871 unification. The internal conflicts within the country which Bismarck tried to crush were repeated in the 1990s as conflict between west and east. This friction weakened Germany and contributed to its reduced international dominance. We have not become a monolithic power, and this has been welcomed abroad with a mixture of relief and *schadenfreude*. Unified Germany turned out to be a rather immobile entity, not the modernist grenade it became after 1871. This may soothe some of the neighbours, but to me it is a matter of concern. I am not qualified to describe the state of economic and political blockage in detail, but I feel it intensely. We seem to lack innovative spirit. My son, who studied medicine and became interested in basic research, did not find a suitable position and now works in Boston. My elder daughter says Germany is boring and went first to London, then to New York, and is now living in Africa. My younger daughter is still in Berlin working as a physicist at the Technical University. She says that the university system is much less creative than comparable institutions elsewhere.

I am happy that my children can travel, but I am concerned that our country is no longer an attractive place for young people from abroad. Those who do come are repelled by all kinds of bureaucratic impediments and even by the threat of the mob. I do not want to exaggerate this factor. Violent youths are a very small minority and exist in other countries too.

Where now? The conflicts of our first decade were perhaps inevitable after two generations of life in antagonistic political systems, but they should now recede. The challenges that Germany now faces are not the internal differences of mentality but those of the global economy and global ecological crisis. They concern us as a whole, not east and west separately. To tackle them we need to renew the spirit of public commitment of the "normal" citizen that made the 1989 revolt so irresistible. But this cannot easily be done by our existing political parties, which are good at balancing out material interests, but do not seem up to the task of building a democratic civic society.

Radical Islam's failure • Malise Ruthven

JULY 2002

The attacks of 11th September were the last gasps of a moribund Islamist movement. Terror is a sign of failure, deployed when political mobilisation has failed. This is the conclusion drawn by a masterly survey of the modern Islamist movements from Morocco to Indonesia, *Jihad: The Trail of Political Islam* (IB Tauris), by Gilles Kepel. The recurrent violence of the 1990s—the attacks on tourists in Egypt, the Taleban takeover in Afghanistan, the war in Chechnya, the violence in France, the attacks on US targets in Saudi Arabia, Yemen and Africa culminating in 11th September—is "a reflection of the movement's weakness, not its strength."

The reason for this political decline, Kepel argues, resides in the failure of the Islamist movement in most countries to maintain its appeal to its two very different constituencies: the pious middle class of small businessmen and shopkeepers, which looked to the movement to uphold its petit-bourgeois values; and the urban poor, recent immigrants from the countryside, who looked to the Islamist movements to authenticate their values, redress social injustices and to supplement the failings of state welfare. Both of these groups, says Kepel, were "committed to the Shari'a and to the idea of an Islamic state, but they did not view that state in the same way. The poor imbued it with a social-revolutionary content, while the devout middle class saw it as a vehicle for wresting power for themselves from the incumbent elites, without fundamentally disturbing the existing social hierarchies ... The fragile alliance between the urban poor and the devout middle classes, which was held together by intellectuals preaching the doctrines of Islamism, was ill-prepared for any kind of protracted confrontation with the state authorities. But with increasing success, governments figured out ways to pit the two camps against one another, exposing the underlying conflict between their agendas and their shared but vague desire to set up an Islamic state."

The tension between these two constituencies has been so successfully exploited by the authoritarian governments of the Muslim world that many of those intellectuals who once espoused, or even led, the Islamist cause are now insisting that the movement give priority to democracy, regardless of the risk of reversals at the polls. The Islamist luminaries of an earlier generation—Abu Ala Maududi in Indo-Pakistan and Sayyid Qutb in Egypt—argued that democracy was a western invention, incompatible with the "divine sovereignty" enjoined by Islam. Statements to this effect by Ali Benhadj of the Islamic Salvation Front (FIS) were invoked to justify the suppression of democracy by the Algerian military in December 1991, when the FIS seemed set to win the election. The consequence has been a cycle of violence that may have cost as many as 150,000 lives.

A sadder and wiser generation of Islamists has learned the hard way that western democracy has moral qualities that are conspicuous by their absence in Muslim societies. Kepel cites the testimony of Munawar Anees, a former Islamist firebrand and colleague of Anwar Ibrahim. Ibrahim was the Malaysian Islamist leader co-opted into government by Prime Minister Mahathir Mohamad, before being disgraced and imprisoned on charges of sodomy when his movement became too powerful. Anees was himself released from prison and sent into exile in the US only after massive international pressure: "Like so many others in the Muslim world, all my adult life I saw western conspiracies everywhere. I thought the west's sole objective was to keep our heads under water. I now find that my western friends were the ones who saved me, whilst Mahathir, a Muslim, has done everything in his power to destroy me."

The same pattern of co-option and repression by the state is repeated in most of the major Muslim countries. In Pakistan, General Zia al-Haq, the former dictator, used the Islamist doctrines promulgated by Abu Ala Maududi and the Jamaat-e-Islami (JI) party he founded in 1941 as a way of blocking the restoration of democracy. His Islamisation measures pleased the pious middle classes whose support he sought. With members of the JI rising in the public service, they had no desire to rock the boat by allying themselves with the disinherited younger generation. The long-term effects of Zia's policies, however, have been disastrous. By levying *zakat*—the ritual duty of charity normally paid as voluntary donations—on bank deposits, Zia antagonised the Shia minority, who pay *zakat* to their own religious leaders, setting in motion a conflict between the Sunni and Shia militias which persists. Zia's "Islamisation of education" did more than damage Pakistan's economy. The funds from *zakat* contributed directly to the growth of the *madrasas* (seminaries) controlled by the ultra-conservative Deobandi sect, the movement that spawned the Taleban.

Co-option and repression were also evident in Sudan. The programme of Islamisation introduced by Jaafar al-Nimeiri and General Omar al-Bashir, under the influence of the urbane Hasan al-Turabi, leader of the Islamist National Islamic Front (NIF), alienated the non-Muslim south, provoking Africa's longest-running civil war. Bashir used the NIF's programme, which included purges and executions of non-Islamists in the top ranks of the army and civil service, to smash the power of the traditional political parties, dominated by the Sufi (mystical) brotherhoods. The NIF compensated for its lack of mass support by recruiting thugs from the Fallata, a previously marginal group of west Africans. But ten years into the dictatorship, Turabi had served his purpose. In December 1999, Bashir ousted Turabi in a "palace coup."

It is a similar story in Egypt. The Muslim Brotherhood, founded in 1928, was a leading force in the overthrow of the monarchy in July 1952. But Colonel Gamal Abdul Nasser, who assumed full powers the following year, quickly fell out with the Brotherhood, whose leading intellectual, Sayyid Qutb, he imprisoned and executed in 1966 on trumped-up charges of plotting to overthrow the state. The "martyr" Qutb, as Kepel makes clear, is the movement's intellectual godfather, though some latter-day neo-fundamentalists influenced by Saudi Arabia consider his revolutionary interpretations of the Koran religiously suspect. Nasser's falling out with the Brotherhood drove it underground. Unlike in Pakistan, where the secular-minded leadership repeatedly clashed with the Muslim nationalism on which their country had been founded, Nasser was able to rely on the "sheer strength of the Egyptian national identity" to control both the Brotherhood and the religious establishment represented by al-Azhar, the world's foremost Sunni Muslim academy. In the course of time, however, Nasser's successor, Anwar al-Sadat, relaxed Nasser's ban on the Brotherhood, believing that its Islamist ideology would help to contain rebellious youth and act as a source of moral values. The moderate leadership of the Brotherhood, which wanted society to be transformed by preaching not political action, was supported by exiles returning from the Gulf and Saudi Arabia, where many had found patronage by presenting themselves as victims of Nasser's socialism. Thus was laid the foundations of the infamous marriage between the disciples of Qutb and ultra-conservative scholars supported by Saudi Arabia (such as Sheikh Abdullah Bin Baz, notorious for his pre-Copernican cosmology).

A jihadist in the Qutb tradition, the electrical engineer Abd al-Salaam al-Farrag, masterminded the assassination of "Pharaoh" Sadat in October 1981. In *The Neglected Duty*, Farrag attacked the religious establishment for failing in its duty to protect society from the "apostate" Sadat, who had "fed at the tables of imperialism and Zionism" by signing the Camp David accords with Israel. The al-Azhar religious establishment was unanimous in denouncing Sadat's killers, and strenuous efforts were made to prove that the assassination was not warranted by the scriptural sources cited in Farrag's tract.

Despite Sadat's unpopularity, the pious middle class has remained broadly attached to the regime of his successor, Hosni Mubarak. Middle-class Islamists have been allowed to take over many professional associations, including the doctors', engineers' and lawyers' syndicates. Until partly discredited by fraud, Islamic financial institutions grew and flourished, providing a rich network of business connections for the pious bourgeoisie. The Islamic resurgence in Egypt reached its high tide in the autumn of 1992, when the charities under Brotherhood control did a far better job of providing relief and shelter for poor Cairenes afflicted by the earthquake than government bureaucrats, snared in corruption and red tape.

Faced with the danger to his own position posed by the alliance between the radicals in the charities and their middle-class supporters, Mubarak was forced to act. In Imbaba, a vast urban slum with about 1m migrants from Upper Egypt, one of the radical Islamists declared the place an "Islamic Republic." The government sent in 14,000 troops, who stayed for six weeks and arrested some 5,000 people. State money was poured into the area. Faced with the prospect of social improvement, many of the former Islamists changed their tune, deciding to work within the system. Thereafter the radicals were gradually isolated: the attacks on foreign tourists (including the Luxor massacre in 1997) alienated whatever remaining support they had amongst the pious bourgeoisie, many of whom depend on tourism. A majority in the movement declared a ceasefire. A minority, led by the former surgeon Ayman al-Zawahiri, kept up the jihad from exile in Afghanistan, where his faction became part of al Qaeda.

The Egyptian case fits Kepel's thesis like a glove: the terrorism that culminated in the Luxor massacre escalated in proportion to the erosion of the movement's political base after the government takeover. The violence in Algeria, on the other hand, has yet to run its course. At this time of writing, 25 nomads are reported massacred in a village west of Algiers, a few hours before the incumbent National Liberation Front (FLN) managed to get itself re-elected in a low turnout poll (46 per cent), boycotted by the key opposition parties. Kepel traces the Algerian conflict from the 1970s when the hike in oil revenues following the Yom Kippur war enabled the FLN to "buy social pacification by subsidising imported consumer goods." When oil prices collapsed in 1986, half the government's budget was wiped out. The gangs of "hittistes" (slang for unemployed youth) were ripe for recruitment by the radical wing of the Islamic Salvation Front

(FIS), led by the populist preacher, Ali Benhadj. The bazaar merchants of the "pious middle classes" were cultivated by Benhadj's co-leader, Abassi Madani, a university professor who impressed them with his knowledge and style. Abassi reassured the traders that an investment in the FIS would be the best guarantee for future business. The alliance between the two wings of the FIS, however, was fragile, and when the army intervened to prevent it from winning an outright majority in the second round of the parliamentary elections in January 1992, the FIS had already lost 1m votes compared with its performance in the municipal elections the previous year, when it won control of a majority of Algeria's communes.

In any case, the middle classes were beginning to fear the real possibility of an FIS regime. In the municipalities controlled by the FIS, women were forcibly veiled, video stores, liquor shops and other "immoral" establishments were closed. There was abundant testimony to "the civic virtue of the elected FIS officials, in contrast to the corruption, arbitrariness and inefficiency that had formerly prevailed." But what really worried the bazaaris was Benhadj's attacks on France's and Algeria's Francophone elite. The Islamist programme of Arabisation also threatened the identity of the Berbers. This allowed the army to imprison Benhadj and Abassi and to smash the moderate wing of the FIS without encountering serious resistance from the middle classes.

The Islamic Salvation Army (AIS), the military wing of the FIS, and the Armed Islamic Group (GIA), led by veterans from the jihad against communism in Afghanistan, became involved in an increasingly violent war of attrition against the government. But long before 11th September this violence proved counter-productive. The fanaticism and brutality of the "Arab-Afghans" spiralled out of control, with the export of terrorism to France and racketeering and extortion by armed gangs at home. Torn by personal and ideological feuds, the GIA eventually dissolved itself, while the AIS (like most Egyptian jihadists) made a unilateral truce with the state. The pious middle classes that used to support the FIS have been appeased by the passage to a market economy.

The Afghan connection was part of the movement's undoing, not just in Algeria. With Serb aggression against Bosnia's Muslims seen throughout the Muslim world as a new crusade, the extension of the jihad from Afghanistan to Bosnia was inevitable. But unlike in Afghanistan, the rhetoric of jihad and the demand for an Islamic state cut no ice amongst Bosnia's secularised Muslims. The Dayton Accords integrated Bosnia into the European sphere and with the forced departure of the Islamist volunteers, the wider Islamic world lost any influence it might have over Bosnia's future.

The "blowback" thesis tracing the spread of Islamist terrorism to the CIA and Saudi-backed jihad against the Soviet Union in Afghanistan has been thoroughly explored by Ahmed Rashid, John Cooley and others, and much of the ground Kepel covers here is familiar. "The international brigade of jihad veterans, being outside the control of any state, were suddenly available to serve radical Islamist causes anywhere in the world." A key figure linking the Afghan jihadis with the spread of Islamist terror is Abdullah Azam, the Palestinian preacher trained at al-Azhar who, with Osama bin Laden, founded the Peshawar-based Office of Services (MAK), which became the core of al Qaeda (the base or foundation). According to Kepel, the name which has become synonymous with international terrorism originated in the MAK's computer database. It was Azam who argued that after the defeat of the communists in Afghanistan the jihad must extend to other lands that once belonged to Islam. The struggle to expel the Soviets was a prelude for the liberation of Palestine, and other "lost" territories, including Spain.

Osama bin Laden attended Azam's lectures at university in Jedda where he also came under the influence of Muhammad Qutb, brother of the martyred Egyptian. After the Soviet takeover in Afghanistan, Bin Laden followed Azam to Peshawar, acting as a channel for Saudi money while Azam (with CIA support) enlisted jihadis throughout the world, including the US, where he visited 27 states on his recruitment drives. After Azam's assassination in 1989, probably by one of many Afghan arms of the Pakistani intelligence services (ISI), Osama took on his mantle. In line with Qutb's and

Azam's philosophy, the "Afghan-Arabs", who formed the core of al Qaeda, were to be the vanguard of a world Islamist movement. Azam's influence is also visible in the charter of Hamas, the Islamist movement in Israeli-occupied Palestine which used the first intifada to extend its influence. The charter states that "there will be no solution to the Palestinian problem except through jihad," while condemning the PLO's acceptance of the existence of Israel.

The rise of Hamas was fuelled by money from Saudi Arabia and the Gulf. The flow increased at the expense of the PLO after Saddam Hussein's invasion of Kuwait in 1990, which Yasser Arafat had supported from exile in Tunis. The rise of Hamas pushed Israel into signing the Oslo accords in September 1993, under which Arafat came to be installed as president of the Palestinian Authority. Crippled by the collapse in his funding, he was a weak negotiating partner, which suited Israel: as Yitzhak Rabin explained to the Knesset, he aimed to use Arafat as Israel's policeman in those parts of the occupied territories it was finding difficult to control. "The Palestinians ... will rule by their own methods, freeing, and this is most important, the Israeli army soldiers from having to do what they will do." Competition, not only between Hamas and the PLO, but also between Hamas and Islamic Jihad, helped to stoke the fires of the intifada. Only the harshness of the Israeli response kept the conflicts of interest and outlook between the Islamists and the middle-class supporters of the PLO (now the PNA) from splitting the Palestine national movement apart.

The virtue of this excellent book is the broadness of its coverage of the Islamist movements. As a political scientist, however, he is less concerned with exploring the movement's philosophical and theological roots, than with charting the social forces that drive it. Being less interested in religion than *realpolitik*, he underestimates the power of forces less amenable to rational scrutiny. If politics is the "art of the possible," religion is its contrary. The myth and ritual upon which religion is built belong to the realm of the impossible.

In his account of the Iranian revolution, for example, Kepel under-plays the role of Shia eschatology. He shows how the Ayatollah Khomeini kept together the fissiparous alliance consisting of the "wretched" of the shanty towns and the pious bazaari merchants alienated by the Shah's pro-western policies and economic cronyism. This alliance is now falling apart, as a reform-minded parliament sup-ported by the middle classes vies for power and influence with a conservative judiciary. To its credit, however, the Iranian revolution has institutionalised the conflict along constitutional lines. The glue that enabled Khomeini to hold his coalition together was partly the Iran-Iraq war, supported by the Gulf states and (surreptitiously) by the US. But it was also held together by Shiism, a doctrine of revolu-tionary legitimism that, like Christianity, involves the symbolic appropriation of the promised millennium.

The eschatological expectations of Shiism can be brought from mythical time into history with devastating results, as Khomeini demonstrated when he returned to Iran in an Air France jumbo jet to a tumultuous reception of 2m people in February 1979. Many ordinary Iranians saw him as the "Hidden Imam" who returns, like Christ, at the end of time to bring justice and peace to the world. But as with Christianity, the eschatological time-bomb at the heart of the tradition can be defused by arguing, like St Augustine, that the prom-ised kingdom is a *spiritual* one, not to be realised on earth; alternatively it can be deferred indefinitely, while the Awaited One's representatives confine themselves to matters moral and spiritual. Since Khomeini's death in 1989, there has been an unacknowledged secularisation of Iranian society, with a growing number of clergy returning to more traditional, quietist interpretations of Islam.

Shiism, like Christianity, is built on political failure. The founding figures of both—Jesus and Ali ibn Abi Talib with his son Hussein—are martyrs whose failure to achieve a worldly revolution allowed an apocalyptic idea to be subsumed into an act of ritual sacrifice. The rit-ualisation and spiritualisation of a failed prophesy or the deferment of the apocalypse, far from leading to a religious tradition's extinction, may be the condition of its survival. Like Christianity, Shiism, especially in its Ismaili versions, has proved adaptable to varied histor-ical conditions precisely because it contains within itself the hermeneutics of accommodation, a deferral of salvation. Similar resources exist within the Sunni mainstream, especially in the Sufi brotherhoods. But as Kepel shows, both Sufism and Shiism have been subjected to relentless harassment and suppression by the forces of "petro-Islam" exported from Saudi Arabia and the Gulf, as well as by the Islamists themselves.

The apocalyptic strand in Sunnism is not institutionalised under the management of a disciplined, educated hierarchy, as in Shiism. Since Ottoman times the authority of the *ulama* has come under the progressive control of the state. But the religious leaders who issued fatwas (legal rulings) at the convenience of governments were ignored by Islamist leaders such as Shukri Mustafa, founder of the Takfir wa'l Hijra group in Egypt. As Kepel shows, the Sunni Islamists hold widely differing views about the meaning of the Shari'a and how to set about the creation of a truly Islamic state.

Most, if not all these movements, however, do share a common theological position which may be described as the Argument from Manifest Success (AMS). The Prophet Muhammad, according to this argument, triumphed over his enemies through battle as well as by preaching. Building on his victories and his faith in God, his succes-sors, the guided caliphs, conquered most of west Asia and north Africa as well as Spain. In this view, the truth of Islam was vindicated through its historical achievement in creating what would become a great world civilisation. The AMS is consonant with the doctrine according to which Islam supersedes the previous revelations of Judaism and Christianity. The problem with the AMS, when held in its most strident Saudi-sponsored versions, is what to do when history starts going wrong. In the late middle ages, the loss of Spain to Islam could be offset against the gains in the Levant, with the collapse of the Latin kingdoms founded by the Crusaders. By 1920, however, almost all the Islamic world had come under direct or indirect European rule. Muslims, as Bernard Lewis details in his fascinating essay, began to ask themselves *What went wrong?* (Weidenfeld & Nicolson).

Unfortunately, the answer did not include a critical revaluation of the religious tradition, as occurred in the west after the Reformation with the gradual emergence of theological liberalism. The sacred text of the Koran and the Traditions of the Holy Prophet were too embedded in the culture to allow for a fundamental reappraisal that would trace the roots of failure to the religion of Islam itself. Rather, it was insisted in numerous discourses to the sultans that the rebellions in Greece and the Balkans and the losses to Russia were the result of Muslims being punished for straying from the path ordained by God—a diagnosis and prescription, Lewis notes, that still finds wide acceptance. Like other Muslim sovereigns the Ottomans thought they could acquire the technical knowledge that would enable them to defend their society without tampering with the eternal word of God. The necessary accommodations with the knowledge of the infidels was difficult enough. First to appear was the "previously unthinkable doctrine that true believers must follow infidels in military organisation and the conduct of warfare." Then, even more painfully, the *ulama* had to accept infidel teachers for Muslim pupils, "an innovation of staggering magnitude in a civilisation that for more than a millennium had been accustomed to despise the outer infidels and barbarians as having nothing of any value to contribute." They also had to accept infidel allies in wars against other infidels.

By the mid-19th century, the classic disdain for the non-Muslim world had eroded to the point where Turkish newspapers were covering foreign events such as the American civil war. Lewis shows how ideas of political freedom began to make headway in the 19th century, along with systems of law imported from Europe. Once the colonial powers had trained up a class of clerics to work in their offices and counting houses in European languages, imperialism was doomed. Lewis ascribes the failures of most post-colonial governments in the western part of the Muslim world to the wrong economic priorities: "In the west, one makes money in the market, and uses it to buy or influence power. In the east one seizes power, and uses it to make money. Morally there is no difference between the two, but their impact on the economy and the polity is very different."

Despite its wit and pungency, Lewis's analysis is somewhat limited. The failure of European-style polities in west Asia, whether Soviet one-party states or western-style democracies, is best explained by reference to the persistence of networks of kinship and patronage allied to the vastly increased police apparatus available to modern states. Lewis's invocation of past attitudes of cultural supremacy, the "wrong" economic priorities or differences in the status of women are only part of the story, however important. The "string of shabby tyrannies, from traditional autocracies to new style dictatorships" which govern most Muslim countries depend on factors—such as personality cults disseminated through visual media and the ubiquity of the security services—which were not available to rulers in the past. Surprisingly, Lewis pays more attention to Muslim resistance to western music than to the impact of photography and visual representation in a traditionally aniconic culture. In contrast to Islam, Christianity externalised its mythologies by giving them visual form, fostering the process whereby the image came to be separated from its content. The brilliant, abstract, geometric patternings of Islamic art may have opened a window into the mind of God, but they did not encourage visual scepticism: every Baghdad store has its picture of "Brother Saddam," who is indeed watching, like Big Brother, because in a culture conditioned by centuries of aniconism, the portrait still conveys an element of the person.

Lewis's conclusion is bleaker than Kepel's. "Compared with its millennial rival, Christendom, the world of Islam has become poor, weak and ignorant." The failures of Islam are compounded by the successes of non-western countries such as Japan, India and South Korea. "Following is bad enough. Limping in the rear is far worse. By all the standards that matter in the modern world—economic development and job creation, literacy and educational and scientific achievement, political freedom and respect for human rights—what was once a mighty civilisation has indeed fallen low." Western imperialism is inevitably held to blame. Now that the French and British have departed, the "Americans" and "the Jews" are the scapegoats. "If the peoples of the middle east continue on their present path, the suicide bomber may become a metaphor for the whole region, and there will be no escape from a downward spiral of hate and self-pity, poverty and oppression, culminating sooner or later in yet another alien domination."

The gloomy prognosis may be applied, *a fortiori*, to Pakistan, an economic and social disaster zone, when compared with its rival, the "polytheist" or "pagan" India. More ominously even than in Israel-Palestine, the apocalyptic mood in Pakistan centres on the "Islamic bomb," to which there are now flower-decked shrines in all their major cities. Like the attacks on New York and Washington, Pakistani bomb-worship is a demonstration of nihilistic theological despair. Since the God of Manifest Success has so signally failed to deliver, we must kill ourselves—taking with us as many of our enemies as we can.

America's demon in the cellar • Anatol Lieven

MARCH 2004

America enjoys more global power than any previous state. Following the death of communism as an alternative path of modernisation, it dominates the world not only militarily but also culturally and economically, and derives immense benefit from the present world system. According to all precedents, therefore, the US ought to be behaving as a conservative hegemon, defending the existing international order and spreading its values by example. Indeed, this is exactly how it did behave for most of the period between 1989 and 11th September 2001. Not marching on Baghdad in the first Gulf war, seeking to persuade the Ukraine to stay in the Soviet Union, intervening with great reluctance in the Balkans—these were all the actions of a mostly status quo power.

So why did a country which, after the attacks of 11th September, had the chance to lead an alliance of all the major states—including Muslim ones—against Islamist terrorism choose instead to pursue policies which divided the west, further alienated the Muslim world and exposed America itself to increased danger? Why has it been drawn towards the role of an unsatisfied and even revolutionary power, kicking to pieces the hill of which it is the king? The most important reason lies in the character of American nationalism.

Nationalism is not the usual prism through which recent American behaviour has been viewed. Critics, at home and abroad, have tended to focus on what has been called American imperialism. The US today does harbour important forces which can be called imperialist, and whose members in the past two years have, for the first time, even begun to describe America as an empire. However, though large in influence, these people are few in number. They are to be found above all in over-lapping sections of the intelligentsia and the foreign policy and security establishments, and even there they are far from predominant.

But unlike large numbers of Englishmen, Frenchmen and others at the time of their empires, the vast majority of Americans do not think of their country as imperialist, or as possessing an empire. As the after-math of the Iraq war seems to be demonstrating, they are also not prepared to make the commitments and sacrifices which would be nec-essary to maintain a direct empire in the middle east and elsewhere.

Moreover, unlike previous empires, the US national identity, and what has been called the "American creed," are founded on adher-ence to democracy. However imperfectly democracy may be practised at home, and hypocritically preached abroad, this democratic faith does set real limits on how far the US can exert direct rule over other peoples. America is therefore more an indirect empire, closer to the Dutch in the East Indies than the British in India.

In presenting its imperial plans to the American people, therefore, the Bush administration—like others before it—has been careful to package them both as part of a benevolent strategy of spreading American values of democracy and freedom and as an essential part of the defence of the American nation itself.

A great many Americans are not only intensely nationalistic, but also bellicose in their response to any perceived attack on their country: "Don't Tread on Me!" as the rattlesnake on the American revolutionary flag declared. Coupled with an intense national solipsism and ignorance of the outside world, this has allowed an unwise extension of the "war on terror" from its original—and legitimate— targets in al Qaeda and the Taleban to embrace the Ba'athist regime in Iraq, and possibly other regimes in the future. This nationalism has also been turned against a range of proposals that have been portrayed as hurting the US or infringing its national sovereignty, from the international criminal court to proposed restrictions on greenhouse gas emissions.

Most Americans genuinely believe all this to be a matter of self-defence—of their economy, their "way of life," their freedoms or the nation itself. The US under George W Bush is indeed driving towards empire, but the domestic political fuel being fed into the imperial engine is that of a wounded and vengeful nationalism. After 9/11, this sentiment is entirely sincere as far as most Americans are concerned and all the more dangerous for that; there is probably no more dangerous element in the nationalist mix than a righteous sense of victimhood. This is a sentiment which has in the past helped wreck Germany, Serbia and numerous other countries, and is now in the process of gravely harming Israel.

A relatively benign version of indirect US imperial dominance is by no means unacceptable to many people round the world—both because they often have neighbours whom they fear more than America, and because their leaders are increasingly integrated into a global capitalist elite whose values are largely defined by those of America. But American imperial power in the service of narrow American and Israeli nationalism is a very different matter, and an unstable base for hegemony. It involves power over the world without any responsibility for global problems and without any responsiveness to others' concerns.

Why "nationalism" rather than "patriotism" as a description of this phenomenon in America? The answer is provided by one of the fathers of the neoconservative tradition in the US, Irving Kristol: "Patriotism springs from love of the nation's past; nationalism arises out of hope for the nation's future, distinctive greatness ..."

Kristol here echoed the classic distinction between patriotism and nationalism drawn by Kenneth Minogue, the historian of nationalism. Minogue defined patriotism as essentially conservative, a desire to defend your country as it actually is; whereas nationalism is a devotion to an ideal, abstract, unrealised notion of your country, often coupled with a belief in some wider national mission to humanity. In America today, there is certainly a very strong element of patriotism, of attachment to American institutions and to America as it is, but as Kristol's words indicate, there is also a revolutionary element, a commitment to a messianic version of the nation and its role in the world. This element links the US nationalism of today to the "unsatisfied," late-arriving nationalisms of Germany, Italy and Russia, rather than the satisfied and status quo patriotism of the British, and thereby helps explain the strangely Wilhelmine air of US policy and attitudes.

If one strand of nationalism is radical because it looks to "the nation's future, distinctive greatness," another is radical because it looks back, to a vanished and idealised national past. This strand is associated with the world of the Republican right, and especially the Christian right, with its rhetoric of "taking back" America, and restoring an older, purer society. This longstanding tendency in the country's culture and politics reflects the continuing conservative religiosity of many Americans; it has also always been an expression of social, economic and ethnic anxieties.

These anxieties stem originally from the progressive loss of control over society by the original white Anglo-Saxon and Scots Irish settlers. Connected to this are class anxieties—in the past, the hostility of the small towns and countryside to the new immigrant-populated cities; today, the decline of the traditional white working class as a result of economic change, globalisation, and the retreat of industry. In America, the supremely victorious nation of the modern age, large numbers of citizens feel defeated. This gives many American nationalists their mean and defensive edge, so curiously at variance with America's image and self-image as a land of success, openness, wealth and generosity. America also contains one large and important region with a legacy of crushing military and political defeat: the white south.

This too is a familiar pattern in other nationalisms. In Europe, radical conservatism and nationalism stemmed from classes and groups in actual or perceived decline as a result of socio-economic change. One way of looking at American nationalism, and America's troubled relationship with the contemporary world, is indeed to understand that many Americans are in revolt against the world which America itself has made. Many middle and lower-income Americans are deeply troubled by the effects of globalisation and the immigration which comes in its train, while conservative religious Americans are appalled by the effects of modern American mass culture on family life and traditional values.

The US is in part simply an old European state which avoided the catastrophes that nationalism brought upon Europe in the 20th century. Its nationalism thus retains an intensity which Europeans have had kicked out of them by history. Seventy-two per cent of Americans say they are "very proud" of their nationality, compared to 49 per cent of Britons, 39 per cent of Italians and just 20 per cent of the Dutch.

But the dangers of unreflective nationalist sentiments remain all too obvious. Nationalism thrives on irrational hatreds, and the portrayal of other nations or ethno-religious groups as irredeemably wicked and hostile. Yesterday this was true of the attitudes of many American nationalists to the Soviet Union. Today it risks becoming the case with regard to the Arab and Muslim worlds, or to any country which defies American wishes. The run-up to the war in Iraq saw an astonishing explosion of chauvinism directed against France and Germany.

In a striking essay on anti-Americanism in *Foreign Policy* (September/October 2003), Fouad Ajami unwittingly summed up the central danger of American nationalism for the US and the world. He dismissed out of hand the evidence of Pew, Gallup and other polling organisations showing that hostility to America had mounted as a result of the policies of the Bush administration. Instead, Ajami argued that across the world—not just the Arab and Muslim worlds, but across Europe, Asia and Latin America too—anti-Americanism is an ingrained response to America's wealth, success and modernity, which are forcing other countries to adapt their systems. The essay suggested that US policies are completely irrelevant, and the sympathy displayed by France and other countries after 9/11 was completely hypocritical: "To maintain France's sympathy, and that of *Le Monde*, the US would have had to turn the other cheek to the murderers of al Qaeda, spare the Taleban, and engage the Muslim world in some high civilisational dialogue. But who needs high approval ratings in Marseille?"

Ajami's argument was taken up in cruder form by the right-wing commentator Charles Krauthammer in a piece for *Time* magazine. He both attacked "the world" and sought to tar his domestic political opponents with the same anti-American brush:

> The world apparently likes the US when it is on its knees.
> From that the Democrats deduce a foreign policy—remain
> on our knees, humble and supplicant, and enjoy the applause
> and "support" of the world ... The search for logic in anti-
> Americanism is fruitless. It is in the air the world breathes.
> Its roots are envy and self-loathing—by peoples who,
> yearning for modernity but having failed at it, find their
> one satisfaction in despising modernity's great exemplar.
> On 11th September, they gave it a rest for one day. Big deal.

But if these arguments are valid how do the writers explain the shift in opinion in Britain between the war in Afghanistan (which public opinion strongly supported) and the war in Iraq? Is British society, too, supposed to be congenitally anti-American and an example of failed modernity? Try applying the logic of these arguments to other national enmities. Many Poles do not much like Russians and probably never will, for historical reasons. Does this mean that Polish-Russian relations would be unaffected by new Russian policies which Poland saw as hostile to its interests? The global hegemon is bound to attract some enmity and hostility, but the point is that its policies towards the rest of the world can exacerbate or diminish such hostility, and increase or decrease the perceived legitimacy of its actions.

Like all such nationalist discourses, these arguments are intended to free America from moral responsibility for the consequences of its actions, and so leave it free to do anything. To this end facts are falsified or ignored (for example, that France strongly supported the US in Afghanistan), and usual standards of evidence suspended.

Other nations are declared to be irrationally, incorrigibly and unchangingly hostile. This being so, it is obviously pointless to seek compromises with them or to try to accommodate their interests and views. And because they are irrational and barbarous, America is free to dictate to them or even conquer them for their own good. This is precisely the discourse of nationalists in the leading European states towards each other and lesser breeds before 1914, which helped drag Europe into the great catastrophes of the 20th century. It was also a central part of the twisted discourse of antisemitism.

Nationalism often encourages its proponents to cultivate not only specific national hatreds, but also hostility to all ideals, goals, movements, laws and institutions which aim to transcend the nation and speak for the general interests of mankind. These are dubbed empty and naive utopianism, when contrasted with the tough realism of the nationalists.

But this sort of nationalism is in many ways antithetical to what Gunnar Myrdal, Samuel Huntington and others have called the "American creed," that optimistic thesis about America which America presents to itself and the rest of the world. The thesis is made up of a set of universalist principles which have included liberty, democracy, law, egalitarianism, individualism, populism, laissez-faire economics and general "progress." Associated with these has been an almost religious respect for US institutions, and above all the constitution. In recent decades, to these principles have been added—in public at least—racial equality and cultural pluralism. During the 1990s, the "Washington consensus" of belief in the supreme value of free markets also became part of the creed.

These principles are of inestimable value both to America and mankind. Along with the appeal of US economic success and mass culture, they form the basis of American "soft power" in the world.

On them rests America's role as a great civilising empire: the heir to Rome, China and the early Muslim caliphate. But they also contain two immense flaws, which are implicit in the term "creed." The first is that they provide a fertile seedbed for nationalist messianism. The second is that precisely because they are so generally held within America, they contribute to a worrying degree of national conformism, and an inability to understand or to acknowledge the legitimacy of other cultures.

The antithesis to the American creed is made up of different elements, all of which share a vision of America based in a particular American religious or ethnic culture. Among them is the kind of chauvinist, Cromwellian Protestant fundamentalism displayed by General Jerry Boykin and his like. Boykin's widely reported beliefs about America's God being stronger than the God of Islam and the direct intervention of the devil in human affairs come straight from the 17th century.

Closely related to this religious tradition are the attitudes which some have dubbed "Jacksonian nationalism," after the populist and military hero President Andrew Jackson (1767–1845). This is the world of the traditional white south and the frontier. It stems from the aggrieved, defeated, white America of which I became aware during a stay in the deep south many years ago. Over time, this tradition has forged alliances with sections of other white ethnic groups who have brought to the US their own traditions of defeat, oppression and consequent bellicosity: the Catholic Irish, and more recently the Jews. Michael Lind and others have described the importance of this southern tradition in the policies and attitudes of the Bush administration.

Of course, the nature of this tradition and its hate figures have changed over time. In the mid-19th century, the nativist "know nothings" dreamed of a return to an earlier Anglo-Saxon and Scots-Irish Protestant America without Irish Catholics and without the growth of the new capitalism. In the early 20th century, Protestant nativists dreamed of a white Protestant America without the automobile (or at least its back seat) and its effects on sexual morality. Today, much of the white lower-middle and working classes dream of an idealised version of the Eisenhower years of the 1950s, before the sexual revolution and the rise of blacks, gays, feminists and other groups. Such nostalgia suffused the language of the "Republican revolution" of the mid-1990s.

This dream has often included a mixture of isolationism and aggressive nationalism. Republican hardliners like Senators Robert Taft and Herman Welker in the late 1940s and early 1950s were aggressively anti-communist and yet also hostile to Nato, the Marshall plan and other pillars of the world anti-communist struggle. Some have seen in this stance the covert resentment of many German Americans at the second world war, especially in parts of the midwest. The politics of Joseph McCarthy, who was Irish-German by descent, reflected a continuing resentment at Roosevelt and his foreign policy elite for entering the war against Germany and on the side of Britain.

One characteristic that has helped give many modern nationalisms their great strength—and their edge over socialism, even before the socialist economic model collapsed—is the ability to ingest and draw energy from a wide range of collective and even personal grievances. But it is the edgy, socially and economically insecure petty bourgeoisie, terrified of sinking into the proletariat, that is the classic group in the genesis of radical nationalism. Sometimes it is flanked by the ruined farmer, forced into the city and horrified by what he finds there.

To situate American nationalism in this context would seem to fly in the face of every stereotype of America as the epitome of successful modernisation, and—with relatively rare and brief interruptions like the great depression—of widespread and steadily growing prosperity; as a country which, far from embodying ancient and endangered social and cultural traditions, has virtually founded its identity on continual change and the continual rejection of the past— including the immediate past.

This is indeed a central part of American culture; and it is the vision projected by US consumerism and the media, advertising and industrial interests which power it. As a portrait of the US as a whole, however, it is misleading, and has contributed greatly to the bewilderment with which the rest of the world—dazzled by the advertising —looks upon the US.

Where the principles of the American creed are universalist, the Jacksonian tradition stresses closed communities defined by race, religion and ethnicity. Where the creed stresses democracy and justice, and more recently tolerance and pluralism, the Jacksonian tradition is characterised by ruthless violence against racial enemies, both by US state forces and groups spontaneously formed from local society. Blacks in the south and native Americans on the frontier were suppressed or dispossessed not chiefly by the state, but by white militia and vigilante groups.

The tradition is also closely linked to a religious fundamentalism that rejects key elements of modernity, is indeed largely pre-modern in much of its culture, and is deeply mixed up with a millenarianism which draws its view of history, and the middle east in particular, from the books of Isaiah, Daniel and Revelation. Attorney General John Ashcroft or General Boykin would have been completely at home in the ranks of Cromwell's Ironsides, from whom their religious ideology is descended. Ethnically, culturally and historically, this tradition stems from precisely the same roots as the Ulster Protestantism of Ian Paisley. But Ulster is the only place in western Europe where this fusion of fundamentalist religion, politics and nationalism still exists. In the US, it is all too common.

In a country which presents itself as the epitome of modernity, the presence of 17th-century Protestant fundamentalists is, to put it mildly, somewhat anomalous. The clash between these two cultures generates some of the atmosphere of hatred in US domestic politics, which in turn spills over into American attitudes to the outside world.

If the American creed is affirmative and progressive, the Protestant fundamentalist tradition today is profoundly reactionary. However, like many pre-modern cultures, it also embraces values of undying importance which the rest of modern America is in danger of losing: honesty, community, loyalty to family, hospitality, personal honour, dignity and courage. This helps to account for the curious mixture of chauvinism, imperial ambition and democratising idealism which has driven the Bush administration.

US support for Israel has been justified to the American public in terms of the American creed: that Israel should be helped because it is "the only democracy in the middle east." But the US -Israeli relationship, and Israeli influence in the US, have certainly played an important part in the wider growth of nationalist attitudes in the US in recent times and in weakening the commitment of the (often Jewish) American liberal intelligentsia to internationalism. The gap between perceptions of the Israeli-Palestinian conflict among most of the dominant US political, media and intellectual elites, and perceptions of this conflict in the rest of the world, is now immense. And the international isolation of America over the Israeli-Palestinian conflict more or less forces those who support US and Israeli policies to take the view that America is so morally superior to all other countries that its opinions naturally outweigh them: first on Israel, but by implication on every other issue on which the US has a strong position. In Madeleine Albright's words, "America is taller than other nations and therefore sees further."

I do not want to sound too pessimistic. Many Americans are, after all, profoundly opposed to the tendencies which I have outlined, and are profoundly committed not only to democracy, but also to pluralism and the rule of law, internationally as well as domestically. American democratic values and institutions have immense and enduring strength. In the past, these values and institutions have always given the US a kind of self-correcting mechanism. Periods of intense chauvinism such as the panic leading to the passage of the Aliens and Sedition Acts in the 1790s, the "know nothings" of the 1840s, the anti-German hysteria of the first world war, the anti-Japanese chauvinism of the second, and McCarthyism in the 1950s, have been followed by a return to a more tolerant and pluralist equilibrium. Chauvinist and bellicose nationalism, though always present, has not become the US norm and has not led to democratic institutions being replaced by authoritarian ones.

There are good grounds to hope that this will also be the case in future. But there are also grounds for concern. One is obviously that the rise of international Islamist terrorism means that, for the first time in almost two centuries (the nuclear threat of the cold war excepted), the American mainland is under real threat of attack, with all that this would mean for bellicose nationalism. September 11th knocked US pluralist democracy off balance. Further attacks might increase the list, and make it permanent.

Another doubt hangs over the future of the economy. Of critical importance in returning the US to an even keel has been the capacity of the economy to recover from its periodic crises, and to provide steadily rising living standards to a large majority of Americans. Over the past four decades, however, the decline of industry, and the effects of globalisation, have thrown this capacity into question.

For large sections of the white middle class—the constituency which in the end decides America's political course—real incomes have stagnated or declined, even as mass immigration has resumed, while the top section of American society has become immeasurably richer. If this decline and growing social polarisation continue in the decades to come, then the experience of other nations and nation-alisms provides some truly sinister warnings of what the consequences may be for American pluralist democracy, as well as for America's international behaviour.

America today needs to rediscover some of the lessons it learned from Vietnam—without, I hope, having to lose tens of thousands of American lives in the process. Among them is that, in the belated recognition of Robespierre, "People don't usually like armed mission-aries." But perhaps most important of all, Americans should have both more confidence in, and more concern for, the example they set to the world, through their institutions and their values. It is this example which forms the basis of America's "soft power," and which thereby makes possible a form of US hegemony by consent. It is these institutions and values which constitute America's "civilisational empire," heir to that of Rome, and which, like the values of Rome, will endure long after the American empire, and even the US itself,

have disappeared. The image of America as an economically successful pluralist democracy, open to all races, and basically peaceful, is so
powerful because it is largely true. Americans must make sure it goes
on being true.

The coming of Shia Iraq • Bartle Bull

NOVEMBER 2004

The 100-mile drive from Baghdad to Najaf usually takes about
three hours. It is hot country with low dusty towns and villages
built of mud brick. About halfway along the road there is a turn to
the right marked by an arch in the form of a pair of swords meeting
at the tips. They are double-tipped swords, curved like those of the
Imam Ali, whose defeat in war in 657 was the founding event of
the Shia faith. The turning leads to Karbala but the bridge on the
way was blown up during last year's invasion and has not been
repaired.

Iraqis call the middle part of this route the Bermuda triangle, on
account of the kidnappings, ambushes and roadside bombs that
happen there. This is Shia country, but along the road there are two
adjacent towns called Mahmoudiya and Latifiya with Sunni minorities of maybe 25 or 30 per cent. Saddam Hussein used to give extra
support to such pockets of Sunnis. He knew that his co-religionists in
places like these had a special stake in supporting his rule: they felt surrounded, which they were, and embattled, which they would become
if the Ba'athist order were ever upended. With jobs, construction and
money, Saddam took extra pains to secure their loyalty. The Shias
dominate the population here south of Baghdad, but today it is Sunni
violence that sets the tone.

On a broader national scale, Iraq's 60 per cent Shia majority faces
a challenge similar to that posed by this local Sunni insurgency at the
gateway to the holiest Shia cities: Najaf and Karbala. With the
approach of the elections scheduled for January, the Shias are looking

forward to their first chance to run their affairs since the Ottomans conquered southern Mesopotamia in 1534. But Sunnis, after five centuries as the ruling minority, do not want to let it happen.

In Najaf, an hour south of the Bermuda triangle, the Shias themselves have raised two insurrections this year, one from April to June and the other in August. The uprisings pitted the supporters of radical young cleric Muqtada al-Sadr against the US-led occupation but also highlighted major schisms within the Shia community. Iraqis have lots of theories about why these uprisings began. Some Shias blame trigger-happy Spanish troops upset by the Madrid bombings. Others blame the replacement of the US first infantry division by the more gung-ho 11th marine expeditionary unit. Some say Muqtada's men are thugs who prefer a criminal environment, or martyrs protecting Shia Islam's holiest places, or fundamentalists gunning for a theocracy, or simply the voice of a miserably poor community that has not seen the democracy or the improved life it was promised.

The real reason is likely to be that Muqtada was fighting for tactical advantage within the Shia community, seizing momentum from the older, conservative clerical establishment—and all the while earning cross-sectarian credit as Iraq's most vocal anti-occupation nationalist. Muqtada is certainly attuned to the January elections and the opportunity they represent. As the fighting faded in Najaf at the end of the most recent uprising, men at his headquarters next to the Imam Ali shrine showed me a photocopy of an agreement between him and Grand Ayatollah Ali al-Sistani, bearing the seals of the two men. Among Muqtada's five commitments was a promise to "participate actively in the political process" and "work co-operatively" towards the elections. In a little-noticed development of profound importance for the prospects of Iraqi democracy, Muqtada is currently making good on that promise under the guidance of the secular Shia politician Ahmed Chalabi.

An angry and fearful Sunni minority, an occupation whose presence seems, in the eyes of many Shias, to taint the progress it promulgates, and divisions within their own ranks: these are the main challenges for the Shias as Iraq looks ahead to January. The response of Iraq's majority sect to these issues will determine the next phase of Iraq's transition.

It would be wrong to refer to Iraq's 15m-odd Shias as a "community." The very notion of Shia identity in Iraq, of a sense of self-awareness shared across tribal, economic, political and even religious strata, is problematic.

Before the expansion of the Iraqi oil industry radically changed the country's demography in the 1950s and 1960s, there were three principal Shia elites. The largest, and quietest, was made up of tribal chiefs looked up to by the nomads and farmers of the country's southern half—from the marshes in the southeast, across the "land between the rivers" and into the vast desert bordering Arabia.

A second elite was the religious establishment in the cluster of holy cities south of Baghdad—Najaf, Karbala and to a lesser extent Kufa. Largely hereditary, often competing with Iranian cities such as Qom for global leadership of the sect, and entwined with the local hierarchy of merchant families, Iraq's Shia clerical aristocracy traditionally eschewed participation in government but nonetheless exerted much influence.

The merchant class formed a third elite. The merchants of the holy cities had an interest in maintaining the international flow of pilgrims and corpses to Shia Islam's most revered shrines and cemeteries. In bigger towns like Baghdad and Basra, a more secular middle class of tradesmen and, later, financiers and courtiers, strove for influence under the Sunni-dominated rule of the Ottomans, the British and the Iraqi monarchy.

In the 1950s, it all began to change. The urban boom that accompanied the expansion of the Iraqi oil industry led vast hordes of the rural poor into the big cities. By 1961, Wilfred Thesiger was writing about the Shia marsh Arabs sucked into an "old-fashioned gold rush … the stampede to the towns … this mass immigration." He loathed the drain of nomads into big cities, and especially mourned the fate of the young boys who heeded the siren call of progress. Those who did leave the marshes or the countryside, said Thesiger, "like hundreds of thousands of others in Iraq ... probably ended by selling newspapers or Coca-Cola in Basra or Baghdad, as well as stealing from cars and pimping for taxi drivers."

Today, the Shias of Iraq are largely an urban people, and the majority of them lead dreary lives in very unpleasant slums. Their sons are doing just what Thesiger predicted. Or they are fighting the Americans. Only a quarter of Iraq's Shias attend mosques regularly, but their dismal material existences and the physical insecurity in some parts of the country are leading to increasingly intense religious identification. And unlike their tribal forebears in the marshes and deserts only 50 years ago, these people are not quiet. Muqtada al-Sadr is their voice.

On the road to Najaf, you leave the Bermuda triangle behind when you pass the final eucalyptus grove of Latifiya. Before you reach that point, there is always a blood-congealing traffic jam that snarls the main crossroads during daylight. In the mornings, the slow-crawl congestion provides a chance for a long look at the roadside police station, its roof blasted off and its walls scorched. On its half-standing concrete curtain wall, spray-painted Arabic script proclaims: "We will kill all the dogs who work with the Americans. We will kill the slaves of dollars. We will kick the dirty Americans out of our country."

In the late afternoons the traffic comes to a full stop, as there has almost always been a bomb or an ambush ahead. If you are a foreigner in the back of a car, it makes sense to lie down. After half an hour of silent promises that you will never travel that road again, you and your companions might squeeze through the bottleneck created by a new crater in the road. Or if the jam is really bad, you might turn off on to the dirt roads between the eucalyptus trees and the maize, and hope that the obscuring dust is protection enough as you crawl through the rebel Sunni countryside where the two French journalists, captured on the main road in August, are said to be held.

Then at last there is the final eucalyptus grove, where the traffic pattern changes again: pedal-to-the-floor on a straight road, swerving past slower vehicles until the last trees slip past. Now you are in Shia country proper and you feel safer, for there is a big difference between Sunni and Shia violence in Iraq.

The basic formula is simple. The Shias, with 55–60 per cent of the population, want elections as soon as possible. The Sunnis, with 15–20 per cent of the population, fear democracy. And the Kurds, with another 15–20 per cent, will play along politely while they wait in their mountains for someone to make the wrong move that either forces or allows them to complete their independence.

History adds passion to these dry numbers. Iraq's Shias have lived under mostly Sunni rule since their first imam, Ali, was deposed from the caliphate in 657, 25 years after the death of Muhammad. The Ottoman conquest in 1534 brought rule by local Sunnis in the service of the global caliphate based in Istanbul. When the British were given the mandate to rule in 1920, they relied on Sunnis. In 1932, when Iraq was granted independence, the British brought in a Sunni monarchy. Sunni officers overthrew the monarchy in 1958 and Saddam's Ba'ath party took over in 1968. (Saddam, already effective leader, became president 11 years later.) He ruled for 30 years with his Sunni clique of national socialists and tribal cronies. After these five centuries of sub-ordination, there is today a wrenching urgency in Shia politics. The long wait may finally be over.

The Sunni position is equally inflamed by the past. After five cen-turies of rule, the Sunnis hate the sudden prospect of relegation to a parliamentary presence not much larger than that of Britain's Liberal Democrats. Iraq's Sunnis have already lost the material privileges—better jobs, places at universities, more services in their towns—that Saddam gave them for 30-odd years. Predictably, it is those who have lost most who are reacting most violently to the notion of ratifying these changes in January: senior party officials, clansmen from Saddam's home town of Tikrit, members high and low of Saddam's enormous apparatus of violence, residents of isolated Sunni pockets such as the Bermuda triangle towns.

A relatively orderly autumn means elections in January. For the Ba'athists and Salafis—the revanchist outlaws and the Islamist fundamentalists—who perpetrate Iraq's Sunni violence, such an outcome is unacceptable. Chaos is what they need.

Thus Sunni violence is more a matter of terrorism than of insurgency. It is Sunnis who carry out the spectacular, media-driven acts of violence: the car bombs, the suicide attacks on queues of police recruits or children celebrating a new sewage facility, the abduction of aid workers, the assassination of foreign workers like Ken Bigley who are helping to rebuild the country. For the Ba'athists and Salafis, tiny and electorally hopeless minorities within a larger Sunni minority, driving out the occupation is not the priority. It gives them their *raison d'être*, and in Falluja it has even given them salaries and uniforms. Their real target is the reconstruction of Iraq.

This should not be a surprise. For the Sunni extremists, and for the moderates who collude with their silent support, Iraq is a Shia country waiting to happen. Nobody—not the Baghdad government, the occupation, the UN, the Shias themselves—is explaining to them that "democracy" does not have to mean the "tyranny of the majority." Grand Ayatollah Ali al-Sistani, the 74-year-old grand spiritual leader of the Shias, contributed to the Sunni fears this summer by insisting that the UN resolution laying out a framework for the occupation and the electoral and constitutional processes ignore Iraq's federalist interim constitution. He has since made noises about minority rights under a Shia-dominated democracy, but Sunnis remain profoundly worried.

The Shia violence in Iraq is very different from the Sunni version. It is truly an insurgency. Instead of targeting Iraqis, aid workers, lorry drivers and infrastructure, it targets occupation forces. The weapons of the Shia insurrection are Kalashnikovs and modified Katyusha launch tubes—rather than the car bomb and the camcorder. During the last Najaf siege, a British journalist and French documentary-maker were kidnapped by Shias in separate incidents in southern Iraq. Muqtada al-Sadr quickly secured their release. When Shias near Basra started attacking the oil pipelines, Muqtada's office in Najaf made them stop. The Shia rebels want the occupation out but they share the occupation's main objective: a stable, democratic Iraq.

Muqtada's forces are called the Mahdi army and the black they wear is the colour of the Imam Muhammad al-Mahdi. The last of the Shias' 12 imams, the Mahdi disappeared in an act of divine concealment in Samarra in the 9th century. His return, when it comes, will bring an age of justice.

Until then, Shiism must define itself by grievance. The faith began with the rejection, betrayal, and murder of Imam Ali by Muslim political rivals in the 7th century. Ali's followers claimed that Ali, as Muhammad's closest male relative, should have been ruler of the Islamic community. Thus for the next 1,000 years the world of Islam was ruled by a series of caliphs whose power the Shias considered illegitimate. According to the Shias, all but one of their 12 imams—Ali and his heirs—were murdered by the Sunni caliphs. The final imam was the only one to escape: the Mahdi, hidden by God, until whose return there can be no justice.

In the time of Ali and for 19 years after his death, the Shiah-i-Ali (party of Ali) was largely a political movement expressing disaffection with the worldly power of the caliphate. That changed with the second of Shiism's two great founding moments: the massacre of Ali's son Hussein and a small group of followers at Karbala in 680. Most of the murders of the Shia imams at the hands of the Sunnis were nasty little assassinations. Poison was the main weapon. Hussein's death at Karbala was different, bigger and somehow more shocking. It was the first time that the family of the Prophet had been martyred in an all-out slaughter involving large groups.

The searing events at Karbala turned the Shiah-i-Ali, the political movement of the dispossessed, into a fully-fledged sect. Today the Shias account for 10 per cent of Muslims worldwide. They commemorate Hussein's martyrdom and the complicity of their forebears in annual pilgrimages and passion plays. In February they will be back on the streets of Karbala in their millions for the day of Ashura. Weeping and howling, flagellating themselves and others, they will be beating their chests and foreheads, cutting their own scalps, celebrating guilt and oppression with white clothes, swords and blood.

Ali is said to be buried in a tomb at the famous shrine in Najaf. The city is also home to the four-man council of grand ayatollahs, which provides scholarly and spiritual leadership to Shias around the world. (Iranian Shiism, because of its close connection with the Iranian state, is currently somewhat separate from the global faith.) Najaf's cemetery, the Valley of Peace, offering an eternity in close proximity to the Imam Ali, is where all Shias aspire to be buried. With 5m graves, Shiism's holiest city is the largest concentration of death on earth.

On any road to Najaf you will usually see vehicles with coffins strapped to their roofs, bringing bodies for burial in the precinct of Ali. The corpses have been coming in every day for a millennium in an endless pilgrimage of the dead. They come from India and Pakistan, from Lebanon, Iran, the Gulf, the Caucasus and north Africa. Heading south from Baghdad on any morning after a night of fighting in Sadr City, the capital's vast Shia slum, you can find yourself looking across the streaming tarmac at a pick-up truck full of Mahdi fighters bringing a dead friend to his resting place. You will know them by their black beards and black T-shirts, and you will see their anger even if you can't hear it as they mouth their chants and incantations through the wind and dust.

In August, many like them went south to Najaf to die as well as to be buried. For three weeks the cemetery became a battlefield and the city became a cemetery. The graveyard is like a small city anyway: five square miles of alleys and narrow lanes between tombs and mausoleums that look like tiny houses. The crypts and catafalques were killing zones for the Mahdi army and the US marines and cavalry this summer. Neither side worried much about the eternal rest of those who had already died—the underground tombs in the Valley of Peace were littered with cigarette butts and streaked toilet paper. Above, empty brown US military food packets were blowing around in the dust among the hundreds of olive green ordnance shells. A packet of strawberry milkshake sat ripped open atop a grave, its white powder spilled out on the flat tombstone. Tank treads have laid lines of rubble along the narrow paths.

For all the violence in this city of the dead, I saw only two graves that had been destroyed completely. While I was nearby, two middle-aged men arrived. They searched through the detritus of the two graves and then held up a pair of tablets, each bearing the name of a man from near Karbala. "This is my father's grave," said one of them. He was crying. "Why did he have to die twice?" he asked.

At the height of the August violence in Najaf, crowds surged through the streets and the Iraqi police and national guard careened about in lorries and SUVs, AKs bristling out of windows or over rails probably made for sheep. Dozens had been killed in Najaf and nearby Kufa that morning and the day before (one never knows the real numbers in Iraq). There seemed to be gunfire everywhere and puddles of blood were still red on the pavements. Ambulance drivers were refusing to take Shia wounded to the hospital—for the good of the wounded. They said the Iraqi police were executing the wounded as partisans.

With an Iraqi friend I ducked through a doorway and into the front room of a house. There were four men inside. On the walls there were posters of Muqtada al-Sadr and his father, Ayatollah Muhammad Sadiq al-Sadr, murdered by Saddam in 1999. The posters showed the al-Sadrs looking fierce or wise, superimposed upon backgrounds of vast crowds, with slogans and images of masked gunmen dressed in black. The main thing I noticed about my hosts, these Muqtada supporters, is that they were not all that young, and we were not in a slum. I wondered where their pictures of Sistani were. The people of Najaf were supposed to be relatively conservative.

"Spiritually, Sistani is undisputed," they told me. (Muqtada is at the very bottom of Shiism's very hierarchical clerical ladder.) "But the political leadership is entirely Muqtada al-Sadr. Muqtada is the only true nationalist in Iraq—like his father before him." Muqtada's father had led the Shia resistance to Saddam in the 1980s and 1990s. In contrast to his Iranian-born, naturally cautious contemporary Ali al-Sistani, Muhammad Sadiq al-Sadr was a home-grown Arab who mobilised the poor through a wide network in mosques and communities, preaching to hundreds of thousands at his fiery Friday prayers.

I have often heard this refrain among the Shia: Sistani, they say, is our spiritual leader, but our problems are political, and only Muqtada speaks to those.

In the heart of the old city stands the holy shrine of Imam Ali. Across the street, fire trucks were hosing blood from the shrine's broad forecourt. An old man told me that 150 people had been buried in front of us when the building above them collapsed. Some were still alive yesterday, banging on a metal door.

In the devastation around us there was a peculiar beauty: shards of glass spun and suspended in windows like mobiles, bright orange awnings flapping dreamily in a light breeze, and a sparkling everywhere underfoot. When Shias pray, they often put a little tablet, made from Karbala clay, on the ground towards Mecca. When they bow forward, their heads touch the holy earth. Piles of these tablets, wrapped up in white paper with jaunty red strings, lay in broken heaps outside the shrine.

On a later visit to Najaf, looking ahead to the elections planned for the end of January, I visited the offices of Muqtada himself in a couple of rundown houses in an alley next to the Imam Ali shrine. I wanted to know what sort of an Iraq his people envisioned. There were reports from his year-long rule in the centre of Najaf that the Mahdi army was a Taleban-in-waiting.

Ahmed Sheybani is one of Muqtada's top three advisers. He is thin, and dresses all in white. He is 34, which makes him five to ten years older than his boss (Muqtada claims to be 31 but is widely believed to be younger). Sheybani spoke nervously, with glazed eyes that never looked at me. "Ninety per cent of this country is Islamic," he told me, "so naturally the new regime would be considered Islamic. But this would not be intolerant Islamic rule. It will respect the rights of minorities. It will not oblige Sunnis to abide by Shia law, or Christians to behave like Muslims. The most important thing is to protect the rights of minorities. Alcohol is permitted for Christians, for example. It should be permitted for Christians to go to church, or Jews to the synagogue.

"Within the Shia community, drinking or playing music will be punished if it is public or provocative, just as for Christians to have more than one wife is forbidden. Islamic law will be applied to Islamic women. Women should be in all professions, but they would have to wear a scarf. Women are like gems. If you see a precious stone in a precious case, you will want it more than if you see it in a cheap case. Look at your Virgin Mary—she covered her head.

"It will be normal to have different levels of law. In America, for example, they have federal law and state law. For the Kurds, their independence is forbidden internationally. Their army should be under the central government, but in other matters we are comfortable with federalism within a unified Iraq."

In the alley outside Muqtada's offices it looked as if they were preparing for an earthquake, not government. Medical supplies lined the narrow space: glass ampoules of potassium chloride from France, bandages from the Korean International Co-operation Agency, intravenous glucose from Egypt, Great Northern beans from US Aid. In late September, Sheybani was arrested by US marines in a 2am raid on the alley. He has not been released.

Among religious Shias in Iraq, the older clerical establishment of Najaf represents the opposite end of the spectrum to Muqtada's people. While religious authority is not hereditary in Shia Islam, it has tended to function that way over the centuries. Muqtada comes from a clerical lineage as distinguished and ancient as any in global Shiism—but his father was a rabble-rousing man of the people and so is he. Muqtada's people are blamed by everyone except themselves for the murder of Sistani's advocate, the moderate cleric Abdul Majid al-Khoei, when he returned in April 2003. No love was lost in the old days between the Khoei-Sistani camp and Muqtada's father.

Radwan Killidar is the 41-year-old hereditary keeper of the keys of the Najaf shrine, the 11th in his family to hold the position. According to Radwan, the Mahdi army took the shrine by force earlier this year.

At the beginning of 2004, Muqtada's people came in from
Sadr City, Kufa, everywhere, and took over Najaf. They

took the keys to the shrine from my deputy. They told him: "You've got children, why make them orphans?" My people are part of the religious establishment, so they don't carry weapons. I had given them directions not to spill one drop of blood. Within a couple of months the Mahdi army had made the shrine their base. They sacked my people, beat them. Before they took over, Najaf was a thriving city. Muslims came from all over the world—from the Gulf, India, Iran, Pakistan. Now the lives of Najafis have been ruined.

If the Mahdi army was a nationalist movement they would not have signed up with Iran. I have seen their food and medicine. It is all Iranian. Meanwhile I have been in Najaf for one year and I never saw the Spanish or the Americans anywhere near the shrine. In fact, I haven't seen them much at all.

I think we *are* talking about a Taleban-in-waiting. I have heard of people in Najaf being called to the Shari‘a courts and when they refused to go they were shot outside their doors.

Twenty years before the fall of Saddam thrust Sistani and his camp into politics, Iraq had two main Shia parties: the Da‘wa and the Supreme Council for the Revolution in Iraq (SCIRI). Both have joined the various Iraqi political structures arranged by the occupation, and in so doing have lost support with the most militant Shia "street."

The Da‘wa, or "Call," fought for 30 years against the Ba‘ath party following Iraq's pseudo-communist revolution in 1958. Muhammad Bakir al-Sadr was its chief founder. In 1980, in the aftermath of activities inspired by Iran's successful Shia revolution the previous year, he became the first grand ayatollah in modern history to be executed. Over the next 23 years, as Saddam's regime identified Shia activism with the Da‘wa, about 60,000 Shias were executed under a decree making Da‘wa membership punishable by death. The Da‘wa is split today, but in May Ibrahim Jaffari, the leader of its main faction, was rated the third most important public figure in Iraq (after Sistani and

Muqtada) in a *Financial Times* poll. As one of Iraq's two vice-presidents, Jaffari has more personal support than anyone else in the Iraqi government. He could well command 10 per cent of the Iraqi electorate. His party has huge prestige from its suffering and its long record of struggle, but is essentially moderate with regard to Islam. It has not seized the post-invasion opportunities as aggressively as Muqtada, and its more measured approach might well endear it to the elusive "silent majority." That said, the youthful and urban demographics of Iraq's Shias render the very existence of a "silent majority" debatable.

SCIRI is a coalition of sorts that was founded as an Iranian initiative in 1982. During Saddam's time the Iranian connection gave SCIRI the advantage of a safe haven, plus training facilities for its military wing, the Badr Brigades, a militia that at the time of the March 2003 invasion numbered around 10,000 men in uniform. The Iranian connection has since made it difficult for SCIRI to claim legitimacy in the eyes of Iraqis, but the group does enjoy residual respect. When its leader Muhammad Baqir al-Hakim was killed by a giant car bomb outside the holy shrine in Najaf in August 2003, 100,000 Shias mourned him in the city's streets. Since his death, or maybe long before, the wind seems to have left SCIRI's sails. The head of its newspaper in Baghdad explained his party's flaccid condition to me thus: "SCIRI appeals to educated individuals who believe in a united Iraq without sectarianism or partisanship. We are not a party but a movement capable of containing multiple directions within a humanitarian framework." He thought that SCIRI would run jointly "with Da'wa and other Shia parties" at the January elections. SCIRI will be a player, but not a prime mover.

Najaf is the spiritual capital of Iraqi Shias, and a constant cockpit for the ebbs and flows of their fortunes. But Sadr City is where the demographic heft lies. As Iraq's pre-eminent slum, it is also the place that embodies the energy of Iraqi Shia politics. With 3m people, it comprises half of all of Baghdad, almost 25 per cent of Iraq's Shia population, and over 10 per cent of the entire country.

In daylight, Sadr City can be a relatively straightforward slum. The sidewalks seem an endless alternation of puddles and rubbish. The animals of the barnyard are everywhere, beast and fowl resting in shade, drinking from rusting oil drums, picking through the drifts of rubbish, fleeing children. It is as if some ancient bucolic life had been laid down accidentally on top of the sewage and the broken streets: people and animals in a concrete arcadia where the loamy soil is trash a foot thick and the babbling brook is a gutter. Only the horses look alright—sad animals, but handsome-boned and not skinny.

The physiology of war is ubiquitous: walls pocked with bullet holes like bad acne, beards of blackened concrete around the windows of gutted houses, lampposts knocked over by Bradleys and crooked like withered limbs. Even now, long after the end of the August uprising, there is fighting in Sadr City every night as the Americans probe the edges of the slum or "thunder run" in their tanks down the boulevards.

On rooftops and in the streets there are many Shia flags, mostly green and black. These flags always—in Najaf, too, and elsewhere—seem to have frayed or cut edges and to be on long thin poles that slant over at an angle that looks both romantic and sinister. The green ones are for Ali and his martyrdom. The black ones are for al-Mahdi and the hope of his return. Black is the colour of Shia optimism.

Like any slum, Sadr City is full of children. The youngest play war games and the oldest direct traffic for the Mahdi army. Thesiger would have approved. It was better than selling Coca-Cola.

Muqtada al-Sadr's baby face and beard are on posters everywhere. The only other face you will see on a wall in Sadr City is his father. The many residents I have spoken to have all told me that in an election they will simply follow Muqtada's wishes. If there is no election, they won't mind unless Muqtada minds. If he minds, they will mind a lot.

Despite the nightly fighting in the city that bears his father's name, Muqtada is reaching an accommodation with Iraq's political process. While he and the occupation loathe each other, they have common cause on the matter of most importance to them. Unlike the Sunnis, with their fears about a democracy that has not proved that it can guarantee them anything, Muqtada and the Americans both want a quiet vote in January.

In September, a member of Muqtada's four-man inner circle for political planning told me that the movement was planning to form a political party and run in the January elections. They were still working out the details, but if true, this would be a mammoth boost for the democratic project. They even had a working name: the Al-Mahdi party. Early in October, Muqtada's people went public with these intentions, telling the *New York Times*, "We are ready to enter the democratic process."

The Al-Mahdi party, with its connotations of wild eyes and Kalashnikovs, is now out. The Patriotic Alliance is in. It is a masterful name—inclusive, positive and entirely unobjectionable. It is not the sort of name that would emerge naturally from Muqtada's dirty back alley in Najaf. It bears the imprint of Iraq's most intelligent politician and the emerging leader of the entire Shia political current: Ahmed Chalabi.

Chalabi's comeback is no surprise. The flux and chaos of Iraqi politics sail straight into his sweet spot. The yogi-like Sistani in the Najaf alley he never leaves, dozy old SCIRI, earnest Da'wa, the pimply Mahdi army, a dozen frenetic little sub-groups, all floundering with a new system called constitutional democracy that has not been quite settled yet and that none of them has ever really had to understand— it is all Karbala clay in the hands of a master sculptor.

Iraqis know that Chalabi is the one man alive without whom Saddam would still be their ruler. And from the moment of Saddam's fall, just as leading up to it, Chalabi has done everything right. He has publicly (if not necessarily privately) fallen out with Washington over a featherweight intelligence stink involving Iran. The world has watched the Allawi government vandalise his house and issue a ludicrous arrest warrant accusing him of counterfeiting Iraq's worthless old currency. Shortly before I last spoke to Chalabi, he had survived an ambush that killed two of his guards at Mahmudiya in the Bermuda triangle.

Saddam, Washington, Allawi, the Sunnis: Chalabi has the right enemies. When I pointed this out to him at his house in Baghdad last month he laughed and said: "That's not a bad thing." Equally importantly, he has the right friends. A member, like Allawi, of a leading family from Baghdad's secular Shia merchant class (Chalabi means "head merchant") he has been assiduously strengthening his position among his fellow Shias. The Mahmoudiya ambush took place after a meeting in Najaf between Chalabi and Sistani. Chalabi claims to have met with Sistani "ten or 12 times"—far more than any other political figure could claim—and he is one of the few Iraqi politicians to have been granted a meeting with Muqtada.

Meanwhile, Chalabi played an active role in the parleying that brought an end to the Shia revolts in Najaf this spring and summer, and has created two Shia groups—the Shia house and the Shia political council—that bring Iraq's Shia political movements and parties together under a loose "umbrella" reminiscent of Chalabi's Iraqi National Congress (INC) during the last years of Saddam.

Chalabi's unified Shia front, running as a single list, is likely to capture close to the full Shia 60 per cent at January's elections. The likely breakdown of this 60 per cent is as follows: 25 per cent for Muqtada's party, 15 per cent for the Da'wa, 10 per cent for SCIRI and 10 per cent for other parties such as the INC, Allawi's Iraqi National Accord, the two Iraqi Hizbollah parties, and others. The two Kurdish parties, the KDP and PUK, which will gain around 20 per cent of the total vote, may also join the list. The main Sunni grouping is likely to be the Association of Islamic Scholars, which has so far ruled out participating in the elections but is likely to change its mind. A few secular parties, including the Iraqi Communist party, are likely to put themselves forward. Former senior Ba'athists and members of Saddam's agencies of repression are barred from standing.

When I saw Chalabi last, he had just arranged for Ali Smeasim, Muqtada's top lieutenant, to visit the Kurds in their capital at Sulaimani. Muqtada's people have since reached out to various Sunni Arab groups, and he has met with Chalabi's Shia political council ten times or more. This unlikely sensei and young samurai, the desert fox and the backstreet preacher, seem to be getting along very well.

This is more bad news for the Sunnis. So deep is the identity basis for politics in Iraq, and so persuasive are Chalabi's coalition-building skills, that Muqtada is far more likely to team up with fellow Shias, even if they are relatively moderate, than with fellow revolutionaries across the sectarian divide.

Talking to Chalabi is a pleasure. He has a sense of humour, which is rare enough in Iraq (although people on the street do sometimes ask my Iraqi friends how much they are planning to sell me for), and a frankness below the politician's surface that can make a meeting feel like an enjoyable conversation rather than a lecture or a battle. When he says, for example, "My position is to involve the people who resisted Saddam," he is doing much more than legitimising former exiles such as himself. He is referring to Muqtada, scion of a martyred father, and the old Shia parties that were slaughtered in the 1991 uprisings, and the Kurds who gave the INC an army through the 1990s. Unfortunately, "the people who resisted Saddam" also means "everyone but the Sunnis."

The formula can still work, however. We have seen the vision, spelled out to me by Muqtada's people in Najaf, of different communities enjoying a degree of freedom and separation: "The most important thing is to protect the rights of minorities ... We are comfortable with federalism within a unified Iraq ...." The message is credible so far. While Muqtada's number three—Sheybani—was explaining it to me in Najaf, his number two was in the north explaining it to the Kurds. And Sistani seems to be a guarantee standing behind the rhetoric of the more active players.

Under Chalabi's tutelage, this pragmatism is bound to grow. As he says, "It's a fiction to think that the Iraqi government will ever be strong enough to force a certain system on any big group of people. We can't start killing people just because they want to run their own affairs." Iraq's interim constitution allows any three or more of the country's 18 provinces to form a federal unit. Chalabi says there is no reason why Iraq should not divide into six of these, or three.

In the meantime Iraqis have a lot of voting ahead of them. The 275-member national assembly to be elected in January will draft a constitution by August, which will be put to a referendum two months later. By December 2005, elections under the new constitution are due. The January election will be held by proportional representation under a national party list system, which sidesteps the problem of lack of local political organisation. There will be about 30,000 voting booths scattered across the 275 electoral districts, with everyone voting for the same party lists. A quarter of seats are reserved for women.

If Iraq's Shias cannot persuade the Sunnis that they are sincere about minority rights in these elections, the Sunni attempt to derail the January election will grow more intense. "Sistani has been very firm about his desire to see these elections take place," says Chalabi.

Seyid Hazem al Araji, Muqtada's top man in Baghdad, reinforces that view. Before his recent incarceration by the Americans, he told me that if there were any delay to the elections, "There will be doomsday."

Iraq's Shias have been waiting 500 years, indeed since the murder of Ali, and now their time is here.

BRITAIN

"We bid you welcome, our brother from beyond the stars. But don't, even for a moment, think that you'll be entitled to any kind of state benefit"

Lyllapur to Luton • Sarfraz Manzoor

DECEMBER 2001

I grew up in a working-class family in a working-class town. During the 1970s and 1980s, Luton was a charmless place of terraced houses and manufacturing industry. It was celebrated for two things: an airport that was a national joke, and the Vauxhall car factory which had been in the town since 1905. Because the plant provided work for the unskilled it was ideal for the town's immigrants. Among those employed on the line at Vauxhall was my father. He had emigrated from Pakistan in the early 1960s, leaving behind his wife, two young children and a modest career in the civil service in Karachi for the potential of a more rewarding life in a country he had never visited and whose language he did not speak.

When he arrived in England, my father was 30, the same age I am now. I was born in Lyllapur, a village just outside Lahore in the Punjabi-speaking north, but we later moved to Karachi, in the Urdu-speaking south. My parents and older brother and sister continued to speak Punjabi as their first language, which I understand but cannot speak. They speak to me in Urdu.

After 11 years of working in Britain, my father had saved enough money to bring the rest of us to join him. I arrived with my brother, sister and mother in May 1974, one month shy of my third birthday. My earliest memory is of my family moving into our first proper home on Selbourne Road in Luton's Bury Park district. My father worked at the factory and my mother made dresses at home on an old Singer sewing machine. Every week a man would come and pick up what she had made and pay us a few pennies for each dress. Dressmaking was a common way for Asian women to earn money because it did not require them to leave the house. My mother made all her own clothes and so did most of the women she knew. As a young boy, I would help her by folding the finished dresses and tying them into bundles, while my older brother and sister went to school.

To my father, Pakistan was always home and England was where work had taken him. His was a utilitarian sense of nationality, founded on economics. His dealings with white people were limited and almost entirely professional: the people he worked with on the production line, the bank manager and later the stockbroker. "The thing about white people," my father used to tell me, "is that no matter how long you work with them, they will never invite you to their homes." Yet he never invited them to our home either.

For my father, coming to Britain offered opportunities that were not available in Pakistan, but it also presented the danger that his children would forget who they were. He was worried that, exposed to western ideas, we would stop thinking of ourselves as Muslim or Pakistani and instead become just Brits with brown faces. He dreamed of us having the best this country could offer—education, the prospect of well paid work—but he wanted us to remain uncontaminated by its worst aspects: parents languishing in old people's homes, children who think they are individuals and not their father's sons and daughters. His faith in progress through hard work led him to come to Britain when all his siblings remained in Pakistan. It was a credo that was hammered into us as children. I grew up watching *Panorama*, *The Money Programme* and the nightly news. I was probably the only person in my junior school whose father read the *Financial Times*. It is not surprising that I ended up working as a journalist. But my father died before I got my first job in his beloved world of current affairs.

When I was eight, our family moved from the overwhelmingly Asian Bury Park to the overwhelmingly white Marsh Farm estate. I joined a new school, where I was almost the only Muslim. At that age it never occurred to me that this three mile move would have any implications for my "identity." Most of my memories of school are happy. I remember, one afternoon, aged about 11, walking home with my best friend Scott. I was envious that Scott had grandparents and uncles who came to his house, whereas I only had my immediate family. What would I do, I asked him, if something dreadful happened to my mother or father? Scott replied as if the question hardly merited pondering. "My mum and dad would adopt you and we would be brothers."

To my parents, however, my identity certainly was important. Because we lived apart from most Asians in town, I wasn't sent to mosque on Fridays, nor did I go to Islamic classes after school. But when I was 11 my mother began to teach me Arabic and written Urdu, which use the same alphabet. I would come home and spend an hour or so with her, trying to get to grips with this strange script. By the age of 12, I had completed the Koran. In the evenings my mother would tell me incredible stories about the prophet and describe Mecca, and how millions go there on the pilgrimage. I was captivated and couldn't wait to tell my school friends what I had heard. Somehow, though, they seemed less impressed than I was.

Naturally there were moments of tension in my childhood, like a friend telling me that his dad did not allow "Pakis" into his home. I knew I was different, of course. None of the people whose books I read, or saw on television, looked like me. I had the same dreams as my friends; only mine seemed less likely to come true. I dealt with this by burying myself in books. I would visit Marsh Farm library and read about astronomy, da Vinci, Dr Who.

My other outlet was music. We didn't have a record player at home, but I had a personal radio. On Tuesdays, Gary Davies would start the Top 40 rundown during my English class, and I would sit with my hands on the side of my head, the radio in my pocket and headphone wire weaving up through my shirt and out of my sleeves. "Why do you listen to their music when you have your own?" my father would ask. For me, there was no divide between "us" and "them." At home I would watch the latest Amitabh Bachchan film on video with my family, and at weekends sneak off to catch the new Clint Eastwood at the ABC. I would listen to the songs of Lata and Mohammad Rafi with my mother and Madonna and Michael Jackson with my friends. I was sliding between worlds and still no sign of an identity crisis.

On religious days like the festival of Eid, I would go to mosque. I copied the movements of those around me, not understanding the meaning behind the motions. During Ramadan, when I was 15 and 16, I would try to fast for at least some of that month. But it made lessons, and especially PE, tiring. By the time I started college, I had abandoned even trying to give up food. With each Ramadan, my parents' sense of disappointment grew. But for me, Islam was like the melody of an old song; over time it became ever harder to remember.

I was 16 years old when I met a boy in a turban who was listening to Bruce Springsteen. He gave me a few tapes to listen to and the music I heard influenced me more than anything I had encountered outside the world of my family. This was something new: music that was a way of confronting life rather than running away from it. Over the next few months I, the Muslim boy, and Amolak, the Sikh, would spend hours in the common room discussing Springsteen's music. It took the place of a religion. Amolak and I thought of the songs as maps of how to live and how to be. *Born to Run, Darkness on the Edge of Town, Tunnel of Love*: these albums amounted to a moral and personal compass. Towards the end of a bootleg tape of the 1985 Born in the USA tour, I heard Springsteen say, "it's easy to let the best of yourself slip away."

Specifically, Bruce Springsteen gave me the promise of America. With it came the civil rights movement, the speeches of Martin Luther King, Rosa Parks, Emmett Till and Public Enemy. I felt that I was on the same side as those who marched in Selma and Montgomery. I found it easier to be a black American by empathy than to be British. Naturally, I failed Norman Tebbit's cricket test by supporting Pakistan. Yet if Tebbit had asked a supplementary question—not just who would I support, but who would I *play* for?—the ambivalence of my feelings would have been starker. My answer would have been England. I did not feel an emotional bond, but England was where my ambitions lay.

America, meanwhile, contained no such fine distinctions. It represented a broader sense of identity. To my father, this adoration of Americana was confirmation of his worst fears. The Faustian pact of coming to Britain had played out: the souls of his children had been robbed by the west. Even years later he would express regret he had ever come.

The night before I went to university in Manchester (chosen because Ben Elton had gone there and because it was far from Luton) I sat with my mother in the living room of our house. "Promise me you won't be far away in your heart," she said.

I ended up spending six years in Manchester. There I was accountable neither to my family nor my Luton background and freedom once tasted is hard to relinquish. I grew more distant from my Muslim self; not by design but because nothing that interested me seemed to be what other Muslims were into. When I went to gigs, I was invariably the only non-white person there. Where were the other Asian Oasis fans? To my parents, I was an embarrassment. I was not working, I refused to come home to Luton, and I didn't grow out of my love of western music.

One day, aged 23, I went to Afflecks Palace in Manchester city centre and spent £80 and three hours having extensions woven into my hair. The impact was almost instant. Girls would offer me their phone numbers, I would be asked if I could supply Ecstasy pills and I'd get searched before going into nightclubs. When my father realised that I was not just wearing a fancy hat, he was mortified. He thought I was trying to be black. On visits home I would be banished upstairs. My sister would bring food to my room. I only had the extensions removed after my father died; it did not seem appropriate to attend his funeral in dreadlocks.

By the time I moved back south and started work I was almost as much of a multicultural tourist as my white friends. I called myself a Muslim because I did not drink and did not eat non-halal meat. But I would take the things I liked about my religion and heritage: the strength of the family unit, a sense of global community, the food. And I would leave the parts I was uncomfortable with: arranged marriages, overbearing deference, bad haircuts. It felt good to be surfing cultures. Someone should have told me that there is no such thing as a free saag aloo.

The cell phone pulsed in my pocket. "Have you heard!?" The twin towers had just been hit. It was Amolak. Fourteen years on from sixth form college, and Amolak is a shaven-headed investment banker (the Springsteen song "Independence Day" had inspired him to lose the turban). I am a journalist with Channel Four News.

I was on the train to Luton to see my mother. By the time the taxi driver dropped me off at home reports of the Pentagon attack were coming in. Watching with my mother, who cannot understand English, I kept up a running translation of the commentary. She began to cry. "All those people, all they were trying to do was go to work." I explained that a Muslim might have been responsible, maybe bin Laden. "That man is no Muslim," she snapped back.

The following day, reports came in of attacks on Arab Americans in the US and racist incidents in Britain. Not far from my London flat an Afghan taxi driver was beaten so violently that he was paralysed from the neck down. The bank Amolak works for had offices in the World Trade Center; his friends survived but he was so shaken that he couldn't speak to me for days. Later he told me of feeling threatened while out in Luton; his father, who still wears the beard and turban of his religion, had been taunted.

Meanwhile, I cancelled a flight to New York and a planned driving trip in the US. America had always offered me the prize of anonymity; now it was gone. Despite having spent half my life in a love affair with the country, it wasn't to America that I turned to understand what it means to be a secular Muslim. In my job I operate as a middle-class liberal, largely insulated from the realities of the place I came from. I have enjoyed good opportunities in Britain and luck since I left Luton. It was time to go back to school.

John Ramm has been teaching politics at Luton Sixth Form College for 23 years. It feels like a long time since I was his 17-year-old student. He was witty and inspiring then. It felt strange to be turning to him for help again, but he was open to my suggestion that I return to college and talk to a new generation of his students. Twelve years after leaving, I was going back to my old classroom. Even as I walked in to college, I could see things had changed. When I was there, we all wore western clothes. Now, there are far more Asian kids and most wear traditional dress. The boys walk unselfconsciously in flowing kurtas, and the girls wear silky shalwar kameez underneath their Diesel denim jackets.

In a class of 25 there are only half a dozen white faces. The fear for my father's generation was that with assimilation would come dilution. He thought that as subsequent generations of British Muslims were born and raised in this country it would become ever harder to preserve their distinct Islamic identity. The third generation would be trapped in an existential no-man's land, neither connected to the motherland nor wholly accepted in the adopted land. Here, however, it looks like a misplaced fear. These young men and women have grown up by doing the reverse: intensifying their affiliation to countries they have never set foot in, yet able to be far more assertive than I ever was about their right to live in Britain.

John makes a short introduction and throws the class open to me. I show them a short film of mine, which deals with how the networks had covered the breaking news of 11th September. I switch off the tape to an audible exhalation; I am talking to a class acutely attuned to the transforming nature of what took place that day. John leaves me alone with the kids. He had felt that they would open up to me in a way that would be impossible with a white outsider.

I imagined confronting an uncertain group of young men and women—perhaps made angry by the sharpening of insecurities after 11th September. Instead, I find a group of confident, articulate teenagers displaying an odd mix of paranoia and scepticism. To every question I ask them, they have questions for me, and not only about the war. In fact, they want to know who the hell I think I am …

That was the week Luton made the front pages. Reports that two men from the town had died while fighting for the Taleban had brought reporters and television crews in search of suburban martyrs.

I did not find any in this class but none of the Muslim students believed that bin Laden was responsible for New York and Washington. "Where's the evidence?" demanded one. Another said, "innocent till proved guilty, that's their law."

Others muttered about Timothy McVeigh. They were scornful of Tony Blair and his quoting of the Koran. They put more credence on circulated e-mails than what they saw on television, or read in newspapers. One girl told the Mossad plot story, in which 5,000 Jews were told not to turn up to work on the day of the attacks.

Some of their scepticism was well directed. They saw the recent portrayal of Luton in the media as an example of how interviews can be distorted. They were suspicious of how I would represent them. Perhaps most telling, was their worry of how recent events might affect their job prospects. "People are going to be suspicious of letting Muslims get into high positions," said Sabia.

"I think you are an amazing person," she added suddenly. I flushed with pride, and began to say that the reason I had come was to give something back; to show the students that you can be working class and Muslim and still get somewhere. Sabia cut me dead. "I think you are amazing," she continued, "because I have never met anyone who tried so hard to blend into white culture." I felt winded.

"If you are a Muslim, why don't you fast?" Hamisa, a tall Kashmiri girl, wanted to know.

"Are you a Muslim because you are a Muslim, or because your parents are?" asked Sultana, a British Bangladeshi Muslim.

My responses came stammeringly. When I was growing up, I found myself saying, things were different. Few of my friends had been especially religious. Just because I listened to Bruce Springsteen and read Philip Roth and watched Woody Allen did not mean I was "denying" anything. I just chose to expose myself to a broader set of influences than some of the people I grew up with. I told my class that they couldn't box people up so neatly. Islam is about tolerance, I added weakly.

"I see what you are saying," Hamisa said slowly. "You're saying that being a Muslim is a very broad category and if we really stretch it out then it's possible to include you too." These were girls who believed in the absolutism of Shari'a law but with very British caveats. Death for adultery was "impractical." They declared that Osama bin Laden was not a proper Muslim and that Afghanistan was not a true Islamic state. "The Taleban practise about three quarters of Islam," Sultana said, "but the missing quarter is really important. It includes things like making sure girls are educated."

The shock passed. I think their views were as much a product of class as religion. They probably hadn't met many middle-class liberal Muslims. "I'm sorry if we offended you," Sultana said sweetly. "I wasn't trying to make out you were a lost case. I was trying to convert you."

Gratitude does not come easy to the young. Sultana and her friends were certainly going to take the best of what Britain had to offer, but they felt no simultaneous need to make compromises. All of them planned to go to university and become professionals: law, finance, journalism. Few seemed to think their colour or religion would make any difference to what they could achieve. Yet when I asked who felt British, among the Muslims in the class not one hand was raised. "I am Pakistani, that is the country of my parents, that's the food I eat and the language I speak," Iftikahar said. But what has Pakistan ever given you? I found myself asking. What about the fact that if you get a job it will be because a British person gave it to you? "Religion comes before nationality," Sabia answered. "I'm British because that is my nationality; but Islam is who I am."

I asked them what they thought was the best thing about Britain. "Clean water," suggested Sabia. "Pavements," said Hamisa. "In Pakistan the roads are crap." This was another version of the utilitarian attitude towards nationhood that my father had. Some said that while they may not feel British, neither did they feel Pakistani. In their attachment to their religion they had carved out a place for themselves which was different from that of both my generation and my parents' but which shared characteristics from both. They had absorbed elements of western culture—the music, the ambition—but from my parents' generation retained a sense that they were different and proud of it. Previously educated in a predominantly white school,

Sultana wears a headscarf by choice, though her mother does not. "I started to wear it because I wanted to know who I am." For her, there was no tension between being British and being Muslim because "you can mix it very well." I asked her what she thought was British about her personality. "My liberalness," she replied. "My culture is Islam and my lifestyle is British." She wants to become a lawyer. Her friends Sabia and Hamisa are also planning on getting degrees. They say their parents have told them that there is no way they can get married until they have an education and jobs.

"I am the oldest child," Sultana said. "My dad wants me to have all the things he would want his oldest son to have." It is a long way down the British-Muslim road from what my father would have wanted for my sisters. But in other ways he would have been pleased with these young men and women, perhaps more pleased than he ever was with me.

I left my old class envious, impressed and disappointed. I was jealous that so many of them believed in something and had a faith they had found for themselves. It might be a misguided, intolerant and untested faith; but it explained the world to them and helped them understand their place in it. It is a faith that is part of me, even if I do not possess it.

I was impressed that the students I met were so relaxed about who they were, so well-informed and could argue their corner so forcefully. At 17 years old they seemed more certain of themselves, not only than I was at 17, but more certain than I am now. Perhaps I had let the best of myself slip away.

Yet I was also disappointed that they started from the notion that to integrate is weak. Maybe these students were luxuriating in the certainties of youth. They seemed only distantly aware of how vulnerable they are. What happens when they leave Luton? "I don't know how I am going to survive in university," Sabia confessed. "All those white people. I don't know what I am going to say to them."

My mother was pleased when I told her what had occurred in class; she seemed relieved that the faith and the culture in which she and my father had brought us up still retained a potency for the generation after us. That night I met up with Amolak and other old friends I had been to college with. They were alarmed by my account, but not surprised. We felt so much older than our years, peering across a gulf at teenagers who were just half a generation away. It was only next morning it struck me that there were also other Asians in that Luton club: men with designer jeans and expensive haircuts, beautiful young women with cropped tops and tattoos, all dancing and drinking and laughing and singing. They too were from Luton; they too were young; some, doubtless, were Muslim. Who was the future, I wondered: the students or the clubbers?

1997: annus memorabilis • Geoffrey Wheatcroft
JANURY 1998

Has there been a stranger or more vivid year in our lifetime than 1997? Two separate weeks are unforgettable: the first week in May and the first week in September. Most of us remember David Mellor and Michael Portillo losing their seats in the small hours of 2nd May, during that astonishing Labour landslide. Everyone remembers the death of Diana: the Sunday itself and the extraordinary mood in London that week, culminating in the bizarre funeral service in Westminster Abbey on 6th September, with Earl Spencer's ferocious (and, as it turned out, hubristic) harangue.

The past year has been called epochal. In his new book *This Time: Our Constitutional Revolution*, Anthony Barnett argues that: "The year 1997 has altered Britain for good: politically, institutionally and emotionally." And apart from the familiar call for modernisation, decentralisation and a written constitution, Barnett directly links the Labour landslide and the public response to Diana's death. Likewise, the playwright David Edgar thinks that "the reason why so many people found that 6th September echoed 1st May was not just the roses and the sunshine (and David Dimbleby); it was an echo of the demand of the British people at the general election that the brute, metallic logic of the market be constrained by a sense of moral responsibility. This time there wasn't a ballot box in which to put that message, but it was posted none the less."

Even if you think (as I do) that this is tosh, it is significant tosh. Even if you thought that "Diana Week" was an unattractive and rather frightening display of mass hysteria and false emotion, it was without doubt an amazing phenomenon. Even if you smile at the steady disillusionment which has followed the exalted post-election mood, something about 1997 needs explaining.

The story of our time, it has been said, is that the right has won politically, but the left has won culturally. This profound truth reached its consummation in Britain in 1997—and it linked those two weeks.

Over the past decade we have seen the collapse of communism in Russia and eastern Europe; and a series of other defeats for the left. As Isaiah Berlin observed not long before his death, Europe is living through the first period since 1789 when there is no large project of the left. But he should have said: no *political* project. Engels's "kingdom of freedom" is a vanished dream, and so are far less drastic versions of egalitarianism. The Labour party's socialist-redistributive Clause IV has been replaced with a touchy-feely, almost meaningless list of "Aims and Values" which read like the mission statement of a multi-national corporation keen to impress with its tender-hearted social awareness. Eighty years ago, when Sidney Webb helped to draft Labour's first properly socialist constitution, the left *thought*. Now it *feels*.

A Labour victory on 1st May was easily predicted, but no one—certainly not Tony Blair—foresaw its scale. Of course no one foresaw Diana Week either, because nobody had thought of her dying, let alone in the luridly baroque circumstances of that early morning in Paris. It was the shock which took away our breath—and our judgement.

After Diana's death, a great deal of what already seems breathtaking nonsense was written. For David Edgar, Diana Week was "open, soft, organic and—as the candles lit up London in the small hours of Saturday—turned night into day. It was also, essentially, collective … The people who made what Martin Jacques has dubbed the 'floral revolution' were engaged in a political act." Edgar and Jacques would both call themselves men of the left. They do not realise how sharply their women's-mag drooling makes the point about cultural victory compensating for political defeat.

Look back at the May election with brute, metallic logic. There were many good reasons for voting Labour, but most of them were negative. The simplest was that, as Ian Buruma put it in *Prospect*, we did not want to become a one-party democracy like Japan under the Liberal Democrats. "Time for a change" was a perfectly sensible instinct. One party had been in office for 18 years, quite long enough. The historic mission of Thatcherism had long since been fulfilled. The Tories were worn-out and shabby, the country was fed up with them, and they were fed up with themselves, almost longing to be thrown out. Thrown out they duly were.

But look closer. There is an element of fantasy about the claims made for 1st May. Labour's huge majority was a result of technical causes: the Tory vote collapsed from just over 14m to just under 10m. The British had at last learned the art of tactical voting, and the first-past-the-post system produced its grossly exaggerated effect. Many prime ministers in countries with proportional representation, from Italy to Israel, wish they could achieve a clear parliamentary majority, let alone the 63 per cent of seats Labour won, with 43 per cent of the votes.

Look closer still. That 43 per cent is no larger than the proportion of the popular vote which the Tories won in 1992. At 13.6m, Labour's actual tally of votes was smaller than the Tories' at three out of the four preceding elections. More remarkably, it was smaller than the number of people who voted Labour as far back as 1951.

Perhaps the most telling—and ominous—fact about the election of 1997 was that it saw the lowest turnout since 1935: less than 72 per cent. This is 12 percentage points below the 84 per cent turnout in 1951; and it is a sombre reflection on what has happened to our democracy over half a century. It means that many people are disenchanted with politicians and bored by politics; and it means that fewer than one citizen in three voted Labour.

Two weeks before the election, even a commentator as perceptive as Robert Harris could write that "these are revolutionary times," thus deftly identifying just what the times were not. The voters were so nervous about Labour that in 1992 they returned the Tories led by John Major during a severe economic slump—circumstances in which it was quite a feat for Labour to lose. People waited, in fact, until they could safely vote Labour without the least chance of any revolutionary effect at all.

Why were the British people voting to constrain the brute logic of the market, when they had conspicuously not done so at the previous four elections? Surely it was because Blair offered them market economics powdered with caring rhetoric; Thatcherism with a human face; a kinder, gentler version of the previous government (not hard to achieve), whose policies would be pursued by a more plausible and agreeable bunch of ministers (not hard either). When they collaborated in a landslide comparable with the Liberal one of nine decades earlier, the voters may have unconsciously guessed that 1997 would indeed echo 1906, when:

> The accursed power which stands on Privilege
> (And goes with Women, and Champagne and Bridge)
> Broke—and Democracy resumed her reign:
> (Which goes with Bridge, and Women and Champagne).

Wipe that smile off your face, brother. The 1997 election was historic, all right: a great historic defeat for socialism. Victory was achieved by the first Labour leader in 80 years who does not even pretend to be a socialist, who can scarcely conceal his loathing of most of his party's emotional roots, from the unions to the Celtic fringe to the left, and who does not bother to call himself a man of the left. (He is a "radical centrist," whatever that may be.) Blair is indeed further to the right not only than any previous Labour leader, but arguably further than some postwar Tory leaders such as Harold Macmillan. He has rejected the core beliefs which have distinguished left-of-centre politics throughout this century and throughout the world: economic planning and redistributive taxation.

But if the new government existentially illustrates the victory of the right, it also expresses the cultural victory of the left. The cabinet which is unpicking the welfare state contains several women and one gay man, several of them, on the evidence so far, chosen for symbolic rather than practical value. Chris Smith is a true cultural leftist, with his warblings about a people's Wimbledon, a people's lottery and a people's opera. And Blair, who talks of himself, not very convincingly, as a man of the rock generation, forced the unfortunate Lionel Jospin to have lunch in a room decked out by Terence Conran in the horrible Canary Wharf, and uses the culturally catchy but politically empty rhetoric of "modernisation" and a "young country."

This political–cultural dichotomy also underlaid the extraordinary events of Diana Week. I was one of those who felt utterly excluded that week, and I was grateful that writers as diverse as Richard Littlejohn and Joan Smith also said that they felt they had been living in a foreign country or on a distant planet. We outsiders were bemused, unable to participate in the tidal wave of emotion, unable to feel grief.

Shock, yes; sorrow and regret, even a pang of guilt at my unsympathetic response to Diana during her life, at things I had said, thought and written about her. But I could not feel grief, not in the sense that I felt when my mother died, or a few close friends. This disturbed me— until a man from Leeds revealed on a radio phone-in: "My wife died in April … and I've shed more tears for Diana than I did for my wife." Another man said that he felt more grief for Diana than he had at his father's death. My own coolness then seemed to me better than those radio callers' emotional derangement; but I also began to grasp what was going on. I skittishly told a friend that there would be visions of Diana before the week was out—and so there were.

Painful as all this is to anyone who claims the inheritance of the Enlightenment, it fits the theme of the cultural against the political. And it helps explain the most preposterous thing of all about Diana: how she became a heroine of the left in general (or what passes for it in this country) and of feminism in particular.

After Diana's Oscar-deserving performance on *Panorama* in 1995, I remarked to a colleague how gruesome it had been. She agreed, but added: "Suzanne Moore will be all over her." Sure enough, two days

later the sparky columnist filled a spread in the *Guardian* with an adu-
latory tribute. Her theme was taken up by Julie Burchill, who claimed
that Diana was an advocate for republicanism and for woman power.

Wipe that smile of your face, sister. The canonisation of St Diana
painfully illustrates the decline of feminism—of rational political feminism, that is. Did Mary Wollstonecraft and Emily Pankhurst live for
this: the adulation of a hysterical and self-pitying pin-up, as intellectually dense as she was emotionally manipulative?

Feminism once meant the vindication of the rights of women:
political feminism demanded that women should enjoy full legal and
political rights, should be free to compete with men on equal terms,
should be free to take control of their lives. It meant that women were
no longer obliged only to *be*, but could *do* as well.

Not any more, if Moore and Burchill are correct. The rights of
women they vindicate are the rights to suffer, to feel bitter, and to make
trouble. Diana was a perfect example of a woman who never *did* anything—were any of her speeches composed by herself unaided, and
would anyone have listened to them if she had married another man?—
but simply *was*. Above all, she was a victim, for which she is canonised.

Absurd as all this may seem, it doubtless touches on a psychological
truth. Like all formal political progressivism, political feminism could
be emotionally obtuse. It forgot "How small, of all that human hearts
endure / That part that laws or kings can cause or cure," which is at
least as true of female as of male hearts. Women could be enfran-
chised, could become QCs, professors of Latin, racehorse trainers or
prime ministers. But they would still want to consummate physical
passion. They would still want to bear and love babies. They would
still know that life is a tragic and arduous struggle. And they would still
find that men can be rats.

This was Diana's importance. Even if to us literal-minded, old-
fashioned feminists she seemed a ludicrous role model for her sex, she
spoke, as Simon Jenkins wrote, to and for many women for whom
political emancipation had proved almost irrelevant. "She was spokes-
woman for those with impossible husbands, worried about their
appearance, wrestling with divorce, career, children, trying to match

impossible expectations. And all the while she was searching for love and security." She spoke, that is, for a cultural but depoliticised "women's movement" of the heart, not of the head; of feeling, not of thinking.

Again and again throughout Diana Week I thought of "Herod's Prophecy," WH Auden's haunting vision of the coming age in which

> Reason will be replaced by revelation ... Knowledge will degenerate into a riot of subjective visions—feelings in the solar plexus induced by undernourishment, angelic images generated by fever or drugs, dream warnings inspired by the sound of falling water. Whole cosmogonies will be created out of some forgotten personal resentment, complete epics written in private languages, the daubs of schoolchildren ranked above the greatest masterpieces ...
>
> Idealism will be replaced by materialism ... Diverted from its normal outlet in patriotism and civic or family pride, the need of the masses for some visible Idol to worship will be driven into totally unsociable channels where no education can reach it. Divine honours will be paid to shallow depressions in the earth, domestic pets, ruined windmills, or malignant tumours ...
>
> Justice will be replaced by Pity as the cardinal human virtue ... The New Aristocracy will consist exclusively of hermits, bums and permanent invalids. The rough diamond, the consumptive whore, the bandit who is good to his mother, the epileptic girl who has a way with animals will be the heroes and heroines of the New Tragedy, when the general, the statesman and the philosopher will have become the butt of every farce and satire.

That soliloquy was quoted by Robert Hughes in *The Culture of Complaint*, his pasquinade against political correctness. Whether or not he rings true in 1990s America, Auden exactly describes London in the first week of September 1997. If not quite a consumptive whore,

Diana was a bimbette who loved hugging Aids victims; she had enjoyed visions of a sort induced by eating disorders; she was the idol of the unsociable and uneducable masses; she was the heroine of the New Tragedy.

Seen in this light, the appropriation of Diana reveals the distinction between a political left—which once believed in justice, and for whom Diana could only have been an object of derision—and a cultural left which thinks that pity is the primary value, and which esteems Diana accordingly.

If the election of 1997 was a historic defeat for British socialism, the elevation of Diana as populist heroine illustrates more broadly and even more starkly the bankruptcy of the political left. Tony Blair's "people's princess" was not merely fatuous. To anyone of the traditional left it would have seemed as offensively oxymoronic as the claim (made in a television interview) by Ian Corfield of the Fabian Society that Diana was loved because she represented a "genuine feeling of meritocracy." She did *what*? The daughter of a rich dipsomaniac earl, whose highest academic achievement was a school prize for best-kept hamster, who married a prince, and who died during (and in a sense because of) a liaison with a coke-snorting, starlet-bonking playboy?

To make the point clearer still, as 1997 neared its end there was another episode which highlighted the dichotomy between the political and the cultural: the huge Commons majority for a Bill to outlaw fox-hunting. No one noticed how remote this is from the conflict of left and right in a traditional political sense. The most eminent "anti" of the century, after all, was Adolf Hitler, a vegetarian whose Reich banned the hunting he abhorred, and one of the best known opponents of hunting today is Alan Clark MP, who has a Rottweiler called Eva Braun—no doubt forbidden to chase bunnies. Equally, better educated fox-hunting men know that Engels hunted with the Cheshire. And more than 50 years ago, George Orwell contrasted the British progressive attitude "towards hunting, shooting and the like" with the fact that "Lenin, Stalin and Trotsky were all of them keen sportsmen" who loved nothing more than to bag a few bears or deer.

But then, compare two Labour governments and two parliaments: those of 1945 and 1997. Under Attlee, Labour believed in socialism and taxed the rich heavily to pay for the welfare state, but it let them enjoy their sports. Under Blair, a government which—as every Labour MP knows—is not remotely socialist has sworn not to raise income taxes, come what may of the welfare state. By way of compensation, MPs can indulge in a little pointless cultural leftism by outlawing a sport still associated with a gentry which barely exists.

A century ago, William Harcourt said: "We are all socialists now." We are none of us socialists any more, it seems, least of all in Tony Blair's cabinet. But we can cuddle toy foxes like Mike Foster, we can mope over Diana, we can simper about flower power. It's a strange end to an old song. Not all of us will mourn the death of socialism; the death of the Enlightenment would be another matter.

A story of justice • Philip Collins

MAY 2001

After a term of office, are we any closer to taking the measure of this government? There have been endless task forces and the shelves of every department groan under the weight of thick booklets full of targets set. Yet the charge of inactivity, of a wasted term, persists. The Blair government is afflicted by a kind of reverse *gestalt*. It all adds up to something, but we don't quite know what.

In one sense, refusing to formulate too clearly a set of grand political objectives is understandable. Old Labour was so cumbersome because it was ideologically glued together. Instead, we have a managerial state which does what works, in an endless series of partnerships with market and third sector organisations. But works to do what, exactly?

The Clinton tenure is a lesson in the danger of politics without a lodestar. Clinton proved himself a first-rate political strategist. But what was his legacy? How far did his administrations change the US? This is a question of which the Blair government seems very much aware. Its four years have been punctuated by fitful striving for intellectual purpose under the rubric of the third way.

But, curiously, although the prime minister now stresses that the third way is "social democracy renewed," there has been little attempt to supply a renewed story about social justice. Meanwhile, the old left continues to conduct a stale argument focused on reducing income equality, which wins few converts and scorns what have been real achievements. The latest British Social Attitudes survey shows that, although 80 per cent of the population agree that the gap is too large between those on high and low incomes, only 37 per cent of people want active government redistribution—a remarkable example of willing the end but not the means.

There is a further problem for a story of justice based on substantially reducing income equality—it is impossible to achieve. The tendency of market economies to distribute rewards unequally has become even more marked recently, as returns to skill and education continue to grow disproportionately. Between 1979 and 1998/9 the income of the bottom tenth rose by 6 per cent in real terms, while the income of the top tenth rose by 82 per cent. The effect of the government raising income at the bottom—which it has—is that it simply slows the pace at which incomes are growing more unequal.

A realistic centre-left needs a new story about fairness, which takes account of economic realities and public opinion but also connects to a notion of the good society. Where is this story going to come from? It is a commonplace to say that there are no big ideas left in politics. Yet the last 30 years have seen a renaissance in academic political theory. In Thomas Nagel's phrase, John Rawls's *A Theory of Justice* "changed the subject" when it appeared in 1971. Yet for all the influence it has had on public policy argument in Britain, it might not have been written.

This is not because people in government have no interest in ideas. We have a prime minister who speculates about utilitarianism versus natural law and a famously erudite chancellor. The truth is that most academic political theory and sociology is dry and without regard for political constraint. Even good ideas may not translate into policy.

Rawls's famous "difference principle" states that income inequalities are only justified when they improve the lot of people at the bottom of the pile. But how do we know when an income difference will accomplish this?

A useful test of any proposition is that if its opposite makes you laugh, then you are saying something banal or absurd. We prefer things which work. As opposed to things which don't? This is just a way of avoiding the force of Isaiah Berlin's dictum that not all good things can be had at once. When the things that we want collide, tough choices occur. Then governments need an intellectual compass.

The refusal to engage in tough philosophical combat means that Blair (indeed, any senior politician) was bound to fall out with the academy (see John Lloyd's "Falling Out" on the disenchantment of the left intelligentsia with New Labour, *Prospect* October 1999). Political theory is, among other things, a quest for definition. If that is one of its weaknesses, it is also the case that nothing sensible can be said until we have arrived at definitions. At its best, political theory operates a sort of clearing house. It can show us that if we commit to so much of *this*, we can commit to only so much of *that*. But the breadth of the Blair coalition means that definitions are left unsharpened. As has been pointed out before, New Labour is *systematically* murky.

This essay seeks to shine some light into the murky hole in New Labour's thinking about equality, poverty and meritocracy, and tries to fit them into a new political narrative. It also looks at what is happening to these concepts, as far as they are measurable, in the real world. It concludes, tentatively, that the government does have a story it can tell, but that its theory needs to catch up with its practice. From a centre-left view, its social policy record has been sound, if not sparkling. The government's true failure has been poetic—New Labour is a republic from which the poets have been banished. Behind the numbers lies no vision of the "good life," even in outline.

In February this year, Tony Blair did offer a picture of his government's good society: "The mission of any second term must be this: to break down the barriers that hold people back, to create real upward mobility, a society that is open and genuinely based on merit and the equal worth of all ... Opening up the economy and society to merit and talent is the radical second term agenda." Stakeholding and communitarianism have come and gone, but meritocracy could endure. It is easy to grasp and in theory it is already established as part of the ideology of all market democracies.

Moving from the aspiration of meritocracy to something closer to its reality is a huge task, one which will take several generations and involve complex compromises with other political "goods"—notably liberty (in particular the liberty of the wealthy). Nevertheless, here is a potentially compelling story of a society in which position and opportunity are related to talent, not social origins. This will require a set of policies to meet the two most important requirements of a meritocracy: extensive social mobility in both directions and a high level of provision at the bottom.

Meritocracy is almost, but not quite, synonymous with the more familiar phrase "equality of opportunity." Both are premised on mass democracies with high levels of social provision and low barriers between social groups (whether based on class or ethnicity). Both combine social justice with economic efficiency; it is efficient to get the best people into the right jobs and that requires ladders upwards for bright children from poor homes. But it is possible to believe in equality of opportunity and reject meritocracy—indeed, this is Rawls's position. Meritocracy implies that people should be rewarded according to their talent—the first violinist should get paid more than the second, and so on. Rawls's egalitarianism rejects meritocracy; he argues that the distribution of talent is a "genetic lottery" which does not in itself deserve reward. Yet this offends a common-sense view of justice which includes an idea of merit—a talented footballer or doctor should be paid more than a less talented one (though talent is hard to measure). In fact, we do admire people for qualities they inherited. And it is hard to disentangle talent from effort, so by rewarding superior performance we also reward graft.

There is, of course, a darker side to meritocracy, pointed out by Michael Young (in *The Rise of the Meritocracy*) and others. Those who form the meritocratic elite may claim an even larger slice of the cake than inherited elites, while those at the bottom of the pile may feel even more miserable if they are there on merit. Young's dystopia is a long way off; we can afford to become far more meritocratic before we face a tyranny of the intelligent. Nevertheless, we ought to be reluctant meritocrats, or rather meritocrats for whom a large rump of failures is an impediment to meritocracy, not a necessary consequence of it. As the prime minister said in February: "Meritocracy is not wrong. It is insufficient."

Meritocracy must be accompanied by a universal idea of equality of respect which transcends an individual's ability. Such quasi-religious assertions about human worth often sound pious when repeated in political speeches. In some ways they assert no more than the founding assumption of all liberal democracies: that all citizens have the vote and rights regardless of ability or income, and that all should be equal before the law. In other ways such assertions are plain wrong: we do *not* all deserve equal respect. There are some bad people out there—those, for example, who kill or rob. The most we can say is that people are due respect until they prove unworthy of it. None the less, the banner of universal respect is an important one—especially in a society with widening income differentials. It reaffirms that there are ways of judging people apart from income. For the effective provision of social support and ladders of opportunity, it is also vital that the agents of the state treat each individual equally and with as much respect as possible.

Here we have the beginnings of a story which might form a "minimum programme" for any centre-left government—a stress on high, universal, social standards (especially of income and education); and a pursuit of meritocracy without abandoning the less successful. The government has made a good deal of progress on this programme through its emphasis on performance in schools, targeted increases in welfare spending and labour market policy.

In the past four years we have seen a mandatory floor set for wages, an unusually active labour market policy and a healthy growth in jobs (although the last two are not necessarily related). The New Deal programmes, the employment zones and the job transition service are all attempts to improve the employability of the least skilled. Moreover, since May 1997, the working families tax credit, the increased threshold for national insurance contributions, and the 10 per cent lower rate of tax, have meant that the working poor have benefited more than any other group as a result of government tax and welfare policies. A family with one working adult has had an average rise in income of £24 per week. The bottom tenth as a whole, many of whom are not in work, have done less well, although an Institute for Fiscal Studies study has shown that their post-tax income is 8.8 per cent higher on average as a direct result of policy announced since May 1997. This figure would be higher were it not for the regressive changes to indirect taxation in the form of tobacco and fuel duties. Apart from the latter, tax policy has been clearly progressive. Sixteen per cent of the population and 19.9 per cent of children are now classified as poor, using a variation on the definition of an income below half of the average. David Piachaud and Holly Sutherland have subtracted the effects of government policy to show that these numbers would have been 19.1 per cent and 26.3 per cent respectively—840,000 children are in households which are relatively and absolutely better off.

No doubt swifter progress could have been made and some of the improvement is the result of an unusually strong economy. But this surely represents a few shuffling steps towards a better, fairer, society. Not so, says the left and much of the social policy establishment—what matters is what has happened to income inequality. Here the story is less good. It seems the rich are still getting richer. Assuming constant earnings, the richest 30 per cent have experienced, as a direct result of government policy, a fall of 0.7 per cent in their average household income. But this drop has been more than counterbalanced by the growth in private sector earnings for higher earners of around 7 per cent per year. So income inequality has increased, notwithstanding a fair amount of progressive policy. If we are to judge the government on progress towards income equality, then it has failed.

Raymond Plant has written that the left and the right differ crucially on these questions: the right-wing position is that poverty is
alleviated as soon as the income of the poor rises in absolute terms,
and the left-wing stance is that it is the gap between the rich and the
poor which really matters. This is a classic case of the best being the
enemy of the good. To say that improving life chances for the least-
well-off represents failure because of a surge in bonuses in the City of
London is absurd. A residual utopianism of the left seems to be
kindled into life by this issue.

That is not to say that we should be completely satisfied with that
minimum programme of a high social floor plus meritocracy. We
need a "maximum programme" too—one which seeks to narrow the
gap between rich and poor, which wants to challenge concentrations
of private privilege in health and education, and even challenge
market outcomes. One reason for this is that if the gap in income and
life-style between top and bottom grows *too* wide, it could undermine
the possibility of meritocracy. (John Goldthorpe has shown that the
societies with least income inequality, such as Sweden and Norway,
tend to have the most social mobility. The US has a myth of mobility,
but in reality less than Britain.) The maximum programme by
definition will not be fully achievable, especially given the nature of
the modern international economy, but it represents an aspiration.
The important *political* point is that it should be seen as an evolution
from the minimum programme, not a contradiction of it. I now want
to examine how minimum and maximum might converse with one
another, by considering poverty and social mobility.

First, the poverty debate. Taking the official definition of poverty
as living on less than half of average income, you would expect
that with a reasonably uniform spread of income, about 25 per cent of
households would fall into this category. This is indeed the case. For a
childless couple it means a weekly income of about £130.

We need to be aware, though, that the official definition is measuring not poverty but income dispersal and can lead to notable
absurdities. A strict apostle of income equality will currently be

wishing for a further plunge in world stock markets. A recession, during which national income falls, closes the gap between rich and poor and thus, strictly speaking, reduces poverty even though *everyone* is worse off. The opposite also occurs. Poverty increased in the late 1980s when average income shot up. So a government could significantly raise incomes for the losers from the market economy and still see official poverty rise, because the winners did even better.

However, if the definition of poverty as inequality seems to miss out something important about poverty, then the claim from the right, that the label of "poor" should be reserved strictly for the destitute, seems to define poverty out of existence altogether. Poverty is, indeed, a partly relative experience. The set of goods which constitute poverty in any given society is inescapably relative to the expectations reasonable in that society at that moment in history. Humans are the only species whose needs have a history. The definition of poverty is rightly different now from what it was for Charles Booth. Poverty in Britain is different from poverty in Ghana.

This argument is not the impasse it seems. We simply need to supplement the relative definition of poverty with another, based on the extent to which people have access to certain goods. Last year, David Gordon and others produced just such a list for the Joseph Rowntree Foundation. This supplementary conception of poverty, which owes a great deal to Amartya Sen's work on capability deprivation, informs one of the government's most successful initiatives, the social exclusion unit. The very term "social exclusion" moves the argument away from the zero-sum game of income inequality on to life chances—what people need to lead a fuller life. It acknowledges that inequality is an arithmetical property rather than an *experience*: the hunger of the hungry, may be exacerbated by the fact that, somewhere near by, others are fed, but it is not the hunger itself.

If we think about poverty as in part an absolute condition, then this government has a story it can tell with some pride. The New Policy Institute has tracked 50 indicators of social exclusion for the Joseph Rowntree Foundation. They reported that, over the last year, 24 of the indicators were steady and 17 had improved. Overcrowding and low income households without central heating have fallen by a third in the last five years and there was a 28 per cent drop in rough sleeping in 1999. The minimum wage meant that 1.5m people, mostly women, saw their pay increase significantly. Further, the incidence of 11-year-olds failing to achieve level 4 at key stage 2 in English and Maths has fallen by a quarter since 1996. Three quarters of all New Deal employees are still in work. A higher platform for the poor is gradually being constructed. This progressive picture should not be lost—or even denounced—because private sector earnings growth is at the top of the cycle.

The second keystone of the minimum programme is meritocracy softened by a universal equality of respect. Meritocracy is a shop-soiled idea, but taking it seriously would make Britain more just and efficient and it would be popular. So how open a society is Britain now? There is a huge amount of data on this—much of it hard to interpret. Forty-two per cent of men and 36 per cent of women born between 1950 and 1959 have been upwardly mobile, although that is partly because the salariat has grown and the manual working class has shrunk. There is a much larger middle class than there used to be. Hence, 73 per cent of men whose fathers were in the salariat have remained there during a period of considerable mobility from below. Further down the scale there is also a fair amount of mobility, but people move only short distances. Since 1991, researchers at the department of social security have tracked the British Household Panel survey to analyse income mobility. The data shows that although half of those in the bottom fifth of the income scale in 1991 had escaped by 1998, the movement was within a short range. Of that group, less than a quarter had made it into the top 60 per cent seven years later. A more optimistic picture is painted by *Social Trends*, which records that only 55 per cent of adults who were in the top fifth of the income table in 1991 were still there in 1998 and 49 per cent of those in the bottom fifth were there in both years.

The more telling measure is the likelihood of a person born in a low social class making it into a higher bracket. John Goldthorpe and Colin Mills, using the General Household Survey data for 1973-92, found no significant changes in relative social mobility during the last 30 years. The verdict seems to be that the middle class has grown but that relative social mobility is stable. The chances of a talented child from a poor background making it through to the top has changed little over the past 100 years.

There is both a strong and a weak version of the politics of meritocracy—corresponding with the minimum and maximum programmes described earlier. The weak version acknowledges that a meritocracy must coexist with a wide spread of incomes and that people will be able to pass on advantage to their children. The strong version wants to narrow the income gap and close off some opportunities to pass on advantage. The two most serious obstacles to equal life chances are the ability to purchase educational advantage and the right to pass on wealth. These two advantages equip people with skills and resources to take to the labour market and diminish the consequences of failure. But no Labour government has ever seriously considered closing private schools. The official policy remains as it ever was: to improve the state sector so that the rationale of going private disappears. But as long as half of the places at the top universities go to the 7 per cent of children educated privately, a real meritocracy is inconceivable.

A weaker, but more appealing option than trying to close private schools is to work vigilantly on access to higher education and try to build bridges between the public and private sectors—as Peter Lampl's foundations are trying. The facilities of some private schools are increasingly being made available to state pupils, with the active sponsorship of the DfEE, especially in preparation for university. In the state sector itself, resources should be concentrated in two areas: on the talented child from a poor background and on "early years" education. This government has stressed the importance of life-long access to education but the brutal truth is that the earlier the intervention, the greater the effect. A realistic meritocrat will argue for a radical reordering of spending priorities throughout the life cycle. The pattern of education spending in Britain is concentrated on the later years when, in most cases, the damage is already done. (A true egalitarian will object to any concentration of resources on able children, preferring a small improvement for all to ladders upwards for some. But this is a false dichotomy.)

There is plenty we can do within the bounds of possibility. That is not to say that even a minimum programme of meritocratic policy will be easy to implement. Meritocracy has losers—the downwardly mobile—and they will try to hang on to what they have. Opening up private schools also has its limits. The parents of children at fee-paying schools will complain that they are paying for education three times over: once for state schools through the tax system, second, for their own children's school fees and third, for the state school children who are now sharing private school facilities.

Education policy will remain central to a meritocratic government. But there are other ways of rising apart from going to university—one of them is in business. A string of business and enterprise schools has just been announced. Perhaps more important, an attempt is being made to reform the insolvency laws, to remove the stigma of bankruptcy, which is higher in Britain than in most comparable countries. This is no use without access to capital. The social investment task force is experimenting with the provision of capital for high risk ventures in deprived areas.

This also connects to the broader issue of government intervention on accumulated wealth. Wealth alters the burden of risk. It provides capital to fund a good idea, insurance against hard times, or a route into the generation of more wealth, through equities or housing. As the Fabian Society document *Paying for Progress* points out, the distribution of wealth is even more unequal than the distribution of income. The wealthiest 10 per cent own 52 per cent of the nation's wealth—up from 49 per cent in 1982. This is likely to worsen. The use of share options is opening a gap between the public and the private sector workforce. Rising house prices add to the wealth of owners, who are outstripping renters. Britain currently has £381 billion of unmortgaged housing assets and a second generation is now inheriting the houses bequeathed by their parents. At the bottom of the scale, the proportion of households with no savings or capital at all has risen to 10 per cent from 5 per cent 20 years ago. One option to dampen this trend is a wealth tax. The Fabians rejected a wealth tax and proposed an ingenious transformation of inheritance tax into a capital receipts tax, in which the rate declines as the legacy is more widely spread. This is a good, though weaker, option. It raises less revenue and does less to address the trickle-down of privilege, but it is a bridge between aspiration and reality.

Another bridge between the strong and the weak conceptions of a meritocracy bears on the idea of equalising risk across the population. The main reason that the poor are so risk-averse is that the consequences of failure are so much greater because they are protected less by financial insurance. We could add to the capacity for risk, and therefore reward, at the bottom of the income pile, by government loans to the poor and by a judicious use of asset-based initiatives—perhaps paid for out of cutting back the still extensive middle-class welfare state. The "baby bond" suggested by Gavin Kelly and Rachel Lissauer of the IPPR think-tank, and the "capital grant" suggested by Julian Le Grand and David Nissan for the Fabian Society, are ways of altering the burden of risk of the poorest. This argument might even be pushed into the family of "citizen's income" proposals. The purpose of all these policies is that they provide a platform for the least well off to capitalise on an idea, to turn income into wealth, to soften a fall.

This government has been surprisingly reticent about social justice. It has undersold its own successes, especially in raising the social "floor"—fearing, perhaps, the anti-welfare sections of the electorate as well as the left's obsession with reducing income inequality. A second term should see further progress in raising the floor, but also several new initiatives to promote meritocracy. An open, socially mobile society with a high floor of social provision is not an original aspiration; it was broadly the aim of the new liberals in Edwardian days—but it remains far from achieved. It is a realistic, measurable, goal; unlike vague rhetoric about solidarity or community. The idea of "high floor plus meritocracy" gathers together many of the strands of existing government policy and presents a clear, popular, case about what is wrong with the country. It must be complemented by an equality of respect for all those citizens who cannot compete. Furthermore, meritocracy requires that we do not abandon completely the aspirations contained in the "maximum programme." A realistic centre-left should worry less about the income gap than about the life chances of those at the bottom, but it should not disregard the gap entirely—if it becomes too wide, it makes meritocracy even harder to achieve. The dialogue between "minimum" and "maximum" must continue—and in that dialogue lies our outline of the good society.

Rude Britannia • Michael Elliott

MAY 2001

Years ago, when I was a child of nine or ten—this must have been about 1960—I went out to play with my friend John. His father opened the door, and said that he wanted to talk to me. Apparently I'd been using "bad words" in front of John, and he'd repeated them to his little sisters. John's father, a kind and gentle man, was furious. He marched me back home to tell my parents of my misdeeds. Apart from a deep sense of grievance—40 years on, I'm still convinced that it was John who taught *me* the swear words—I knew what was coming next. It duly came; a full-scale dressing down from my mum and dad; suspension of privileges, which meant that I couldn't go and watch Tranmere Rovers for a few weeks; and, on my part, deep, deep guilt.

I wonder if such scenes happen in Britain today? It's hard to imagine that they do; after all, what would be the point? Watch the television, read the newspapers, listen to conversation in the office, at the pub, on the buses and words which not long ago were almost taboo, tumble out of mouths unchecked. Now, Britons seem to use the word "fuck" in the way that an earlier generation would have said "blast." And language is only the half of it. Britain has become a society whose standards of civility seem to have collapsed and where much public behaviour has become astonishingly coarse—a place where aggression, vulgarity and drunkenness are commonplace. Here are a few random incidents from last year:

I'm walking across a side street in Clerkenwell after work, minding my own business. A car screeches to a halt in front of me; the driver winds down the window and screams: "Either cross the fucking road or get out of the fucking way, OK?"

I'm being driven down Curzon Street in the middle of the afternoon, at walking pace. A man in a three-piece suit, obviously drunk, steps in front of the car, which stops. He then whacks his umbrella across the bonnet of the car, leaving a dent; the driver gets out and they have a fight on the pavement.

I'm at Arsenal, watching them play Liverpool. Where I'm sitting, there are as many women and children as men. Behind me, a group of Liverpool supporters keep up an unbroken tirade. Patrick Vieira is a "black cunt," everyone else is a "fucking gobshite."

I'm watching a Channel 4 show one Friday night. Contestants are playing "Mammary Memories." The rules: five women stick their breasts through holes in a screen, and a man has to match the breasts to a face. (The catch: one of the pairs belongs to his girlfriend.)

The sense that incivility has become a distinct social problem is growing. In a recent ICM poll for the *Observer*, people were asked "What makes you most embarrassed when you think of Britain?" By far the most common response, mentioned by 33 per cent of those polled, was "hooligans/lager louts." In the criminal justice system, there is growing interest in the "broken windows" theory of crime generation—the idea that if you leave small acts of anti-social behaviour untended, they will metastasize into genuine issues of public order. The public security measures in the Crime and Disorder Act of 1998 and Jack Straw's determination to address drink-related crime (in the last British Crime Survey, more than half of all violence inflicted by strangers was said to happen under the influence of alcohol) suggest that incivility has become a genuine issue of social policy.

That makes sense; a society which is rude, aggressive and yobbish is a place in which, sooner or later, people will become fearful and unwilling to trust others to behave decently. There's an obvious link here to the burgeoning literature on the importance of social capital, with its modern roots in Robert Putnam's seminal 1995 article "Bowling Alone" (now expanded into a book of the same title). Putnam identified the extent to which traditional American forms of civic and political association had atrophied in modern times. For him and his followers, trust—the sense of reciprocal, generalised dependence—is a crucial attribute of successful societies and economies. Trust thrives in conditions of civility and social capital in conditions of trust. So civility matters. But, as I quickly found out when I started work on this article, it's easier to dislike anti-social behaviour than to measure its impact; and it's easier to do either of those than to figure out how to persuade people to behave better. This is difficult stuff.

At the outset there's a problem of subjectivity: things that offend some of us may not get a rise out of anyone else. The incidents mentioned above left me feeling at best uncomfortable, at worst, threatened; others may have shrugged them off. In a Home Office research paper, "Policing Anti-Social Behaviour," published last year, the authors found that police officers often suggested that "tolerance of certain types of behaviour differed among different sections of the public … middle class areas had different perceptions about what constituted disorderly behaviour than did working class areas." There are similar differences between generations. Although some anti-social behaviour will show up in official crime statistics, much of it will not; there's no law against failing to offer your seat to an old lady on the bus. Indeed, even where there are relevant statistics, they won't always capture a wider social phenomenon. It is well known that "aggressive drinking" has become a pervasive feature of British life, not only in the city centres of Manchester and London, but in smaller towns, too. Yet it's hard to document the phenomenon. Although there was an increase in the number of young people who consumed alcohol in the 1990s, British alcohol consumption per head is stable; it comes in the mid-range of the European countries. Police convictions and cautions for public drunkenness fluctuate wildly in number, changing, presumably, with local police practice. The number cautioned in 1994 (57,890), for example, was almost exactly the same as in 1955 (54,210), but much less than in 1975 (104,452). Make of that what you will.

Doubtless we're all prisoners of our past. I was born in 1951 and grew up in suburban Merseyside. My father was a schoolteacher, my mother a housewife. Their life revolved around local churches—Baptist for my father, Presbyterian for my mother. The house was tee-total and we didn't have a television until Liverpool got to the Cup Final in 1965, though we often watched television at neighbours' houses. So my upbringing may have been a little more decorous than most. Moreover, these days I'm no more than a frequent visitor to Britain; I've spent most of my adult life—and almost all of the last 15 years—in the US. That has coloured my judgements, and not just because, by comparison with London, New York is a rather well-mannered city. There's something about periodic visits to a once-familiar place that heightens your sense of what has changed—changes which, like the slow accretion of rust on exposed metal, may not be noticeable to those closest to them. I've twice written articles about being shocked by the yob culture in Britain, and each time it has been fellow expatriates in New York who have called to say how much their experience mirrors mine. We could all be thin-skinned prigs; but the American journalist who, after five years in Britain, returned to New York last year certainly isn't. I asked her why she left. "In the end," she sighed, "I just got tired of all the drinking."

In any case, the statistics, or lack of them, prove no more than good reporting does. Travel outside Britain and you start to see us as others do. Most Britons regard football hooligans and drunk holidaymakers as aberrant mutants of the genus True Brit. But for many foreigners, the authentic representative of the nation is a young man with a St George's cross painted on his face, wrecking a European café. It doesn't matter where you go—Las Vegas, Florida, Spain, Bangkok, Verbier—bartenders and shopkeepers will tell you that they detest the sight of a group of young British males descending on their establishments. (They're not much keener on British women.) Reporting the handover to China of Hong Kong in 1997, I was ashamed by the reaction of Chinese and American friends when I suggested that many of the young Britons in the territory were interesting examples of a new form of global adventurism. Those who lived in Hong Kong saw something different—a loud, aggressive group who would finish work (whether on the construction site or in financial services) and head for a bar to get legless. There is no other country whose people, when they get together abroad, are so well-known for vomit and violence—not the Germans or French, not the Americans, not the Swedes. That too is a subjective judgement, but when one's own experience is backed up by those of countless others, it takes on the attributes of fact.

Those of us who think that incivility matters face one more objection: is today's anti-social behaviour really that new? Plainly, it isn't. You don't have to go back to Hogarth or Dickens to know that booze, mayhem and riot are as much a part of the national character as cream teas at the vicarage. So are moral panics; each decade since the 1950s has been scandalised by the behaviour of its young: teddy boys, mods and rockers, punks and skinheads, lager louts. And in some respects prosperity has made Britain a more pleasant place. I didn't like the language when I watched Liverpool play Arsenal last year. But the crowd was all seated, and at half-time everyone trooped off to the toilets. When I used to stand on the Kop at Anfield in the 1960s—packed in with 20,000 others—the half-time ritual was rather different. It involved a rolled up *Liverpool Echo* and warm rivulets of piss would be cascading down the terraces within minutes. (One other change in football: at half-time at Highbury, the scallies I was sitting with fired up enormous joints, right under the noses of policemen. We didn't do that in the 1960s.)

Still, we all know that something has changed over the last few decades. In trying to figure out what that might be, George Orwell's wartime essays on England remain a fruitful starting point. When a contemporary politician or commentator, from John Major to Jeremy Paxman, adumbrates on national character, they parse Orwell. So they should; "The Lion and the Unicorn" (1941) and "The English

People" (1947) are astonishing works: written in simple declarative sentences, with themes subtle yet understandable and sentiments recognisable even at distance.

Yet Orwell's world is not ours. The evidence he cited to support his ideas—like that famous passage on "the clatter of clogs in the Lancashire mill-towns ... the old maids biking to Holy Communion through the mists of an autumn morning"—is about another time and place. Just as removed from our experience are the judgements he drew. "The gentleness of the English civilisation is perhaps its most marked characteristic," he wrote. "It is a land where the bus conductors are good-tempered and the policemen carry no revolvers." The spread of middle-class ideas and habits to the working class, Orwell thought, had led to a "general softening of manners ... In tastes, habits, and outlook, the working class and the middle class are drawing closer together."

Think about that claim. Orwell, a man of the left, was describing a process of levelling up with obvious approval. And it's not hard to think of real-life examples: Roy Jenkins, the son of a Welsh miner, became chancellor of Oxford University with an accent as fruity as a summer pudding. The idea that there was something reprehensible about this—that Jenkins and others had lost something by turning their backs on a world of "collarless, unshaven men, with their muscles warped by heavy labour"—would have struck Orwell as absurd. Softened manners were *better* manners; this was progress. Yet sometime in the postwar years—between the end of the Chatterley ban and the Beatles' first LP?—this received wisdom was turned on its head, at least by the left. For the working class to aspire to middle-class manners now became a betrayal. Middle-class children—Mick Jagger, for example—consciously aped working-class habits. I know; I did it myself. My brother, born in 1944, educated at the local grammar school, left for university in 1963 with perfect received pronunciation (which he still has). I left the same school in 1969 with an affected Scouse accent (traces of which I still have). God knows what our parents, who had gratefully left the two-up two-downs of Anfield for a semidetached in the Wirral, thought of it all.

Unlike those conservatives who appropriate him for their own purposes, Orwell found no unbroken line of civil conduct stretching back to Anglo-Saxon times. "The prevailing gentleness of manners," he wrote, "is a recent thing. Within living memory it was impossible for a smartly dressed person to walk down Ratcliff Highway without being assaulted, and an eminent jurist, asked to name a typically English crime, could answer: 'Kicking your wife to death.'"

So the "prevailing gentleness" had not been of long standing. But it was there then—and now it is not. (Try saying "The gentleness of the English civilisation is its most marked characteristic" with a straight face today.) Why did civility go into decline?

The central reason, I think, is the success of consumer capitalism. Civility is one of the Roman virtues, along with restraint, thrift, honour, selflessness and so on. But modern capitalism is far from Roman; the sheer abundance of consumer goods, the boundless pleasures available to us, when coupled with a decline in religious observance, have changed patterns of behaviour all over the developed world. Daniel Bell's *The Cultural Contradictions of Capitalism* (1978) remains the classic analysis of the shift. American capitalism, Bell argued, had once taken its moral compass from the small-town Protestant ethic, which prized the values of thrift, effort, and restraint, and which held in check the hedonistic impulse of capitalism—the urge to get and enjoy more things, now. But the link between capitalism and a moral ethic was broken by metropolitanism and modernity. "The Protestant ethic served to limit sumptuary (though not capital) accumulation," wrote Bell. But by the 1960s, "the Protestant ethic was sundered from bourgeois society, only the hedonism remained, and the capitalist system lost its transcendental ethic ... The cultural, if not moral, justification for capitalism has become hedonism ... pleasure as a way of life."

Britain never had the American folk-memory of small-town virtues. But in a brilliant essay last year in the *Times Literary Supplement*, Ferdinand Mount argued that, in effect, Britain had something whose impact on expected patterns of behaviour was rather similar: the empire. Britain, Mount argued, "underwent a uniquely intense experience of empire, with all its restraints and impassivities and deprivations. It was the empire that taught our ancestors to keep their chins up and their upper lips stiff, and to put public duty before private satisfaction." Some of Mount's imperial virtues—self-denial, fortitude, loyalty—are precisely those which Bell identified with the American Protestant ethic. Just as metropolitanism crushed that ethical sense in America, one might argue, so did the end of empire in Britain.

A concomitant of the end of empire was this: the concept of a "ruling class" no longer made as much sense as it once had. The second world war was a great leveller in more ways than one. Not only did it enforce a degree of common austerity; not only did it expose the sheer waste and stupidity of a class-ridden society. Above all, it sounded the death-knell of empire, even if it was nationalists in Singapore and India who heard the bell toll first and understood its meaning. The war and the end of empire, in their turn, contributed to a post-1945 decline in class-based deference to figures of authority and their values. In a 1988 Centre for Policy Studies address at the Conservative party conference (later a pamphlet), Peregrine Worsthorne looked back to the days when "Almost everybody respectably dressed and speaking with the right kind of accent ... was an authority figure able to over-awe merely by his or her presence." But that world did not survive the changes in Britain between 1945 and 1970: decolonisation, the welfare state, the long economic boom, the permissive society, Kenneth Tynan saying "fuck" on the BBC, swinging London, and a growing multiculturalism, especially in the larger cities. These and other changes have for most of us, in most ways, made Britain a better place to live. And here we get the first inkling of a nagging possibility to which we will return: incivility may be one of the prices we have paid for Britain to become a more vibrant, interesting, and dynamic society. Or, to quote Mount once more, "an almost insanely open-minded, casually reckless place."

That's the big picture but there are plenty of small brush strokes worth considering. To a visitor, one of the most striking changes in modern Britain over the last 20 years has been the extent to which it has become a society which takes its pleasure outdoors. Drunkenness, violence and bad language have always been with us; but until the 1980s, they tended to happen inside pubs or behind lace curtains. Now that is not the case. For once, the moment of change can be precisely dated; it came in the summer of 1980, with the opening of the rehabilitated piazza in Covent Garden. In the late 1970s, I used to walk to work through the old Covent Garden, a place of boarded-up warehouses and decrepit, gloomy streets. One sunny day, the wraps were taken off the old flower market. There they were: stalls, cafés, pubs, wine-bars, soon followed by jugglers, street-artists, restaurants, all tumbling out of the confines of the piazza. Where central London led, everyone else soon followed. From the Albert Dock in Liverpool to Canal Street Basin in Birmingham, the rehabilitation of old industrial space was accompanied by an explosion of opportunities to eat, drink and be merry. Couple this with the relaxation of British licensing laws in the early 1990s, and the stage was set for an all-day chance, gratefully taken, to down a skinful in the open air. Has this made Britain a more pleasant and relaxed place? Undoubtedly. But it's had a downside. Milanese or Parisians may know how to handle café society without scaring the horses, but—so far at least—Londoners and Brummies don't.

Precisely because incivility seems entwined with the modernisation and liberalisation of Britain, no serious political constituency has ever wanted to tackle its causes. The Thatcher and Major governments spoke as if good manners were important to them. So why didn't they do something about it? Why was there never a British version, say, of William Bennett, Ronald Reagan's education secretary, who loudly made the case that standards of social behaviour had slipped and that government could do something to reverse it?

In essence, it was because Bell's contest between hedonism and self-restraint had by then been resolved, and hedonism had won. Thatcher tried to stem the tide only once. In 1982, at the suggestion of that modern Zelig, Ferdinand Mount, then head of the Downing Street policy unit, Thatcher asked all her ministers to write short personal essays for a cabinet committee called the Family Policy Group.

The idea was to find initiatives which would strengthen the family and support virtuous civil behaviour. The plan was revealed to much hilarity. Most ministers didn't have their heart in it, and those who took it seriously made suggestions—such as school lessons in how to manage pocket money—that were too easy to ridicule. The exercise was abandoned; it was, in any case, doomed. For many of the most articulate supporters of Thatcher—such as Andrew Neil, whose *Sunday Times* editorship in the 1980s was emblematic of the view—the whole point of Thatcherism was to produce a prosperous, classless, society in which rewards went to the able and hard-working, whether or not they threw up on the 8.50 from Liverpool Street. For those sort of Thatcherites, the case that Worsthorne and his fogeyish friends made for good manners was an embarrassment. Worsthorne hoped that the newly rich would assume the responsibilities which are the burden of wealth, helping to address "pressing problems to do with law and order, good behaviour in public places, good manners, social obligation." But such attitudes were too reactionary to be taken seriously in the hedonistic 1980s.

So it has been left to the present government to tackle incivility as an issue. Should it do so? Or should we accept that anti-social behaviour and a more aggressive society are no more than the flipside of welcome changes in British life—that we're bad because we're good? Indeed, I've heard it said that London's global reputation as a wide open city where you can drink, take drugs and have sex around the clock has given it an edge over other places in the race for foreign investment. Moreover, if civility is important because it contributes to social capital, then those of us who are troubled by yob culture have a problem. There is little evidence, so far, to show that Britain is following the path that Putnam ascribes to America. In a careful study in the *British Journal of Political Science* in 1999, Peter Hall found that "aggregate levels of social capital have not declined to an appreciable extent in Britain over the post-war years." Surveys by the National Council of Voluntary Organisations suggest that levels of participation in community activities have not changed much in 20 years, and that charitable giving—which fell off in the early 1990s—has recovered well. (There is some data from the European Values Survey that suggests that levels of trust have declined markedly since the 1960s, but this is not conclusive.)

Perhaps for that reason, there seems little support for a substantive policy response to anti-social behaviour. You can't say that Tony Blair hasn't tried; his family has had its own brush with yob culture, and ever since he was shadow home secretary he has made a point of stressing the importance of civility, even if his ideas—such as the proposal that drunks should be marched to cash machines to pay on-the-spot fines—seem off-the-cuff. None of this has done Blair much good. For Conservatives, a Blair speech on the importance of manners and responsibility is the work of a hypocrite; for his own supporters, especially in the London media village, it is the sermonising of a finger-wagging moralist; proof, as a friend of mine puts it, that Blair is a "sanctimonious git."

I find that judgement on Blair profoundly depressing. At least he's trying to address a question which, outside the clever-clever salons of London, engages the attention of a large number of Britons. Of course, most of the ways in which Britain can address incivility are beyond the ability of politicians to shape. Legislation and new police powers will only get us so far. A number of police forces have set up "quality of life" task forces, designed to take action against behaviour which may have been tolerated before—urinating in the street after the pubs close, for instance. But police officers can't do everything and shouldn't try. In the Home Office research report on anti-social behaviour, a senior officer worried that tough enforcement of the laws might drive a wedge between young people and the police, and unnecessarily criminalise relatively harmless activity.

Yet even accepting the limits to police action against incivility, it seems defeatist to throw in the towel. Parents, teachers, friends, media executives—all of us—could make a small effort to behave in a more considerate, more polite way. If we don't, one day the image of modern Britain as a scruffy, loud, yobbish place will hurt us; and we won't get the international investment on which we depend. I'm from Liverpool, a city which, in my lifetime, has willingly changed its image from a great port to a haven for wisecracking, work-shy, hard-drinking scallywags. You don't think that hurts the city's economic prospects? That it doesn't condemn Scousers to more years of stunted life-chances?

There's nothing preordained about incivility in the modern world. Yobbishness degrades and divides us. It's the counsel of despair, surely, to argue that we've got to take the rough with the smooth; that social aggression is the inevitable consequence of an open, meritocratic, liberal Britain. We used to be better than that and we can be again.

Notes from underground • Dan Kuper

DECEMBER 2004

O f all the reasons the underground service grinds to a halt, from signal failures to insufficient staff to derailments, none has as much impact as a suicide. Almost everyone gets involved. The police, ambulance and firemen all pitch up; the underground's own emergency response unit, station staff, station managers and train managers all crowd around on the platform and try variously to save the person, move the person and clean up bits of the person.

How the tube got its reputation as a good spot for suicides is a mystery. It is a completely stupid choice. A large number of jumpers don't die immediately and plenty don't die at all. Those that are successful often manage because they get themselves crushed between the far wall and the train, instead of on the rails. It is very far from clinical. At the first "one-under" I attended, the woman was still alive underneath the train, screaming and trying to get up. The image stayed with me for years.

The drivers take the brunt of the trauma, frequently—ridiculously —blaming themselves for not stopping in time. Each takes it differently, of course, but quite a few never drive a train again, suffering nightmares and flashbacks for months. Others put it behind them, although, as one said to me, you never look at crowded rush-hour platforms in the same way again. A few have seen quite a number in their time, which is not so surprising when you consider that there is on average about one a week.

Not that all jumpers are inconsiderate. At one east London station, a man was seen placing an envelope under a stone on the platform before leaping in front of a train. When they opened the envelope, they found a £20 note and a slip of paper saying, "Say sorry to the driver, this is to buy him a drink."

On the other hand, some staff are very blasé about the whole thing. A story has been told of how two drivers threw a dummy in front of a train driven by a mate, who then got a few weeks off sick. One driver told me that after someone jumped in front of his train, he told the police, "Her arm went there and her leg went over there." The police-woman came back and said to him, "She had nice shoes, didn't she?"

Drivers who witness a suicide are at least entitled to money from a compensation fund and a couple of months off, which is an improve-ment on the old days, when they used to get three days standing spare while they waited to find out if they would be charged with manslaughter. This would normally have been in case they were drunk, but that was the rule rather than the exception in those days (see "Notes from underground," November 2004).

There is no compensation for the station staff who have to deal with the aftermath. It is one of those infrequent occasions when station supervisors earn their money; a week of drinking tea and reading the paper is suddenly transformed into a high-stress morning, running about like the proverbial blue-arsed fly, chaos all around and the smell of singed flesh in your nostrils.

The emergency crews, though, put it all in perspective, charging down to the scene without blinking, cracking jokes as they rummage around bits of brain. It almost makes you feel ashamed at taking a week or two off yourself. Not that ashamed, obviously.

After the initial burst, however, the supervisor has only one import-ant job left—a job so vital that it was impressed on me several times when I was learning the procedure. When the body is brought off the track and the police are going through the pockets, the supervisor needs to pay close attention to what they find—not because of any magpie tendencies on the part of the police, but because they want to see if the person had a ticket. Perhaps, I said when I first heard this, they want to claim a penalty fare off the undertaker. But apparently many bereaved families try to sue the underground—on what grounds I can't imagine—and if the person was travelling without a ticket the lawsuit is automatically null and void. So the lesson is clear: if you're going to kill yourself on the tube, at least buy a ticket. In the circumstances, it only needs to be a platform ticket.

The underground might seem thoughtless and clumsy hurrying to get the victim tidied out of the way, but it is appreciated by people in the train behind, stuck in a tunnel. (The service is usually running again in an hour.)

Upstairs, the public are normally understanding, it being one of those few occasions when it isn't entirely our fault. Not always, of course. A woman once berated us for incompetence at the station gates. "Why did this happen?" she demanded. My colleague told her that the victim had been very depressed. She replied, "Well, who wouldn't be, with that escalator out again."

Doctors often ask to be of help, but the ambulance crew is sufficient. A priest once tried too. I looked at him for a second and said, "No, there's no room down there. They don't need help."

"Spiritual help?" he persisted, standing right in the way of the entrance.

"No thanks," I repeated. "There's nothing you could do I'm afraid."

"Well I could pray," he said.

"Well pray over there, will you?"

He didn't stick around long.

Too diverse? • David Goodhart

FEBRUARY 2004

B ritain in the 1950s was a country stratified by class and region. But in most of its cities, suburbs, towns and villages there was a good chance of predicting the attitudes, even the behaviour, of the people living in your immediate neighbourhood.

In many parts of Britain today that is no longer true. The country has long since ceased to be Orwell's "family" (albeit with the wrong members in charge). To some people this is a cause of regret and disorientation—a change which they associate with the growing incivility of modern urban life. To others it is a sign of the inevitable, and welcome, march of modernity. After three centuries of homogenisation through industrialisation, urbanisation, nation-building and war, the British have become freer and more varied. Fifty years of peace, wealth and mobility have allowed a greater diversity in lifestyles and values. To this "value diversity" has been added ethnic diversity through two big waves of immigration: first the mainly commonwealth immigration from the West Indies and Asia in the 1950s and 1960s, followed by asylum-driven migrants from Europe, Africa and the greater middle east in the late 1990s.

The diversity, individualism and mobility that characterise developed economies—especially in the era of globalisation—mean that more of our lives is spent among strangers. Ever since the invention of agriculture 10,000 years ago, humans have been used to dealing with people from beyond their own extended kin groups. The difference now in a developed country like Britain is that we not only live among stranger citizens but we must *share* with them. We share public services and parts of our income in the welfare state, we share public spaces in towns and cities where we are squashed together on buses, trains and tubes, and we share in a democratic conversation—filtered by the media—about the collective choices we wish to make. All such acts of sharing are more smoothly and generously negotiated if we can take for granted a limited set of common values and assumptions. But as Britain becomes more diverse that common culture is being eroded.

And therein lies one of the central dilemmas of political life in developed societies: sharing and solidarity can conflict with diversity. This is an especially acute dilemma for progressives who want plenty of both solidarity—high social cohesion and generous welfare paid out of a progressive tax system—*and* diversity—equal respect for a wide range of peoples, values and ways of life. The tension between the two values is a reminder that serious politics is about trade-offs. It also suggests that the left's recent love affair with diversity may come at the expense of the values and even the people that it once championed.

It was the Conservative politician David Willetts who drew my attention to the "progressive dilemma." Speaking at a roundtable on welfare reform (*Prospect*, March 1998), he said: "The basis on which you can extract large sums of money in tax and pay it out in benefits is that most people think the recipients are people like themselves, facing difficulties which they themselves could face. If values become more diverse, if lifestyles become more differentiated, then it becomes more difficult to sustain the legitimacy of a universal risk-pooling welfare state. People ask, 'Why should I pay for them when they are doing things I wouldn't do?' This is America versus Sweden. You can have a Swedish welfare state provided that you are a homogeneous society with intensely shared values. In the US you have a very diverse, individualistic society where people feel fewer obligations to fellow citizens. Progressives want diversity but they thereby undermine part of the moral consensus on which a large welfare state rests."

These words alerted me to how the progressive dilemma lurks beneath many aspects of current politics: national tax and redistribution policies; the asylum and immigration debate; development aid budgets; EU integration and spending on the poorer southern and east European states; and even the tensions between America (built on political ideals and mass immigration) and Europe (based on nation states with core ethnic-linguistic solidarities).

Thinking about the conflict between solidarity and diversity is another way of asking a question as old as human society itself: who is my brother? With whom do I share mutual obligations? The traditional conservative Burkean view is that our affinities ripple out from our families and localities, to the nation and not very far beyond. That view is pitted against a liberal universalist one which sees us in some sense equally obligated to all human beings—an idea associated with the universalist aspects of Christianity and Islam, with Kantian universalism and with left-wing internationalism. Science is neutral in this dispute, or rather it stands on both sides of the argument. Evolutionary psychology stresses both the universality of most human traits and—through the notion of kin selection and reciprocal altruism—the instinct to favour our own. Social psychologists also argue that the tendency to perceive in-groups and out-groups is innate. In any case, Burkeans claim to have common sense on their side. They argue that we feel more comfortable with, and are readier to share with, and sacrifice for, those with whom we have shared histories and similar values. To put it bluntly—most of us prefer our own kind.

The category "own kind" or in-group will set alarm bells ringing in the minds of many readers. So it is worth stressing what preferring our own kind does *not* mean, even for a Burkean. It does not mean that we are necessarily hostile to other kinds or cannot empathise with outsiders. (There are those who do dislike other kinds but in Britain they seem to be quite a small minority.) In complex societies, most of us belong simultaneously to many in-groups—family, profession, class, hobby, locality, nation—and an ability to move with ease between groups is a sign of maturity. An in-group is not, except in the case of families, a natural or biological category and the people who are deemed to belong to it can change quickly, as we saw so disastrously in Bosnia. Certainly, those we include in our in-group could be a pretty diverse crowd, especially in a city like London.

Moreover, modern liberal societies cannot be based on a simple assertion of group identity—the very idea of the rule of law, of equal legal treatment for everyone regardless of religion, wealth, gender or ethnicity, conflicts with it. On the other hand, if you deny the assumption that humans are social, group-based primates with constraints, however imprecise, on their willingness to share, you find yourself having to defend some implausible positions: for example that we should spend as much on development aid as on the NHS, or that Britain should have no immigration controls at all. The implicit "calculus of affinity" in media reporting of disasters is easily mocked —two dead Britons will get the same space as 200 Spaniards or 2,000 Somalis. Yet every day we make similar calculations in the distribution of our own resources. Even a well-off, liberal-minded Briton who already donates to charities will spend, say, £200 on a child's birthday party, knowing that such money could, in the right hands, save the life of a child in the third world. The extent of our obligation to those to whom we are not connected through either kinship or citizenship is in part a purely private, charitable decision. But it also has policy implications, and not just in the field of development aid. For example, significant NHS resources are spent each year on foreign visitors, especially in London. Many of us might agree in theory that the needs of desperate outsiders are often greater than our own. But we would object if our own parent or child received inferior treatment because of resources consumed by non-citizens.

Is it possible to reconcile these observations about human preferences with our increasingly open, fluid and value-diverse societies? At one level, yes. Our liberal democracies still work fairly well; indeed it is one of the achievements of modernity that people have learned to tolerate and share with people very unlike themselves. (Until the 20th century, today's welfare state would have been considered contrary to human nature.) On the other hand, the logic of solidarity, with its tendency to draw boundaries, and the logic of diversity, with its tendency to cross them, do at times pull apart. Thanks to the erosion of collective norms and identities, in particular of class and nation, and the recent surge of immigration into Europe, this may be such a time.

The modern idea of citizenship goes some way to accommodating the tension between solidarity and diversity. Citizenship is not an ethnic concept but an abstract political idea—implying equal legal, political and social rights (and duties) for people inhabiting a given national space. But for most of us citizenship is also something automatic, something we are born into—arising out of a shared history, shared experiences, and, often, shared suffering.

Both aspects of citizenship—the abstract and the automatic—imply a notion of mutual obligation. Critics have argued that any idea of national community is anachronistic—swept away by globalisation, individualism and migration—but it still has political resonance. When politicians talk about the "British people" they refer not just to a set of individuals with specific rights and duties but to a group of people with a special commitment to one another. Membership in such a community implies acceptance of moral rules, however fuzzy, which underpin the laws and welfare systems of the state.

In the rhetoric of the modern liberal state, the glue of ethnicity ("people who look and talk like us") has been replaced with the glue of values ("people who think and behave like us"). But British values grow, in part, out of a specific history and even geography. Too rapid a change in the make-up of a community not only changes the present, it also, potentially, changes our link with the past. As Bob Rowthorn wrote (*Prospect*, February 2003), we may lose a sense of responsibility for our own history—the good things and shameful things in it—if too many citizens no longer identify with it.

Is this a problem? Surely Britain in 2004 has become too diverse and complex to give expression to a common culture in the present, let alone the past. Diversity in this context is usually code for ethnic difference. But that is only one part of the diversity story, albeit the easiest to quantify and most emotionally charged. The progressive dilemma is also revealed in the value and generational rifts that emerged with such force in the 1960s. At the *Prospect* roundtable mentioned above, Patricia Hewitt, now a Labour cabinet minister, recalled an example of generational conflict from her Leicester constituency. She was canvassing on a council estate when an elderly white couple saw her Labour rosette and one of them said, "We're not voting Labour—you hand taxpayers' money to our daughter." She apparently lived on a nearby estate, with three children all by different fathers, and her parents had cut her off. (Evidence that even close genetic ties do not always produce solidarity.)

Greater diversity can produce real conflicts of values and interests, but it also generates unjustified fears. Exposure to a wider spread of lifestyles, plus more mobility and better education, has helped to combat some of those fears—a trend reinforced by popular culture and the expansion of higher education (graduates are notably more tolerant than non-graduates). There is less overt homophobia, sexism or racism (and much more racial intermarriage) in Britain than 30 years ago and racial discrimination is the most politically sensitive form of unfairness. But 31 per cent of people still admit to being racially prejudiced. Researchers such as Isaac Marks at London's Institute of Psychiatry warn that it is not possible to neatly divide the population between a small group of xenophobes and the rest. Feelings of suspicion and hostility towards outsiders are latent in most of us.

The visibility of ethnic difference means that it often overshadows other forms of diversity. Changes in the ethnic composition of a city or neighbourhood can come to stand for the wider changes of modern life. Some expressions of racism, especially by old people, can be read as declarations of dismay at the passing of old ways of life (though this makes it no less unpleasant to be on the receiving end). The different appearance of many immigrants is an outward reminder that they are, at least initially, strangers. If welfare states demand that we pay into a common fund on which we can all draw at times of need, it is important that we feel that most people have made the same effort to be self-supporting and will not take advantage. We need to be reassured that strangers, especially those from other countries, have the same idea of reciprocity as we do. Absorbing outsiders into a community worthy of the name takes time.

Negotiating the tension between solidarity and diversity is at the heart of politics. But both left and right have, for different reasons, downplayed the issue. The left is reluctant to acknowledge a conflict between values it cherishes; it is ready to stress the erosion of community from "bad" forms of diversity such as market individualism but not from "good" forms of diversity such as sexual freedom and immigration. And the right, in Britain at least, has sidestepped the conflict, partly because it is less interested in solidarity than the left, but also because it is still trying to prove that it is comfortable with diversity.

But is there any hard evidence that the progressive dilemma actually exists in the real world of political and social choices? In most EU states the percentage of GDP taken in tax is still at historically high levels, despite the increase in diversity of all kinds. Yet it is also true that Scandinavian countries with the biggest welfare states have been the most socially and ethnically homogeneous states in the west. By the same token the welfare state has always been weaker in the individualistic, ethnically divided US compared with more homogeneous Europe. And the three bursts of welfarist legislation that the US did see—Roosevelt's New Deal, Truman's Fair Deal and Johnson's Great Society—came during the long pause in mass immigration between the first world war and 1968. (They were also, clearly, a response to the depression and two world wars.)

In their 2001 Harvard Institute of Economic Research paper "Why Doesn't the US Have a European-style Welfare State?" Alberto Alesina, Edward Glaeser and Bruce Sacerdote argue that the answer is that too many people at the bottom of the pile in the US are black or Hispanic. Across the US as a whole, 70 per cent of the population are non-Hispanic whites—but of those in poverty only 46 per cent are non-Hispanic whites. So a disproportionate amount of tax income spent on welfare is going to minorities. The paper also finds that US states that are more ethnically fragmented than average spend less on social services. The authors conclude that Americans think of the poor as members of a different group, whereas Europeans still think of the poor as members of the same group. Robert Putnam, the analyst of social capital, has also found a link between high ethnic mix and low trust in the US. There is some British evidence supporting this link too. Researchers at Mori found that the average level of satisfaction with local authorities declines steeply as the extent of ethnic fragmentation increases.

Finally, Sweden and Denmark may provide a social laboratory for the solidarity/diversity trade-off in the coming years. Starting from similar positions as homogeneous countries with high levels of redistribution, they have taken rather different approaches to immigration over the past few years. Although both countries place great stress on integrating outsiders, Sweden has adopted a moderately multicultural outlook. It has also adapted its economy somewhat, reducing job protection for older native males in order to create more low-wage jobs for immigrants in the public sector. About 12 per cent of Swedes are now foreign-born and it is expected that by 2015 about 25 per cent of under-18s will be either foreign-born or the children of the foreign-born. This is a radical change and Sweden is adapting to it rather well. But not all Swedes are happy about it.

Denmark has a more restrictive approach to immigration. Only 6 per cent of the population is foreign-born and native Danes enjoy superior welfare benefits to incomers. If the solidarity/diversity trade-off is a real one and current trends continue, then one would expect in, say, 20 years' time that Sweden will have a less redistributive welfare state than Denmark; or rather that Denmark will have a more developed two-tier welfare state with higher benefits for insiders, while Sweden will have a universal but less generous system.

What are the main objections, at least from the left, to this argument about solidarity and diversity? Multiculturalists stress Britain's multiple diversities, of class and region, which preceded recent waves of immigration. They also argue that all humans share similar needs and a common interest in ensuring they are met with minimum conflict; this, they say, can now be done through human rights laws. And hostility to diversity, they conclude, is usually a form of "false consciousness."

Critics of the dilemma also say, rightly, that the moral norms underpinning a community need not be hard for outsiders to comply with: broad common standards of right and wrong, some agreement on the nature of marriage and the family, respect for law, and some consensus about the role of religion in public life. Moreover, they add, there are places such as Canada (or Australia) which happily combine European-style welfare with an officially multicultural politics. London, too, has US levels of ethnic diversity but is probably the most left-wing part of Britain.

In the autumn 2003 issue of the US magazine *Dissent*, two academics, Keith Banting and Will Kymlicka, show that there is no link between the adoption of multiculturalist policies in countries like Canada, Sweden and Britain, and the erosion of the welfare state. But many of the policies they describe are either too technical (allowing dual citizenship) or too anodyne (existence of a government body to consult minorities) to stimulate serious tax resistance. They also assume too swift a reaction to growing diversity—these are forces that take effect over decades, if not generations. Similarly, two British academics, Bhikhu Parekh and Ali Rattansi, have offered a critique of the solidarity vs diversity thesis (partly in response to *Prospect* articles) which also assumes an implausibly rapid connection between social cause and effect. They argue that because the expansion of Britain's welfare state in the late 1940s coincided with the first big wave of non-white immigration into Britain, ethnic diversity cannot be a drag on solidarity. But the post-1945 welfare state was the result of at least 100 years of experience and agitation. The arrival of a small number of immigrants in the 1940s and 1950s was unlikely to have much bearing on that history.

A further point made by the multiculturalists is more telling. They argue that a single national story is not a sound base for a common culture because it has always been contested by class, region and religion. But that does not mean there is no such thing as national history, nor does it mean that the stress on the binding force of a shared history (or historical institutions like parliament) condemns immigrants to a second-class citizenship. Newcomers should be encouraged to adopt the history of their new country as part of the process of moving from immigrant "them" to citizen "us." Helpfully, Britain's story includes, through empire, the story of many of our immigrants—empire soldiers, for example, fought in many of the wars that created modern Britain.

I would add a further qualification to the progressive dilemma. Attitudes to welfare have, for many people, become more instrumental: I pay so much in, the state gives me this in return. As we grow richer the ties that used to bind workers together in a risk-pooling welfare state (first locally, later nationally) have loosened—"generosity" is more abstract and compulsory, a matter of enlightened self-interest rather than mutual obligation. Moreover, welfare is less redistributive than most people imagine—most of the tax paid out by citizens comes back to them in one form or another so the amount of the average person's income going to someone they might consider undeserving is small. This, however, does little to allay anxieties based on *perceptions* rather than fiscal truths. And poor whites, who have relatively little, are more likely to resent even small transfers compared with those on higher incomes.

Despite these qualifications it still seems to me that those who value solidarity should take care that it is not eroded by a refusal to acknowledge the constraints upon it. The politician who has recently laid most stress on those constraints, especially in relation to immigration, is the home secretary, David Blunkett. He has spoken about the need for more integration of some immigrant communities—especially Muslim ones—while continuing to welcome high levels of net immigration into Britain of over 150,000 a year.

Supporters of large-scale immigration now focus on the quantifiable economic benefits, appealing to the self-interest rather than the idealism of the host population. While it is true that moderate levels of immigration can be beneficial—neither the NHS nor the building industry could survive without it—many of the claimed benefits of *mass* immigration are challenged by economists such as Adair Turner and Richard Layard. It is clear, for example, that immigration is no long-term solution to an ageing population for the simple reason that immigrants grow old too. Keeping the current age structure constant over the next 50 years, and assuming today's birth rate, would require 60m immigrants. Managing an ageing society requires a package of later retirement, rising productivity and limited immigration. Large-scale immigration of unskilled workers does allow native workers to bypass the dirtiest and least rewarding jobs but it also increases inequality, does little for per capita growth, and skews benefits to employers and the better-off.

But large-scale immigration, especially if it happens rapidly, is not just about economics; it is about those less tangible things to do with identity and mutual obligation—which have been eroded from other directions too. And it can create real—as opposed to just imagined—conflicts of interest. One example is the immigration-related struggles over public housing in many of Britain's big cities in the 1970s and 1980s. In places like London's east end the right to a decent council house had always been regarded as part of the inheritance of the respectable working class. When immigrants began to arrive in the 1960s they did not have the contacts to get on the housing list and so often ended up in low quality private housing. Many people saw the injustice of this and decided to change the rules: henceforth the criterion of universal need came to supplant good contacts. So if a Bangladeshi couple with children were in poor accommodation they would qualify for a certain number of housing points, allowing them to jump ahead of young local white couples who had been on the list for years. This was, of course, unpopular with many whites. Similar clashes between *group* based notions of justice and *universally* applied human rights are unavoidable in welfare states with increasingly diverse people.

The "thickest" solidarities are now often found among ethnic minority groups themselves in response to real or perceived discrimination. This can be another source of resentment for poor whites who look on enviously from their own fragmented neighbourhoods as minorities recreate some of the mutual support and sense of community that was once a feature of British working-class life. Paradoxically, it may be this erosion of feelings of mutuality among the British majority that has made it easier to absorb minorities. The degree of antagonism between groups tends to be proportional to the degree of co-operation within groups. Relative to the other big European nations, Britain's sense of national culture and solidarity has arguably been rather weak—diluted by class, empire, the four different nations within the state, the north-south divide, and even the long shadow of US culture. That weakness of national solidarity, exemplified by the "stand-offishness" of suburban England, may have created a bulwark against extreme nationalism. We are more tolerant than, say, France because we don't care enough about each other to resent the arrival of the other.

When solidarity and diversity pull against each other, which side should public policy favour? Diversity can increasingly look after itself—the underlying drift of social and economic development favours it. Solidarity, on the other hand, thrives at times of adversity, hence its high point just after the second world war and its steady decline ever since as affluence, mobility, value diversity and (in some areas) immigration have loosened the ties of a common culture. Public policy should therefore tend to favour solidarity in four broad areas.

Immigration and asylum. About 9 per cent of British residents are now from ethnic minorities, rising to almost one third in London. On current trends about one fifth of the population will come from an ethnic minority by 2050, albeit many of them fourth or fifth generation. Thanks to the race riots in northern English towns in 2001, the fear of radical Islam after 9/11, and anxieties about the rise in asylum-led immigration from the mid-1990s (exacerbated by the popular press), immigration has shot up the list of voter concerns, and according to Mori 56 per cent of people (including 90 per cent of poor whites and even a large minority of immigrants) now believe there are too many immigrants in Britain. This is thanks partly to the overburdened asylum system, which forces refugees on to welfare and prevents them from working legally for at least two years—a system calculated to provoke maximum hostility from ordinary Britons with their acute sensitivity to free riding. As soon as the system is under control and undeserving applicants are swiftly removed or redirected to legitimate migration channels, the ban on working should be reduced to six months or abolished. A properly managed asylum system will sharply reduce the heat in the whole race and immigration debate.

Immigrants come in all shapes and sizes. From the American banker or Indian software engineer to the Somali asylum seeker—from the most desirable to the most burdensome, at least in the short term. Immigrants who plan to stay should be encouraged to become Britons as far as that is compatible with holding on to some core aspects of their own culture. In return for learning the language, getting a job and paying taxes, and abiding by the laws and norms of the host society, immigrants must be given a stake in the system and incentives to become good citizens. (While it is desirable to increase minority participation at the higher end of the labour market, the use of quotas and affirmative action seems to have been counter-productive in the US.) Immigrants from the same place are bound to want to congregate together but policy should try to prevent that consolidating into segregation across all the main areas of life: residence, school, workplace, church. In any case, the laissez-faire approach of the postwar period in which ethnic minority citizens were not encouraged to join the common culture (although many did) should be buried. Citizenship ceremonies, language lessons and the mentoring of new citizens should help to create a British version of the old US melting pot. This third way on identity can be distinguished from the coercive assimilationism of the nationalist right, which rejects any element of foreign culture, and from multiculturalism, which rejects a common culture.

Is there a "tipping point" somewhere between Britain's 9 per cent ethnic minority population and America's 30 per cent, which creates a wholly different US-style society—with sharp ethnic divisions, a weak welfare state and low political participation? No one knows, but it is a plausible assumption. And for that tipping point to be avoided and for feelings of solidarity towards incomers not to be overstretched it is important to reassure the majority that the system of entering the country and becoming a citizen is under control and that there is an honest debate about the scale, speed and kind of immigration. It is one thing to welcome smart, aspiring Indians or east Asians. But it is not clear to many people why it is such a good idea to welcome people from poor parts of the developing world with little experience of urbanisation, secularism or western values.

Welfare policy. A generous welfare state is not compatible with open borders and possibly not even with US-style mass immigration. Europe is not America. One of the reasons for the fragmentation and individualism of American life is that it is a vast country. In Europe, with its higher population density and planning controls, the rules have to be different. We are condemned to share—the rich cannot ignore the poor, the indigenous cannot ignore the immigrant—but that does not mean people are always happy to share. A universal, human rights-based approach to welfare ignores the fact that the rights claimed by one group do not automatically generate the obligation to accept them, or pay for them, on the part of another group—as we saw with the elderly couple in Leicester. If we want high tax and redistribution, especially with the extra welfare demands of an ageing population, then in a world of stranger citizens taxpayers need reassurance that their money is being spent on people for whose circumstances they have some sympathy. For that reason, welfare should become more overtly conditional. The rules must be transparent and blind to ethnicity, religion, sexuality and so on, but *not* blind to behaviour. People who consistently break the rules of civilised behaviour should not receive unconditional benefits.

The "localisation" of more tax and redistribution would make it possible to see how and on whom our taxes are spent. More controversially, there is also a case—as Meghnad Desai has argued—for introducing a two-tier welfare system. Purely economic migrants or certain kinds of refugees could be allowed temporary residence, the right to work (but not to vote) and be given access to only limited parts of the welfare state, while permanent migrants who make the effort to become citizens would get full access to welfare. A two-tier welfare state might reduce pressure on the asylum system and also help to deracialise citizenship—white middle-class bankers and Asian shopkeepers would have full British citizenship, while white Slovenian temporary workers would not. Such a two-tier system is emerging in Denmark. Indeed it already applies to some extent in Britain: migrants on work permits and spouses during the two-year probationary period cannot get most benefits. If we want to combine social solidarity with relatively high immigration, there is also a strong case for ID cards both on logistical grounds and as a badge of citizenship that transcends narrower group and ethnic loyalties.

Culture. Good societies need places like London and New York as well as the more homogeneous, stable, small and medium-size towns of middle Britain or the American midwest. But the emphasis, in culture and the media, should be on maintaining a single national conversation at a time when the viewing and listening public is becoming more fragmented and shared public belief systems have largely disappeared. In Britain, that means strong support for the "social glue" role of the BBC. (The glue once provided by religion no longer works, and in any case cannot include immigrants of different faiths.) The teaching of multi-ethnic citizenship in schools is a welcome step. But too many children leave school with no sense of their national history. The teaching of British history, and in particular the history of the empire and of subsequent immigration into Britain, should be a central part of the school curriculum. At the same time, immigrants should be encouraged to become part of the British "we," even while bringing their own very different perspective on its formation.

Politics and Language. Multiculturalists argue that the binding power of the liberal nation state has been eroded from within by value diversity and from without by the arrival of immigrant communities with other loyalties. But the nation state remains irreplaceable as the site for democratic participation and it is hard to imagine how else one can organise welfare states and redistribution except through national tax and public spending. Moreover, since the arrival of immigrant groups from non-liberal or illiberal cultures it has become clear that to remain liberal the state may have to prescribe a clearer hierarchy of values. The US has tried to resolve the tension between liberalism and pluralism by developing a powerful national myth. Even if this were desirable in Britain, it is probably not possible to emulate. Indeed, the idea of fostering a common culture, in any strong sense, may no longer be possible either. One only has to try listing what the elements of a common culture might be to realise how hard it would be to legislate for. That does not mean that the idea must be abandoned; rather, it should inform public policy as an underlying assumption rather than a specific set of policies. Immigration and welfare policies, for example, should be designed to reduce the fear of free riding, and the symbolic aspects of citizenship should be reinforced; they matter more in a society when tacit understandings and solidarities can no longer be taken for granted. Why not, for example, a British national holiday or a state of the union address?

Lifestyle diversity and high immigration bring cultural and economic benefits but can erode feelings of mutual obligation, reduce willingness to pay tax and encourage a retreat from the public domain. In the decades ahead European politics itself may start to shift on this axis, with left and right being eclipsed by value-based culture wars and movements for and against diversity. Social democratic parties risk being torn apart in such circumstances, partly on class lines: recent British Social Attitudes reports have made clear the middle class and the working class converge on issues of tax and economic management, but diverge on diversity issues.

The anxieties triggered by the asylum seeker inflow into Britain now seem to be fading. But they are not just a media invention; a sharp economic downturn or a serious terrorist attack might easily call them up again. Progressives need to think more clearly about these issues to avoid being engulfed by them. And to that end they must try to develop a new language in which to address the anxieties, one that transcends the thin and abstract language of universal rights on the one hand and the defensive, nativist language of group identity on the other. Too often the language of liberal universalism that dominates public debate ignores the real affinities of place and people. These affinities are not obstacles to be overcome on the road to the good society; they are one of its foundation stones. People will always favour their own families and communities; it is the task of a realistic liberalism to strive for a definition of community that is wide enough to include people from many different backgrounds, without being so wide as to become meaningless.

Family matters • Melanie Phillips vs Polly Toynbee

JUNE 1996

26th April 1996

Dear Polly,

It feels most odd to be writing this letter to you across what appears to be a chasm of thinking that divides us. Odd because although we are both working mothers and for years were colleagues at the *Guardian*, we now find ourselves on opposing sides in this great debate about the family. We've never talked about it, nor have we written directly about each other's views. But I know from personal experience that this issue more than any other is a bitter battleground. What makes it so explosive is that the family is about not living as an atomised individual. Yet we live in an individualistic culture which sets as our highest goal the achievement of personal happiness. The family sets extremely inconvenient limits to that individualism. Most people do still aspire to a traditional family life, in which they marry and raise their own children. But more and more people are rejecting the limitations of loyalty, fidelity, duty and responsibility that such a life entails.

You know as well as I do the statistics showing the burgeoning rates of divorce, cohabitation, babies born out of wedlock and so on. These trends are to be regretted because of the damage they entail both to individuals and to our wider civic fabric. As these trends unfold, more and more cultural commentators—academics, journalists, pressure group activists, politicians—are becoming players, through their own lives, in the drama of the fragmenting family. Partly for this reason, the conclusion that "the family isn't deteriorating, only changing" is not reached from a dispassionate examination of the evidence. Time after time, I have observed ostensible policy discussions about the family which lightly camouflage a justification of personal experience. It is also a discussion which is—ludicrously—politically polarised, with defenders of the traditional family pilloried as reactionaries. True, people like myself wish to "conserve" certain values and structures without which I think we cannot live in a civilised way. But that doesn't make us any more reactionary than those green conservationists who wish to protect the physical environment from the depredations of selfish individualism. Being green is seen as laudable; but defending the *moral* ecology is beyond the pale.

My starting point has been the damage caused to most children (not all) by the fracturing of their home life. This seems to me undeniable from looking at schools, prisons or child psychiatric clinics. Of course some children from intact families have troubled home lives. But children from fractured families do worse in every area of life, relatively speaking, than those from intact families. This has been amply demonstrated in research studies here and in the US. Yet I have seen this evidence regularly distorted and ignored by people who usually turn out to be justifying personal circumstances about which they feel guilty. "What do these people want?" an angry academic once asked me about advocates of the traditional family. "Do they want unhappy parents to stay together?" Of course the traditionalists were correct as far as the facts were concerned, he conceded; but where did that get us? Nowhere! And why was everyone so concerned about the rights of the child? What about the rights of the adult? His unprofessional tirade only became intelligible once I discovered that he was going through a messy and acrimonious divorce himself.

This is essentially a struggle between adults who want the freedom to live as they please and the interests of children who need stability, attachments and security. The idea that marriage break-up is good for children because it brings conflict to an end is demonstrably false. I don't believe that all marriages must endure whatever the circumstances; some should undoubtedly end, in the interests of the adults or the children involved. I am merely alarmed that people have become far too casual about relationships, that commitment has been redefined as a transitory arrangement that can be ended for adult convenience, without reference to the consequences for children. Not all children from fragmented families are harmed, but the dice are loaded against them. I am concerned not just for them but for the civic values of our societies which are learned within the family. I believe that other people matter, that altruism is important and that duty and responsibility keep a civilised society together. These values are damaged where family life is too easily abandoned in the interests of individual fulfilment. We lost these values from political life in 1979. To me, the unbridled self-interest unleashed by libertarian Tory economics finds its unacceptable mirror image in the social libertarianism of the fragmented family.

You may have wondered over the past few years why I appeared to have become embattled within the liberal culture to which I still subscribe. This is why.

With best wishes,

Melanie

1st May 1996

Dear Melanie,

Over the years I have read your columns with growing surprise and dismay. I am not particularly interested in whether we can define the moral agenda as being essentially of the left or right, though I realise that your left wing past urges you to square the two. Tony Blair has laid such vociferous claim to moral and family values that I think it no longer a left/right question. Perhaps you are right to say that "moral decay" set in with Thatcherite selfishness. Perhaps the Tories are right in dating the "collapse of the family" from the libidinous 1960s.

I doubt, though, that couples entering on marriage full of optimism or couples enduring the pain of divorce are busy examining their ideological credentials. It's a bit of a low blow to accuse your critics of using specious arguments to justify their own bad marital behaviour. For the record, I am a widow and was married to my husband for 22 years; like you and your husband, neither of us was ever divorced. But you are right in one way: I do draw on my own personal experience of divorce and family to offer a less alarmist view of how families can still prosper after divorce so long as adults behave in a civilised way and treat their children well.

My mother was divorced twice; I was brought up with assorted half-siblings and we all saw each other regularly. My father and his wife visited often; whatever tensions there were, we were protected from them. We are still a close family, meeting twice a week. My children are surrounded by half-uncles, half-aunts and these relationships provide a rich and fulfilling family life for my fatherless children. I think I, too, had a rich and fulfilling childhood with a father and stepfather, neither of whom counted much in comparison with my all-important mother. In many families, fathers are all but absent, and most of literature and autobiography describes a distant relationship. The quality of life with the mother matters more.

Now you may say that it is more likely that a child will receive love and security from a stable family, with its two natural parents; you might be right. But what if you are? What on earth can anyone actually do to force people to stay married? Unless you propose some moral Cromwellian revolution I do not think you will persuade people to return to a life where marriage is destiny. Good people make honest mistakes and as a result make one another miserable in bad marriages. I regard their right to divorce as more important than many other civil liberties, from freedom of speech to the freedom to vote. Yoking the miserable together for eternity because of some youthful folly is a cruelty we will simply not return to. It was achieved in the past by economic and social pressures, above all by shame—of a kind I hope we shall not see again.

You suggest that those who divorce are feckless, reckless sexual adventurers who just want to have fun. The evidence suggests otherwise. The best research is from Professor Gwynn Davis's study of divorcing couples. He was struck by how much unhappiness people endured for how long before finally deciding to part. Divorce lawyers attest to the same thing. That is hardly surprising, since the penalties for divorce are high—a man loses his home and daily contact with his children, they both lose a lot of money and the woman struggles to bring up children alone. And yet they do it, because the alternative is worse. The myth of the "savable" marriage, to be rescued by Labour's compulsory counselling, is just political point scoring.

Marriage does not necessarily make good mothers, nor divorce make bad ones. In divorce there is a wide difference between children who do well and those who do badly, depending on whether they keep in touch with both parents, are protected from bitter rows and have enough love and security. Your energy would be better spent on finding ways to teach people to be better parents, rather than trying to get them to stay together. I don't see this as any kind of "liberal" ideology, just common sense.

Yours ever,

Polly

3rd May 1996

Dear Polly,

Divorce does not merely liberate people who are dreadfully unhappy in marriage. It also sanctions opportunistic behaviour, including walking out on the family in pursuit of personal fulfilment, leaving behind a devastated spouse and children, or breaking up someone else's marriage and harming someone else's spouse and children.

Divorce should be available for those whose marriages really are intolerable. But the problem is we're redefining intolerability to include the merely less than perfect. That redefinition has been fuelled in part by a failure to acknowledge the consequences of separation—financial, practical and emotional—for ourselves, our spouses or our children. It works for some; and good luck to them. But many divorced people say they now regret embarking on a course, the consequences of which they never fully appreciated.

You say you hope shame is a thing of the past. But I think people *should* be ashamed if they cause pain and misery to other people. Are you really saying that if people cheat on their spouses, abandon their children or help break up someone else's family they should feel no shame? That's tantamount to saying people should kiss goodbye to a moral sense. If we believe that moral codes are essential for a civilised society—and I'm sure you do—then we surely need to express our disapproval when people behave badly towards each other.

I don't want to force people to stay married. But marriage is being progressively written out of the script. I'd like people to list a rather more realistic set of factors in their personal happiness balance sheets when making their family choices. Maybe the fragmenting family *is* an irreversible social revolution. But it's being fuelled by the fantasy that people can have all the benefits of marriage without any of the hard work. You suggest we should emphasise not marriage but good parenting and children's need for love and security. But the care and commitment that are the essentials of good parenting depend upon the parent living with the child. To support children, we should support marriage—precisely the purpose for which it was invented. With best wishes,

Melanie

5th May 1996

Dear Melanie,

We see the world through very different eyes. I detect in your writing a rather grim moral fortitude, in which this vale of tears is to be struggled through with little expectation of happiness. Your words suggest that we can make something of this miserable world only if we do the right thing, so at least on our deathbed we can congratulate ourselves that the moral certainties have been fulfilled, pain endured and justice done to all. That is not ignoble, but it is not enough. It is not the view of life I would wish to hand down to my children. I would urge them to reach out for more, because so much more is offered—great happiness, even brief moments of unmixed joy, alongside misery and times when it all seems meaningless. If I were unhappily married you would, I suppose, urge me to put up with it for the sake of the children. Why? Because children draw much of their future view of life from their parents' values. But they would then feel the weight of a dour, loveless and quarrelsome marriage—a sad model for them to carry through life and burdening them with the sense that they should be grateful to their unhappy parents for staying together. Your intent, I suppose, would be to impress the same moral values on them, so that when they grew up they too would eschew pleasure for duty. They too would endure unhappy marriages. Even unto the tenth generation each would take up the chains forged by their parents.

In real life people rarely separate without great pain and years of unhappiness. Your picture of people casually sauntering out of marriages in search of sexual adventure is largely untrue. Most people are not compulsive ecstasy-seekers: simple contentment is hard enough to come by and people are grateful when they find it.

I still cannot see how these very personal decisions are a matter for public policy. But for all your hand-wringing, you never say what you want governments to do about it.

Yours ever,

Polly

6th May 1996

Dear Polly,

All I am saying is that selfish behaviour causes pain and sometimes harm to vulnerable people left in its wake, and therefore people should think twice before behaving in such a way if they want to live in a civilised society. Is that really so unacceptable to you? Clearly it is. It appears that for you, the duty to avoid harming others wherever possible is a passport to hell. I'm simply staggered by your equation of responsibility with personal misery. We all want our children to be happy. But are you really teaching your children that they should grasp happiness even where it may do actual harm?

I am concerned with the happiness of children and am very aware that for most (not all) children in voluntarily disrupted families, being brought up without a father, or with a succession of "fathers," is a recipe for maladjustment that can last well into their adult lives. That's the burden they bear. Sometimes such disruption is the lesser of two evils. But it must be avoided wherever possible. As for policies, I'm forever writing about how law or welfare does or doesn't support family life. But what the state can do is limited. People will only adjust their behaviour if their perspective changes about its likely consequences. This is hearts and minds stuff.

With best wishes,

Melanie

Dear Melanie,

Self-restraint and altruism are sometimes misplaced. Lifetimes can be wasted in self-sacrifice that turns out to have done no one else much good. Children are frequently not grateful for it later in life and it can leave the bitterest of empty nests.

All the same, we share much the same moral universe. We both try to instill into our children the same values: treating others well and recognising social responsibilities.

I like your confidence in the power of our newspaper pens to change hearts and minds. In the great cacophony of words, I wonder what effect we really have? I tend to think the job of journalism is to describe the world for our readers, rather than try to change their views.

What concerns me most is the failure of politicians to focus on solutions to the problems caused by divorce, which you rightly identify. How much hot air is wasted in parliament exhorting people to stay married—spitting in the wind of social change. They should be seeking practical remedies instead.

While you are right that most research shows that children of divorce do worse, you must also know that to compare them with children of happy marriages is meaningless; and to compare them with the children of unhappily married couples who stay together for their sake is methodologically impossible. But we do know that there is a great difference between those children who do very well and those who do badly after divorce. Policy makers should give attention to the far more fruitful business of helping all children of divorce do as well as the best. I think your grin and bear it message will go the way of Canute's feet and I'm tempted to send you a pair of galoshes.

With very best wishes,

Polly

Tories on the couch • John O'Sulllivan

OCTOBER 2002

Until a few years ago, if anyone had predicted a nervous break-down for the Tory party, it would have looked something like the scene in *Brief Encounter* in which an unhappy Celia Johnson rushes out of the station buffet to the edge of the platform just before the London express is scheduled to race past. For a few moments she hesi-tates—an emotional maelstrom in a fetching hat—then the express hurtles by and resolves the crisis for her. She returns to collect her packages and to take the local train home to her children and decent stick of a husband. Only the Rachmaninov soundtrack reminds us of the Freudian truth that, like all civilisation, home counties decency is founded on repression.

Emotional repression is rather out of style in today's Tory party. Even when ostensibly important policy questions are under discus-sion—as when Michael Portillo wanted William Hague to disavow Lady Thatcher's views on multiculturalism the week before the 2001 election—the participants lose all sense of proportion. Portillo's insis-tence that Lady Thatcher's mild critique would destroy the party's reputation for racial decency was followed by the lightest of media interest in what she had said but an avid curiosity in his attack.

Most of the time, the rows were not about policies at all but about internal loyalties and the presentation of policies. This high-strung debate continues even now. A high percentage of the pamphlets, essays, speeches, and articles in what is supposedly a debate on policy consists of sour denunciations of other factions in the party as morally repugnant, existential doubts about whether any form of conser-vatism is viable in a postmodern society and passionate but tellingly vague appeals for the total transmogrification of the Tory party into—well, into something quite unlike its present or recent self.

All of this, magnified by unsympathetic media, resembles less the "rethinking" that the party has conducted on previous occasions than a collective nervous breakdown, in which thinking of any kind becomes diverted into obsessive-compulsive acts of guilt and accusation. That the carnivore Tories of all parties should have been reduced to this state testifies to the psychological buffeting they have received in the last 12 years. Consider the following symptoms:

Repressed guilt. Their descent into breakdown began with the defenestration of Margaret Thatcher which prevented the integration of her achievements and ideas into the party's history and self-image in the uncomplicated way that Churchill's celebratory retirement permitted. Thereafter, she was both cause and symbol of the party's divisions. Her admirers were astonished at the party's coolness to its greatest peacetime leader. Anti-Thatcherites announced her political irrelevance with increasing desperation. She herself was able to command headlines with comments made at private gatherings. Successive party leaders have wanted to claim her achievements, with qualifications, and to establish their distance from her, provided it was not too far. This ambivalence is likely to continue, despite her withdrawal from public life, until the issues that provoked the rebellion against her recede into history.

Conflict avoidance. But those issues, especially Europe, remain points of division. The immediate post-Thatcher party leadership under John Major assumed that the party could be "managed" into accepting Britain's participation in ever-closer European integration. That judgement wrecked Major's premiership. Subsequently, the Eurosceptics gained control of the party at all levels, even including the shadow cabinet after the 1997 defeat, both because they reflected grassroots Tory opinion and because their predictions about how the EU would develop proved to be more accurate than those of the Major leadership. Major's resistance to this trend maximised internal turmoil. But the painful rows that ensued seem to have instilled a nervousness of open disagreement. Although the Eurosceptics now dominate the party, they seem strangely exhausted and reluctant to drive home their victory.

Loss of self-esteem. Not coincidentally, Europe was also behind the single greatest policy disaster that struck the Major government: its forced exit from the Exchange Rate Mechanism. Major had made

ERM membership the centrepiece of his economic policy even though it was clearly importing Germany's deflation and thus aggravating a domestic recession. He even won an election against the odds by assuring the voters that this was the tough economic medicine needed to restore prosperity. Yet when Britain was ejected from the ERM by the currency markets the British economy promptly began a rapid recovery. What "Black Wednesday" had done was to destroy one of the Tory party's most valuable assets—its reputation for financial and economic competence. This produced the extraordinary paradox that the more the economy prospered, the less credit the Major government received. The Tories were unable to explain why they deserved credit for the recovery based, as it was, on the collapse of the ERM they had declared to be a vital support. Having been re-elected in a recession in 1992, it lost by a landslide during a boom in 1997.

Sudden (but not unexplained) rejection. That landslide was a deep shock. Tories believed that they were the natural party of government in modern Britain. The collapse of communism, and the accompanying intellectual collapse of socialism, had fortified that belief. And, however odd it now seems, their complacency went deep. Of course, the drift of the Major years, the in-fighting over Europe, the serio-comic Tory scandals of the mid-1990s and the revival of New Labour had forced the more realistic Tories to accept that defeat was likely in 1997. Some even relished the prospect as an opportunity for recuperation, rethinking and revenge. But almost none of them had expected the scale of the defeat. It transformed them in one night from a government to a parliamentary rump. The shock of doubt and self-loathing has held them in its grip ever since.

Manic depression. William Hague's leadership was the next victim of this mood—both its despair and its moments of groundless optimism. In reality, the British people were largely uninterested in the Tories after they had been ejected from office. British public opinion had, in effect, fallen in love with Tony Blair and New Labour and it fluctuated solely in response to the successes and failures of the new government. This continued until the 2001 general election when the voters gave Blair what may have been the most unenthusiastic landslide in political history—granting him a second term in order that he might fulfil the promise to improve public services that he had self-evidently failed to redeem in his first term. But the Tories, used to being the centre of attention since 1979, interpreted the opinion polls and the 2001 result as reactions to their *own* exercises in policy-making and image redefinition. Instead of taking advantage of the public's lack of interest to invest in a long-term programme of policy reformulation, they fixated on the short-term impact of new initiatives. And when the voters returned Blair for a second term, they embraced the masochistic interpretation that the election had been primarily a rejection of themselves—and promptly fell to quarrelling over who in the asylum deserved most blame.

Project envy. At first it seemed that this dispute might be resolved quickly by the Tory leadership election. But the election was soon transformed from a conventional fight between pro and anti-Europeans into a curious contest between sense and sensibility; Michael Portillo advocating sensibility and everyone else his own version of sense. Party images are deeply imprinted in the voters. Almost irrespective of current policies, they feel that Labour is the party of sensibility and the Tories that of sense. It is almost always futile to attempt large cultural transformations of the kind seemingly advocated by the Portillistas. This scepticism was apparently confirmed when Iain Duncan Smith emerged as the new leader. Yet Duncan Smith too was soon talking up sensibility, and the party was being urged to be inclusive and nice, and to reject those who whored after the darker gods of class, nation, race or moral authoritarianism. A hunt for extremists to expel was duly launched. It is hard not to interpret this as a feeble imitation of the New Labour "project." Unfortunately for this logic, genuine political extremists had dominated parts of the Labour party until the New Labour revolution, whereas Tory "extremists" were either supporters of capital punishment (a penalty supported by two-thirds of the electorate) or refugees from an Ealing comedy. Some born-again Portillistas might have liked to include unreconstructed Thatcherites in a purge of extremists, but that would scarcely have been an imitation of the Blair project, which was rooted in converting Labour to market economics. The Blair project was itself an imitation of what Blairites believed to be the successful "ideological" project of Thatcherism. The Tories were reduced to imitating an imitation of themselves—and getting it seriously wrong. There is a postmodern novel in this somewhere, but not a manifesto.

E merging from these emotional traumas, gradually seeking to cope again, the Tory party under Duncan Smith seems to have decided on a three-pronged political strategy. It is determined to win the niceness stakes, to repackage itself as a party better suited to improve public services than New Labour, and to demonstrate that it is a party of normal people free of any "obsessions" with matters like tax-cutting and Europe.

Any political consultant, however, would have to advise caution on all these scores. John Major is still regarded as nice by the majority of voters. But his niceness was established at the expense of his fellow conservatives, who are regarded as nasty for disagreeing with him. Nor did he persuade the voters to go to the lengths of actually voting for him in 1997, since competence, authority and sensible policies are even more valuable qualities in a government than niceness—and Major's government lacked two and a half of them. If the Tory party is to recover, it must tackle practical problems in practical ways. Voters will be open to liking the Tories only after they have reasons to pay attention to them on other grounds.

Insofar as a policy of improving public services is an expression of such reality-based politics, it is a modest advance. Insofar as it is part of a cultural makeover of the Tory party, it is doomed to disappoint. Voters "know" at a fairly deep level that Tory MPs do not "care" as much as Labour MPs—just as they "know" that Labour MPs are not as patriotic as Tory MPs. The only thing likely to alter these deeply rooted perceptions is events in the real world. If a Labour government picks fights and wins wars for Britain, then it might challenge the Tory hold on patriotism—and Blair's decision to join the US in attacking Iraq might conceivably achieve that, if his own backbenchers do not spoil his efforts. In the same way, a Tory government might begin to reverse the party's "uncaring" image if it were to succeed in raising standards in health or education. But a Tory opposition cannot do anything so profound because it can only propose reforms—and talk is cheap in politics. Indeed, if improving public services becomes the main election appeal of the Tory party, it will have succeeded in the perverse project of concentrating voter attention on Labour's traditional strong points. A successful political party is one that concentrates the minds of voters on issues where it has a natural advantage.

For the Tories, those issues historically include opposition to government waste and over-regulation; tax reduction and support for private enterprise; defence and patriotism. If they have temporarily lost the issue of economic competence, that should encourage them to stress some of the others, such as patriotism—which, in current circumstances, equals "Europe." Europe has the additional advantage that it enables the party to exploit not only patriotism but also opposition to government waste and over-regulation (not to mention outright fraud in the EU). Hardly mentioning such a central issue as Europe is far more "obsessive" than dealing with it straightforwardly. Exactly the same applies to tax cuts and over-regulation. For the Tories to allow themselves to be morally bullied by the media and New Labour into avoiding the precise issues where the voters think them most competent or trustworthy is simply silly. And if they coolly decide that some of these issues are no longer productive of votes, then they need to seek new issues where the right has a natural advantage.

To a significant number of Tories, however, all such arguments are no longer the stuff of politics. They have taken the nation's pulse, detected a growing warmth in the blood, and proposed a more emotional style of politics. Here what matters is not getting the right policy on health, but getting the right words on it—words that will persuade people that you are at one with the more relaxed, libertarian, multi-ethnic culture of modern Britain. This is the message of Portilloism. And although Portillo's politics of sensibility was squarely beaten by the rival versions of sense offered by Duncan Smith and Kenneth Clarke, he seems in defeat to have converted the victor to his cause. Apostles of Portilloism now hold the high ground in central office.

Portilloism is one of those doctrines that becomes less intelligible the more one understands it. It is not so much a programme, more a disposition, an attitude, an openness to emotions, experiences, and other people that manages all the same to be extremely self-regarding. It is, in short, the Dianification of Toryism. This comparison is made explicit by Andrew Cooper in one of the best essays in a recent collection *A Blue Tomorrow*:

> In 1997 Hague—aptly representing the attitude of
> most Tories—showed that he simply didn't understand
> what Diana represented in British life, and therefore had
> no comprehension of how the nation would react to her
> death. Not getting the point of Diana was a
> motif for our cultural out-of-touchness. The revulsion
> of most Tories at the weepy pose struck by Blair—which
> brilliantly anticipated the unprecedented collective
> grieving that was about to follow—underlined the point.
> He got it. We didn't.

Except, as we now know, that collective grieving was not the majority view at all. It was rammed down the throats of many people who disliked the way it was exploited to attack the Queen and launch a cultural revolution. The revolution did not "take" and Labour's New Sensitive Britain retreated until, at the Queen Mother's funeral and the jubilee celebrations, it vanished altogether. Those fiestas of out-of-touchness revealed a *different* national self-understanding, a set of cultural sympathies that is both older and newer than the Diana cult—home and colonial, multi-ethnic yet accessible to the most traditional Tory, and based on institutions that expand to accommodate new arrivals—symbolised by the grandchildren of New Commonwealth immigrants singing "Land of Hope and Glory."

What is more, they involved emotions that point directly to Tory conclusions. They affirmed a distinctive national identity, the monarchy, a historical grand narrative that reconciles conqueror and conquered on terms of modern equality, the encouragement of continuing links between this country and its former colonies, and a political tradition of ordered liberty. It is hard to see exactly where the emotions celebrated in the Portillista canon lead us. What policies do emotional openness or "inclusiveness" dictate? When it comes to specific proposals, most analyses keep coming back to gender and race quotas for candidate shortlists. But the real significance of such ideas is not that they bring more strivers from minority backgrounds into the magic circle, but that they shift the selection of candidates from local people to the national political elite. What is then likely to happen is that identikit candidates, ethnically varied but politically uniform, will rise smoothly into parliament.

Portillista politics is large and generous-sounding, but missing the last page where all will be explained. One sometimes entertains the fantasy that Duncan Smith will lead a Portillo-esque party into the next election on the slogan "We must love one another or die," while Blair leads the nation in a chorus of "We don't want to fight, but by jingo if we do/We've got the men, we've got the ships, we've got the money too."

What these fanciful politics reveal is how the Tory party is still struggling to make sense of the post-cold war world. It is odd but true that the left adapted much more quickly to post-communism than the right. Social democratic parties won power throughout the west, apparently against the tide, by presenting themselves as more likely than the capitalist parties to administer capitalism compassionately. It is only in the last year that the right has been able to put together coalitions that win majority support without relying on the dying appeal of anti-communism.

Those coalitions have brought together three broad electoral groups: economic conservatives and classical liberals, both wedded to the free market; moral traditionalists; and patriots or nationalists (according to taste). Parties that obtain support from all three groups generally win elections; if they lose even one group, the left wins. Tories have no grounds for complacency towards any of the three.

Take nationalist voters. In recent years, mainstream conservative parties have lost the support of nationalist voters throughout the west.

Indeed, very often they have rejected such support in order to reassure "modernising" elites that they were untainted by xenophobia. As a result, in a large number of countries, new parties have sprung up to appeal to these scorned groups on such issues as crime, immigration and loss of sovereignty to supra-national bodies. A brief list of these parties illuminates the danger to mainstream parties: the Reform party in Canada, the Progress Party in Denmark, Pim Fortuyn's party in the Netherlands, the National Front in France, the New Zealand First party, the One Nation party in Australia, the Freedom Party in Austria, the National Alliance in Italy, and on and on. Their votes range from about 8 per cent (Australia) to almost 30 per cent (Austria). Their effect is to divide the right and allow the left to slip into power.

At first glance, the Tory hold on nationalists looks strong by comparison. In 2001, the United Kingdom Independence Party won only 1.5 per cent of the national vote—and 2.5 per cent on average of the votes in the seats they contested in the Tory heartland. But that was a high percentage for a fourth party in Britain and the UKIP vote will rise if the Tories prove half-hearted in defending British identity and institutions.

And there are some signs of this. As well as shrinking from a fight over Europe, the Tories have also been reluctant since the election to raise such issues as crime, immigration and asylum seekers. This seems to be part of their attempt to shed an image that is alleged to be racist and intolerant. But they may also believe these to be issues of the past when, in reality, they are the issues of the future. Immigration is a different issue from when Enoch Powell first raised it. In the hands of Pim Fortuyn, restricting immigration became a defence of liberal values against the intolerance of Muslim immigrants and the cowardice of the establishment. David Blunkett has responded to it in just these terms. And public concern about both the rising numbers and the possible cultural incompatibility of immigrants is rising.

As for moral traditionalists (aka moral authoritarians) they face two rebuffs: Tory policy is gradually drifting away from them on such matters as drugs and family values, and some libertarians argue that the party would gain ground if it were to drive them out altogether.

That last seems a counterproductive solution, for moral traditionalists bring more votes to the Tory party than economic libertarians do. Though it is hard to assess their relative electoral strengths directly, the operation of continental proportional representation gives us some clues: neo-liberal parties like the German FDP generally get something like 6 to 8 per cent of the total vote, which is considerably less than the percentage of moral traditionalists. A decent respect must therefore be paid to the latter's opinions even when they are rejected. It might mean, for instance, arguing the case for any limited drug decriminalisation not on grounds of liberty, but on the very strong evidence that the drug war on balance imposes heavier costs on society than the drug problem it affects, but fails, to solve. Besides, the moral traditionalists are often right and their voice is essential to the counterpoint of Toryism. The evidence is unambiguous that single parenthood is worse for children than a family that includes two parents. And although it may be politically risky to say as much in a society with so many single parents, a party that genuinely cares about the welfare of children must be prepared to tell the inconvenient truth.

Finally, economic libertarians are nervous that Toryism's philosophical preference for limited government and low tax rates has been sacrificed to a dubious political imperative of improving public services that is anyway uncertain of achievement. All in all, the party needs to keep its links to its core supporters in better repair.

But the Tory party's main problem at present is that it has nothing particular to say—or rather that it has nothing general to say. As Matthew Parris wrote a few years ago, Tories in the Commons pursue a variety of causes, but the causes do not seem to proceed from a common set of principles. You cannot give a short answer to the question: what do the Tories stand for these days? And that is partly because they cannot give a short answer to the question: what is it we stand against?

Two years ago in the Keith Joseph Memorial Lecture, I answered that question by suggesting that the Tories should stand against the gradual erosion of democracy that was proceeding below the radar screens of everyday politics. Serious then, this democratic deficit has widened as power has been steadily transferred from elected parliaments to non-elected courts, bureaucracies and NGOs.

Francis Fukuyama recently pointed out that one cause of the rifts between Europe and the US is their different view of the source of democratic legitimacy. Europe believes that it flows down from "a willowy, disembodied international level" whereas the US sees it as flowing upwards from "concrete, legitimate democratic publics." Yet as Fukuyama observes, this European view positively "invites abuse on the part of elites who are then free to interpret the will of the international community to suit their own preferences." We see this every day in the EU and in UN conferences like the recent summit on sustainable development, which make far-ranging commitments on matters which voters have never considered.

John Fonte of the Hudson Institute has analysed the ideology that unifies "the elites"—the academics, lawyers, NGO spokesmen, foundation executives, judges and international civil servants—who wield this unaccountable power. What Fonte calls "transnational progressivism" is a coherent body of thought which, while presenting itself as a development of democracy, is in fact an alternative to it. In place of majority rule in a sovereign democratic state, it substitutes permanent negotiations between ethnic groups; in place of citizenship in the nation state, it offers several citizenships in overlapping jurisdictions; in place of international law to regulate relations between states, it establishes non-accountable legal and regulatory bodies that deal directly with citizens and companies. It is a system in which power is located everywhere and nowhere and is therefore beyond the control of democratic parliaments.

This is a challenge to constitutional democracy, which insulates its beneficiaries from political competition and its decisions from challenge. There is little prospect, however, that New Labour will oppose these anti-democratic forces, or even admit their existence, because it is too closely enmeshed in the structures of this supra-national regulatory Leviathan to consider its real political character in a clear-sighted way. So the way is open for the Tories to make the defence of democracy the underlying theme that gives coherence to all their other policies. Not only that, defending democracy makes great political theatre since it boasts a stage villain in the political elites who seek to escape democratic constraints. It would provide constant opportunities for principled opposition—since once you are sensitised to the erosion of democracy, it seems to crop up everywhere. It would satisfy the very different tastes of nationalists (the defence of sovereignty), economic libertarians (opposition to international regulation), and moral traditionalists (distaste for the UN's moral agendas). Like the long opposition to Soviet communism, it would elevate the daily business of politics to a morally higher and more strenuous level. On top of everything else, it really is the right thing to do.

Too many students? • Alison Wolf

JULY 2002

In the past 15 years Britain has acquired a full-blown system of mass higher education. Over 40 per cent of 18 year olds are set to enter higher education and the target is for 50 per cent to do so by 2010.

This should make many people happy. British education has for years been haunted by stories of relative backwardness. In enrolment and graduation rates for higher education we have now overtaken most of the developed world. But people are not happy. Indeed, British higher education starts the 21st century in a despondent mood.

Over £8 billion a year of public money is channelled into higher education. We must be getting *something* from this, whether it is faster economic growth, a fairer society or more cultured citizens. But we need to clarify what it is that we are getting—and what, if things are going wrong, can be done about them.

The most important fact about university education is easy to spot. University pays—at least it pays the individual. On average, all over the world, graduates are the ones who succeed, in terms of pay and employment. The average earnings gap between those with some higher education and those who never finished upper secondary school ranges from over half as much again in egalitarian Scandinavia to double for the OECD as a whole, and more than double in Britain and the US. Further, throughout the world, a growing proportion of good jobs are now graduate only.

Yet there is no clear link between student numbers and growth rates, GDP per head or productivity. Switzerland, at the top of the income tree, has the lowest university participation rates in the OECD; while the US, also near the top, has the highest. Big increases in university numbers are at least as likely to follow periods of rapid growth as they are to precede them: Japan is a prime example.

Employers sometimes do need graduate skills, but often they simply use graduate entry as a way of "screening" applicants: that is, targeting people who have shown application, and are assumed to be in the top half of the cohort intellectually. This is rational behaviour for employers, if not much to do with the "knowledge society."

But if the 1.9m students and 172 full degree institutions in our new mass system are not about labour market skills, might they at least be making Britain a more open and equal society?

Selecting people on the basis of objectively measured results, not by connection and family inheritance, has been one of the great achievements of democratic societies. Surely one result of mass university education is to deepen this trend. It may mean that degrees operate as a entry ticket to many jobs that don't need them. But isn't this better than the alternative—management trainees who know a member of the board, articled clerks whose parents can pay the fees, promotion from the ranks dependent on favouritism?

As a victory for fairness, however, this one doesn't stand much scrutiny. In every developed country, expanding higher education has done less for equal opportunity than one might expect—whilst steering large subsidies towards the middle classes.

It is true that the absolute chances of a child from a working-class family attending university have increased substantially since the 1950s or indeed the 1970s—from about 1 in 50 to 1 in 20 to something close to 1 in 6. But the chances for a middle-class child have grown far more in that same 50 years—from about 1 in 10 to 1 in 2 for children with teachers or middle managers as parents, and from 1 in 5 to pretty near universal for the children of the upper middle classes. The result is a student body in which the proportion of undergraduates from non-manual homes is exactly the same as it was before either the expansion of "old" universities in the 1960s, or the creation of the polytechnics. This is in part because the manual working class now forms a smaller part of the overall population than in 1965; but it is mostly because of differential access.

Hammering away at our universities to admit more students from state rather than independent schools—as New Labour has been doing—misses the major point. This is not a case of haves against have-nots, with pampered middle-class kids on the independent school team and dedicated but disadvantaged working-class pupils on the state one. London-based politicians and journalists see it that way because in central London (and some other large cities) the middle classes have abandoned the state system. In most of the country, they have not—so what we actually have are two sets of applicants of which one (the independent schools) is *entirely* middle class and the other (the state schools) is *overwhelmingly* middle class.

The gap between middle-class children and the rest opens up well before university application. Children who make it into the sixth form with equivalent GCSE grades have the same chances of A level success, regardless of background. But the chances of getting decent GCSEs depend enormously on your family and local school. Only one in seven children from semi-skilled and unskilled homes gets two or more A levels; and with almost all of them already going to university, there is no reservoir of qualified, disadvantaged students to draw on.

Financial barriers *do* exist for poorer students, although they are far more about living expenses than fees. The British taxpayer spends over £4,000 per student per year on the universities' infrastructure and teaching staff. Fees were re-introduced by Labour in 1998 to augment this: even so, the most any student contributes to the cost of his or her degree course is around £1,000 a year. Moreover, although you would never guess it from the rhetoric of student leaders or the self-satisfaction of the Welsh assembly and Scottish parliament, the children of the poor do not pay fees; not even in benighted England. The fees that are so reviled are not paid by anyone with a family income under £20,000, after which a sliding scale kicks in. However, poor students are more averse to taking loans than middle-class ones: which isn't surprising, given their lack of financial cushion. Middle-class students often borrow up to the limit. So when Labour abolished means-tested grants in favour of (subsidised) loans, this did have a disincentive effect on low-income students.

But this underlines, once again, how the middle classes are the major beneficiaries of mass higher education. They are the ones who meet the entry criteria in vast numbers. They obtain higher education overwhelmingly at taxpayers' expense. They benefit over a lifetime, through far higher salaries and far lower risks of unemployment. They may even benefit through wider interests, wider experiences and the intrinsic benefits of study.

Thanks to the "cohort studies" which track British children born in 1958, 1970 and 2000, we are able to look at how the experiences of successive generations have changed. Between the first two groups—born just 12 years apart—there is a big difference. The incomes of the 1970 cohort are twice as strongly determined by parental income as they were for the 1958-born. A major reason is that education is itself increasingly tied to family income. So it is hard to argue that a mass university system is creating a fairer society. Indeed, the opposite seems to be the case: university helps to "lock-in" middle-class advantage in the career system.

Nor is Britain unique or even a particularly bad case of a general phenomenon. In France, entrance into the most selective institutions is dominated by students from a dozen or so lycées which cater to a metropolitan upper-middle class elite. In Japan's best universities, the percentage of students from high-income homes has increased since the 1960s. It is often claimed that top US universities are less exclusive than Britain's, but this is not true. Harvard offers generous aid to cover its annual fees of around £17,000 plus board and lodging of £7,000, as do other top colleges. But less than one in five US students from a poor background attends a private institution, while almost half of those from families in the top income decile do.

If today's universities are not a response to economic need, or a fair way of sorting out the most talented and deserving, then what has society received for its money? Have we, at least, got a more skilled population? A more cultured one? People who are better citizens? Maybe. There is evidence that university-educated adults are healthier and less prone to depression than their peers. They are also more involved in the community, more likely to vote and less cynical about political parties. On the other hand, the rise of the universities coincides with a period in which broadsheet newspaper sales have fallen and anxiety about "dumbing down" has grown.

More seriously, we don't really know what our new graduates will be like, because the findings cited above are for previous generations. And our mass system is not just the same as in the past, only bigger. After 25 years in which funding per student has more than halved and staff-student ratios have fallen from 1:8 and 1:9 in the mid-1970s to between 1:17 and 1:18 now, it is a *different* system. Of course, student experiences vary because British universities have very different histories and resources to draw on. The "old" universities have established libraries, attractive campuses, and affluent alumni. They can cross-subsidise their facilities from research funding, which is very unequally distributed. Research reputations are what underpins the hierarchy of British universities: the result is that Imperial College can ask applicants for three or more A grades at A level for courses in chemistry or engineering, while other universities are accepting two Es. This year the former polytechnics (in England), which only entered the research field since becoming universities in 1992, received about £64.5m of the £940m higher education funding for research. The big four—Cambridge, Oxford, UCL and Imperial—received £260m between them.

Research success buys better facilities and attracts better staff, but it also makes research, not teaching, the priority: and Britain surely can't need 100,000 academics producing largely unread journal articles. The learning of skills demands the teaching of them, even when the skills are such generic ones as "communication," or "IT" or "making presentations." The argument for expanding higher education is always expressed in terms of the skills students will acquire; not as a back route to creating and funding 200 research institutions. This is certainly the logic for the uniform way the teaching of students is funded: universities all get so much per student, depending on the nature of their course—more for medicine and science, less for humanities (which is why new universities average less per student than the old).

Less money per student means less time per student. This is a problem because what promotes learning is individual feedback on students' work. Worse, in a growing economy, people, unlike machines, get more expensive. If you raise academic pay in line with that in the economy the cost of expanding higher education rises dramatically. If you squeeze academics' pay then you buy time—but when they retire (as at least one in five will in the next decade), it will be hard to replace them with people of equal ability. A new lecturer at an old university now earns about the same as a new policeman.

So within universities an atmosphere of financial "crisis" is endemic. In England alone, at least 50 institutions of higher education are now running at a loss. Yet the cost of higher education goes on rising simply because of its expansion, creating endless spending battles within government.

So why doesn't government call a halt? Partly because expanding the universities turned out to be popular. Partly because it was taken by surprise. The first large university expansion in the 1960s was the subject of a government report (Robbins) which was widely debated, carefully implemented, and followed by a period of stability. The growth of the late 1980s and 1990s was less well conceived. For example, one key change in the Treasury funding mechanism, allowing universities to expand in response to demand, produced growth in student numbers which took government by surprise.

However, policies have also been the result of two beliefs which are deeply implanted in the modern state and which act as obstacles to clear thinking about what universities should be. The first is the belief that educating more people will somehow in itself raise economic growth rates. The second is the belief in "free education." This slogan has powerful resonances in democratic societies. It is easy to whip up indignation at the idea that young people might be excluded from university by the barrier of fees and debt, with the subtext that this marks a return to the class-ridden past when money, not merit, opened doors. Labour's somewhat egalitarian attempts to chip away at the middle-class welfare state in higher education is all too easily caricatured as its opposite.

The argument that education is a universal entitlement, and should be free at all levels to anyone, has had an enormous impact on higher education's development, not least because, when joined to a mass system, it guarantees low funding per student. This impact has been particularly evident in the countries of continental Europe; and, as Britain has acquired a mass system, our universities have moved much closer to the European model.

European universities are large, state-run and funded at a uniform level, with a commitment to egalitarian provision. Uniformity has advantages—no Oxbridge-style rows about access—but obvious disadvantages too. Large public systems demand standardised recruitment and salary conditions—and their size means those salaries will be low. With uniform pay and conditions, you get an excellent scholar here, a dedicated teacher there, but no possibility for institutions to build up a critical mass of excellent staff, top-class research facilities, and a global reputation. And European university systems are nationalised industries. Consequently they devote large portions of their time to relations with the public agencies and politicians.

As British higher education has ballooned, higher costs and greater public visibility have brought more detailed political control here too. Centrally established bodies now inspect internal procedures, lay down "benchmark standards" for degrees, provide ring-fenced grants for government initiatives, and monitor the composition of student bodies. The cost in academics' time and motivation is high.

If our mass university system were doing an effective job of enriching us, or promoting social justice, then one might argue for accepting the burden of centralised uniformity, and the loss of excellence, as acceptable costs. But one can make no such argument. Should we, in that case, continue towards increasingly centralised, highly subsidised and largely uniform mass provision provided by a low-paid workforce? Do we have an alternative?

The main alternative is to opt for a model based on competition, private funding and inequality—but also of innovation, scholarship and world-class research in the best institutions. Such a system can certainly be combined with a level of teaching quality in all institutions which is no worse than students receive under the uniform model. But this is a difficult approach for democratic politicians to select. It is one thing to inherit a highly diverse system of public and private universities, as the Americans have, and quite another to encourage divergent funding in a de facto nationalised one, against a backdrop of political opportunism and voter anger.

The US now boasts the vast majority of universities with any sort of global reputation. It dominates the Nobel prizes in science and economics, and attracts the world's best academics and graduate students. Creating such universities is incompatible with central control, and requires freedom for universities to set their own agendas, to hire their own staff at salaries they decide, to compete for students—and, above all, to set their own fees. Fees have to play a large role in funding. They are the only way, in a mass system, to secure high levels of quality; and they recognise the fact that a university education is, first and foremost, of benefit to individuals.

The simplest option for Britain would be to edge towards a more explicitly two-tier system—a mass publicly funded system with a part-privately funded British Ivy League on the top (with plentiful assistance for poorer students). This requires only modestly steady nerves; the difficult decision was made in the 1990s, when the Labour front bench accepted the need for fees. Enrolment figures have, since then, failed to plummet (contrary to many predictions); and since elite universities' graduates earn more than those from other institutions, politicians can surely argue that they should pay more for the privilege too.

But an "Ivy League" plus the rest sounds uncomfortably like the old system of grammar and secondary moderns, and it would need careful handling to avoid a political backlash. It would also mean relinquishing control in a way that governments find hard to do, even when it is in their interests to.

If, instead, we carry on as we are with increasingly uniform mass provision, and low funding per student, we will lose any universities which can claim world class. We will also lose many of the foreign students currently attracted here. That won't matter to the world at large. One huge, competitive, world dominant system may be all humanity needs to keep research and knowledge generation boiling—and we have that already in the US.

Should we, the British, care? Yes we should. Carrying on as we are means spending vast sums on institutions that have uncertain economic benefits for the country as a whole; yet cannot offer the sort of high-quality education provided by their older, smaller predecessors. We will not be doing much for social justice, though we will be subsidising a desirable private good: and in so doing, drawing funds away from schools and other social programmes which can help to improve equality of opportunity. We will have lost some great institutions, the creators and guardians of high culture. And we will have done this because we failed to ask ourselves what mass higher education is for.

Afghan in the dock • James Fergusson

MAY 2004

Gulabuddin was always the likeliest of the three arrivals from Afghanistan to make a mess of his life in London, although none of us could have predicted how spectacularly. His depression should have been lifted by the success of his recent asylum appeal. Perhaps it had been—perhaps his subsequent behaviour was a last spontaneous act of *joie de vivre* before the arrival of his wife and children. Yet what he did was so illogical, so stupidly risky, it was hard to avoid the conclusion that he was still not quite right in the head.

I didn't know him well. I was only connected to him via his cousin, Mir, my interpreter and fixer from the days when I worked as a freelance journalist in Afghanistan. I had helped Mir gain asylum in Britain three years earlier. His work for me and other western journalists, notably Lionel David of the BBC, had put his life in danger. I thought that we westerners collectively owed him at least that much. He was clever, resourceful and spoke good English—a fine example of a well born and well educated Pashtun. So it wasn't too long before he established himself and settled down in a smart east London council flat. The complication was his family.

In the summer of 2000, a year before the problems began, two of Mir's brothers and his cousin Gulabuddin had without my knowledge smuggled themselves into England in the standard way, arriving at Dover in the back of a truck. Mir was thrilled. As with most Afghans, family was sacred to him; he lived through it and for it. The thought of seeing his relatives again had sustained him through many lonely nights in this alien city, and if he could not return to them, then they would have to come to him. I felt ambiguous about the arrival of the newcomers. On the one hand I understood that eventual family reunion was the likeliest, and perhaps only, means by which Mir would ever be happy again. On the other, I inwardly groaned at the memory of the home office paperwork and court appearances I had undertaken on Mir's behalf. The thought of repeating this dreary cycle in triplicate did not appeal.

Unlike Mir, the newcomers spoke little English and struggled to adapt to their new life—particularly Gulabuddin, the eldest of them. Back in Afghanistan, he had been a respected professor of mathematics. Here, however, he felt less than nothing. He pined for the wife and three children he had been forced to leave behind, and sank into despondency. I had seen him slobbing around Mir's flat, which he seldom left. His uncertain mental state was exacerbated by what had happened to him back home. The Taleban had applied electrodes to the soles of his feet, and beaten him so badly that he still passed blood in his urine. At one stage he had been locked in a partially flooded cell with a rotting corpse for company.

I was in my office in Mayfair when Mir rang.

"I don't know what to do. It's my idiot cousin. He's done something ... werry stupid and he is in prison now. The police arrested him and he gave a false name. James, I am so ashamed. I can't tell anyone."

It seemed that Gulabuddin, without telling his cousins, had been making some extra cash by minicabbing around the east end. On the previous Friday he had picked up a passenger from a wine bar, a young white female, who was now alleging that Gulabuddin had "done things" to her in the back of the car.

"What sort of things, Mir? What are we talking about here—sexual assault?"

"Something like this," Mir muttered.

"You mean it's more serious? Did he rape her? What did the police say?"

"He says he never did it. He says that she was leading all the time and that he just followed."

"But the charge is rape?"

It was rape. I began thinking furiously what this might signify—for Gulabuddin's own future, for the future of his wife and three children, for the chances of the family's reunion, anywhere, ever. If convicted, would the home office seek to deport him? It seemed a reasonable bet. Even if he were allowed to stay, his name would surely be added to the police register of sex offenders. There would be no chance of his working as a teacher. There was also the little matter of what several years on the sex offenders' wing of a British prison might do to him.

Could he really have raped someone? He was a gentle man, but also powerfully built. He had not seen his wife for over two years. On a summer's night with an attractive white woman in the back of the car, probably drunk, perhaps appearing to be available—who was to say he had not succumbed to a moment of male madness and done something terrible?

I was sure that his young cousins were incapable of such a crime. They were more disciplined, more saturated in the strict mores of their Pashtun upbringing. They understood the risks of misbehaving in Britain, the fragility of their status here. Gulabuddin was not focused. He was bored and frustrated. The secret minicabbing sounded like a desire for independence and a chance to get away from the claustrophobia of Mir's flat. The fact that he gave the police a false name sounded ominous too.

"I am so angry with him," Mir continued, with shame in his voice. "I don't understand why he didn't go to a prostitute if he wanted to do this. I didn't want to tell you. But yesterday they moved him from the police station to some other place. Pent … Penting something. A big prison for proper criminals."

"Pentonville?"

"Pentonville, yeah."

"Who else knows? Have you told your family?"

"Only my little brother Musa. I can't tell my father. It would kill him. Do you know the penalty for adultery in Afghanistan?"

It was stoning to death, of course. And nowhere were the injunctions of Shari'a law more zealously or literally followed than in modern Afghanistan. Worse still, the Shari'a law punishments were decreed by the Muslim clergy—and the head of Gulabuddin's family was a senior Shari'a judge. This was already a personal disaster for Gulabuddin, even if he were ultimately acquitted of rape in an English court.

I recalled a conversation I had had the year before with Kahar Walji, a solicitor specialising in asylum in Dollis Hill. His words suddenly seemed eerily prescient. He had, he said, handled 3–4,000 Afghan asylum cases in the previous five years. Since he was generally an asylum-seeker's first and only contact with the English legal system, they usually came back to him when they got into trouble with the police. Yet in the whole five years that he had been dealing with Afghans he had handled fewer than a dozen serious crime cases.

"They are good citizens. Very law-abiding," he said, leaning back in his tilting chair. "They assimilate well. They are the most adaptable people."

"What about the criminal cases?" I asked, perhaps expecting him to mention involvement in heroin smuggling or the funding of terrorists.

"In almost every case the charge has been sexual assault," said Walji, and he didn't doubt the reason: "It's the media's influence. They see western women on television—and they get the wrong notion. They think women here are loose and … asking for it, if you understand me." His sexual assault clients were also of a type: "Waiters, minicab drivers—I've had two of those—they are often in jobs that bring them into a lot of contact with women. Especially drunk women. They think, 'she wants me to squeeze her breasts.' And so sometimes they try it."

"What's the defence? Do you try to explain the culture gap to the judge?"

"That never works. The judges always say the same thing. The driver of a minicab is in a fiduciary position vis à vis his passenger, with a duty of care. It's a principle of English common law. They take a dim view of anyone who breaches that trust."

The only light in the darkness was Mir's conviction that his cousin had not raped the woman. He had spoken to Gulabuddin in a police cell before his transfer to Pentonville, where he swore by the beard of the Prophet that he was innocent.

Gulabuddin's version of what happened was this: it was one o'clock on a Saturday morning and he was driving the woman to her home. On the way she made several mobile phone calls to a man on night shift at her office. Although Gulabuddin's English was still poor, he understood just enough to work out that she had a crush on this man, and that the man wasn't interested. But she had plainly drunk a few glasses of wine, and persisted with the calls. Halfway home she ordered Gulabuddin to make a detour to her office. She intended to visit the man she fancied, on the pretext of retrieving her umbrella. In the office car park she made a further telephone call, but she was refused admittance to the building. She then remained in the back of the car for over an hour, lovelorn and maudlin, fretting to the half-comprehending Gulabuddin about her uninterested lover.

Eventually, Gulabuddin suggested that she should either get out or let him take her home, but she refused to move. So he got out and opened her door, whereupon she invited him to join her on the back seat. He regretted it deeply now, but he had allowed her to pull him in. He had no idea why she had phoned the police once she had finally got out of the car, although he suspected it was a ruse to gain attention from the man who had spurned her.

"And you really believe him?" I asked Mir when he had related all this.

"James, I made him look me in the eye," he replied. "He swore he did not do this thing."

"I'd like to hear it for myself. Can we see him?"

It took a fortnight to arrange the visit to Pentonville prison. Mir's arrival in the visitor centre on the Caledonian Road was shadowed as usual by Musa. We filled in forms and progressed through a gloomy maze of bullet-proof doors, emerging at last into the cavernous visiting hall. The inmates sat at tables arranged in long rows, dozens and dozens of them, most of them black, the mostly white prison guards patrolling the spaces in between like teachers in an exam hall. The prisoners were separated from their visitors by a crenellated partition that came no higher than the waist, making it easy to lean across to kiss or touch a wife, girlfriend or child. There were moments of intense intimacy going on all around.

Prisoner number JM4810 was dressed like all the others in a grey tracksuit and red nylon bib. He rose to greet us with a faint smile, murmuring something as he shook my hand in the formal way, placing his right hand on his heart and ushering me to sit. Mir indicated a vending machine and asked if I wanted tea. Even here they were clinging to their traditions like mariners to a shipwreck.

"What I want," I said, "is to hear what happened from Gulabuddin. Right away—all of it, in detail."

Gulabuddin's story took almost an hour to tell. Mir had to pass on everything in English, and there were frequent interruptions. Musa could not stop himself from haranguing Gulabuddin, jabbing the table with a forefinger. Ordinarily this would have been considered impertinence towards an elder and Mir would have brought him to heel like a naughty puppy, but he didn't intervene because he was furious with his cousin too. By the end of his narrative Gulabuddin could barely raise his eyes from the table.

Yet his version of events was impressively consistent with the one related by Mir, and he gave no indication that he was guilty of rape. There was even a plausible explanation for why he had given the police a false name. His Afghan driving licence entitled him to drive a private car in Britain, but insurance companies did not cover mini-cabbing on such a licence. His solution was a classic example of Afghan resourcefulness: he falsified a British driving licence, turning himself into an anonymous London Pakistani: Zahid Amin Khan, place of birth Rawalpindi, now resident at the patently false address of 88 Noor Shah Avenue, London SW18. It later emerged that 18 of the 32 drivers at E–Z Cars, the minicab office that Gulabuddin worked for, had done the same as he had.

I pushed Gulabuddin hard on the details.

"Why did you let her pull you into the cab like that?" Mir translated. Gulabuddin simply shrugged.

"Was she pretty?"

The answer was long and evidently lyrical. An almost nostalgic look flitted across Gulabuddin's face.

"He says she had hair the colour of dates," said Mir.

"Of dates. And then what? Who undid your—you know. Your fly." Emphatically: "She did."

"And what was she wearing? A skirt, or trousers?"

"Trousers."

"And did you pull down her trousers?"

"No. She did."

Suddenly, a violent scuffle broke out nearby between guards and another visitor, over an attempt to pass drugs to an inmate. Gulabuddin broke off from his story, musing about how much heroin he had seen in the prison. "All from Afghanistan," he added with the ghost of a smile. He was probably right: at least 80 per cent of all heroin in Europe originates in Afghanistan. Pentonville, one of

Britain's busiest prisons, is hopelessly overcrowded, and lacks sufficient guards. The previous week this shortage had caused a riot on D wing, and it had taken an emergency draft of 350 police officers to coax them back inside.

"Tree hundred fifty," Gulabuddin exclaimed, strangely impressed by the Met's big turnout. It was only slightly encouraging that he was at last starting to learn a bit of English.

"I hope you weren't involved."

"No. I am on R wing—R for Rumi," he added, rolling his r's preposterously.

I caught the reference, and smiled. His cousins often quoted Jalaluddin Rumi, a 13th-century mystic and poet who was born in Balkh, where the family used to go on picnics. Rumi spent most of his life in modern-day Turkey, but the Afghans regard him as one of their own. His verse displays a mixture of sensuality and spiritual rigour that is distinctly Asian in character. It is laconic, almost aphoristic, and seems to lose little in the translation from the Persian. It is also perfect prison poetry, what Mir called *qaza-ye ruh*, sustenance for the soul.

> Weep like the waterwheel,
> That green herbs may spring up
> From the courtyard of your soul.
> If you wish for tears,
> Have mercy on one who sheds tears;
> If you wish mercy, show mercy to the weak.
> The world is a prison and we are the prisoners:
> Dig a hole in the prison and let yourself out!

Visiting time was soon over, and the brothers parted from their cousin without much apparent emotion. As we stood to leave, however, Gulabuddin said one thing more in an insistent voice.

"He says he wants to stand trial because he knows in his heart that he is innocent," Mir translated tonelessly. "He says that England is a fair country with a strong legal system and that justice is sure to prevail if Allah wills it." Gulabuddin's faith in the justice system was worryingly naive. He was going to have to work hard to prove his innocence, which would be far from obvious to a typical English jury. It was clear that he hadn't begun to understand how much trouble he was in. But the conviction behind his assertion of innocence was impressive, and in the end I was persuaded he didn't belong in Pentonville. So out in the prison car park I offered to stand bail for him.

The solicitors had warned that in the unlikely event of bail being granted it would probably be set at around £10,000. It was an impossible sum for the brothers to raise, but I had enough savings to risk it, and the money would be recoverable after the trial, providing Gulabuddin turned up for it. When Mir had arrived in London I had undertaken to help him only in the event of emergency. This surely qualified. I was certain that Gulabuddin's best chance of resuming a normal life was to get out of prison as soon as possible. But Mir looked at me blankly before turning away and conferring with Musa. Musa listened, then answered emphatically in the negative.

"Don't you want your cousin to get out of here?"

"Musa thinks they should throw away the key and leave him in there forever," Mir answered for him.

"You can't be serious."

"Not forever—maybe just for two weeks more. He's not showing proper shame for this thing."

"You mean you think he did it?"

"Not the rape," Mir shook his head impatiently. "The adultery. I told him, if he had done this in Afghanistan he would be under the ground by now."

"But he's not in Afghanistan any more!"

"Adultery is serious," Mir continued, "werry serious. The Prophet (peace be upon him) says there are only three circumstances in which a Muslim must be executed. If he turns his back on Islam and his community; a life for a life; or if a married person commits adultery. It is even the same for you. Did not Allah say to your Moses, thou shalt not commit adultery?"

"Not on pain of death," I protested. It was amazing how easily Mir could still switch into mullah-speak.

"Gulabuddin has dishonoured me in London," he continued. "He has dishonoured my family. He has gone minicabbing without telling me while Musa has worked hard in a pizza shop."

Musa nodded self-righteously.

"Man, your prisons are too soft. He's sitting around in there watching television all day."

There wasn't that much television available in Pentonville, but Mir's broader point was unarguable. I had seen for myself the medieval conditions in Afghanistan's jails. Overcrowding, stifling heat, stygian darkness and beatings were the norm; and all of this family had experienced them at first hand.

"It may be better than in Afghanistan, but this prison is still not a good place to be," I said. "Shouldn't we at least lodge an application for bail?"

Mir was unmoved. "Two weeks more," he said.

Six weeks went by before Gulabuddin was granted a bail hearing. It was held in a courtroom at the Old Bailey. My doubts about the police-nominated lawyers were confirmed when their appointed barrister failed to show up. A substitute arrived at the last moment with a fold-up bicycle under his arm, panting for breath, his bald head sweating. He knew almost nothing about the case, and couldn't even pronounce Gulabuddin's name. Yet the judge responded as well as could be hoped. I stood to attention in my pinstripe suit and he looked me up and down, visibly surprised by a bail application in a case such as this.

"May I ask," he said, "how you know the accused?"

He was prepared to grant bail, a small victory in itself, but there was one problem. If Gulabuddin was bailed, he could not return home because his flat was too close to that of his alleged victim. The judge would not countenance the possibility of a chance meeting between the two of them ahead of the trial. But up popped the bald barrister.

"My lord," he said, "I haven't actually raised this possibility with Mr Fergusson, but you will see from the papers before you that he lives several miles from the area in question, on the other side of London. Would it be acceptable to your lordship if the accused were to stay with him pending trial?"

"Well, Mr Fergusson?" said his lordship. "Would that proposition be acceptable to you?"

I squirmed, conscious of Mir watching from high above in the public gallery. "I mean, yes of course, in principle, your honour, although … I can foresee certain difficulties with that solution." I lived in a one-bedroom flat, and the trial could be months away. Did I really want a depressed Afghan refugee sleeping on my sofa for all that time? But the judge saved me.

"No," he said, with a wry shake of the head. "It isn't fair to impose a condition like that on the bailor. Come back in a week, and if you can provide an alternative address then I will grant bail as appropriate."

"Thanks a lot," I said to the barrister afterwards.

"Yes, sorry about that. But it's a good result. I never thought he'd get bail, it's rare in rape cases. Must have been the suit you're wearing."

Mir knew plenty of people who would willingly have put Gulabuddin up, but he was reluctant to approach any of them because to do so would mean letting them in on a shameful secret. The potential damage to his family's reputation was a theme that he returned to again and again. In east London he had already circulated a cover story, telling inquirers that Gulabuddin had been imprisoned for minicabbing without a proper licence—a fiction that caused a minor panic among the local Asian minicabbing community. He would later tell his father in Pakistan that Gulabuddin had run over and killed a child, and risked a long prison sentence as a result. Theirs was a topsy-turvy moral universe, in which it was preferable by far to be guilty of manslaughter than of adultery. In the end, however, Mir had to choose between Gulabuddin spending several months more in prison or his immediate release. He finally saw reason, and after much deliberation selected a mild-mannered Tajik, a chef from Kabul whom he had once helped with some immigration paperwork. He swore him to secrecy, and the Tajik made a room ready for

Gulabuddin in his house in Norwood, southeast London. Bail was duly granted. I rode out to Stratford magistrates court to deliver a cheque, a trial date was set for December 2002, and Gulabuddin was released the same day.

The trial date gave the Afghans a goal to aim for, but there was no doubt that everything had begun to militate against the westward migration of Mir's extended family. Gulabuddin's wife and children could not come to Britain now, not with a crown case pending against him. It would be at least four months before normality resumed, even assuming that Gulabuddin was acquitted. The problem with this delay was spelled out by Anna Stein, an immigration lawyer who had previously helped the family. It was already two years since the last members of the family had left central Asia, and nothing particularly terrible had happened to the relatives left behind. The more time that went by, the harder it would be to argue their case for asylum to the authorities. The government was tightening its asylum conditions all the time. With the removal of the Taleban and the establishment of Hamid Karzai's regime in Kabul, the home office had just cancelled its policy of automatically accepting asylum seekers from Afghanistan —a policy that had lasted for more than 20 years.

The trial was slow to get under way once the day finally came. There were two false starts caused by the inadequacy of the Old Bailey interpreters. The first one, a young Kabuli woman who had been brought up in Birmingham, was too embarrassed to deal with the seamy details of a rape case. By the time the trial was over, six different interpreters had sat with Gulabuddin in the dock. Mir had hoped to keep the affair secret from London's Afghan community, but that hope looked more forlorn with every personnel change.

The trial began at the end of 2002 and lasted for five days. Lionel David and I had been recruited as character witnesses, which meant that we were unable to watch the proceedings until after we had testified, but to begin with, things seemed to be going well. We learned that the testimony of the complainant, Maureen Rivers, had been so poor that the prosecution counsel was visibly disheartened.

Maureen Rivers naturally had her own version of what had happened that hot summer night, but after close examination of certain prosecution documents it looked full of discrepancies to me. She now maintained that she had diverted the taxi to her office not in order to go and surprise the night worker she fancied (which was what she had told the police operator who answered her 999 call), but because she was alarmed by Gulabuddin's improper behaviour in the course of the journey. She claimed he had used the phrase "I'm going to give you some loving"—which was implausible, given Gulabuddin's poor English—and that she had gone to the office to seek refuge. But if that was true, then surely she would have got out of the car at once upon reaching her destination. Instead, she sat in the car for more than an hour, chatting to the scarcely comprehending Gulabuddin and phoning the unrelenting man in the office on her mobile. Lenora, our defence barrister, had the phone company records that showed the exact time and duration of the calls. She called him six times in 45 minutes. Furthermore, the man in the office who had received those calls had testified that there had been no cry for help from Maureen, no sense that anything was wrong. She just wanted to see him, and he had told her to go home because she sounded drunk.

Gulabuddin's description of her hair—the colour of dates—had led me to picture a slim, pretty secretary, but there was nothing particularly attractive about the real Maureen. Even Gulabuddin now struggled to explain why he had been tempted.

"I was just an animal," he murmured, shaking his head with shame. At the end of the day of her testimony, Lionel and I took Gulabuddin and Mir out of the Old Bailey for a pep talk and debrief. As we crossed the road, a pressman ambushed us and began to take photographs. There had been a big press pack waiting by the entrance all week hoping for a shot of the defendant in a high-profile trial in another courtroom, but I had hoped they wouldn't bother with us. I held a bag in front of Gulabuddin's face, but the photographer skipped backwards down the street ahead of us, his camera twisting and turning, a ritual bizarrely familiar from television news.

"Can they really do that?" asked Mir once we were installed in the sanctuary of a nearby wine bar.

"I'm afraid they can in this country," I said.

As Lionel brought them a Coke each I noticed that Gulabuddin's hands were shaking uncontrollably. He hadn't slept at all the previous night.

"He's not looking well," I commented to Mir.

"I know. He's ashamed of this thing now," he said.

"You will go easy on him, won't you? He's got to be on form to-morrow."

"Don't worry. He knows he is in big trouble. He knew from the moment he saw the size of this place," Mir said, jerking his head towards the Old Bailey.

But Gulabuddin messed up his testimony. At the recess the following day the prosecution counsel emerged from the court-room with a spring in her step, and Lenora with a doleful face. "I can't understand it," Lenora said. "He was so good at explaining himself in my chambers. I'm putting the same sort of questions to him as before but the answers are just completely different."

So different, indeed, that she wondered if there was yet another problem with the interpreter. Mir had been in the public gallery, and also thought this might be the case. It was a Friday. When the court reconvened after lunch, Lenora voiced her concerns and requested the trial be adjourned until Monday so that she could have the tran-scripts independently verified over the weekend. The judge agreed with reluctance, evidently irritated by the delays that the interpreter problems had already caused. But the translation service company that checked the transcripts could find nothing wrong, and the judge's irritation turned into a suspicion that the adjournment had been a delaying tactic by the defence. Nevertheless, when the trial recom-menced, it did so with yet another nervous interpreter in the dock.

We didn't dare tell Gulabuddin that the press were now on to the story. Lionel had checked the news agency wires in his office at the BBC and found an item headed "Afghan minicab driver pounces on fare." The newspapers hadn't picked it up yet, but further shameful publicity was now a strong possibility.

Worse, the judge and jury, already detained for longer than they should have been in this trial, had begun to turn against Gulabuddin. In court he was almost as inconsistent as Rivers. He mumbled ineffectively, cowed by the glare of the jury. I could see how the shame he felt might easily be mistaken for guilt. He stammered that he had been prevented from resisting his passenger's advances by the pain in his back, a line of defence that Lenora had never heard before and would certainly have advised against if she had. His back was strong enough for him to get in and out of a car, after all, and his defence depended on proving that whatever happened between him and Rivers had been consensual. There was another problem. The judge latched on to the fact that Gulabuddin had been driving a minicab under a false identity. Lenora tried to argue that her client was not on trial for this lesser crime—indeed, the police had not even charged him with it—but the judge insisted that it shed light on the defendant's moral character.

Never mind the fact that Gulabuddin's car was properly taxed and registered in his real name. "This man admits that he has been living a lie," said the judge. Why should the court believe anything he said?

By the time I took the stand, my heart hammering, the defence was drowning. At the start of the trial Lenora had confidently addressed Gulabuddin as "professor," but she was now referring to him as "Mr." Her confidence had taken a knock, and the prosecution smelled blood.

"Mr Fergusson," the beak-nosed prosecutor said. "You told us that the defendant was a professor of mathematics in Afghanistan; who told you that?"

"My knowledge of him as a professor predates this case by many years," I replied, startled.

The prosecutor smiled thinly. "But you do not know that yourself, in any event?"

"I've never been taught by him in a classroom, no."

The fact that Gulabuddin was a maths professor and not the freeloading asylum-seeking peasant of popular imagination was supposed to be one of his defence's strong points. Britain's state schools were infamously short of teachers. Didn't that make him precisely the kind of immigrant that the country needed? At Lenora's prompting I gave the court a long description of Gulabuddin's background, the importance of status to his family, the harshness of the *Pashtunwali* moral code and the respect that was traditionally accorded to women. The point was to demonstrate that an Afghan brought up in such circumstances and in such a culture was very unlikely to have committed rape, and that even adultery represented a gross aberration for him. But my exposition was quickly turned against the defence.

"So if somebody like this man committed adultery, he would know that he was committing a grave sin?" the judge suddenly interjected.

I had to agree.

"I asked you the question because you put him on moral high ground. On his own account he has abandoned that in this country."

"If it was consensual sex, I don't see why he has, necessarily," I said, struggling on. "He is not in Afghanistan … the moral ground is a different place in Afghanistan than it is here, is it not?"

This was bad. You could hear the jury's sharp intake of breath. The judge gave me a piercing look. "He has abandoned the moral high ground in this country, and that does not surprise you?"

In that moment I felt certain that Gulabuddin was already a condemned man. I left the witness box feeling like some sort of social delinquent. How extraordinary, the judge seemed subtly to have implied, that this man even knows the accused.

Lenora summed up the defence well. She had a kind, expressive face, and she believed Gulabuddin to be innocent. "There are a lot of stereotypes involved here," she said. "Asylum seekers, minicab rape, the fact that the accused is an Afghan. Don't be influenced by these." She homed in on the many discrepancies in Maureen Rivers's testimony, and made the jury reread the relevant passages in the transcript of her 999 phone call. When Mir turned around from the pew in front and asked, "Is it good?" I felt confident enough to give him a thumbs-up sign. But the judge's summing-up that followed seemed to cancel out Lenora's good work.

"Sympathy plays no part in your considerations," he told the jury. "Put out of your mind any form of sympathy for the girl and what she says she has gone through. Also put out of your mind any form of sympathy for the defendant because he comes from a good family, and so on and so forth."

By calling Maureen Rivers a "girl" he had already begun to tip the balance in her favour. On and on it went in a similar vein, with Maureen Rivers's version given an hour out of the hour and a half that the summing-up lasted: the innocent "girl" versus "the man who had been living a lie."

The prosecution contended that Gulabuddin had lied about his back pain, lied about the precise location of the attack, lied about being pulled into the back of the car. Ultimately it was a case of his word against hers; and in court, her word had evidently been every bit as plausible as his.

Medical examination of the pair proved that sex had occurred. There was little firm evidence to support rape, yet the judge seemed to linger over the medical report's most suggestive passages, so that Mir buried his head in his hands. His words seemed almost calculated to shock. He said the complainant had internal abrasions that were "consistent with sexual intercourse of a rough or energetic kind." There was fresh bruising "consistent with rough sex in a confined space." He also mentioned how the doctors had found "a milky secretion deep down inside her," even though the complainant had said she thought "her attacker," as the judge was at this point describing Gulabuddin, had not ejaculated. Once again it seemed pretty clear what the judge thought, even though the "excessive whitish creamy discharge" that the doctors found on the complainant's vaginal wall was suggestive to them of thrush.

The jury's verdict was imminent. Gulabuddin was allowed to accompany us to the canteen only if escorted by a court employee, a grandmotherly solicitor's clerk. In the canteen, Gulabuddin began to cry, a single hot tear that rolled down his cheek and splashed on the table. Mir looked away.

"Aw, come on dearie," said the clerk, giving him a tissue. "It might never happen."

Gulabuddin turned his back to blow his nose and remained facing away, his head down and his shoulders heaving. Mir sat upright, shook his head impassively and said nothing. "Oh dear," sighed the clerk. "It's always difficult before the verdict, I know." She was a wise old bird whose chatter about the countless rape trials she had seen might have been obtrusive but was actually comforting.

"I was raped myself once, you know," she added matter-of-factly. "Gang-raped, actually. A couple of Italians slipped a Mickey Finn in me drink when I was on holiday ... I was a girl at the time, not even eighteen. I didn't know anything. They caught the bastards but that was a proper rape, not like this business. I think the law's very tough on men these days. It's such a shame. He's a very nice man," she added, nodding at Gulabuddin's silently trembling back.

They found him guilty. The jury had elected the foreman I'd hoped for, the kindly-looking older man with the cardigan and glasses, but obviously I'd read him wrong. In fact I'd read all of them wrong.

"Guilty," he said in a sonorous voice put on for the occasion. The tension in the courtroom deflated at last. Lenora rose wearily and pleaded for sentencing to be deferred pending a psychiatric report (which was reluctantly granted) and applied for bail pending that examination (which was peremptorily refused).

"Very well," nodded the judge. "Take him down."

I caught Gulabuddin's eye for the final time and shrugged hopelessly. His face was white and there was a wild look in his eyes, and he stumbled as he turned so that the Securicor guards stepped forward to support him by the elbows. He lost all self-control at their touch and began to struggle desperately, clutching on to the banister as he vanished down through the floor, weeping openly now. There was a gothic clanking of keys and bolts being slid back and a final, animal howl of despair that was cut short by the slamming of a heavy metal door. The jurors looked momentarily shocked by this Faustian descent. But the judge quickly reassured them.

"I must thank the jury for their time and good work in this difficult case," he said pleasantly, "particularly the jury member who I know has been anxious to get off on holiday."

The jury beamed back their gratitude, as pleased as a patted dog. Mir twisted around in the seat in front of me and shook his head. He said: "My father will say that I did not look after my family properly."

I thought of the old man in Peshawar, still under the impression that his nephew was in trouble for running somebody over. It was going to be difficult to keep the truth from him now. Then the judge announced that he wanted to deal with what he called a "side issue"— the ease with which the defendant had been able to drive a minicab without insurance. The press box was packed, and I suddenly understood that the judge wanted to publicise this case. He expounded jovially on the subject of photo-ID driving licences and the *Evening Standard* duly ran an article the following day, the first of many to come in the national press, complete with a photograph of Gulabuddin in his seedy suit. "Refugee posed as cab driver before raping woman in car," ran the headline.

"Merry Christmas," said the judge as he dismissed the jury. The ruination of Gulabuddin was complete.

ARTS & LETTERS

"I'm sorry, miss. But you're meandering clockwise at a
counterclockwise exhibit"

Young British Artists • Matthew Collings vs Brian Sewell

APRIL 2002

22nd February 2002

Hello Brian,

May I start by saying what a valuable cultural figure I think you are?

We have been asked to consider a question which I think is probably the wrong one: "does contemporary British art have anything to say which is not just about itself."

We have also been asked to address issues of conceptual art; the way people criticise or celebrate art forms without being familiar with their provenance; the forces of commerce, celebrity and patronage; and the difficulties of art criticism.

The fact is that modernism and post-modernism are self-referential. There is no point crying about it; this is the art that society produces.

In the case of art criticism and the problem of judging whether a thing is good or not, I believe that, because art is a structure and a system, the more you look at it, the more you see something in it. You find things in the system that have a value. This requires a leap of faith. But if you're hostile to the idea of it, then you are not going to get anything out of it.

As to conceptual art, it only lasted a few years, from the mid-1960s into the early 1970s, and was largely about criticising the premises of modernism. It elevated figures like Marcel Duchamp, who was already dead by 1968, but whom it valued for being intellectual rather than visual. Conceptual art is really a 1960s thing, it's connected to anti-war movements, civil liberties, being against the establishment and so on. Within a few years, it became a stale academic type of art and faded away. But then conceptual art in the Ivan Massow sense—where you just say any nonsense that comes into your head in order to get attention —returned as the catch-all title for the art we now have in the spotlight.

This new type of art is multi-form, and has a broader range of subject matter than the old 1960s type. But although it has a dubious kind of "popularity" about it (whereas the original didn't have any popularity at all) it is still part of the modernism/post-modernism system, in that it is self-referential. What mostly separates it from modernism is its adherents' lack of belief in anything at all.

This new art's "ideas" aren't really ideas at all. It is popular because it's scandalous, and scandal is something our age finds fascinating, though in a distanced, emotionally vacant way.

All this relates to the issue of what people find to celebrate or hate in current art. There is nothing in art that says it should be popular, or that it gets better when it is popular. And its meanings don't change because it's popular, they just get discussed in more distorted and ulti-mately meaningless ways. People have to try to think for themselves, which requires an effort. Personally, I think Tracey Emin's blankets are good. They have a kind of pleasing, lopsided composition. I never think much about what the words on the blankets say. I find the senti-ments slightly boring, because too familiar and banal.

Regarding patronage, commerce and celebrity, the first two are not of much interest, since nothing changes there. The last is important because it's a peculiar horror of modern life. And, again, Emin comes into it, since, regrettably, she has become the most popular sign of the decline of something that might originally have been creative (that is, the whole young British artist phenomenon) into something that is too easy. The point of art is that it should make demands on you.
Best wishes,
Matthew Collings

PS I read your review of the Royal Academy's "Paris" show the other day and found it both hilarious and accurate. It's a hideous, deflating exhibition, and you have to marvel at the curatorial skills that could make some of the greatest artists the world has ever known seem depressing.

24th February 2002

Dear Collings,

Flattery may have got you where you now are in terms of television, publication and celebrity, but with me the parsnips remain unbuttered.

Your letter is unworthy of you, tedious, vapid, flatulent and contains no substance into which the terrier may sink his teeth. You make a play with knowledge (does the term modernism, and its multiple derivatives, have any meaning now?) to reassure those of the Serota tendency that you know their jabberwocky and are, perhaps, on their side—I say *perhaps* because you have learned your television lesson well and, like most presenters, know never to commit yourself, always to sit on the fence while making a show of enthusiasm.

You were brought into this world by Peter Fuller, editor of *Modern Painters*, to be his court fool, his jester, and a merry joker you have proved to be. The trouble is, that neither the readers of that now benighted journal, nor you, realised that your only purpose on its pages was as a foil, a leavening, for Fuller's peculiar polemics. Television, a medium that when it concerns itself with visual art is run entirely by ignoramuses, then took you up and made you what you are.

In your way you perfectly represent the current state of art criticism. Twenty years ago I thought that the collective noun for art critics should be a creep or crawl, so evidently did they sing for their canapés and Chablis, so necessary to their incomes were the payments for their laudatory essays in dealers' catalogues. Twenty years ago, much in cash and kind was earned by compliant critics prepared to lick arse, but things have changed; the cash and carry aspect of the business has run down, the volume is much reduced and the *quid pro quo* much cheaper for the patron. The demand is less for services than for absolute loyalty to the tiny clique that now runs the visual arts in Britain. This means that those who are critical of Serota, for example, are excluded from the radio programmes of the BBC and all television channels. You do not belong to the generation of critics who benefited in kind, but you are very much the obedient contemporary critic, watching your back and never blotting your copybook.

I raise these points in response to your claim that art is a structure and system into which the more one looks, the more one sees. That art itself is either a structure or a system in any deliberate or even art historical sense, is to me an incomprehensible notion; perhaps you mistake art for the systems in which it is confined by ex-polytechnic theorists, none of whom has an aesthetic bone in his body. This is like confusing Wren's ingenious scaffolding for St Paul's with the cathedral itself. As for your assertion that the more one looks, the more one sees —as in Rothko's shallow canvases, no doubt—the only possible response to that is that you have swallowed Roger Fry's pathetic instruction (in his 1934 lecture on American art) that we must look at all art in "a state of passive receptiveness … ready to vibrate in harmony with it." Neither vibration nor harmony comes easily to Jack Russell terriers, but the Richard Corks of this world are adept at it.

And there's the rub. Vibrating critics are incapable of criticism. They unquestioningly accept as art all that is given them by the Arts Council, Serota, a tiny bunch of canny dealers, and now the Royal Academy. Most of them, having no grounding in art history, know nothing of what they see in historical exhibitions—witness the Royal Academy's "Genius of Rome," in which half the paintings catalogued as by Caravaggio were copies, replicas, ruins or nothing to do with him, yet all got equally extravagant billing. How many of our critics are able to argue with the National Gallery's chronology of Cuyp's paintings, and how many are qualified to comment on their over-scrubbed condition? How many, moving nearer to your chosen period, could make informed judgements of two current exhibitions in which it is rooted, the "Fifties" show at the Barbican or the "Paris" show at the Academy? Most comment on those from younger critics revealed abysmal ignorance.

Critics are lazy. I read with dismaying frequency their rehashes of press releases. They are no better than the jurors in *Alice in Wonderland*, treating every word as if it were dictation. "Your duty," Marina Vaizey lectured me for my failure to review an utterly trivial exhibition, "is to signpost, not express your own opinion. Tell us it's there, describe it. That's all."

But it is not all. When as a boy I questioned the literal truth of transubstantiation, my parish priest said, "Bring everything to the bar of your own judgement," and I have done so ever since. It removed the cornerstone of my faith, but was better advice than any given me later —and it answers the point you make that art "requires a leap of faith." It does not. Rembrandt's self-portraits require no such leap, nor Velazquez's roped and naked assistant posing as Christ in the National Gallery, nor Goya's joyful cannibal, nor Picasso's lugubrious *Demoiselles*; only such presentations as the Emin bed and Hirst shark require your leap—and with these you see the Serota dictatorship in action, the faithful welcomed and the sceptic scourged. Serota does not permit debate; his response to adverse comment is, "He would say that, wouldn't he?" If Serota had any confidence in the material he promotes, he would invite me and David Lee, the editor of *Jackdaw*, on to the jury of the Turner Prize, certain that he could convince us with intellectual and aesthetic argument.

You raise the spectre of popular opinion. Lord, save us from it. If the National Gallery were in the hands of popular opinion it would be filled with the works of LS Lowry and Beryl Cook. We need the Reithian view, always pitching above the heads of the ignorant so that we can draw them on (not below, so that they feel comfortable). I want those who know nothing about art to be fed with caviar and oysters, so to speak, to acquire taste, to feel the heart stop at a sight too beautiful to bear, to sense a thrill as powerfully as a kick in the stomach, to weep at a work of art as they might at a performance of *Tristan und Isolde*, to experience the catharsis of Stendhal syndrome. Hirst, at an exhibition in the ICA some years ago, hinted that he might one day produce art with such power, but he has fallen by the wayside; Emin, however, showed no promise and fell into the ditch. That we know anything of either is nothing to do with art, but is entirely due to the manipulations by which adventurers become and stay celebrities. You must beware of this yourself.

Yours avuncularly,

Brian Sewell

26th February 2002

Crikey, Brian!

You say all the anguished stuff in the first half of your letter is something to do with your shock at the notion, in my letter, that art might be "a structure or a system." I meant modern and contemporary art. But, of course, any art is part of a system, otherwise what would your job on the *Evening Standard* be? Could anyone do it, even someone who thought Beryl Cook should be in the National Gallery? What system of ideas and meanings do you draw on to make an educated guess that some Caravaggios in the Royal Academy are "fakes or ruins," if not that of the baroque?

I don't think it is shocking to say that modern art is self-contained. You don't either, since you criticise that art for not being self-evident, whereas you see pre-modern masterpieces as available to all. Apparently, though, they are not completely available, since you feel Reithian lectures are necessary to educate the ignorant.

Modernism is the term that describes the broad cultural movement out of which contemporary art has grown. "Conceptual art" is an art-critical term from late modernism, describing a type of art that values the mind over the eye, and is connected to an ideology of social revolution. It comes from the 1960s. It is misleading as a term for the generality of current art, not least because of its connection to an anti-establishment ethos (no art today is anti-establishment); but it is mainly inaccurate because the type of contemporary art it is supposed to describe—Turner Prize art, or what you call Serota tendency art—isn't focused upon the mind or the intellect. It's not primarily visual either but, contrary to your fumings, it's not actually anti-aesthetic. It's just that the aesthetic is usually daft, not serious.

Terminology matters, even if you choose to dispense with it. Much of the stuff in your art column is rather striking and weird, by the standards of everyday usage. Heaven forbid this should merely be to draw attention to yourself. I assume it's there to say why art is important. In your letter you use words like "joyful" and "lugubrious" in connection with cannibals and cubism; and you relate Stendhal syndrome (a tendency to swoon from an excess of feeling in front of artworks) to early Damien Hirst. This is all unusual and jarring, as is your 18th-century pomp manner in general, but it is amusing, and you get your points across with it.

Many people mistakenly assume they know what Renaissance art is. They are familiar with it from Christmas cards, but they don't know the symbolism (whether it's flowers and skulls, or squares and circles in the composition) they don't know the religious and mythological meanings, the patrons, or the historical background. It takes a bit of learning to know those things. Should they do more work? Yes. But they are lucky because they have got you, with all your connoisseurship, to do that for them.

Yet one thing about contemporary art is that it doesn't need traditional connoisseurship. In fact, it leaves the connoisseur with hardly any power-role at all, because it doesn't depend on a special knowledge of dates and attributions and so on, nor on knowledge of a period which is not our own. It only requires familiarity with a set of codes. These codes are to do with broad ideas of content and, for the past 15 years or so, they have increasingly overlapped with pop culture. That is, the forms may be fragmented and unconventional (though they have gone on to become conventional), but the subjects are familiar to all.

You feel it's you against the trendies, but I'm constantly told off for being rude about the trendies, too. I complain about their faith in zombie-like language. Knowing the codes of contemporary art doesn't require any great cleverness, so it is annoying when a pseudo-clever language is used to discuss it. The purpose of this language is only to intimidate people. I also complain about their recent obsession with literalism and a low grade form of narrative—that is, the return of cloying Victorian illustrative morality painting, only in the form of installations with politically correct homilies instead of paintings with old-fashioned Christian ones. This is the case with Mona Hatoum's room-size replica of a *mouli legume* in Tate Britain. It is supposed to symbolise profound alienation (because it's so big), only with intimations of the domestic and the feminine (because it's a vegi-mixer). And the same with Jeremy Deller's more light-footed work: actors dressed up as bobbies beat up actors playing miners, and the result is supposed to express involvement with politics.

My points about the art world in my journalism are not as conveniently schmoozing as you imagine. You go on about a conspiracy keeping anyone critical of the director of the Tate off television. But I publicly criticise him and, as you have noticed, I'm on television. Tate Modern is a silly, woolly, empty-headed place. I like art to be serious and playful but Tate Modern is solemn and trivial.

When I like some contemporary art it is because it has successes which are not usually discussed. Behind the pretentiousness of Rachel Whiteread's plaster-cast objects, there is sometimes genuine elegance and loveliness. And it's similar for, say, the different types of black-culture stereotypes in Chris Ofili's paintings—they are funny rather than profound, but his handling of something decorative and ordered actually *is* profound. Occasionally I like this art when it fulfils its own cliché and does it with a bit of flair, as with Martin Creed's lights at last year's Turner Prize, which I thought was the right choice to win. Creed's piece summed-up and parodied the general public's fury at modern art.

Modern art is not a "system" in the sense of an organisation being run by somebody powerful. It's a system because there are frameworks and rules, which make it possible to judge one thing against another. You already know this, in terms of earlier art. You know Goya can be better appreciated the more you know what you're looking at. Understanding more about him and the period he worked in, understanding why there's a cannibal in a Goya painting, makes it more meaningful and marvellous than otherwise. It might even bring on a bit of the vibrating harmony you hate reading about in Roger Fry (you hate it because it's about seeing the same virtues in modernist abstract art as in pre-modern art).

To recognise a system is not to praise everything in the system. One needs to know what the grain is to be against it, or one's opinion isn't of much value. I have always assumed it's an amusing and effective pose on your part when you appear not to be bothered with the intricacies of contemporary-art gabbling, or with the trinkets that are produced for the gabblers to gabble about. Again: I think you're good. Don't whip me just because you want to be whipped back. Stop being a sado-masochistic nutcase and accept a compliment when it's paid to you.

If I wanted to find a weakness in my own argument, I might say "this is the art that society produces" is complacent. Perhaps one ought to change society. In fact, my support for serious, non-ironic abstract painting by artists who are outside of the trendy spotlight (I have recently organised an exhibition showcasing this work) is an attempt to put a spanner in the works.

I know you are an anti-abstractionist. You don't know what to do with it. You can't take the meaninglessness. I'm not particularly mesmerised by Mark Rothko, one of America's most revered abstract painters, and I don't disagree that what is usually said about him is sentimental and unthinking. But your idea that he is always shallow is not a serious observation, but just a reflex twitch. You imply that Fry wrote something (which you find absurd) in 1934 about Rothko's abstracts. Yet at that time, Rothko hadn't really become Rothko. He was still painting nudes and bathing scenes, was very little known even in New York, and was still using his real name, Marcus Rothkowitz.

Much of your letter is feverish. However, you appear to want to say something about aesthetics, not all of which I disagree with. My real disagreement is that the things you yourself appreciate as aesthetic were not always transparently, gorgeously so. History made them so. One finds something aesthetic because one has worked to understand it. That is, it is part of a system that can be learned.
Looking forward to your next go,
Matthew

Come off it, dear boy,

Surely you should not so late in the day attempt to explain modernism
and its derivatives to anyone, least of all to me. It has for far too long
been meaningless and is now merely confusing. I know that Roger Fry
was as ignorant of Rothko as of so many things; it was merely that, in
the context of American art, he commended the business of vibrating
in harmony, and I see that now, not without mischief, as the necessary
exercise for all who seek enchantment in the grim Rothko room of
Bankside. You should read more Fry (a penance, I know), because his
Bloomsbury dominance explains so much wretched British criticism
now, evident in the vibrations of Richard Cork, Charles Darwent and,
occasionally, Richard Dorment.

The trouble with most art since the second world war is that it has
been, when claiming to be modern, merely repetitive. The dynamic
has gone out of it, as with Christ when his robe was touched too often
and deliberately. Duchamp, the joker, the intelligent iconoclast, was
dynamic. Kienholz, who has reasonable claim to have invented both
the installation and the modern written concept (though that goes
back to the neo-Platonists of Quattrocento Florence), was, and indeed
still is, dynamic. Beuys, perhaps the most sincere of late 20th century
artists, was unfailingly dynamic. But the rest was all the flaccid,
gutless, crassly derivative rubbish of the Serota tendency. Compare
the 20th with the 15th century—the latter a hundred years of astonishing advance from late international Gothic to young Michelangelo,
the former a descent from cubism, futurism, expressionism, some
lively forms of post-impressionism and the wild imaginings of surreal-
ism, into a morass of stale third-hand ideas and tenth-rate
presentation by idiots who knew nothing of their recent forebears,
and could not spell "aesthetic" let alone comprehend the meaning of
the word. We are told that they break the barriers of art, that they
bring sculpture down from the podium and painting from the wall,
that they are artists because they think of things and are lauded by
Serota for being cutting-edge when, in truth, they are the vandals of
our age.

Serota is a circus barker for the freakish and grotesque, the fraudulent and phony, and above all the boring and pretentious. If there is a system, Martin Creed's Turner Prize exposed it. Creed got it for being in Serota's regular employment at the Tate, not for the second-hand idea of switching off the lights. It is the determination of Serota, Saatchi and the Arts and British Councils, much assisted by lottery funding, to promote one narrow aspect of visual art at the expense of all others that constitutes the system. The Royal Academy is doing its best to join the bandwagon, so too are the British Museum, the V&A and even the National Gallery with its fatuous patronage of the lunatic and incompetent Kitaj and other nincompoops. The system even extends to handing the curatorship of exhibitions to artists in this sacred circle—Klee diminished in the hands of Bridget Riley, for example. It was a system identified in its infancy by Bryan Robertson in 1965: "The System," he wrote, treating it as a proper noun, "stands for promotion, for publicity, for continual change, for a stepped-up rhythm of production and for a show-business attitude to what used to be a solitary and unpublicised activity." This is still the case, but with the apparatus of television and such presenters as yourself and Melvyn Bragg to lend the system weight. The loss of face and financial investment that must follow telling the truth are too terrifying to contemplate. In pop music, fame and fashion are allowed to come and go, but visual art is a tangible commodity with second-hand value, and a rumpled bed cannot, at £150,000, be as readily discarded as Will Young, Pop Idol of the moment, will be once his moment has passed.

You say that connoisseurship is irrelevant, and that I should not expect to use it when I review exhibitions. This would reduce me to the level of Richard Cork, a glove-puppet of Serota's establishment. I cannot regard art as a mere phenomenon to be reported with the dispassion of a scientist, which is, in some sense, how I see your work on television—entirely without judgement of quality.

In ignorance of Saint Makarios, who forbade all forms of flattery, you pay me compliments but you do not understand me. You say that I am anti-abstractionist: I am not; I own abstract paintings and sculpture and seek the abstract in representational paintings. You say that I do not know what to do with abstract art: but I do, and I give way to no one in enthusiasm for Mondrian's *Boogie-Woogie* paintings. You say that I "can't take the meaninglessness": not so—it is the pointlessness, the wearying lack of wit and quality that I cannot take; but give me a great Kupka and I'll talk you through its meaninglessness with more enthusiasm than I could ever muster for Van Dyck. Does this really suggest a deliberate structure or system in my criticism? I vow that I go to every exhibition without a prejudice and am, in the light of revelation, prepared to change whatever view I hold—as I have with Beuys, Duchamp and Ellsworth Kelly.

I am amused to discover that we are both enshrined in academic history—"Compare the cultural strategies of Brian Sewell and Matthew Collings" was a recent MA question at the Courtauld Institute. A structure, a system, and now a cultural strategy—whatever next?

My parish priest used to sign his letters, "Yours, in friendship"— I am inclined to do the same.
Brian

4th March 2002

Dear Brian,
You claim that I don't make value judgements. I do. I just don't say it in the way you want to hear it.

With art, one tends to find what one is looking for. If you're looking for something that isn't on offer—like ex-ICA chairman Ivan Massow complaining he can't find craft skills in conceptual art—then very likely you will feel that there's nothing there. Which is to return to the original point—stories that art might have to tell which are beyond art itself. I have just seen an exhibition by Colin Lowe and Roddy Thomson which was very eloquent about modern life and as dynamic as anything by Joseph Beuys. It included a work about Lowe's father. From the grainy enlarged photo of him used for the work, he seems to be a hospitalised basket case, an alcoholic. Dressed in pyjamas, with a towel round his head, he has a Bin Laden look. There was beer-and-winemaking equipment at the back of the installation, with tubes of red wine connecting, hospital drip-like, to the dad's body. What were the associations? A taboo about alcohol, an ill patriarch and another, more threatening patriarch. It was a story about sickness; quirky, witty and concise.

In a previous age you might have found these qualities in a play. It might have been done as a narrative. But it wasn't, because the story-tellers are artists. The themes were spelled out in a visual way: the aesthetic came from it being right.

I agree that, compared to the Renaissance, this is a depraved and idiotic cultural period we're living in. But I still want to look for what is serious in my own time.
Best wishes,
Matthew

5th March 2002

Dear Matthew,
Like you, I long to be thrilled, moved and sated by a contemporary work of art; unlike you and, at twice your age, with a far longer view, I am filled with pessimism unrelieved. Apart from your final, optimistic note, your concluding letter makes little sense.

Art must be more than happy or unhappy accident, must not depend wholly on the whimsies of a "curator of interpretation" (the title given to the puppet at the Tate). You must not drag Ivan Massow into this argument, a poor deluded boy who knows nothing about art and even less about the art world. His only value here is the impatient honesty of his gut reaction—an honesty unknown in the work of critics who dance on the pin-head of contemporary art and have neither scholarship nor historical perspective.

In your second paragraph, you describe a commonplace of photography and video rather than an ancestral art form, and we have seen it a thousand times before—at £20,000 if it is by Bill Viola, £20 if by a student in any of our state academies, with not much to choose between the two in quality. Photography and video (ideal stuff for the provision of pretentious longueurs on BBC4 and Artsworld) belong on television, or with advertisements in the cinema, not in art galleries. You, I fear, have surrendered to the propagandists and now faithfully believe the One Commandment of Contemporary Art: "If a man declares himself to be an artist, then whatever he produces is necessarily art." I have no doubt that this is engraved over the door of your privy.

Affectionately (in my way),

Brian

Worst of England • Andrew Marr

JULY 2000

The survival of the novel is rather surprising. As a developing form the novel was pretty much exhausted a lifetime ago—by, say, 1922, the year in which *Ulysses* was published and Kingsley Amis was born. As with figurative painting, the "modern" novel would twist and struggle to find a way forward and then more or less give up. But whereas the visual arts turned to *new* forms—pop images, video and installations, the stuff of Tate Modern—the novel settled back into its early-modern or classical form and kept on going. Philip Roth's last three novels, for instance, *American Pastoral, I Married a Communist* and *The Human Stain,* are rich, high works of a completely traditional kind (silver age if not golden age); they would be completely comprehensible in terms of form, if not history, to a contemporary reader of, say, Emile Zola or Henry James. The experimental novels produced with such excitement by modernists—Celine, Wyndham Lewis, William Burroughs, the French new wave, Woolf, and so on—have gone nowhere.

Why is this? "Because they were all bloody unreadable," would presumably be Kingsley Amis's answer. That is not true and, in any case, the triumph of the conventional novel form is a standing refutation of the cultural pessimism that informed Kingsley Amis's curmudgeonly opinion. More likely, it is to do with the different markets. A Damien Hirst can become successful with the patronage of a single Saatchi, but a novelist needs to find hundreds of thousands of individual patrons in order to live well.

The truth is, the novel remains the handiest tool for millions of us to use when thinking about our lives and their shape—the novels of childhood, of early sex and sentimental education, of family and divorce, the novels of bereavement, old age and loss. Film rarely does this job. It does spectacle and horror, escapism and jokes, but not life. The novel's nearest rival is the television soap opera; it has bigger audiences but a vacant glossiness and a necessary absence of catharsis. No, the chances are that if you are averagely intelligent and educated you will think about your generation, and what is happening to it, through the eyes of serious novelists—John Updike, Ian McEwan, PD James, Alasdair Gray, Iris Murdoch—very much as the Victorians did. Because of this the novel is required to update its information; the surrounding furniture of music, sexual ritual, social atmosphere, political worry and fashion, everything from emails to Aids, has to be right for new readers to turn a page and think, "yes ... that's how it is now, for me, for us." The great novelists of the canon are essential for an educated mind, but we need the contemporary tellers, too. And the achievements of the latter—the reports they send back to the rest of us about how we're all getting on—shape our imaginations and choices too.

This is a long way of saying that novelists matter, more than journalists or film-makers, and is a prelude to the subject of this essay: the Amises. It was going to be an essay on failure, but it has turned out rather differently. Its origin was a semi-flip remark I made to the editor of *Prospect* a few months ago, to the effect that for me the two Amises were "the worst of England" and their half-century of snarl and sneer was the most interesting thing in recent literary life.

Some of this, at any rate, I still stand by. To attack Martin Amis's novels, as distinct from his dentistry, hauteur, alleged greed and so on, is to invite the wrath of a large protective shield of Martists in newspapers, literature and publishing. It's not done. But surely I am not the only person who has been sent by newspaper reviews to the latest great, wise, hilarious, life-enhancing Martin Amis novel, only to find myself consumed by nausea and boredom after a few chapters. Not all his novels, admittedly: *London Fields*, his best by far, and *Time's Arrow*, a single good idea sustained right through with manic intellectual energy, will stay on the bookshelf. But *Money, Success, Night Train?* Utterly brilliant phrases, sentences of pure verbal genius, fine paragraphs, so-so pages and, taking them all in all, sloughs of despond, every one of them. As for *The Information* ... a stinker, no?

Kingsley was a different matter. Nobody with any ear for the English language could resist *Lucky Jim* or *The Old Devils*. But the succession of women-baiting, self-consciously bufferish performances (the very worst were *Stanley and the Women* and *Russian Hide and Seek*) which came garlanded with squeaks of delight from the puff-merchants of the press, plus his apparently serious loathings of great contemporaries, foreigners, Jews and so on, put him beyond the pale.

What slightly spoils this diatribe, however, is that to prepare for it I went back to Kingsley Amis's novels and enjoyed myself more than was convenient for my purposes. *Jake's Thing*, for instance, famously rancid with misogyny, turns out, on re-reading, to be surprisingly tender in parts, and intensely moving on the humiliations of impotence. *The Old Devils* will last as long as novels do; but it is not the only brilliant treatment of old age—*Ending Up* is one of the most delicately tragic funny books I have ever read. And so on.

Then came Martin's memoir *Experience*, certainly the oddest but also one of the best books he has written. It has terrible flaws and jarring notes, but it is utterly compulsive too. Early on, he throws a pre-emptive punch at any mere critic. There is a good, structural reason, he writes, "why novelists should excite corrosiveness in the press ... When you write about a composer, you do not reach for your violin ... But when you write about a novelist, an exponent of prose narrative, then you write a prose narrative. And what was the extent of your hopes for *your* prose—bookchat, interviews, gossip? Valued reader, it is not for me to say this is envy. It is for you to say this is envy. And envy never comes to the ball dressed as Envy. It comes dressed as something else: Asceticism, High Standards, Common Sense ..."

This is, of course, mere bullying. The case of Martin Amis would not matter a tinker's cuss if he was not one of the finest prose performers alive. There are plenty of examples in *Experience*. His account of his father falling over on a traffic island in the Edgware Road (pages 338 to 339 in the hardback) is a masterpiece of funny-sad writing. So yes: envy. No one who relishes a sinewy sentence and a compacted block of thought, compressed and kneaded into surprising freshness, could resist the tribute of envy. The force is with him.

But that makes what he does with that force even more important. Yes: he has had a lot of rubbish written about him. But to imply that Martin Amis's talent should put him beyond criticism is nonsense on stilts, with a scowling mask and an ostrich-feathered hat.

In fact it is a little worse than that. You live your professional life in and around a public family. You have your media and literary friends —polemicists as powerful as Christopher Hitchens and James Fenton, many literary editors, about 5,000 admiring younger writers, your father's circles of poets and critics. As you say, you've been name-dropping ever since you first said "dad." You would not have grown and thrived without your great gift but none of the rest has exactly stalled the career, has it?

You have played your image alongside your novels: the tough-kid 1970s literary hooligan, the snooker lout, the charmed circle of brilliant mates, the private slang leaking into the books, the film star friends, the famous women. There has been a violently coloured penumbra around the actual books which has been, let's face it, part of the deal. Martin Amis is no Salinger, not a man to lock himself away in the forest. And now, in the memoir, we have further material thrust upon us: the Fred West connection, the lost-and-found daughter, the divorce and remarriage, the struggle with and then loss of the remarkable father. And it is all recounted in prose which, while thinned down with white spirit, is still close enough to the clotted writing of his novels for an idle reader to confuse fact and fiction. To turn around now, with injured innocence, and complain about media intrusion into your private life, about "how often my free will has been compromised by fame"—well, it's rather late in the day, that's all. Whatever Martin Amis's problem has been, too much publicity it ain't.

What, then? The problem is evasion, a cold obliqueness to life which is accomplished in the novels through bravura writing at the expense of closure, genuine catharsis or structure. The energy is intense but febrile, like an opera crammed with thrilling arias but without a plot, heroine or jot of real emotion. This would not matter much, perhaps—after all, nobody is obliged to read the books— except for the suspicion that the problem of Martin Amis is the problem of British men of his generation—many of us, anyway. Like his dad, he is good enough to represent more than himself; he is the message as well as the messenger.

Here is a crude proposition. Kingsley Amis was the worse man but the better writer. That, of course, is a generational judgement made by a 40-year-old. Kingsley Amis had the characteristic virtues and vices of British males of his time; he was still driven, even tormented, by the old British protestant work-ethic, but he was, as his son notes, a baby all his life. The self-pity, the mixture of spite against women and utter reliance on them, the morose hostility to outsiders, the blub-blub pessimism about his country, the conservative timidity in cultural matters, the booze-bottle as teat ... none of this is attractive, and it is ruthlessly self-exposed in his letters.

Kingsley Amis may have been a living caricature: the club-man who had little time for "abroad," the vigorous fucker and drinker who managed to feel oppressed by "the permissive society," the poet and prose-master who made much of his enthusiasm for dirty limericks and Dick Francis. But he was also somehow emblematic. His post-1945 England was indeed a country that had lost its way and its confidence, a nation of anti-modernists, of mildly resentful, hard-working, women-hating, culturally conservative men redeemed—some of the time—by their quiet, stoical courage and humour. Larkin, bleaker and more courageous than most, was their poet, and Kingsley Amis, funnier than most, was their novelist, and both men were confident about who they were. They were not, in the French phrase, comfortable in their skins—that was part of the point—but they were self-assuredly uncomfortable. This confidence gave Larkin's poetry its deadly compression, those killer closures; and it gave Amis's novels their comic structure, their resonant conclusions. These were books which knew where they were going.

Where did this leave Martin Amis? One clear clue is provided in *Experience*, which contains, interleaved through its disjointed narrative, a series of letters he wrote as a teenager to his father and step-mother, Elizabeth Jane Howard. Though he cringes from them now, they are precociously fluent for a schoolboy: "Thanks awfully for your letter. So we all appear to be working like fucking fools. I seem to be flitting manically from brash self-confidence to whimpering depression; the English is all very fine, but the Latin I find difficult, tedious and elaborately unrewarding ... In my last few days in London I read *Middlemarch* (in three days), *The Trial* (Kafka is a fucking fool—in one day) ... Much as I'd love to see you both, it does seem that I'll be doing too much fire-ironing and pie-fingering (I'm sure Jane could adapt that to one of her swirling mixed metaphors), to be able to get away ..." The fluency, of course, is borrowed. Young Martin's breezy rhythm is remarkably close to his father's.

He arrives, therefore, as a young writer, with the gift of astonishing loquacity but also the son of a certain kind of Englishman who was, for post-1960s youth, utterly redundant. Kingsley Amis, however, seems to have been a hard man to rebel against—too funny, too tolerant and too lacking in fatherly discipline in the first place. So Martin develops that encrusted rococo English he's famous for, sentences that preen and double up and go nowhere—a perfect cover for the inherited fluency. His novels don't have the self-confident structure of his father's. He creates low-life grotesques and Hogarthian caricatures to replace the plausible, shrewd, just-caricatures of the Kingsley Amis books. He is less naked than his father, less fully confronting life's trouble.

Some things don't change: Kingsley Amis's most compelling novelistic gift was his ear, his talent for mimicry which resurfaces, untouched, in his son's work. Both are masters of reported inarticulacy. Also, the son, like the father, abandons his family and is tormented by the choice. The son drinks and screws and surrounds himself with a reliable band of male friends to share in-jokes; it's a snooker club, not the Garrick, but the principle is the same. Julian Barnes seems to perform a similar role for Martin to the one Philip Larkin played for Kingsley, until the rift over Martin dropping Barnes's wife as his agent. The Kingsley-Larkin friendship also cooled, although less dramatically, and then triumphantly revived later in the two men's lives. In Martin Amis's account of that "delightful" rejuvenation, with the return of old endearments and verbal energy, there is perhaps a wistful message for Barnes.

So the son is like the father in much, but he has the liberal politics, the more generous attitude to women (although I still think he's a poor writer of female character), and the more confused attitude to his own identity which all go with his generation. Again, there is a wider message. Millions of men of roughly his age, say from their mid-thirties to their mid-fifties, broke out of the shell of British postwar maleness, its puritanism and pessimism, its misogyny and insularity, only to find themselves adrift and confused, freed from their fathers but not free, lacking a robust sense of self or purpose. Like Martin Amis, they are not very good at stability, and seem younger at 50 than their parents were at 30. Like him, but unlike their Americo-sceptic fathers, many of them are fixated by US culture. They—we—reject the big picture and struggle to make sense of anything much.

This revolt against structure and therefore meaning is exemplified in *Experience*, which dodges awkwardly through space and time. There is, after all, an almost too-perfect Shakespearean plot buried in the book: the daughter lost and found; the good cousin lost to unspeakable evil, and not redeemed; the father lost and the other father found; the wife and children abandoned and the wife and children found. The hero errs, is human, is tested (by a dentist) and is reborn. There is even the comic underplot, featuring a comic villain, Eric Jacobs, the biographer.

Experience sets hares running and fails to follow them. It ends on a jarringly discordant and weak account of a trip to death camps in

Poland and evades questions any reasonable reader wants to know about. There is a picture of a baby which "cannot be named for structural reasons"—yet dammit, there are no pictures of the main tragic protagonist, Martin Amis's teeth. He concludes: "My life, it seems to me, is ridiculously shapeless. I know what makes a good narrative, and lives don't have much of that—pattern and balance, form, completion, commensurateness."

But nor, characteristically, do Amis's novels; structure and meaning are joined at the hip, but Martin Amis has always had a structure problem. His novels start, continue and finish; they rarely travel or conclude; they lack completion. Why is this? *Experience* is a book haunted by at least two other books, Kingsley Amis's own *Memoirs* (and, less so, his *Letters*); and Saul Bellow's *Ravelstein*. Bellow is a surrogate father to Amis; that friendship, Bellow's recent illness and quotes from drafts of *Ravelstein* recur constantly in *Experience*. And *Ravelstein* is also a book made on the disputed ground between memoir and fiction, a novel bearing an uncanny closeness to a portrait of Bellow's friend Allan Bloom, author of *The Closing of the American Mind*, who died of Aids.

Ravelstein, however, is a book of tremendous confidence: poised and beautifully formed, a model, in Amis's words, of pattern and balance, form completion, commensurateness. It is spare; but full of sinewy wisdom, a judgement flying high above the ground and missing nothing. The same could be said for late Roth, DeLillo, Ford, and some Updike. Somehow, the male American novelist has an openness to history, to the wider culture and a sense of men's condition that the British male novelist does not—certainly including Amis, who is probably the most conscious of the American issue. Is it because of the grandeur and glamour of "the American century" or the easily mocked but triumphant cultural earnestness of part of the US elite? At any rate, our story seems smaller by comparison, our male imagination (for this does not apply to female novelists or less so) inward, pinched, shrivelled, unconfident. And perhaps it is just that Amis is too good a novelist not to reflect those cultural failures—a man whose stylishness is doomed to fail because of his time and place. The dodginess and brokenness of Experience is the brokenness of the experience of many of us.

I am not saying that the Americans are optimistic in a simple way, just big in every way. Philip Roth, whom Amis (rightly) attacked for his postmodern, writing-about-writing novels of the Zuckerman era, has since managed to give triumphant shape to lives lived, to have the boldness and courage to spread his empathy, to make judgements on good people struggling with fate, and to achieve closure. This doesn't mean a neat, happy, invigorating or simple conclusion. But for some reason, Roth and other male Americans have an openness and a breadth of historical understanding which allows them to make old-fashioned well-built novels about the genuine catastrophe—the one which happens to all of us—while British male novelists have been twisting away into genre and grotesquerie. Not true, I know, of people disdained by the literary set, such as Nick Hornby or Tony Parsons. But it is true of the most talented, Martin Amis above all.

His father is dead. His father's letters, the last great slew of his writing, are published. The shadow of postwar man, with all its virtue and failure, is lifting from the country. The worst of England, and some of the best. Now Martin has started to write a little straighter—to look his life if not in the eye, at least in the face. Is it possible that he, like Roth, will move beyond a mediocre middle age into a triumphant late flowering? He has the gift and the intelligence, but has he the generosity to get beyond the old evasions, the coldness, the camouflage of that deadly, fish-eyed stylishness? If he does, a generation will be the richer for it.

Jesters on the box • David Herman

JANUARY 2004

Last May the Guardian television critic, Gareth McLean, reviewed the Channel 4 production of John Adams's opera *The Death of Klinghoffer*. McLean was underwhelmed. "It wasn't that *The Death of*

Klinghoffer was bad, it just wasn't really my thing." He went on to consider ITV's *The Forsyte Saga*. "Damian Lewis and Rupert Graves are very, very good as Soames and Jolyon."

It is impossible to imagine anyone but a television critic writing like this. Who else would think that "wasn't really my thing" or "very, very good" is criticism? Can you see Michael Billington reviewing a play, or Philip French reviewing a film, and resorting to language like this? It is inconceivable in any other kind of cultural criticism, but routine in television criticism. Why is television criticism so bad?

No other form of cultural criticism resembles it. Film criticism has David Thomson and Anthony Lane. In theatre criticism we have Sheridan Morley and John Lahr. On art, think of Robert Hughes or John Berger. The list of major literary critics is long. But television criticism? Who, today, writes about television with the erudition of French, the polemical energy of Kenneth Tynan or Hans Keller? There is no FR Leavis of television criticism, no Andrew Sarris or Pauline Kael. It's not just a matter of individual names. The point is that no television critic has introduced any kind of conceptual innovation, or has revolutionised the subject. Tynan championed the angry young men of postwar theatre. Which television journalist has fought for a particular group of directors or producers and put them on the map? Sarris introduced the notion of the auteur into film criticism. Which television critic has introduced a single idea, other than making fun of David Vine? Leavis's *The Great Tradition* became the canon of literary studies in schools for decades. Which television critic has defined a great tradition in television?

Television critics have no distinctive critical language, either borrowed or created, and no sense of a larger context. No television critic makes connections between television and the larger culture in the way literary critics like Raymond Williams, Edward Said and George Steiner have routinely done. Programmes are reviewed as if they have no context, either in television or in society at large. Of course, some of these other critics were writing about high literature for an educated audience. Television is the most popular of all the new mass media, and television critics, even in broadsheet newspapers, can't assume the kind of specialist knowledge of someone interested in Samuel Beckett or Joseph Conrad. But then look at the references in rock reviews or film articles. These critics are not illiterate and they don't assume their readers are. Or compare television critics with theatre critics, and try to remember the last time you read someone writing about Jack Rosenthal or Alan Bennett in the way you would routinely expect Michael Billington, say, to write about Pinter. When reviewing a new play or a new production of an old play, any theatre critic would, as a matter of course, refer knowledgeably to past productions, make comparisons with previous plays or the work of other contemporary playwrights. But where, in television criticism, are the references to great producers like Rudolph Cartier, Adrian Malone or Mike Dibb, to the early television dramas of Ian McEwan, Mike Leigh or David Hare, or to past episodes of *Monitor* or *Aquarius?* Television is reviewed as if it has no past. Granada's recent two-part drama about Henry VIII was discussed as if no one would remember a famous series from 30 years ago. Comparisons would be fascinating: the different kinds of studio filming, the wordiness and intellectual ambition of the BBC series compared with the Tudor soap opera served up by Granada, the sheer length of the six BBC programmes, compared with ITV's fear of committing to six successive Sundays at peak time. All of this spoke volumes about how television culture has changed in such a short time.

Similarly, where were the informed comparisons between Granada's *Forsyte Saga* and BBC2's famous production? When critics raved about Steven Poliakoff's *The Lost Prince*, who compared it with his earlier television work—dramas like *Hitting Town* (1976) or *Bloody Kids* (1980)? All of this would be the mere minimum in any other area of arts reviewing but seems too much to ask of television criticism.

Television critics still write as if programmes are created by one person—the presenter in the case of a factual programme, or the writer if it is a drama. As a result, they have no way of explaining the diversity of a series like Andrew Graham-Dixon's history of British art, when the opening programme on medieval art was clearly better than one or two of the later ones because it was directed by Paul Tickell, one of the best arts directors around. Similarly, the scripts of

Simon Schama's *History of Britain* varied, not because Schama had his ups and downs, but because some of the producers were more experienced and more knowledgeable than others. Think of the long-term relationships of producers like Kenith Trodd with Dennis Potter, of Jonathan Stedall with Alan Bennett, or of Mike Dibb with John Berger, and ask when was the last time you saw a television critic discuss the oeuvre of such producers?

This ignorance is especially surprising given that the battle over the importance of television has been won. For years, television was patronised by newspapers and academics. It was too ephemeral, too trivial. The left, too, was suspicious of it. The first issue of the *New Left Review* in 1960 had articles on cinema, theatre, pop music and a review of *Lolita*, but nothing on television.

That debate is over. Half a century of great programmes has killed the condescension. Television has been central to the lives of two generations, and yet the gap between the importance, at times the greatness, of the medium, and the banality of the newspaper coverage is still staggering. In the meantime, critics have gone down several different blind alleys.

First, is the court jester approach to television reviewing. It didn't start with Clive James, but his ten years as *Observer* television critic have cast a long shadow over the subsequent 20 years of criticism. His pieces on David Vine and assorted BBC sports commentators, on Sue Ellen and American soap operas, belong to any anthology of 20th-century humorous writing. No one has so relished the banality of bad television. It's a tradition admirably continued by AA Gill, Victor Lewis-Smith and Nancy Banks-Smith.

James's collected reviews capture the feel of the 1970s as well as any other book, and on the big issues he was usually right. He knew the BBC was being ridiculous when it withdrew EP Thompson's invitation to give the 1981 Dimbleby lecture or banned *Brimstone and Treacle*. James also knew that while good art is better than schlock, good schlock is often better than bad art—what he called "the higher trash." "Anaemic high art is less worth having than low art with guts," he wrote in a review of a BBC1 production of Michael Tippett's oratorio *A Child of Our Time*. He hated it all: "the caftans, the roll-neck sweaters, the portentous sets and the sententious lines." *Roots* was on in the same week. James concluded his review, "People who couldn't begin to understand *A Child of Our Time* will have no trouble remembering what happened to Kunta Kinte."

However, there are serious problems with James's legacy. First, his successors aren't as well read or as funny as James. The bigger problem, though, is that despite the wit, erudition and decent moral judgements, James didn't write television criticism. He might as well have been writing about literature, film or football. It would have been just as funny and every bit as clever and would probably have sold just as many copies of the *Observer*. This is not smart hindsight. Several contemporaries roasted James for his lack of engagement with the medium. In the *New Statesman* in 1977, Dennis Potter wrote that James only picked on easy targets like sports commentators, beauty queens and Richard Nixon. Your technique, wrote Potter to James, "depends on the deft snigger, your wit on the easy victim, your passing solemnity on assent to what is generally assented to." James's television column was "the best oiled, most spectacular schlock-crusher in the business but nothing very much more." Writing in the *Listener* in 1984, Mike Poole also took James to task for his jokey tone and "cleverdickery" but, above all, for his "blimpish hostility to experiment."

It is true: landmark programmes slipped through his net (*Men of Ideas*, *World at War*) or got short shrift. There was a saloon-bar philistinism, a knee-jerk hostility to Marxists, theorists and avant-garde figures of any kind. No highbrow has been so resolutely middlebrow in his tastes. Ingmar Bergman, Bertolt Brecht and Tippett, in particular, get the full emperor's new clothes treatment. James dismissed any attempt to theorise about television—or anything else. The problem is that this left him nowhere to go when he wanted to discuss television programmes more seriously. James began his review of *Holocaust* by saying, "It can't be done and perhaps ought never to have been attempted, but if you leave those questions aside then there should be room to admit the possibility that *Holocaust* (BBC1) wasn't really all that bad." On the direction of one of Alan Bennett's best television plays, *Me, I'm Afraid of Virginia Woolf*, James offered one sentence: "Stephen Frears directed with his usual sure touch." Discussing Richard Eyre's role in Ian McEwan's *The Imitation Game*, all James could manage was "Eyre directed with an unfailing touch." On Jack Rosenthal's *The Knowledge* we got a few predictable lines about taxi drivers, and James ended with, "Some of the acting was nearly as unsubtle as some of the writing, but the thing worked."

British television criticism emerged in the 1950s and 1960s, with critics like Philip Purser at the *Sunday Telegraph*, TC Worsley at the *FT* and Peter Black at the *Daily Mail*. It was a time when literary criticism, in particular Leavis, loomed large over British culture and literary criticism has dominated the way we think about television ever since. It is worth recalling that Purser wrote several novels and that Worsley went to Spain with Stephen Spender and wrote a pamphlet on education with WH Auden.

In his essay in the *Listener* on the state of television criticism, Poole noted this literary bias of so much television criticism: "Clive James leaves the *Observer* to complete his first novel. He is replaced by Julian Barnes, whose column at the *Statesman* is, in turn, taken over by another novelist, William Boyd, who subsequently leaves to be replaced by the poet Hugo Williams ... Barnes's vacation replacement at the *Observer* is none other than Martin Amis; while the considerably younger novelist Adam Mars-Jones understudies at the *Sunday Times* ... One of the *Times*'s television reviewers is Peter Ackroyd ..."

These writers, and other television critics, used literary criticism as a way of writing about television. Programmes were discussed as if they had a single author, so Eyre and Frears, two of the best television drama directors of the past 30 years, became spear carriers in James's reviews. Realism, or better still naturalism, was the accepted mode of television and any form of experimentalism was treated with suspicion. Most of the books written about television are about dramas and writers. Other genres only have the same prestige if they have a big-name presenter (Schama, David Starkey) or a "name" director (Molly Dineen, Rex Bloomstein or Roger Graef).

Television criticism became part of a more general belles-lettrism, usually written by people without any experience of television production. The template for this belles-lettrism is the newspaper book review: lots of literary and intellectual references, a bit of history, sensible politics and earnest morals, the occasional aperçu or deft one-liner doing the job of criticism.

Take a recent review by AA Gill, considered by many as James's successor. In his *Sunday Times* column of 23rd November he starts with Channel 4's "Adult at 14" week—lots of moral judgement and comments on New Labour hysteria about paedophilia, and Roy Jenkins liberalism. "The truth," writes Gill, "is ... early sex is a messy, uncomfortable, cold and disappointing experience that is best got out of the way as quickly as possible. Nobody who has had sex as a grown-up would swap it for sex as an adolescent. The one thing teenagers really don't need is David Blunkett in bed with them."

This is supposed to be a review of a television programme, "a good and timely documentary," *Sex Before 16 – Why the Law Is Failing*. Why is it a "good" documentary? We will never know, although we are told that the reporter, Miranda Sawyer, "is comfortable and watchable in front of a camera." This is classic belles-lettrism: lots of opinions and a slack, inert bit of value judgement. Then we're on to BBC1's drama about Charles II. "One of the great delusions about television is that its audiences care about historical accuracy," begins Gill provocatively. "Historical truth is relative and shifting." I wonder whether Gill's father, Michael Gill, would have agreed when he was working as a producer on *Civilisation*, Alistair Cooke's *America* and *Face of Russia*?

Television criticism has on occasion wandered off the jokey belles-lettrist path. One was a cul-de-sac called theory or media studies. It took off in various universities and at the British Film Institute in the 1970s and 1980s, and quickly became an almost unreadable mush of Marxist theories of ideology, Brechtian aesthetics and French theory, with a bit of Tony Garnett and Ken Loach thrown in. The jargon was awful. "Initially," wrote Charlotte Brunsdon in an essay on *Crossroads* in *Screen* in 1981, "I should like to make a distinction between the subject positions that a text constructs and the social subjects who may or may not take these positions up." Ten years later, John Caughie wrote a piece called "Adorno's Reproach: Repetition, Difference and Television Genre," also for *Screen*, which includes sentences like this: "Thus Houston attempts to think through the difference which television's textual specificity presents to theories of the psychoanalytic and semiotic subject, while recognising at the same time the interrelationship between that specificity and the specificities of institution and viewing."

It is not hard to see why this kind of work remained marginal in the culture at large. At its best, however, it took television seriously and challenged our commonsense assumptions about television and culture, especially about notions of realism and naturalism.

Some of the best insights from these theorists were taken on board by a group of television critics writing in the late 1970s and early 1980s. Critics like Mike Poole, John Wyver, Paul Kerr, Carl Gardner and John Dugdale grew up on television, and started to write for *Time Out, City Limits, Screen* and the *Listener* under Russell Twisk during the early Thatcher years. Poole and Wyver together wrote a book about the television plays of Trevor Griffiths, *Powerplays*, which is one of the best books ever written about television. These writers knew their theory but wrote clear and accessible prose for a wider readership. They were left-wing, interested in theories of ideology, and wrote widely about television, from Sydney Newman to science programmes, from US cop shows to the final episode of *Z Cars*. Like James they were keen to take the unserious seriously, but were also aware of the political and historical context of programmes. Most of them moved into television later in the 1980s with considerable success, but they have had no real heirs.

The generation that followed—Mark Lawson, Andrew Billen (*New Statesman*), Tom Sutcliffe (*Independent*), Stuart Jeffries (*Guardian*) and Victor Lewis-Smith at the *Evening Standard*, among them—are television-literate and some have direct experience of making programmes. They are both less political and less interested in theory than the BFI theorists at *Screen* or the group at *Time Out* and the *Listener* and their writing has turned back to the Clive James belles-lettrist tradition: clever, funny, accessible takes on individual programmes with individual authors.

In his account of the history of television criticism, Mike Poole argued that "Fleet Street has never known what to do with television." As a result, we have ended up with television criticism as we know it today: a strange pantomime horse of Leavisite lit crit and funny one-liners. What is strange is that all television criticism now should be like this. Isn't it time for one newspaper or magazine, somewhere, to try something different and find a new way of writing about television?

Europe's lost stories • Julian Evans
JULY 2004

In Douglas Coupland's 1993 novel *Shampoo Planet*, his hero Tyler Johnson escapes his US west coast hometown to spend a summer in Europe. He writes home with disappointment: "Europe lacks the possibility of metamorphosis. Europe is like a beautiful baby with super-distinctive features who, while beautiful, is also kind of depressing because you know exactly what the child will look like at 20, at 40, at 99. No mystery." This is an anti-old world judgement that fits Tyler's punk self-image (a fawn at play in the hectic fields of US consumerism). Returning to America, Tyler himself eventually metamorphoses enough to sell out completely, finding a position with a global leisure corporation in Los Angeles. Before he does, he qualifies his analysis of Europe in less self-conscious, more honest words. What is wrong with Europe, he adds, is that its efforts to be modern always flop. What constitutes modern? "France has never heard of Sunday shopping."

For British readers, Tyler's opinion may seem trite, interesting only as part of Coupland's wider critique of America. But we are in a curious position vis à vis such remarks all the same. As Europeans possessing a cultural heritage as immovable as any on the Continent, do we shrug them off? Or do we agree with Tyler? The cultural position is similar to the one we find ourselves in politically, divided between a tensile connection to Europe and a desire to shear away and emulate the (over)confident gestures of our younger, bigger brother. Narrow "cultural" down to "literary" and we can go further. The shearing has happened: in the past half century, Anglo-Saxon literary attitudes have shifted decisively away from Europe, westwards (and southwards) to the US, Latin America and the Commonwealth.

At the same time, we inhabit a political and economic union, now of 25 member states, that has made our idea of Europe more synecdoche than reality. The "Europe" we evoke today is usually an entity concerned with Brussels or Strasbourg, or UEFA. The Europe we live in is acquiring something homogenised about it, and may run counter to our cultural needs. While departments in Brussels administer initiatives to preserve dying languages, their colleagues in other departments are doing their best to turn us into lifestyle consumers of identical stamp. The Czech writer Ludvík Vaculík, a respected opponent of Czechoslovak communism, wrote recently of the European Union's drive to disseminate a philosophy only of affluence: "The EU is not advancing human awareness and the development of Europeans but, on the contrary, will prove a major obstacle to them." We live balanced between nostalgia for the Continent's past, and a present whose ideology is unmistakably economic: a virtual Europe of museums and folklore, a material Europe of second homes and city breaks. The closest comparison that occurs to me, *pace* Tyler, is of Europe as a Disneyland or Seahaven. So the question is not: how modern are we? We are, in Tyler's terms, supremely modern. The question, rather, is how much vitality—how much potential for metamorphosis—is left of the threads that have bound Europe since the Renaissance?

Some terms need to be defined. The roots of modern Europe belong not to the EEC or the second world war, but to the 16th century, and in particular to the dangerous anarchists who were the draughtsmen of our commonality: Rabelais, Erasmus, Cervantes. Their humanist bandwagon was a perilous vehicle to board; their exuberance in driving it straight at the edifice of religious orthodoxy had its desperate side. But as a result of their writing, a continent departed in search of its identity. We still give shape to that pursuit through the mongrel art form of the Renaissance to which Rabelais and, more formally, Cervantes gave birth: the novel. Without the novel, there would be no Europe. (Three hundred years later, when 70-odd years of cold war division produced a gulf across Europe, the Lithuanian poet Tomas Venclova noted that Europe continued to exist in the east only by virtue of its novelists and poets.) Again and again in the European masterpieces—*Don Quixote* (Cervantes), *Gil Blas de Santillane* (Alain-René Le Sage), *Tristram Shandy* (Sterne), *Michael Kohlhaas* (Kleist), *Either/Or* (Kierkegaard), *Madame Bovary* (Flaubert), *In Search of Lost Time* (Proust), *In the Penal Colony* (Kafka), *Confessions of Zeno* (Svevo), *Man Without Qualities* (Robert Musil)—we have discovered not just our connectedness but the keys to modernity itself: to modes of thought and feeling that did not exist until writers gave them expression.

That shortlist ends 50 years ago. With the shift in British literary outlook away from European modernism and the successors of Sartre and Camus, our last continental icons, and towards the American postwar realists—Updike and Roth, Mailer, Bellow and Morrison—what is our position now towards continental Europe? What ought it to be, as political union expands? How to talk about it?

We lost interest in the Continent, it is said, from a combination of Americanophilia and Anglo-Saxon insularity. This is not so. The extinction of literary intimacy with mainland Europe came only after the British reading public had been an exemplary European reading public for more than three centuries. Thomas Shelton's 1612 English translation of *Don Quixote* was the first in Europe; the English received Cervantes and other European fiction writers of the 17th and 18th centuries (Mme de La Fayette, Voltaire, Rousseau, Diderot, Laclos, Goethe, Kleist) with remarkable admiration. The *Quixote* became so popular in Britain that in the 18th century new translations were published every few years. Among the most popular were Peter Motteux's (1700), Charles Jervas's (1742) and Tobias Smollett's (1755), whose version ran to 13 editions. More revealing still is Smollett's comment in the *Continuation of the Complete History of England* (1760) of the kinship between Cervantes and Henry Fielding: "The genius of Cervantes was transfused into the novels of Fielding, who painted the characters, and ridiculed the follies of life with equal strength, humour and propriety."

The 18th century, that most admirable epoch of novelistic playfulness, was ruled by the spirit of Cervantes and the homage paid to his memory by Fielding, Smollett and Sterne—all of them to some extent attempting (and succeeding) to fashion an English *Quixote*, equal to the original in comedy, character, digression, and fictitiousness. This aesthetic convergence was to continue for more than a century. Dickens and Thackeray converted Quixote's horizontal, ideological wanderings into fiction that journeyed vertically, aspirationally, up and down class (as Balzac, Stendhal and Flaubert did in France). This is no neat geometry, but the tangible result of Cervantes having conceived his novel as a journey and of his first imitator, the Frenchman Le Sage using, in *Gil Blas de Santillane*, the road as a means for his hero to seek out both a means of advancement and an identity.

At the beginning of the 20th century, a remarkable change occurred. Remarkable because, as Europe's half century of wars began, the novel—chief vehicle for its cherished and carefully bequeathed humanism—abruptly abandoned aspiration to replace it with escape, resistance, fear. Theme was mirrored in form. The novel, once about telling a story, began to be about the difficulty of telling a story. From 1919 onwards, as Paul Fussell notes in *Abroad*, his survey of literary travelling between the wars, the whole of Europe was "frontier-obsessed and ... map-mad." The road of the novel now stopped at the border. A sample of British novel titles from the 1930s amply illustrates this neurotic preoccupation with frontiers, trains and anxiety: Christopher Isherwood's *Mr Norris Changes Trains*, Graham Greene's *Stamboul Train*, Edward Upward's *Journey to the Border*, Eric Ambler's *Journey into Fear*.

The Continent disintegrated. Its themes coalesced into a single concern: how to deal with fracture? Here Britain was in an anomalous position. It had undeniably shared in horror from the time of the first of the new 20th-century borders—the murderous "front" of 1914 that demarcated the line between Allies and Central Powers. Even so, in a specific sense, it did not suffer: its borders were not compromised in either world war. The literary gap between Britain and the Continent dates from that time.

It is an old saw that the difference between British and continental novelists is that we can do narrative and they cannot. This may contain a seed of truth, but not because of our superiority. If true, it is because our lives—our narratives—were not disrupted by war to the extent that those of the Poles were, or the French, Germans, Italians, Hungarians; of most mainland European nations. That aesthetic break—the schism of *form*—between British and continental writing has little to do with native taste or British "insularity," but emerged from a condition of history. In Warsaw in 2001, I interviewed the Polish novelist Tadeusz Konwicki in his Stalin-era flat. To Poles who had experienced Hitler's war and had then to deal with Stalin's communists, he said, conventional narrative made no sense. "My generation time and again had to face the possibility of their lives being threatened. Traditional narrative structure could not express the psychological insight of the situations we found ourselves in."

What befell occupied, annexed, border-compromised Europeans made linear narrative jar as thuddingly on them as the "experimental" fictions of postwar Europe jarred on British sensibilities. In the 1950s, where France had Nathalie Sarraute's *Portrait of A Man Unknown* (1947) and Alain Robbe-Grillet's *The Erasers* (1953), Britain had Evelyn Waugh's *Sword of Honour* trilogy (1952–61). Nevertheless, the experiments of the French *nouveau roman*, and its associated European formal exploits, were not an ultimate cause of British readers turning to America in the 1960s. What took them there was America's own vitality, an evolving narrative force in which one can see an unbroken vital line stretching from Scott Fitzgerald's America in *The Great Gatsby* to Thomas Pynchon's in *Mason & Dixon*. History had caused continental Europe's faith in narrative to falter in its stride; in the US (as, variously, in Latin America and the Commonwealth) there was no pause in the gallop. A great, unbordered expanse of narrative lay all around.

What went wrong in the old world? I fed, from inky school bench onwards, on Maupassant, Flaubert, Zola, Céline, Sartre, Camus, Proust; my youthful spirit was bottled in the poetry of Nerval, Baudelaire and Valery Larbaud. It was French literature that represented the greatest of the Continent; and it was France's decline that occluded our interest in Europe.

But wait: isn't the idea that French fiction declined merely a figment of British ignorance? Surely the French would declare the reverse—that the novel advanced on the Continent while Britain got caught in a formal cul-de-sac. The *nouveau roman*—exploring a subjective, randomised world of objects and sensations—dismissed the narrative novel's "dubious relationship" with the world. Alain Robbe-Grillet, theorist of the new movement, declared in *For a New Novel* (1963): "How could style have remained motionless, fixed, when everything around it was in evolution—even revolution—during the last 150 years? ... [Novels] survive only to the degree that they have left the past behind them and heralded the future." In Robbe-Grillet's time it was important to be modern, and even we—the British!—championed the *nouveaux romanciers* because the conservatives attacked them. But Robbe-Grillet was also the villain of the piece, a writer of prodigious skill at publicity but mediocre judgement (how could he otherwise have consented to write the text for David Hamilton's collection of vaselined erotica, *Dreams of Young Girls?*). In March 2004, he finally attained membership of the Académie Française. One academician, Michel Déon, wrote to me afterwards, "It's amusing to think that for 30 years this agronomist ran a thing called the *nouveau roman* which may have made his fortune but which ruined the reputation of the French novel outside France."

The *nouveau roman* arrogated literary gravity, fell into an impoverished emotional minimalism and produced a generation of "novels" that were no thicker than a box of restaurant matches. The result almost fatally undermined French fiction throughout the 1970s and 1980s. During the 1980s, I worked as an editor for a London publisher (by coincidence the publishers of Sartre and Camus 20 years before). Each spring, I would do the rounds of the Paris houses to see what was being published. The answer was plenty, but practically nothing worth translating. In eight years I brought back two worthwhile French novels, one by Michel Déon, another by Patrick Besson.

France's self-absorption, its imperial pretension to be the regulator of the literary world (an ambition linked, I think, to wartime defeat), helped divert British interest elsewhere. Significantly, at around the same time, a new aesthetic from further east began to open up—defined by Milan Kundera. If the novel is a European form, it is more accurately a western European form, and only later central and eastern European (and Russian). It came to central Europe in the second half of the 19th century, and central European novelists impinged only slowly on western consciousness. Neither Kafka (died 1924) nor Musil (died 1942) was widely recognised as a writer of European rank until after 1945. The collected works of Joseph Roth (died 1939), the great elegist of the tottering circus of Austria-Hungary, were not published in German until 1956. (In Britain, we began to read Roth only in the mid-1980s.) Kundera, first translated into English in 1970 with *The Joke*, was the exception, and his rapid ascendancy became the key to British readers' entry into the aesthetic identity of central Europe—a unity of small nations cyclically kidnapped by "protective powers" and other tyrannies.

Still, it was a one-man show. British readers did not really become familiar with the centre and east of Europe. Is this where our error truly lies? On the west of the Continent, the novel may have been shrinking; but in the east, this was not the case; there we do need to answer a charge of ignorance.

I emphasise this because the novelists of central and eastern Europe succeeded more far-reachingly than any of their western counterparts (except perhaps James Joyce) in making visible the modern era. Just as Cervantes's first lesson was to have Don Quixote discover that the world did not resemble what he had read about it in books, both Kafka, with his cosmos of impasse, and Musil, with his salutary collection of loose ends, indicated how Europe at the peak of its civilisation was also at its most untrustworthy and discontinuous. There is, surely, a 21st-century resonance there. The world did not change forever due to 9/11, as many commentators had it. Its fragility had already been perfectly set down in the 20th century by other writers from that aesthetic crucible—Andri'c, Broch, Canetti, Čapek, Gombrowicz, Hašek, Hrabal, Kadare, Kertész, Kiš, Konwicki, Kosztolányi, Krleža, Milosz, Svevo. What these writers also have in common with us in Britain is that, though their stories may seem strange, their Europe is our ancestral Europe: a continent of picaresque risk, in which the individual is sent out to venture everything, exactly as Britain's fictional forebears were—our Crusoes and Gullivers, Joneses and Shandys—a few centuries ago.

Europe is not merely a stadium of competing aesthetics. A country's literature is like an unofficial foreign policy, an expression of its specific interests. We need to feel that specificity in our ourselves and in others. If we lose touch with it, we—Europe as a whole—will turn into a kind of atopia, a nowhere built in the image of an airport. Through its specific geographies—Portugal, Greece, the Netherlands, Sweden, Estonia, and so on—the novel creates its metaphors, and a mosaic of places where human emotions can lodge. Through its attempts to retell specific histories, it tries to earth its own, and our, fears.

Why don't the British know more of this carnival of locality? There are problems of remoteness, obscurity, language—of translation. There is a thick domestic fog of media and publicity; thousands of books claiming readers' attention. Should readers really be demanding a constant redistribution of literary priorities? An ongoing complaint, to be heard at translators' conferences and European publishers' lunches, is that British publishers are not interested in fiction in translation. Of the 100,000 books published annually in Britain, the complainers charge, only a miserable 3–4 per cent are translated. This criticism has its origins in a nostalgia for those pre-1970 glory days of European (French, German, Spanish and Italian) translation, and the bizarre assumption that publishers have some kind of high duty to bring translated fiction to British readers.

And yet, all of the central European writers mentioned above *have* been translated, and can be found on Amazon or www.abebooks. co.uk. The complaint about translation may be justified in a few cases. There is no defence for not having translated the collected stories of Alexandros Papadiamantis, the pioneer of modern Greek prose, nor for passing over the Hungarian novelist Lajos Grendel, nor the novels of the Latvian Nora Ikstena or the Estonian Peeter Sauter. And it may be fair to say that British publishers are too ready to forswear quality in favour of commercial turnover. But corporation-dominated publishing, with us now for more than 30 years, is not terribly committed to authors, whatever their nation. Reputations rise and fall for a variety of often arbitrary reasons. I think of the brief moment of fame for Balkan writers during the wars in Yugoslavia. Recently, I could not find in bookshops or on Amazon a single British-sourced translation of the novels of the Yugoslav novelist Danilo Kiš, though Faber and Penguin once published several of his works and Joseph Brodsky considered his novel *Garden, Ashes* "the best book produced on the continent in the postwar period."

What more are publishers supposed to do? Every work of continental fiction published in English is the result of individual enthusiasm. The Harvill Press, Britain's most dedicated publisher of translated fiction, has contributed to the reputations of many European novelists. Christopher MacLehose, its publisher, established in Britain the Portuguese José Saramago, later a Nobel laureate, and the Swedish crime writer Henning Mankell. Smaller publishers— Arcadia, Bitter Lemon, Canongate, Carcanet, Dedalus, Mare's Nest, Peter Owen, Pushkin Press, Serpent's Tail—continue to publish books they care for. Do the publishers' critics want a centralised translation publishing programme?

When continental European critics and publishers complain that their British counterparts are uninterested in translation, they usually avoid a more difficult task—that of interrogating the fiction to discover whether it is worth translating. During the 1970s and 1980s, the British who, to some extent, had reason to be proud of their fictional record, were none the less frequently asking, "Why are the Americans so much better than us?" Elsewhere in western Europe, and France in particular, such self-criticism was non-existent. A recent book by a professor at the University of Grenoble, Pierre Jourde, has at last attacked this cycle of self-adulation. In *La Littérature sans Estomac* ("literature without guts"), an assault on the promotion of literary mediocrity, Jourde singles out cliques like that of *Le Monde des Livres*, presided over by Philippe Sollers, guru of the literary left. "In the precious world of contemporary literary life, writers—a weird species of mammal—graze calmly beneath the gaze of gawping onlookers in their cultural enclosures," Jourde writes. "In their dreams, they 'disturb,' they anger those in power and upset the established order … In fact, no one is attacking them, and they are not hurting anybody."

My advice to the Euro-plaintiffs would be to try another strategy. What is it that the Continent's writers have to say? What might it be exciting to have cultural conversations about? About freedom? About the nature of democracy or modernity; about the value of history? They might conclude that proselytising on behalf of, say, the Albanian Ismail Kadare, the Portuguese José Saramago, the Pole Magdalena Tulli, the Swede Jan Henrik Swahn, the Estonian Jaan Kross, might produce better results than complaining.

There are, too, the accusations against British readers: that they are useless at other languages, that Anglophone culture is dumbly Americocentric. But shouldn't we rather be pitied? The English-speaking world is large and multi-continental. And, even at home, the world looms large. London contains the largest collection of linguistic groups on the planet. Of course, many Britons do speak another language; just not necessarily a European one. The charge that the British are uninterested in what is going on beyond our tidal waters is an odd fantasy.

Fifty years is the blink of an eye in the history of the novel. After Cervantes published the *Quixote*, Spain was so overwhelmed it took 250 years to produce another novel. In France, the French novel once again has a voice, in the shape of the disaffected editor of a review, *Perpendiculaire*, who in 1994 published his pointedly titled first novel, *Extension du Domaine de la Lutte* ("extension of the domain of the struggle"), published in English as *Whatever*. Michel Houellebecq— Balzac's representative in the globalised world—has said of his second novel, *Atomised*, an incendiary attack on the French left, that: "The idea which prevailed was that a book was a style, a writer was a style, only a style. In my book there is more sociology than psychology, and that's new." Not quite, but every French novelist of the 19th century would have known what he meant.

What is the novel, and what is it for? It is a metaphor in the form of a story that renders the world legible. It has no pedigree, only a blueprint that came out of the old, opiate landscape of La Mancha almost 400 years ago. It is self-renewing; hard-wired for resistance to propaganda, orthodoxy, massification, fakery, bullshit. The vitality of the European novel—or perhaps I should say the European vitality of the novel—rests on an insistence: that we question historical experience, seeking the individual in the communal, the communal in the individual. That seeking is bound to be inconclusive, because the sense of who we are is not fixed, but an engagement with reality. What kind of engagement? A novel, perhaps more than any artistic form, is a work made by an individual for an individual. It is a request, from writer to reader: here I am as a human being. Do you recognise anything? Are we both human beings? When a writer of Houellebecq's singularity asks that question, the British are clearly willing to listen. Have we missed opportunities to listen more widely? Undoubtedly. Have we been excessively engrossed by American fiction? Perhaps. Has our ear for the European novel been damaged? If it has, it is a reparation easily made. Now is a good moment. After accessions and elections, we can turn our back on euro-Europe with equanimity, and await new fiction, where a continent of localness can still be found.

As for Tyler Johnson, he may think he knows what the child will look like in 99 years' time, but unless he reads its novels, he will have no idea what might yet metamorphose.

Norman's conquest • Rowan Moore

MARCH 2002

Norman Foster is the single most successful British architect in history, whether success is measured by the size of office, fame, honours, global reach or number of projects. His is a heroic life story, which has taken him from working-class Manchester to the House of Lords. He has achieved a near-monopoly of the monuments of millennial London—enough to constitute a city in themselves—designing such essential urban objects as the city hall, two skyscrapers, the bridge, the football stadium, the town square, the train station and the headquarters of a supermarket chain (as well as hectares of office space and flats). And this is to say nothing of the icons and airports he has bestowed on Hong Kong, Berlin, Barcelona, Nîmes, Frankfurt, Tokyo, Singapore, Glasgow, Cambridge and Omaha, Nebraska. Few, if any, living Britons have the international stature in their fields that Foster has in his.

He has achieved this as a modernist architect in a notoriously conservative country, a mere decade after the traditionalism of Prince Charles seemed all-conquering and as an outsider in this allegedly class-ridden land. How? The short answer is talent and determination. Yet these alone cannot explain his appeal to institutions as diverse as the British Museum, Wembley stadium, Sainsbury's, the Royal Academy and the mayoralty of London. It would be nice to believe that they have all suddenly been converted to beautiful and radical architecture; nice but, alas, not plausible.

There's a second mystery, which is Foster's ability to be supremely skilful in some aspects of architecture, and club-footed in others. Despite its wobble, the Millennium Bridge is a structure of grace and precision, as are the roofs of Hong Kong and Stansted airports. His Reichstag pulls off the fraught symbolic task of representing the new Germany. In Bilbao, after the adrenalin rush of Frank Gehry's Guggenheim, spirits are soothed by the calmer perfection of the *fosteritos*—glass, hooded entrances designed for the city's metro.

At the same time, though, he is capable of the ponderous and malfunctioning faculty of law in Cambridge, where hard surfaces and an aversion to inserting partitions meant that readers in the library were distracted by the clatter of drinks machines and conversation from communal areas. When a committee from London arrived with the intention of giving the building an award, a 30-minute tirade from the head of the faculty persuaded them otherwise.

The simple objection to Foster's architecture is that it is cold and boring; but he gets into worse trouble when he tries too hard to be sensuous and interesting. Arbitrary lumps and bumps appear, at odds with the lucid rationality that is Foster's most famous strength. The hovering egg of his Greater London Authority lacks relevance either to London or to its political role.

Sometimes strength and weakness appear in the same Foster building, as in the British Museum's Great Court. Look up and you see a virtuoso structure, glass and steel breathed upwards in a complex bubble. But look around, and you see beige, respectable stone arranged with deadening symmetry. A pompous double stair rises to almost nowhere amid a shapeless plenitude of space. Stone is cut and polished with such precision as to look like plastic (though, ironically, it was a supplier's imprecise definition of Portland stone which led to the row about the south portico). Never, as Will Self said, has a finished building looked so much like its computer visualisation.

There is a pattern here. Brilliance and invention are applied to aerial things, to the abstract rules of structural engineering, to places beyond inhabitation. At ground level, in the zone of complex human activity, the design resorts to generalities and platitudes. So here's a hypothesis: Foster is popular because he supplies the look of innovation without the pain of actually changing anything; the establishment likes him because he lets it feel daring at minimal emotional expense; he is the purveyor of radical architecture for people who want no such thing.

Norman Foster is happiest when not in contact with the ground. He flies gliders and jets and lives in a penthouse over the Thames. Asked by the BBC to name his favourite building, he chose a Boeing 747. As a child, he spent solitary hours at the controls of imaginary aircraft; as an adult, he described his vision of a future London for the television cameras, while looking down on it from a helicopter. His very first building, designed with Richard Rogers, was the Cockpit, a tiny study in a Cornwall garden whose basic principle—glassy above, solid below—would be replicated at vast scale in projects like Hong Kong airport. Airports, and the American Air Museum in Duxford, are among his most eloquent buildings.

His buildings want to take off, too. His hero is Buckminster Fuller, who fantasised that giant domes could cover much of Manhattan, creating immense, climate-controlled zones. Foster took up the idea and repeatedly reworked the idea of the big roof sitting lightly on the ground, the British Museum's Great Court being the latest variation. Recently, he has taken to wrapping Fuller-esque triangulated structures around seemingly unsuitable building types, like his "erotic gherkin" skyscraper for the insurance company Swiss Re. In the British Museum, the Reichstag and the Royal Academy's Sackler Galleries, light, crisp modernity is juxtaposed with crumbly, heavy antiquity. Old and new are kept apart with what are known as "negative details"— gaps or recesses that underplay the junction. Unexpectedly, Foster buildings can involve a lot of digging, but the object of this underground construction seems to be more to neutralise the subterranean than to engage with it. When Foster uses materials of the earth, like stone and concrete, he makes them smooth and pale.

He treats human material in a similar way, talking of "flexible" space, in which all things are possible, coupled with the ideal of the democratic workplace. In Foster's office by the Thames, everyone works in the same space, from junior staff to Foster himself, even if the boss has a location rather more equal than others. As the pilot, he sits at the end of the oblong fuselage, in which the staff sit like passengers in parallel rows.

In Foster's plans, people are often represented as myriad dots gathering at critical points like iron filings round a magnet. Or else they merge into arrows denoting movement, identical to the arrows denoting air flows in Foster's diagrams of ventilation systems.

There are dreams here of escape, of purity and of control; beautiful dreams with a sinister potential. As a boy Foster was an awkward loner, who could not ride a bike until he was 13. Once he learned, he would flee the dull streets of Levenshulme for the Lake District. Flying is the next step. To fly is to be raised above a troubling world and is a supreme form of control. "It is difficult," he wrote, "to separate the spiritual uplift of the experience of flight from the satisfaction of delicately balancing the physical forces involved in the process."

Those things Foster can control completely, like a roof, he makes perfect. Those things he cannot, like the messy ground level, he seeks to neutralise. There is a fear of friction, an aversion to touch. The sense that dominates is the distancing one of sight. Architecture is chiefly a visual medium, but Foster's work relies to an extreme degree on the power of the look.

I know I'm ugly," barked Foster at *Foundation* magazine's art director, "but if you publish these photos I'll never talk to Stuart Lipton again." Lipton is a property developer and a client of Foster's; *Foundation* was a magazine paid for by Lipton's company. I was its editor. We had a polite article about Foster, with portraits by the photographer Nigel Parry, whose style is frank. Under the conventions of such publishing Foster had sight of the photos, and a gentler, blander Norman appeared in print.

This incident was about human imperfection. And control—the control of look, which Foster seeks in all aspects of his business. There is, for example, a typeface, designed by Foster's friend the late Otl Aicher, which is used not only for the signage in his buildings, and in his company literature, but also for books written *about* him. Publishers are coralled into his corporate identity.

He exerts an extraordinary influence over British architectural critics, the most acute of whom will give him an easy ride. When the Great Court opened, it was left to the non-specialist writers to make the sharp remarks, while the specialists (myself included) blathered about soaring roofs. It's not only because there is kudos to be had from curating Foster exhibitions, or editing his books. Nor is it just that the critics and Foster have been through the hard times together when Britain seemed set against modern architecture. It is because he wants their support and the power of his will is not to be underestimated.

Critics flit between whichever explanation of his work—practical or aesthetic—will best serve to praise him. In *Norman Foster: A Global Architecture*, Martin Pawley admires the high-tech functionalism of

Foster's Glasgow conference centre, an ultra-cheap building made possible by clever design. Yet, when he discusses the Hong Kong and Shanghai Bank, which was the most expensive office building in the world, Pawley shifts to art-historian mode, noting the "elegance" and "clarity" of the structure. Here, he's not concerned with how the building works, but how it looks.

Repeatedly with Foster, look triumphs. The Reichstag and GLA buildings are said to be "democratic" because their glass-walled debating chambers allow the public to see their representatives; but it would be hearing, not seeing, that might expose them to scrutiny. The words "elegant" and "spectacular"—abstract, visual, empty words—are often used about his work. There are also the random metaphors, used in praise and criticism: the Millennium Bridge is a "blade of light," the Swiss Re tower is a "gherkin," the GLA a "searchlight" or a giant "eye." Why a blade? Why a searchlight? What counts is the interaction between object and eye; the intellect needn't get involved.

We expect architects to make buildings look nice, to raise our spirits by their appearance. Foster rightly insists that if buildings "do not move the heart and mind then they are only addressing one part of their function." But in high architecture, which is usually paid for by the rich and powerful in order to glamorise themselves, there is a slipperiness between enlightenment and deception, a slipperiness that increases when its look is as free-floating as it is in Foster's work.

Norman Foster grew up in a working-class area. His father was the manager of a furniture and pawn shop, then worked nightshifts in an aircraft factory during the war. His mother also worked and much of the time he was on his own. When Foster surmounted his background and got a place at architecture school, he had to pay his way by working as, among other things, a bouncer. He also financed himself with scholarships, one of which got him to Yale, where he met the man who became his friend and only serious British rival, Richard Rogers.

Foster would later speak of discovering an "American world in which everything was possible if you were willing to try hard enough." Back in London, he set up Team 4, a partnership with Richard Rogers,

Rogers's first wife, Su, and Wendy Cheesman, who would marry Norman. The idea was to put the American can-do attitude into practice. Despite mishaps, they built Reliance Controls, an electronics factory in Swindon, which brought them widespread attention.

Team 4 split in 1967. Through the 1970s, in partnership with Wendy, Foster built his reputation with buildings for Fred Olsen in London's docks, for IBM in Hampshire and Middlesex, and for the insurance company Willis Faber Dumas in Ipswich. This was a weary time for British industry and architecture, but Foster lit up both worlds. For Olsen, he didn't just design a building; he rearranged his client's operation. For Willis Faber Dumas, he created a dark, piano-shaped glass building with a grass roof. His works were taut with clarity and intensity. He was a poet in the unpoetic Britain of business parks and metal sheds.

In 1974, he was called to the Smith Square house of Sir Robert and Lady Sainsbury to discuss a museum they wanted to build. He was impressed by their art collection, and a lifetime friendship was formed. The building that resulted, the Sainsbury Centre at East Anglia University, was a variation on his industrial theme, but it was Foster's entrée into the world of cultural buildings. Elegant though it was, it was also Foster's first irrational structure. The illogical museum or establishment building is a type that would recur.

In the 1980s came the Hong Kong and Shanghai Bank, a skyscraper in a faraway place by a practice that had never designed anything higher than three storeys. It required a prodigious effort from Foster and his colleagues, and veterans speak of this time as the most exhilarating of their lives. The building gleams with this effort, its details dense with energy. It is serene, but with compressed restlessness.

Foster's reputation was sealed, though he had still built nothing in central London, and would not until, aged 55, he completed his own offices in Battersea. Two other projects gave the cautious British public an unthreatening introduction to his architecture: Stansted airport (modernism being acceptable for transport buildings) and the Royal Academy's Sackler Galleries, where the new architecture was polite.

In 1989, Wendy died of cancer, a few months after they adopted a son. Foster then had a relationship with the newsreader Anna Ford, introduced to him by Richard Rogers's second wife, Ruth, before marrying Sabiha, also introduced by Ruth. The marriage did not last, and in 1996 Foster married Elena Ochoa, a Spanish television psychotherapist, 25 years his junior.

During the Sabiha period, recession hit and staff were laid off. Ever since, there has been a hunger to acquire more and more commissions. Foster now employs over 600 people and is a rich man. He is also ruthless in pursuit of a job. He beat Santiago Calatrava to the Reichstag commission with an impractical plan to build a giant over-sailing roof. What he built, to Calatrava's anger, was a dome similar to the one Calatrava had proposed. And when the burghers of Cardiff were plotting to oust Zaha Hadid from the job of designing their opera house, Foster was asked to present an alternative plan—despite Richard Rogers's plea that this was unfair on Hadid. Foster sent in designs. He talks of teamwork but plays to win.

So Foster, the awkward loner, has found himself as the architect that the establishment most wants on its side. According to someone who observed Foster's dealings with the British Museum at close quarters, "it was as if Foster was the client, and the museum his consultant." And the boy who experienced the rough underside of industrial society grew up to design steel and glass buildings that are shining, benign versions of the industrial.

They are seen as images of the future, though their primary inspirations were the Crystal Palace and 19th-century railway stations. Some of Foster's buildings are radical, more are conservative, but all get grouped under the broad term "innovative" which, as the world of architecture moves on, becomes harder to sustain. Increasingly, in Foster's work, innovation is represented by bizarre shapes, rather than technical invention. On some projects there are praiseworthy environmental measures, like the generators fuelled on vegetable oil in the Reichstag, or the use of ground water to cool the GLA. But they are tangential to the main business of the building. The social conscience of the architecture is subcontracted to the engineers.

In some ways Foster doesn't seem to quite get real life, and beneath his fixity of purpose he can be uncertain and impressionable. His politics shift under the influence of his friends. As a self-made man he was a natural Thatcherite, and expressed support for her in the 1980s—but cautiously, for his friends were mostly critics. Wendy, passionate about alternative medicine, converted hard-headed Norman to the cause. When he was with Anna Ford, he moved sharply to the left. In 1999, the architecture critic Jonathan Glancey presented Foster's "dynamic, modern worldview" as an inspiration for Blair's New Britain.

But what is disconcerting is the way genuinely pioneering works get grouped under the same rhetoric as conventional ones. In the early projects no one should doubt the sincerity of his desire to better the conditions of workers. The Reichstag does not rethink the German body politic but is streets ahead of most of the smug monuments of new Germany. Its strategy is simple—to insert Fosteresque glassy lightness into the shell of an historically haunted powerhouse, and let the public walk on the roof.

Yet the same architect can produce the GLA headquarters, which was procured by the government in a deal that allowed for no public discussion about what this public institution should be like (a private developer, CIT Group, led the deal). The site's developers will use the GLA as an "anchor tenant" to pull in others. It means that so-called public space around the building will be managed by private security. If people demonstrating against the GLA annoy other tenants, they can be ejected. The old chestnut that transparency equals democracy is offered, even though the GLA's convex form means that the glass reflects the sky, making it opaque. Its bulbous shape is deflective rather than inviting and is lifted, in Foster style, off the ground. Little thought has been given to interaction between the public, their representatives and the press. Rather than engage with the building's purpose, and its site, the architecture is dictated by its look and low-energy design. Foster is thinking global (about CO_2 emissions), but not deigning to act local.

Perhaps the seemingly random metaphors that stick to Foster's buildings are not so random after all. The "giant eye" or "blade of light" are images of control and aggression, as are the eulogies "stunning" and "striking" which Foster attracts. In the 1980s, the trusses of the Hong Kong and Shanghai Bank were compared to Sylvester Stallone's rippling pectorals. Foster works for people with power, who prefer not to declare it, although it slips out in inadvertent imagery.

There is a flaw in Foster's approach to architecture, and it lies in the overpowering desire to be airborne, which directs creativity away from the ground-level complexities of a given project. The real issue of the British Museum Great Court was how to put a lot of retail into a venerable museum. To which the answer was: spectacular glass roof. The real issue of the GLA building is the representation of civic democracy in a privatised environment. To which the answer supplied is: funny shape plus view and a smart cooling system.

This helps the British Museum to get away with not thinking too deeply about its cultural purpose. It helps the Government Office for London to palm off a tokenistic democracy on London. A more engaged, challenging architecture would make this harder, but a more challenging architect would not get the jobs. It is tempting to see the mishaps of some of Foster's projects—the wobbly bridge, the wrong limestone in the British Museum—as the revenge of the actual (of statics and geology) over abstraction; tempting but libellous, except at the level of metaphor, as the blame for these events is far from clear cut.

For all his striving for simplicity, Foster is a complex and contradictory man. For all his aggressive business attitude, he has artistic aspirations. He calls his huge business the "Foster studio" and when he describes his early attraction to architecture it is as an art. His failure lies in an inability to take complexities and contradictions to the source of his own art.

Potter in the past • Richard Jenkyns

OCTOBER 2000

Just in case you don't know: Harry Potter is an orphan who lives with his aunt and uncle in a boring suburb. On his 11th birthday he discovers that he is really a wizard, the child of a magical family. Leaving King's Cross station from the magical platform nine-and-three-quarters, he is transported to Hogwarts School of Witchcraft and Wizardry, where he has various adventures, comic and serious. There are plenty of japes and jokes, but ultimately Harry is engaged in a struggle with a supernatural force of evil, in the person of the Lord Voldemort. In 1997 JK Rowling published *Harry Potter and the Philosopher's Stone*, to be succeeded by *Harry Potter and the Chamber of Secrets*, *Harry Potter and the Prisoner of Azkaban* and *Harry Potter and the Goblet of Fire*. Three more books are promised. In terms of advance publicity and immediate sales, *Goblet of Fire* must be the most successful novel of all time.

The scheme of the child passing from real life into an alternative or fantasy world (and usually returning to reality again) originates, of course, with Lewis Carroll. It has been borrowed time and again since: it is the basis of *Peter Pan*, *The Wonderful Wizard of Oz*, CS Lewis's *Narnia* books and Maurice Sendak's *Where the Wild Things Are*. But Rowling gives an odd twist to this theme. We expect the real world to be prosaic, and the otherworld to be untrammelled by the laws of ordinary nature, but she comes close to reversing this pattern. The Dursleys, Harry's guardian family, are very nasty—fairytale nasty. They are Cinderella's wicked step-parents, keeping Harry in a cupboard under the stairs. Their son Dudley keeps bullying Harry; grotesquely fat and preposterously spoilt, he plays the role of the Ugly Sisters. Harry even has a strange scar on his forehead, like the birthmark which identifies the prince or princess in many a romance. So the real world is made exotically horrible, while by contrast, the running joke about the magical world is that it is as humdrum, bureaucratic and businesslike as anywhere else. It is controlled by a

Ministry of Magic; the Minister wears a green bowler hat and pin-stripe robes. Hogwarts sends out a list of the kit which new boys need to bring with them, just like any other boarding school, although other schools may not ask for a cauldron and a pointed hat. A wizard's arts are acquired not supernaturally but by years of study: the more you swot, the more magic you will be able to do.

This turns upside down the common habit of science fiction. In the hands of a master like HG Wells, the pseudo-science is ingeniously worked out and given a kind of plausibility, but in much second-rate fantasy, from Dracula to Superman, what is presented as science is really magic: though Van Helsing is supposed to be a scientific investigator, only magic can make Dracula turn into a bat, and despite some nonsense about kryptonite and so on, only magic can make a person in human form speed effortlessly through the air or put on underpants in a nanosecond. In the Harry Potter stories, by contrast, what is declared to be magic seems more like an alternative science, an otherworld set of physical laws to be learnt in the classroom. The paradoxical upshot is that these books have rather little magical atmosphere. Rowling's subversive jokiness makes the flying broomsticks and metamorphosing sweets into a series of conjuring tricks or comic turns. The magic does not need to be glamorous, for the glamour lies elsewhere: in escaping the Dursleys, Harry escapes from the start of a fairy story not into reality exactly, but at least into a genre of fiction which purports to be naturalistic—the public school story.

The school story is a peculiarly English genre. The originating work is Thomas Hughes's *Tom Brown's Schooldays* (1857), in which several elements of the genre are already present: the wise, worshipped headmaster (in *Tom Brown*, Dr Arnold; in the *Harry Potter* books, Professor Albus Dumbledore) and the bully (in *Tom Brown*, Flashman; in *Harry Potter*, Draco Malfoy). By the end of the 19th century the school story was an established form, with writers such as Talbot Baines Reed, author of *The Fifth Form at St Dominic's*, turning out a succession of such works. Particularly influential were two men who were not writers for boys: FW Farrar and Rudyard Kipling.

Farrar, who became Dean of Canterbury, was a master at Harrow when he published *Eric, or Little by Little*, in 1858. *St Winifred's* followed in 1862. Only a writer of genuine talent could have produced works as deeply bad as these. Their fetid atmosphere of moral panic and clammy religiosity may seem hardly credible to those who have not read them. The boys are stalked by fearful spiritual perils, signalled in language so impenetrable that the best-brought-up child must have had trouble understanding it.

These books are pervaded by a half-erotic morbidity. In the middle of *Eric*, the most pious boy in the school dies, apparently of terminal priggishness. Later on, Eric's little brother perishes (falling over a cliff) and, lastly, Eric himself. What is most extraordinary about these stories to the modern reader is the blatant exhibition of Farrar's pederastic and sadistic impulses (of which this high-minded man must presumably have been entirely unaware). In *Eric*, one of the masters, the wise and saintly Mr Rose—all too obviously Farrar's idealised vision of himself—publicly beats a miscreant, who writhes, blubbers and begs unavailingly for mercy—while his schoolfellows look on, cheering. (Mr Rose then rushes away to fall on his knees in grateful prayer.) Eric himself, after running away from school, is so savagely flogged by sailors that he dies of his injuries (there is some juicy description of the rope lashing into the boy's naked back and the blood dribbling from his white and tender skin). It is bizarre to think that the young had this stuff pressed on them by their elders.

Like the schools in Farrar's books, Hogwarts is the field for a struggle between supernatural forces of good and evil. That may seem to be mere coincidence, but it is not so entirely, for Farrar's importance is in establishing the public school as a site for dramatic conflict; this tradition, at several removes, has been inherited by Rowling. Kipling's originality, on the other hand, lay in bringing the spirit of antinomianism to the school story. The tales that make up *Stalky & Co* (1899) are not free from Kipling's peculiar nastiness. One of them describes how Stalky and his chums plant a dead cat in the rafters of a rival boys' house so that the stench of its decomposing body will mock their reputation for hygiene. But Kipling's virtue is to recognise that the schoolboy world is its own place, its values independent of adults. Kipling also establishes the much imitated idea of a small gang of cronies (one of whom is often the "intellectual" of the party). Stalky's sidekicks are M'Turk and the bookish Beetle, modelled on Kipling himself. Whether by chance or not, this pattern is replicated in the Potter books, in which the gang consists of Harry and his best friends Ron and the bookish Hermione (who Rowling has said, similarly, contains a good deal of herself).

Stalky has had more effect on the 20th century than is realised. He was an important influence on the young PG Wodehouse, who began as a writer of school stories, and on Frank Richards, who took on a good deal of Kipling's invented schoolboy argot wholesale. "Frank Richards" was actually Charles Hamilton, who almost single-handed for 30 years up to the time of the second world war wrote a weekly story about Greyfriars School in the *Magnet* comic, and St Jim's in the *Gem* (in the latter magazine under the name Martin Clifford). As George Orwell observed in his classic essay "Boys' Weeklies," these magazines were widely read by lower-middle and working-class children, and spread the school story deeply into the popular consciousness. Greyfriars and St Jim's are in many ways reborn in Hogwarts, and indeed some of Rowling's nomenclature has the Frank Richards flavour. At Greyfriars the nasty master is Quelch, who squelches people; at Hogwarts he is Snape, who snaps at them (and is like a snake: the serpent is the emblem of the house in his charge). In the *Gem* and *Magnet* the principal boy villains are Loder, Racke and Crooke; in the Potter books, Malfoy, Crabbe and Goyle.

Richards's Billy Bunter, the Fat Owl of the Remove, brought an element of farce into the school story, but there is a more immediate influence on Rowling's comedy: Nigel Molesworth. The four Molesworth books, written by Geoffrey Willans and brilliantly illustrated by Ronald Searle, came out in the 1950s. These are the misspelled lucubrations of a prep-school boy; there is no narrative as such, but a free flow of satire, parody and fantasy (they are not much like anything else, although the jokes about the syllabus bear some resemblance to *1066 and All That*). I loved them when I was

Molesworth's age, and 40 years on they still seem to me very funny. Childish in a way, they are also highly perceptive: like Osbert Lancaster's last masterpiece, *The Littlehampton Bequest*, this is comedy which says more about the sociology of the English upper or upper-middle class than a dozen academic volumes.

Molesworth is not to be found in *The Oxford Companion to English Literature* (which finds room for Farrar and Frank Richards) or in *The Oxford Dictionary of Quotations*, although I suspect that some of his phrases are among the most quoted, from among books of the last half century. Like Stalky, Molesworth has affected them more than most people know. He is, after *The Diary of a Nobody*, the principal influence on Sue Townsend's *The Secret Diary of Adrian Mole aged 13 and Three Quarters*, a debt acknowledged in her title. And Rowling is evidently another admirer. Nomenclature is again a clue. Molesworth's school is called St Custard's, and there is mention of a public school called Grunts; the influence of both names may be subliminally present in Rowling's Hogwarts. But in fact the borrowing is more direct: in *How to be Topp* there is a cod Latin play, "The Hogwarts," by Marcus Plautus Molesworthus, and Hoggwart is also the name given to the headmaster of Porridge Court, a rival academy. (As far as I know, no one has yet noticed this—a *Prospect* scoop?) Even Harry Potter's appearance, with his round glasses and perpetually untidy hair, seems to be modelled on Molesworth as drawn by Searle. What this *Quellenforschung* indicates is that a wacky, farcical humour is at the heart of Rowling's original conception; it is the later books which increasingly subordinate it to a graver kind of adventure.

Though Rowling is a comedian, she is hardly at all a satirist, and perhaps the most surprising feature of these books is their lusty immersion in the ethos of public-school fiction. We can contrast Hogwarts with another school which is currently under attack from supernatural evil: Sunnydale High. But whereas in *Buffy the Vampire Slayer* the demons have somehow got into a perfectly ordinary Californian high school (well, ordinary except for the presence of a drippy Limey and the absence of drink, drugs and acne), the point of Hogwarts is that it is grand and special. The school is a thousand years old (which makes Winchester seem *arriviste*). If you have enough school spirit, you can read about it in *Hogwarts: A History*. Swotty Hermione's devotion to this volume is presented as faintly absurd but also admirable. The school is housed in a medieval castle, first glimpsed across a stretch of water (like the view of Windsor from Eton, perhaps?). Some of the pupils are from families which have gone to Hogwarts for generations. Even the devil is an old boy, more or less: rather as Captain Hook turned to piracy after failing to get elected to Pop at Eton, so the Lord Voldemort was a pupil at Hogwarts who went off the rails and had to take up cosmic evil instead. At Hogwarts you wear a special uniform—robes. There is a special school sport, called Quidditch (the Eton wall game?). You change into different robes to play this, each house having its own colours (house spirit is very strong at Hogwarts). There is lots of feasting, and plenty of banter in the house common room.

Unusually among school stories, the Potter books genuinely admire academic values, but in a very traditional form. The teachers, who are all called Professor, eat together on a high table at the end of the great hall—a touch of Oxbridge here, or even of Tractarian Oxford: none of the teachers appears to be married. This is a school with compulsory Latin (in effect): the spells, which have to be learnt in class, are all in a kind of garbled Latin (in the latest volume, one is even in real Latin). Even the teachers have Latin names: Albus, Severus, Minerva. Hogwarts, it would appear, is archaic on principle—not only the sole school in Britain without a computer, but a place where you write on rolls of parchment with quill pens. (The love of traditional inefficiency seems to be endemic in the magical world: the unit of currency is the Galleon, with 17 silver Sickles to the Galleon, and 29 Knuts to the Sickle. This is the old £sd system made even more inconvenient, quixotically resistant to the Voldemorts of Brussels.) You travel to Hogwarts not just by railway but by steam train; because wizards can move from place to place in no time at all by using magic, this mode of transport seems quite unnecessary, but it is much more fun.

By contrast, the dreadful Dursleys, outside the magical world, are modern. Mr Dursley works in industry: he is a director of a firm that makes drills, called Grunnings (overtones of "grungy," "grinding"). Dudley Dursley is devoted to computer games. In contrast to them stands the magical Weasley family. Mr Weasley is a gentleman (his family have gone to Hogwarts for generations) and he does a gentleman's job (as a civil servant); and although he works in London, at the Ministry of Magic, the Weasleys live in the style of upper-class bohemianism in the country, in a rambling old house of picturesque charm. Harry's escape from the Dursleys to Hogwarts is a fairy-tale deliverance, but his visit to the Weasleys—one of the most strongly felt episodes in any of the four books—is presented in the terms of a *Bildungsroman*: here he discovers the enchantments that breathe from inherited culture and ease of manner. This is where he can feel at home: the associations of his own name, after all, are traditional, rural, arts-and-crafts: pottery, Beatrix Potter, pottering around. (He shares his christian name, of course, with young royalty.) Aunt Petunia, who is herself called after a suburban flower and lives in Privet Drive, called after a suburban shrub, observes that Harry is a nasty, common name—where has she been?

The social set-up at Hogwarts is also remarkably old-fashioned; it feels less like the 1990s than the 1950s—the Molesworth period. Deference is back. Hogsmeade, the nearest settlement, is a sort of estate village, servicing the posh boys and girls up at the school: we are shown it as a Dickensian Christmas card, with thatched cottages and shops, covered in snow, glimpsed from a cosy interior through the mullioned windows (all credit to Rowling for risking the word "mullioned," though not for the banality of the picture). Hagrid, the faithful retainer at the gates, was once a pupil at Hogwarts, expelled for an offence which for a while is nameless (it turns out that he took the rap for another boy who was actually guilty—a favourite ploy in school fiction). But in leaving the school he has become literally déclassé: whereas everyone else at Hogwarts talks in RP, Hagrid is the one person in the saga who is given a lower-class accent (estuarine? rustic?—it is hard to make out quite what it is meant to be). As a Hogwarts boy or girl you can enjoy sneering at the non-magical multitude as Muggles (oiks)—though this feature of magical life seems to have embarrassed Rowling, who makes some adjustments in her second volume. It is now implied that Muggle is a neutral term, and it is nasty Malfoy who uses the new rude word, "mudblood" and snobbishly boasts about his family's distinction. He derides nice Mr Weasley as a "Muggle-lover." But this does not change things much: liberal tolerance is one of the luxuries of good birth, and Mr Weasley remains unassailably one of the gentry.

In some respects Hogwarts has moved with the times: there is no fagging or beating, and the school is coeducational. In *Philosopher's Stone* it is mentioned that one pupil has dreadlocks, and another is called Parvati Patil; in later instalments the ethnic quota at the school is self-consciously increased. But it is hard not to feel that these kids have got in on assisted places. Despite the co-education, it is also striking how much these books remain boys' stories. There is plenty of the Frank Richards spirit, but not a trace of Angela Brazil or Enid Blyton; if readers did not know that Rowling was female, few would have guessed it.

All the girl characters except one are ciphers. Hermione, introduced as a comic swot, is soon allowed to be one of Harry's best friends, but at the cost of being a schoolboy's idea of a schoolgirl. Molesworth has her number: "gurls," he explains, are "intent, eager, keen ect. in class, and stick their hands up excitedly when the teacher asks a question"—just like Rowling's Hermione. (And since no real child has been christened Hermione in the last 20 years, it may be worth noticing that this is one of the few female names to drop from Molesworth's blotchy pen.) In *Goblet of Fire* Hermione is given sexual stirrings, and angrily protests to the boys that it has taken them four years to notice that she is a girl, but one may feel that it is really Rowling who has only just realised it. In *Chamber of Secrets* it is hilariously soppy for a boy to be keen on a girl—a blush-making secret to be kept well hidden. Rowling changes this in *Goblet of Fire*, but in a half-hearted and pretty unconvincing way.

The enthusiasm of the young, and indeed many of their parents, for this apparently traditionalist stuff may make the neophilia of early-period Blairism seem a little sad. But are the world's children, from

Stuttgart to Sydney, being unwittingly seduced by a reactionary fantasy? I don't think so. It is no more surprising to learn that Rowling has no personal experience of the boarding-school world about which she writes than it is to recognise that PG Wodehouse did not spend his best years shinning down drainpipes with the younger sons of earls. And few people, I think, believe that reading about Bertie Wooster and Lord Emsworth is an indulgence in snob-fantasy (as reading Barbara Cartland is). To enter Wodehouse's world, or Rowling's, is to enter an imaginary structure which does not take itself too seriously. What the popularity of Hogwarts does suggest is that people like a lively modernity to coexist with pleasure in tradition, and that a healthy fondness for the past is one in which genuine affection need not exclude a touch of wry irony. That is not such a bad lesson to learn.

But we may still ask: why has Rowling been so staggeringly successful? In part, the Potter phenomenon can be seen as one of those children's crazes which come and go, like My Little Pony or Teenage Mutant Ninja Turtles or Pokémon. But although there is a touch of truth in this—some children adore Harry Potter because they know they are meant to—there are big differences between the Potter cult and these other crazes. One is that the other crazes were manufactured by marketing men, whereas Harry's fame spread spontaneously, by word of mouth. Another difference is that Harry demands some effort from his devotees, and gets it: lots of children are reading these books, with genuine enjoyment. Essentially, Rowling owes her success to her own talent. Parents amazed to find their children—teenagers included—actually wanting to read a book, can agree that she has earned every one of her millions.

Rowling has that gift, so hard to analyse, of natural story-telling; her narrative is both gripping and amusing. The plots are well-made and ingenious. Actually, there is really only one plot: a whodunnit in which one of the goodies turns out to be a baddy and one of the baddies proves to be a goody after all—all four books pretty much fit this pattern, with minor variations. (When I read *Philosopher's Stone*, I was not expecting the whodunnit element, and the twist in the tale took me by surprise, but by the time I reached *Prisoner of Azkaban* I was able to guess the main plot twist early on.) But if the basic pattern does not vary much, the plots are cleverly worked out, with some entertaining red herrings. Rowling's dialogue is excellent: her adults sound like adults and her children like children, addressing one another robustly, without sentimentality. Above all, she is completely without condescension: she makes you feel not that she is consciously writing for children but that she is telling the kind of story that comes to her naturally. She is not afraid to use words that her readers may not know —but children like to be stretched. Many children's books appeal separately to two audiences: the children hear one thing, the grown-ups another. Children are not meant to pick up the Freudian resonances in Sendak's *Where the Wild Things Are* or the allusions to the great god Pan in *The Wind in the Willows*. But when adults started reading Harry Potter, they found themselves enjoying the same things that their children enjoyed.

Rowling's weakness is in creating character. Harry himself is fine, as his are the eyes through which we see the stories; and he does not need to be a self-standing figure, seen from the outside. Hermione is the best character. Hagrid, the gruff giant who is a big softy at heart, started as a sentimental cliché and has become a crashing bore. Most of the caricature figures are crudely overdone. Those minor characters who are not comic cuts—especially Harry's schoolfellows —hardly deserve to be called characters. The much trailed death, in *Goblet of Fire*, of a character whom "we care about" turned out to be an anticlimax, because we did not care about him. Rowling's lack of talent for creating new characters may be one reason why she now appears to be having difficulty in opening out her story. An entertaining newcomer in *Goblet of Fire*, however, is the yellow journalist Rita Skeeter, schlock reporter for the *Daily Prophet*.

The reviews that I have read reckon *Goblet of Fire* to be at least as good as its three predecessors, but it seems to me a decided falling-off. Quidditch was always one of Rowling's less happy inventions: as a game it makes no sense. It was also a misjudgement to make Harry a sporting hero, dazzlingly good at Quidditch: his proper role is as the untidy little chap in giglamps who somehow saves the day. A hundred pages of the latest book are dominated by the Quidditch world cup; it is quite the feeblest thing Rowling has written. (She seems to have got fed up with the game herself: back at Hogwarts all Quidditch is stopped for a year, on the flimsiest of pretexts.)

The transformation of Quidditch from a Hogwarts game to a world-wide sport is a symptom of a ponderousness which weighs down the new book. The heart of the story, attractively enough, is a quest in which Harry has to pass through a series of ordeals, like Pamina and Tamino in *The Magic Flute*; but it is presented as part of an inter-school competition, with marks awarded by judges. It all seems so earthbound and laborious. Hogwarts is no longer unique: there are similar schools in other countries. Given Rowling's ethnic sensitivity, it is surprising that these are depicted in such hackneyed terms: the French are elegant and feminine, while the half-German, half-Slavic lot are the sinister Reds or Nazis of movie cliché.

The narrative of *Goblet of Fire* includes, startlingly, the news that a female agent of the Ministry of Magic has been tortured to death. Some reviewers have remarked that Rowling's imagination is getting darker, but it may be more that as her comic invention starts to falter she is feeling the need to look for ever more spectacular effects. Voldemort has become much more openly sadistic, but this has the paradoxical effect of making him less devilish. Whereas at the outset, his purpose seemed to be the corruption of the individual soul, his aim is now the acquisition of universal power. He is becoming less like a cosmic force of evil, more like a James Bond world-domination baddie. On the comic level, the new magical showpieces—Portkeys, Blast-Ended Skrewts, and the rest—may also remind us of the later Bond films, in which Q wearily has to come up with ever more elaborate gadgetry.

It is significant that the ontological status of Hogwarts has changed in *Goblet of Fire*. In the earlier books, when you found platform nine-and-three-quarters at King's Cross you entered an alternative universe: it was like Alice passing through the looking-glass, or the wardrobe which leads into Narnia. But now Hogwarts seems to be somewhere in the north of England: we are told that it exists in the space we inhabit—only a bit of magic makes Muggles unable to see it. This is symptomatic of a shift from fairytale to (more conventional) adventure story: the action of the first Potter books took place in wonderland, but it has now been transferred to our own world.

Where will Rowling go next? Over in California, Buffy and her friends have moved on from Sunnydale High to a college with an affirmative action policy on werewolves; and back here, Harry, too, is growing up. The Hogwarts setting is beginning to look like an impediment. One thing which now needs adjustment is the skewed balance between the forces of good and evil. The dénouement of *Philosopher's Stone* is brilliant: Harry's escape from Voldemort proves, unexpectedly, to have been achieved through his own virtue and his dead mother's past self-sacrifice (readers will know why). This is the one moment in the saga when it comes close to the spiritual allegory of Narnia. In the later books, Voldemort and his cronies have enlarged their stature, while the good forces have dwindled into slightly sour comedy: the Ministry of Magic is bureaucratic and partly corrupt, the Council of Magical Law is pusillanimous. Increasingly, Dumbledore is being called on to play the part almost of God: there seems to be nothing beyond or behind him. But although headmasters may be admired, they should not be treated as divine. Like Harry Potter, Rowling has been inventive and resourceful but is now caught by the powers of evil in a trap from which there seems to be no easy escape. It is time for a bit of magic.

The Asian aesthetic • Mark Cousins

NOVEMBER 2004

At the end of August, a Chinese film, *Hero*, topped the US box office chart for the first time, despite already being available on DVD. A lush kung fu film in the manner of *Crouching Tiger, Hidden Dragon*, it was directed by former cinematographer Zhang Yimou. *Screen International* called it "one of the most eagerly awaited films in

Asian film history." It also went to number one in France and cut a swathe through the box office in many Asian countries. This is unheard of, yet Zhang's follow-up, the even more beautiful *House of Flying Daggers*, looks set to follow *Hero*'s extraordinary breakthrough. Shot partly in the rust-red forests of Ukraine, it has already broken box office records in China itself.

Something remarkable is happening in Asian cinema, and Hollywood has cottoned on. "Check out the latest US movie production slate and it is hard to escape the conclusion that Hollywood is turning Japanese," commented the *Guardian* in July. "And Korean. With a dash of Thai and Hong Kong thrown in." No fewer than seven new versions of box office hits from Asia are preparing to go before western cameras. Tom Cruise is developing a remake of the Hong Kong / Thai horror picture *The Eye*; Martin Scorsese is in preproduction with a new version of *Infernal Affairs*, the Hong Kong *policier*; a Japanese thriller, *Dark Water*, is being reworked for Jennifer Connelly; British director Gurinder Chadha is remaking the Korean feminist crime comedy *My Wife is a Gangster*.

This is not the first time that Hollywood's imitation of Asian cinema has seemed like flattery. *Star Wars* borrowed from Kurosawa; the *Matrix* films used Hong Kong fight techniques. But western film industries have never banked on the east to this degree before. Virtually every Hollywood studio has optioned an Asian project. Their interest in the continent's movies has become a groundswell. Part of this is the usual Tinseltown faddiness, but that is not all. *Dark Water*, *The Eye* and *The Ring* films—also being updated in the US— unnerved Hollywood because they beat it at its own game. They found new, subtle, inventive ways of doing what producers in southern California have spent a century perfecting: jangling audiences' nervous systems. From *Frankenstein* to *Jaws* and *The Blair Witch Project*, western cinema has prided itself on being able to electrify filmgoers with novel terrors. All of a sudden, Japan and Korea have stolen its thunder. Directors from these countries are using the power of suggestion, and turning the screw of tension to scare audiences profoundly. They build up tension more slowly, hint at unseen horrors, use sound more evocatively. The American studio system is constantly in search of fresh material and ideas. In the last few years, Asia has been western cinema's new source.

Asian cinema, however, doesn't merit our attention merely because it has captured Hollywood's. Despite the brouhaha caused by Michael Moore's *Fahrenheit 9/11* in Cannes this year, the lasting impression of the festival was the overwhelming beauty of a quartet of films from China, Japan, Hong Kong and Thailand. I have been going to Cannes for well over a decade but had never seen audiences applaud the visual magnificence of an individual scene as they did with *House of Flying Daggers*. Meanwhile, Hirokazu Kore-eda's *Nobody Knows* was one of the greatest works of observation that cinema has produced. And although I had to stand throughout Wong Kar Wai's two-hour *2046*, the world it created was so ravishing I didn't even shift on my feet. Finally, Apichatpong Weerasethakul's *Tropical Malady* delivered one of the festival's greatest coups. While Hollywood can easily ransack Asian horror cinema to renew its own techniques, it is unlikely ever to match the beauty of these four.

How is it that, despite the occasional blink of recognition, the west has remained so blind to Asian cinema for so long? There has always been a sense in which America and Europe owned film. They invented it at the end of the 19th century in unfashionable places like New Jersey, Leeds and the suburbs of Lyons. At first, they saw their clumsy new camera-projectors merely as more profitable versions of Victorian lantern shows. Then the best of the pioneers looked beyond the mechanical and fairground properties of their invention. A few directors, now mostly forgotten, saw that the flickering new medium was more than a *divertissement*. This crass commercial invention began to cross the Rubicon to art. DW Griffith in California glimpsed its grace, German directors used it as an analogue to the human mind and the modernising city, Soviets emphasised its agitational and intellectual properties, and the Italians reconfigured it on an operatic scale.

So heady were these first decades of cinema that America and Europe can be forgiven for assuming that they were the only game in town. In less than 20 years western cinema had grown from nickelodeon to vast rococo picture palace; its unknowns became the most famous people in the world; it made millions. It never occurred to its Wall Street backers that another continent might borrow their magic box and make it its own. But film industries emerged in Tokyo, Shanghai, Hong Kong, Delhi and Bombay, some of which would outgrow those in the west. India made its first feature around 1912 and was producing more than 200 films a year by 1930, Chinese production managed 400 films between 1928 and 1931 alone, and Japan was quicker off the mark—four production companies were established by 1908, four years before Hollywood became a production centre, and by the end of the 1920s, Japan was releasing 400 films a year. Vast production factories were built. On sound stages as grand as anything in Hollywood or Rome, huge sets re-created scenes from Asian history.

In some ways the film industries of the east mirrored their western forbears. Just like scandal-ridden Hollywood, the eastern film world killed the thing it loved, its movie stars. The Chinese actress Ruan Lingyu was as famous and enigmatic as Greta Garbo, yet the Shanghai tabloids hounded her. When she took a fatal overdose in 1935 (aged 25), her funeral procession was three miles long, three women committed suicide during it and the *New York Times* ran a front page story, calling it "the most spectacular funeral of the century." Despite her key role in Chinese cinema in its heyday, she appears in almost no western film encyclopedias. She was better known in America and Europe than almost any other figure from Asian cinema. And yet her fame did not introduce eastern to western cinema in any meaningful way.

In the five years before Ruan's death, her country had produced more than 500 films, mostly conventionally made in studios in Shanghai, without soundtracks. As western film industries refitted for sound, the film industries of China and Japan entered a golden age. Tokyo and Shanghai were as much the centres of movie innovation as southern California. China's best directors—Bu Wancang and Yuan Muzhi—introduced elements of realism to their stories. *The Peach Girl* (1931) and *Street Angel* (1937) respectively are regularly voted among the best ever made in the country. But after 1937, Yuan Muzhi went to Yen'an to work with Mao's communists, and in 1938 the Chinese film industry moved from Shanghai to Hong Kong. There, directors like Wang Weiyi and Zhu Shilin paved the way for the flourishing of Hong Kong cinema in the 1950s and again in the 1970s.

India set a different course. In the west, the arrival of talkies gave birth to a new genre—the musical—but in India, every one of the 5,000 films made between 1931 and the mid-1950s had musical interludes. The effects of this were far-reaching. Movie performers had to be able to dance. There were two parallel star systems—that of actors and that of playback singers. The films were stylistically more wide-ranging than the western musical, encompassing realism and escapist dance within individual sequences, and they were often three hours long rather than Hollywood's 90 minutes.

The cost of such productions, combined with the national reformism of the Congress party, resulted in a distinctive national style of cinema. Performed in Hindi (rather than any of the numerous regional languages) and addressing social and peasant themes in an optimistic and romantic way, "All India films" (the style associated with Bollywood) represented nearly half the continent's annual output of 250–270 movies throughout the 1940s and 1950s. They were often made in Bombay, the centre of what is now known as Bollywood. By the 1970s, annual production in India reached 500 and a decade later it had doubled once more. All India Films, as well as some of the more radical work inspired by the Indian Communist party, found markets in the middle east, Africa and the Soviet Union. By the late 1980s, however, the centre of gravity had moved away from Hindi production in Bombay. Madras began to produce an astonishing ten films a week (more than Los Angeles), and there were around 140 productions a year in Telugu, Tamil and Malayalam.

In Japan, the film industry had long ceased to rival India's in size but was distinctive in two ways. Until the 1930s, commentators called *benshis* attended every screening, standing in front of the audience, clarifying the action and describing characters. Directors did not need to show every aspect of their tale, and tended to produce tableau-like visuals. Even more unusually, its industry was director-led. Whereas in Hollywood, the producer was the central figure—he chose the stories and hired the director and actors—in Tokyo, the director chose the stories and hired the producer and actors. The model was that of an artist and his studio of apprentices. Employed by a studio as an assistant, a future director worked with senior figures, learned his craft, gained authority, until promoted to director with the power to select screenplays and performers.

These radical digressions from the norms of industrial cinema are in part explained by Japan's psychological retreat from 20th-century westernism. Its chauvinistic belief in Japanese superiority led to its invasion of Manchuria in 1931 and China proper in 1937, to catastrophic effect. Yet in the 1930s and 1940s, no national cinema was more artistically accomplished than Japan's. Its directors had considerable freedom, their nation was (over)confident and the result was cinema of the highest order.

The films of Yasujiro Ozu, Kenji Mizoguchi and Mikio Naruse were the greatest of these. Mizoguchi's were usually set in the 19th century and unpicked the social norms which impeded the liberties of the female characters whom he chose as his focus. From *Osaka Elegy* (1936) to *Ugetsu Monogatari* (1953) and beyond, he evolved a sinuous way of moving his camera in and around a scene, advancing towards significant details but often retreating at moments of confrontation or emotion. No one had used the camera with such finesse before. Great western directors like Vincent Minnelli and Bernardo Bertolucci would borrow his techniques.

Perhaps significantly, given the political climate, Mikio Naruse's best films were also beautifully controlled accounts of women's lives. Even more important for film history, however, is the work of the great Ozu. Born in Tokyo in 1903, he rebelled at school, watched lots of American film comedies in the 1920s, and imported their boisterous irreverence into his own work. Then he rejected much of their physicality and from *I Was Born, But...* (1932), embarked on a string of domestic films about middle-class families which are the most poised and resigned in world cinema. Brilliantly cast and judged, Ozu's films

—the most famous is *Tokyo Story* (1953)—went further than Mizoguchi's emotional reserve. Where Hollywood cranked up drama, Ozu avoided it. His camera seldom moved. It nestled at seated height, framing people square on, listening quietly to their articulations. This sounds boring, but the effect is the opposite. The families we see are bracingly alive. Their hard-earned wisdom is deeply moving.

The human elements alone in Ozu's films would have been enough to endear him to many of those in future generations—Wim Wenders in Germany, Hou Hsiao Hsien in Taiwan and Abbas Kiarostami in Iran—who have called him the greatest of film directors. But there was his technique too. Ozu rejected the conventions of editing, cutting not on action but for visual balance. His films analyse the space in which his characters move rather like the cubist paintings of Picasso and Braque—intellectually, unemotionally, from many angles. Even more strikingly, Ozu regularly cut away from his action to a shot of a tree or a kettle or clouds, not to establish a new location but as a moment of repose. Many historians now compare such "pillow shots" to the Buddhist idea that *mu*—empty space or nothing—is itself an element of composition.

By the beginning of the 1950s, and despite the ravages of nationalism, war and independence struggles, the three great Asian powers had national cinemas of distinction. Influenced by western directors, those in the east rethought the medium musically and spatially, making it rapturous or rigorous, according to their own national sensibilities.

Western directors still took no notice. They had new darlings by this stage—directors like Orson Welles, Alfred Hitchcock and Marcel Carne; actors like Ingrid Bergman, Judy Garland, Bob Hope and Humphrey Bogart. But their blindness to Asian cinema was now chronic. Then, in 1951, a film festival in Venice, started by Mussolini's cronies in 1932, awarded its top prize, the Golden Lion, to a Japanese film—Akira Kurosawa's *Rashomon*. Audiences on the Lido couldn't work out what they loved more, the film's ravishing cinematography, or its philosophical disquisition on relativism. *Rashomon* went on to be shown in cosmopolitan cities throughout the west and to win the Oscar for best foreign film. (Japanese films won again in 1954 and 1955.) The floodgates opened. Kurosawa had been crowned. The effect was compounded by his remarkable, cancer-themed *Ikiru*, made two years after *Rashomon*. Lucas, Coppola and Scorsese were soon paying attention.

Japanese cinema was pored over for new discoveries. Kurosawa's *The Seven Samurai* was fêted in 1955 and remade in Hollywood in 1960 as *The Magnificent Seven*. Kurosawa had himself been influenced by John Ford, but at least the flow was now two-way.

India, too, found the limelight. A new master director, Mehboob Khan, gained international acclaim—and an Oscar nomination—for *Mother India*, an epic often compared to *Gone with the Wind*. In their belated rush to raid the treasures of the east, the western cognoscenti even started to take notice of Japan's least showy director, Ozu. Still, it took a while. Despite festival screenings of his work and six of his films being named "best film of the year" in Japan, Ozu was recognised by few people abroad. Eventually, the British Film Institute called him "one of the greatest artists of the 20th century in any medium, in any country." Wim Wenders declared him "a sacred treasure of the cinema."

Watching the Asian films in Cannes this year, I had an idea of what it must have been like in Venice in 1951 or 1954. The sheer loveliness of the breakthrough films of 50 years ago was somehow feminine—certainly delicate, rich, soft, and shallow-focused. Each of the latest new wave of Asian films is highly decorated, tapestry-like, with an emphasis on detail, visual surface, colour and patterning, and centred on a woman, or feminised men.

It comes as no surprise, for example, that Zhang Yimou's *House of Flying Daggers* is so beautiful. His *Raise the Red Lantern* was visually striking and he started as a cinematographer on the breakthrough work of modern Chinese cinema, *Yellow Earth*. *Daggers*, however, may be one of the most photographically distinguished films ever made. In it, the actress Zhang Ziyi, who starred in *Crouching Tiger Hidden Dragon*, plays Mei, a blind dancer in the year 859 who is sympathetic to a revolutionary group threatening the Tang dynasty. An early sequence takes place in a large pavilion decorated entirely by peonies. A local captain suspects that Mei is a subversive and sets her a test. In the pavilion, he surrounds her with 100 vertically mounted drums. She stands in the middle, dressed in a coat of gold silk, embroidered with turquoise chrysanthemums. Presented with dishes of dry beans, the captain flicks one at a drum. The camera follows it though space. As it strikes the taut surface, Mei spins and flicks the enormously long sleeve of her coat in the direction of the sound. It travels as the bean did and strikes the drum in a rococo flourish. Then the captain flicks another bean, and Mei spins and flicks again. Then another. Then a small handful which scatter around the circle of drums. Mei responds to the percussive effect, her sleeves darting and soaring, her face still serene and expressionless, at the centre of the vortex. The bean shots are computer-generated—the most satisfying use of CGI CGI yet. The combination of such cinematic modernity with martial arts choreography, photographic splendour and, centrally, Zhang's enigmatic performance, makes this scene, at once, a classic.

If anything, Hong Kong director Wong Kar Wai's *2046* goes even further. It, too, is a widescreen film of seductively shallow focus, surface patterning and feminine beauty. Zhang Ziyi stars again, this time joined by two other great Chinese actresses, Gong Li and Maggie Cheung. Like Wong's previous film, *In the Mood for Love*, it is an evocative exercise in atmosphere and music, set in Hong Kong in the 1960s. Tony Leung plays a brilliantined writer caught in a destructive web of relationships. Wong and his cinematographers take the colours and lighting of Edward Hopper but reconfigure them into wide, flat, scroll-like images where everything has a melancholic sheen, where women move in slow motion, their stilettos clicking in night-time alleyways. To this Wong adds a futuristic element. A dazzling bullet train rockets forward through time to the world of 2046, a place where robotic people symbolise the empty state of love.

At first glance, the Japanese director Kore-eda's new film, *Nobody Knows*, is different from the aesthetic worlds of Zhang and Wong. Set in present-day Japan, it tells the story of a neglectful mother who rents an apartment with one of her children and who, when she moves in, opens her suitcases to reveal two more. In his way, however, the former documentary director is equally interested in stillness, in shallow focus and in production design. The mother leaves her children, but instead of declining into *Lord of the Flies* chaos, they subtly transform their apartment into a world suitable for themselves: scruffy, but full of play and adventure. *Nobody Knows* is another tapestry film like *Daggers*, but it is about the timeless ways in which children amuse themselves.

Thai director Apichatpong Weerasethakul's film *Tropical Malady* is more enigmatic still. In its first half, a soldier befriends a young peasant man who lives in the country. They drift around, sit talking, grow fond of each other. In one scene the soldier puts his head in his friend's lap, in another the soldier licks his hand. As their growing eroticism looks as if it might become explicit, the peasant walks into the jungle. Then the screen goes black: no sound, no picture, as if the film has broken. Then a second film begins. The actors are the same but their situation is more fable-like. A monkey talks to one of the characters, the other is the spirit of a tiger running naked through the jungle.

Tropical Malady is likely to be seen as one of the most experimental films of its time, but what is again striking is its gentleness and stillness. Though made in very different countries, the films of Weerasethakul, Zhang, Wong and Kore-eda share certain ideas about art. Just as the work of Ozu can be fully understood only by balancing its psychological aspects with more abstract Buddhist questions of space and stillness, so the influence of Buddhism can be seen in these new films. Despite the range of western cinema today, most of it derives from the assumption that movies are narrative chains of cause and effect, that their characters have fears and desires, and that we follow the film by understanding these fears and desires. The new films of Zhang and the others make similar assumptions but are less driven by them and balance questions of selfhood with Zen ideas about negation and equilibrium. This makes their beauty hard to replicate in the west.

But Buddhism is not the whole picture. Another Asian philosophy explains the sense of gender and use of space in these films. Unlike Maoism, which pictured a clear moral opposition between the good workers and bad bosses, and unlike Confucian philosophy, in which masculinity is noble and femininity is not, Taoism is less clear-cut. Morally, it sees good within bad and vice versa. The feminine is a virtue in the same way that emptiness may be for artists.

Every one of the great Asian films in the pipeline evinces Taoist ideas of sex and space. In none of them is gender polarised. In all of them, space is crucial. And the influence is acknowledged. Zhang, for example, has talked about the way Chinese painting has affected his work. His shots are often very wide. Space and landscape weigh as heavily within the frame as the human elements. Art historians have long discussed the Taoist component of such paintings.

Indian cinema, deriving from Hindu aesthetics, is not currently as innovative as that of other Asian countries. Although Indian film continues to be economically successful, and has become synonymous with high spectacle, the Hindu nationalism of the country's recent, backward-looking BJP government has coincided with a spell of cinematic complacency.

As the art form most swayed by money and market, cinema would appear to be too busy to bother with questions of philosophy. Other Asian nations are proving that this is not the case. Just as deep ideas about individual freedom have led to the bracingly driven aspirational cinema of Hollywood, so Buddhism and Taoism explain the distinctiveness of Asian cinema at its best. In Venice in 1951 and Cannes in 2004, audiences left the cinemas with heads full of dazzling images. But the greatness of *Rashomon, Ugetsu, 2046* or *House of Flying Daggers* is, in the end, not to do with imagery at all. Yes, they are pictorially distinctive, but it is their different sense of what a person is, and what space and action are, which makes them new to western eyes.

IDEAS &
POPULAR SCIENCE

"Communism's rubbish. I can't cut a bloody thing with this"

The legacy of the 1960s • Christopher Hitchens vs Peter Hitchens*

MARCH 1998

2nd February 1998

Dear Christopher,

If there is anything worse than a young conservative, it is an old revolutionary. Young Tories are now practically extinct, but the western world is infested with paunchy radicals. My own path—a silly flirtation with revolution in my teens and 20s followed by a comfortable return to Tory certainties in middle age—used to be a cliché. Now I am an exceptionasked, in wondering tones, how I come to be a reactionary. The disturbing thing about the late 1960s is that they are still going on; and we have not had to grow up.

The 1960s were not the emotional spasm they appeared to be, but a genuine upheaval with permanent effects. The year 1968 was not the beginning of this, but it was the moment when all its strands—political, moral, sexual and artistic—were woven most closely together. This was a cultural revolution far more destructive and iconoclastic than the Reformation—and lacking any true liberation. It reduced beloved institutions to rubble, while elevating musical, artistic and literary garbage. It introduced dope into western daily life. Its corrosive effects on language, manners, true human kindness, the education and upbringing of children, have been a disaster to anyone who has

*These are the first two letters of the original six-letter exchange.

the slightest tenderness for the next generation. I regret that I was involved in it at all, and squirm with embarrassment when I recall most of what I said and did. I recognise my responsibility for the loss of things which I should have been cherishing and defending, while I was helping to knock them down.

You ought to agree with me. You went deeper into this than I ever did and understood it better than I. You cannot be pleased by the nurseries of ignorance we call schools and universities. You cannot be glad that heroin is sold openly in pit villages such as Grimethorpe. You cannot be happy that rock music is the nearest most people now get to poetry, or that faith, class and deference have been replaced—not, as you might have hoped, by rational self-confidence, but by the syrupy celebrity worship epitomised in the recent festival of the Goddess Diana.

Nor can you be delighted by the achievements of the political causes, foreign and domestic, that we espoused. Vietnam holds public executions of "economic saboteurs." Africa is an economic and political slum, from Cape Town to Cairo. The Clintons, that perfect counter-culture couple rooted more deeply in the movement than they now care to admit, turn out to be as inspiring in office as Warren Harding, liberated only in the president's unconventional sexual tastes.

The favourite social causes of our generation—unrestricted abortion, easy divorce, radical education, sexual equality, homosexual law reform, the end of censorship and the abolition of capital punishment —have all been victorious. In every single case, the warnings of the crustiest and stupidest conservatives now turn out to have been sober and accurate prophecies. The family is disappearing. Life, born and unborn, is cheaper than it has been for almost two centuries. Millions of women, willingly or not, abandon their children to the care of paid strangers. Sexual tolerance led not to civilised contentment but to demands for legal and moral equality between homosexual partners and married couples. Morality has been replaced by a cold hedonism which promotes sterility rather than fertility.

An ethical person is no longer one who behaves well, but one who publicly conforms to orthodox opinions. As for the liquid manure which gurgles out of Hollywood and television studios, who can now say that Mary Whitehouse did not have a case when she predicted this and warned of its effects? And who can now read the evidence of clerics and literary persons, who declared that *Lady Chatterley's Lover* was a puritan and moral book, without a snigger?

We have not merely changed the rules of politics and morality. With our complacent acceptance of narcotics and our worship of talentless rock music—both of which provide exaltation without effort—we have broken the link between pleasure and reward as well as that between crime and punishment. By mocking the ideal of the gentleman we have elevated ambition and greed, unrestrained by concern for others. Surely this is not what we wanted? We have cut down the forest of custom and law which protected us. Yet to oppose or criticise these changes is to become a lonely dissident.

It is fashionable in Britain at the moment to blame our social decay on Margaret Thatcher and the "cuts" which she failed to make in social spending. As it happens, I accept that both the Thatcher and the Reagan administrations lacked a moral centre, and I believe that this is why they failed to achieve anything lasting. However, the truly serious diseases of our society are the work of our own spoiled generation: we wanted everything designed for our convenience and gratification, chose causes because they made us feel superior to our parents rather than because we were truly concerned about them, and then called our selfish wails a revolution.

Yours fraternally,

Peter

3rd February 1998

Dear Peter,

I think we might start as we mean to go on, and leave my circumference out of it. (After all, in your eyes, I was worse when I was leaner.)

In the autumn of 1996, I was interviewing Václav Havel in Prague. He spoke very warmly of Bill Clinton and declared himself—rather indiscreetly, I thought—in favour of his re-election. "I feel a bond with Mr Clinton," he said. "Like me, he is a man of the 1960s." A definite gloom descended upon me. As a relatively unrepentant *soixante-huitard*, I felt that I could trace some of the filiations connecting 1968 to 1989. Sixty-eighters I had known, or came to know, had become valiant eighty-niners. I mention Adam Michnik, Jan Kavan, Miklos Haraszti, Hans-Magnus Enzensberger, Peter Schneider and the late Rudolf Bahro—not in order to drop illustrious names but to show "where I'm coming from." In the old debate between EP Thompson and Leszek Kolakowski, for example, I always thought that Thompson had the right of it because he believed that some of the 1960s spirit, however unintended, had begun in 1956.

Bill Clinton, on the other hand, has always seemed to me a gruesome combination of baby-boomer narcissism and political correctness. All decades are arbitrary, of course (and I suspect that you would rather periodise history by reigns), but the 1960s did have a definite shape and definition. By its close, in a phrase that I detested at the time, "the personal had become political." Much of what you do not like in the modern world can indeed be blamed on the ethos concealed in that slogan. But it was the exhausted and demoralised *terminus* of the time, rather than its most authentic expression.

I am writing this from my current roost at the University of California at Berkeley. What was the position as viewed from here in the spring of, say, 1967? The college and state authorities claimed the right to invigilate and suppress most forms of political expression. Volunteers from the campus took their lives in their hands if they journeyed—as many did—south of the Mason-Dixon line, where millions of Americans were denied the essentials of citizenship. Meanwhile the university served as a think-tank and laboratory for an unjust war of aggression in Indochina. And much of the state of California was a proving ground for thermonuclear experiments which calmly envisaged the extinction of the human species for the sake of a dishonest superpower quarrel. Thanks in part to a cultural and political rebellion with which the name Berkeley is identified, the extension of civil rights became unstoppable, while a lousy war was actually stopped—in large part by a movement of citizens.

My chief regret, looking back on that period, is that I didn't play a more active part. Two of the great initiatives which also featured locally—the struggle for decent treatment for the Spanish-speaking underclass and the movement for nuclear disarmament—still await their dénouement. I was, I might add, relatively unmoved by the poetry of Allen Ginsberg and totally unmoved by the music of Frank Zappa. But Václav Havel says that these voices came to him as liberators. It's not much of a test of one's broadmindedness to see what he must be driving at.

Take the same moment in Europe and elsewhere and you find that military fascists in Greece have just joined the sub-Nato club comprised of Spain and Portugal; that a British Labour government is capitulating to a racist settler revolt in Southern Rhodesia; that Northern Ireland is a sectarian political protectorate of a cynical "Conservative and Unionist" party and that Israel has taken the leap from tiny David to the role of occupying Goliath. Nelson Mandela has two decades of confinement still ahead of him. At Oxford University, the PPE course ends before the study of Keynes—and official permission must be sought for everything from apparel to the distribution of leaflets, to say nothing of equal overnight rights for heterosexuals in college (male guests had always been allowed). I probably did more to alter the conditions in the last category than in any other, but I did at least witness and applaud and argue for some of the later triumphs in the other areas too, all of which were substantially *soixante-huitard* in origin, and some of which still need more attention of the same kind. I would not take back a word or deed of it.

Nor would I—do you invite me to do so?—restore the ban on DH Lawrence. Furthermore, Zimbabwe and South Africa are much less "slummy" than they would have been under the old dispensation; and Vietnam, if our lot had had any say in the matter, would have become independent in 1945. Grimethorpe was fairly rugged when I saw it last during the miners' strike of 1974, but the prevalence of illegal hard stuff is the work of serious cartels with occasionally frightening friends in high places; hardly the outcome of a flower-child ethic. I am in favour of decriminalisation of all narcotics and also the unfettered availability of all forms of contraception. But I don't get your drift about fertility. Apart from your status as a Jeremiah who sees little hope for our species, do you want the human sexual urge to lead to the production of more bambini? (I realise that, like all Christians and monotheists, you are stuck with the belief that we are (a) created sick and (b) commanded to be well.)

Looking back, I am most of all struck by how little the theories of the ownership of the means of production had to do with the outcome of anything. I wouldn't have believed that at the time. There is also the matter of unintended consequences. (Endless grudge suits about harassment, say, instead of any talk about workplace democracy.) You could reply that I am picking the good bits and leaving the bad bits out. But in order to say that you would have to be a different kind of critic, one who is not merely issuing an undifferentiated Whitehousean lament.

Fraternally,

Christopher

The meaning of the genetics revolution •
Geoff Mulgan
JUNE 2002

Francis Fukuyama's new book, *The Posthuman Future*, is about how science is remaking humanity, and why we should be afraid of what is coming. What most concerns Fukuyama is the prospect that biotechnology will transform what it means to be human. Three sets of changes stand out, each of which will cast profound doubt on some of our most cherished political beliefs: the effects on our personalities of various new kinds of drug; the radical extension of the life span; and the ability of genetic medicine to change and improve human beings.

The first set of changes is almost upon us. Before long, biotechnology will be able to change not only our moods but also the very structure of our personalities. Something of its potential power can be gauged from the influence of drugs like Prozac, Zoloft and Paxil, which have together been taken by some 10 per cent of Americans. Prozac works by increasing the levels of serotonin in the brain and has proven a remarkable cultural as well as medical phenomenon—albeit one on which the evidence is still contested—turning nervous and depressed people into confident, happy and assertive extroverts. Ritalin is another character transformer: the wonder-drug solution to attention deficit disorder. So successful is it that it is now used, usually illegally, by millions of students to increase concentration and energy levels and to fuel feelings of euphoria.

The advocates of both drugs argue that there is a biological cause and a chemical solution to personality problems, and it is true that pharmaceutical remedies to psychological problems have (to the chagrin of some) proved much more effective than many non-pharmaceutical therapies in treating conditions as varied as manic depression and some forms of schizophrenia. The problems arise when you try to draw a line between an illness needing treatment, and an everyday human flaw. Depression, like the inability to concentrate, affects most people to varying degrees. There is nothing intrinsically wrong with redefining such relatively normal problems as pathologies which require therapy. For example, meditation techniques which teach people how to discipline their minds can be effective at holding low-level mental illnesses at bay. But it is all too easy for therapy to turn into social engineering. Fukuyama writes that "there is a disconcerting symmetry between Prozac and Ritalin. The former is prescribed heavily for depressed women lacking in self-esteem; it gives them more of the alpha-male feeling that comes with high serotonin levels. Ritalin on the other hand is prescribed largely for young boys who do not want to sit still in class because nature never designed them that way. Together, the two sexes are gently nudged towards that androgynous median personality, self-satisfied and socially compliant, that is the current politically correct outcome in American society."

Current policy justifies restrictions on drug use mainly on the basis of harm. A truly safe drug that simply makes people feel better, without side-effects, could, paradoxically, be much harder to cope with. Huxley's *Brave New World* is a dystopia precisely because we are so suspicious of chemical routes to happiness, and would like to believe happiness should be at least distantly related to virtue. For the same reasons, we are suspicious of chemical remedies for low self-esteem. Self-esteem should bear some relationship to real qualities of character and achievement (although some people enjoy unreasonably high self-esteem without either achievement or drugs).

The second big impact of biotechnology is likely to be a further radical extension of life itself. The rise in life expectancy over the last century already ranks as one of the great achievements of modern science. When Europe's pension systems were created, very few could hope to live long enough to enjoy them. Now well over 80 per cent of people can expect to live to 65, and well over a quarter are likely to be alive at 85. Combined with falling birth rates, the effect is a big demographic shift: according to the demographer Nicholas Eberstadt by 2050 the median age will be 54 in Germany, 56 in Japan and 58 in Italy.

Much has been written about the impact of these shifts on pensions systems and labour markets; rather less on politics. As Fukuyama points out, the character of societies is likely to be changed by ageing, with more rigidity and resistance to change. Elderly women in particular will emerge as one of the most important blocs of voters and their views—less supportive of defence spending and using force abroad, according to US surveys—will gain in influence.

These arguments can be overdone. In the 1960s, swinging Britain was the oldest society in the world; conservative Japan one of the youngest. There is no simple correlation between age and politics. Yet just as it is intuitively likely that the rising importance of social order and inflation (which causes more harm to older savers than younger borrowers) over the last 20 years reflects ageing societies, so is it reasonable to expect that a further "greying" of society will change the political agenda—for example bolstering the constituency for higher spending on healthcare.

The forecasts on ageing, dramatic as they are, take no account of possible medical advances which could achieve a further sharp rise in life expectancy. Scientists have already identified some of the genetic foundations of mortality: the SIR2 gene, isolated by Leonard Guarente at MIT, plays a decisive role in the longevity of yeast and could possibly lead to ways of extending human lives. Stem cells created through therapeutic cloning could, in theory, be used to generate entirely new body parts identical to the cells in the host body, and so free from immune reactions.

Some scientists doubt whether anyone will ever find a simple key to the ageing process. But even if they are right, governments look certain to be condemned to hard choices. The continuing debate about whether the retirement age should rise in step with longevity may prove to be one of the easier issues. Much tougher ones will include how to manage access to new medical technologies, especially if they turn out to be very expensive, and how to strike the right balance between keeping people alive and keeping them lively (what of the prospect of an extra 50 years of life but no cure for Alzheimer's disease?).

The third big area of advance, and potential difficulty, is genetics. In recent years it has had a largely benign impact on political debate —notably stressing the genetic homogeneity of the human race. But much that may become known in the future will not be so comfortable. The most obvious example is the heritability of intelligence. Although this remains a complex issue because of the interactions of culture and biology, there is now a fairly wide consensus that some 40–50 per cent of many characteristics, including intelligence, are in some sense heritable, which if true has huge implications for how we think about social mobility and opportunity.

Another example is crime. It is easy now to mock the 19th-century Italian professor Cesare Lombroso, who identified a criminal physical type with a sloping head that was a throwback to an earlier stage of human evolution. But this does not mean that criminal behaviour, or characteristics that are associated with it such as impulsiveness, have no genetic basis. The idea that there might be genes for crime has been discredited, not least for ignoring the extent to which crime is socially determined. Yet there is a growing body of evidence which is harder to discount, such as a large study in Denmark which found that identical twins had a 50 per cent chance of sharing criminal behaviour, versus 21 per cent for non-identical. If this sort of finding is accepted, it will be hard to ignore its implications for crime prevention and punishment. One of its effects could be a further challenge to the idea of free will and personal responsibility: for criminals there may be grounds for claiming diminished responsibility, the "genetic defence"; for states there may be grounds for taking pre-emptive action to restrain prospective criminals.

The way we think about sexuality is also likely to change. Imagine, Fukuyama says, that in 20 years time there is reliable evidence that exposure to certain levels of testosterone in the uterus correlates with homosexuality, and that mothers could take a pill to significantly reduce the chances of a child becoming gay. How many parents would take it? How many governments would let them?

Millions of parents have already used amniocentesis and sonograms to diagnose Down's syndrome or cystic fibrosis. Geneticists expect that in the foreseeable future mothers will be able to produce dozens of embryos, screen them for genetic profile and choose the characteristics they want. Cloning may eventually be possible. This spring it was rumoured that three women were pregnant with cloned embryos. If this is true, the children have only a slim chance of survival. But what sounded like science fiction only a few years ago is starting to sound almost commonplace.

Genetic engineering poses huge risks especially given how little we know about how genes interact with each other. For some, this confirms the virtue of the precautionary principle: we should avoid tinkering with complex ecologies that we barely understand. But there will be competing pressures. Parents will often do whatever they can to maximise their children's life chances. Global markets are likely to find legal or illegal ways of linking scientific supply to what may be desperate demand. Governments may conclude that, far from banning the technologies, they should use them to reduce inequalities or raise the IQ of their people.

The above are just a few examples of how biotechnology could change us. They suggest how hard it is likely to be for societies to find their way amidst a confusing scientific and moral landscape. The first half of Fukuyama's book works well, providing a clearly written description of this landscape. Unfortunately, in the second half, as he tries to provide a moral compass, his clear-headed confidence dissolves. The central thesis is straightforward enough: that human nature is so fundamental to our notions of justice, morality and the good life, that any attempts to modify it will have disastrous consequences. Yet each successive step of the argument takes him further from solid ground.

His first challenge is to define human nature. Fukuyama argues that "human nature exists, is a meaningful concept and has provided a stable continuity to our experience as a species." Behavioural genetics and cross-cultural anthropology have, indeed, together done much to paint a picture of a human race that shares many more common traits than earlier generations of relativists allowed. So far, so good. The problems arise however when he tries to load a moral weight on to this picture. The ability to speak, the tendency to bring children up in families, and even belief in God, may all be typical of the human species and not explicable solely in cultural terms, but that does not make them in any strong sense constitutive of human nature. Nor is it clear why we should want to preserve all of these behaviours. Fukuyama weakly concludes that what he calls Factor X, our "essential humanness," is a cluster of characteristics that go to make up a whole.

At no point does Fukuyama answer the most powerful implicit claim of the biotechnologists. If we could—and it is a big "if"—change the behaviour and characteristics of some human populations in ways that were widely accepted as morally advantageous (perhaps with more optimistic, co-operative and less impulsive people on average) would this be a bad thing? After all, our inherited natures were shaped in a radically different environment, and have left us often ill-suited for modern life. There are many reasons for being nervous about any serious attempt to change our nature. But to defend our inherited make-up as the last word in evolution is just dogmatic.

Fukuyama criticises much Enlightenment thinking for having ignored human nature, and rightly argues that no political philosophy can be entirely credible without a coherent view of it. However, he is quite wrong to criticise today's political philosophies on these grounds. Much traditional conservative philosophy has a very clear view of human nature: our vulnerability to evil is the justification for a strong authority to hold us in check. Much socialist and liberal political philosophy is founded on a clear view of human beings as inherently benign and co-operative, just as neoliberalism (and neoclassical economics) is founded on an equally clear view of human beings as primarily self-interested. In none of these cases is the problem the lack of a view of human nature. The problem is rather that these views of human nature are simplistic caricatures, and devoid of any reference to the now very substantial empirical evidence we have about human psychology.

Moreover, it is by no means clear that our deepest understandings of justice, equality and morality *are* firmly founded on human nature. A more accurate claim would be that our deepest understandings of justice, equality and morality have arisen not as reflections of human nature, but rather from the tension between ideals and reality, between our ability to imagine a more perfect world and the "crooked timber" of real people. This tension is dynamic, not static; what Norbert Elias called the civilising process is a story of how some aspects of our nature—impulsive behaviour, violence—have been reined in, while others—discipline, sociability, loyalty to the group, honesty—have been rewarded.

In essence, Fukuyama's argument is a secular version of Pope John Paul II's acknowledgement in 1996 that the church could accept that humans are descended from non-human animals, but that there is an "ontological leap" that occurs somewhere in this process, a point at which the soul is created.

The idea of such a leap is flattering. It implies that we are safe from competition from the computers and artificial intelligence systems which a generation ago might have been expected to challenge our monopoly on recognition and rights. And it provides protection from the claim that animals, particularly those like gorillas which are genetically very close to humans, should be treated as having rights. Unfortunately, despite much effort, it turns out to be very hard to construct a convincing argument in favour of this "leap." As the animal rights theorist Peter Singer has repeatedly shown, if our ideas of rights are founded on a view of human beings' moral capacity then it is illogical to exclude animals that are very similar to us from the domain of rights, just as it is illogical to treat a severely mentally incapacitated adult, or a foetus, as having the same rights as a fully formed adult.

Fukuyama at one point concedes that Singer's position is probably logically stronger than his own, but attacks it instead for where it leads. He argues that if we give up the idea that humans are unique, and that all humans share equally in this uniqueness, or if we allow some people to use genetic engineering to alter their biological nature radically, then we risk destroying the very ideas of equal rights and dignity on which much that is best in our civilisation rests.

This is a big claim which left me unconvinced. Equal dignity and rights are not, and never have been, empirical facts. Some of the authors of the American constitution and the declaration of the rights of man may have believed that all men were literally created equal. But these ideas are much better understood as valuable fictions which encourage people to respect each others' needs and interests, guarantee our protection from oppression and hold diverse communities together. It is quite possible to believe in them, while also recognising how very unequally people are endowed. Greater genetic variability might make it harder to sustain arguments for equal rights, equal treatment or equal opportunity. But it is not self-evident that they would. In any case, it is just as likely that genetic engineering will *reduce* genetic diversity as that it will increase it, just as it is likely that societies with greater genetic knowledge will do more, rather than less, to pool risks. The fact that increased insight into each individual's genetic distinctiveness opens up the prospect of more personalised health care, will strengthen not weaken the case for socialised medicine because the alternative, in which everyone would buy their own insurance based on their own genetic predispositions, runs so counter to any sense of fairness or community. Such an outcome does not require anyone to believe that people are equal; instead it would reflect a majority choice that we would rather live in a society which treats people as if they are of equal worth.

Fukuyama's central claim is that biotechnology will be uniquely dehumanising. In a literal sense he is right; biotechnology will change our nature. But when we describe something as dehumanising we mean that it will destroy our most cherished values, and people's capacity to act as moral beings. This distinction matters because for nearly two centuries successive generations of critics have warned that technologies—the railway, the telephone, the television and the computer—would be dehumanising. Yet when we look back, each of these technologies has done far more to enrich life than to impoverish it, and the worst crimes against humanity have been committed by all-too-human institutions, often with scant support from technology. The very human nature which Fukuyama extols is as likely to threaten us in the future as any technology that we may create.

Fukuyama might have been on stronger ground if he had warned that the effects of biotechnology are likely to be as unequally distributed as those of previous industrial revolutions. But as in his other work, he hardly mentions words like "power" or "interest."

This absence is particularly evident in a final group of chapters which turn to the policy implications of the new technologies. Each year legislatures and politicians devote much time to the task of establishing the rules of a game that few fully understand. A great deal of the argument is polarised between *laissez faire* advocates of scientific progress, and sceptics whose primary purpose is to impede the new technology at all costs. Usually the battles take place in obscure committees and commissions. But the experience in Europe over GM crops shows how quickly issues at the intersection of science, economics and values can burst to the surface.

Most of the pressure for greater regulation is likely to come from consumer groups and environmentalists. However, some of it could come from pragmatic business leaders. Monsanto, for example, asked the first Bush administration to introduce stronger regulatory rules for genetically engineered products, including labelling. The proposal was subsequently dropped, but might have saved them from the disastrous backlash in Europe.

Governments wanting to regulate utilities or financial institutions can make use of an extensive body of theory and years of experience. In biotechnology, by contrast, governments and legislatures are making it up as they go along, mainly guided by the prevailing national climates of opinion. These are surprisingly varied. Britain, for example, has generally opted for cautious optimism, and has legalised therapeutic cloning and the use of stem cells harvested from human embryos. In the US, the religious right has made common cause with the radical left to oppose biotechnology in general and stem cell research in particular. In Germany, the unhappy history of eugenics has led to a very restrictive stance, while many southeast Asian countries have taken a liberal approach, primarily for economic reasons.

The principles which should guide regulators in the future are worryingly elusive. Take for example the argument that therapeutic technologies should be acceptable, whereas technologies for enhancing desirable attributes (like intelligence) should not be. This seems attractive, yet on closer inspection the distinction melts away: why for example should the enhancement of intelligence be so much less acceptable if it takes place in a clinic than in a school?

Fukuyama gives up on the attempt to define the boundaries. Instead, he suggests, we should be thinking about *how* decisions are made. One decision-maker held up as a model is Britain's Human Fertilisation and Embryology Authority. Its main role is to regulate such things as IVF and donor insemination. Its strength is that it brings together the many incommensurable dimensions of human biotechnology—scientific, medical, economic and ethical—in one institution which is responsible for controlling research and regulating what can be done. Crucially, too, it combines lay members, doctors and scientists in a transparent approach to making decisions.

I doubt whether members of the HFEA would share Fukuyama's conclusion that "we want to protect the full range of our complex, evolved natures against attempts at self-modification" and that "we do not want to disrupt either the unity or the continuity of human nature, and thereby the human rights that are based on it." So far they have taken a pragmatic, but ethically sophisticated approach, to ensure that we maximise the benefits and minimise the risks associated with biotechnology. That is surely the best position to take. To describe research on fertility, the preservation and extension of life as dehumanising will strike most people as odd. Similarly, the idea that we should block whole fields of technology just because of what they might do at some point in the future, flies in the face of the rather successful ways in which societies have managed to regulate and shape past technologies, from nuclear power to television.

But many observers will share Fukuyama's anxiety. The new technologies elicit a sense of vertigo, perhaps appropriately since far from coming to an end, history may only just be gathering speed, as humanity learns how to control its own evolution, not just culturally but biologically too.

Anti-social capital • Nicholas Lemann

AUGUST/SEPTEMBER 1996

Why is there such a wide variation in the social and economic health of different regions and ethnic groups and, for that matter, of different societies all over the world?

A Harvard professor, Robert Putnam, has come up with an answer which has aroused academic and political interest on both sides of the Atlantic. It came to him, curiously, studying Italian local government.

Putnam discovered that local authorities in the prosperous north of Italy outperformed the ones in the benighted south. In itself this is not surprising, but the reasons given by Putnam are. In *Making Democracy Work*, he showed that northern success was not simply a case of the rich getting richer; regional government officials, for example, are less well educated in the north than in the south. Instead, he found the north's secret to be a quality that Machiavelli called *virtu civile* ("civic virtue")—an ingrained tendency to form small-scale associations. "Good government in Italy is a by-product of singing groups and soccer clubs," he wrote. Civic virtue both expresses and builds trust and co-operation in the citizenry; it is these qualities—which Putnam called "social capital," borrowing a phrase from Jane Jacobs —that create a fertile ground for political and economic development.

What causes some societies to become more civic-minded than others? In Italy, Putnam said, the north-south difference dates from the 1100s, when the Normans established a centralised, autocratic regime in the south, and a series of autonomous republics arose in the north. The southern system stressed what Putnam called "vertical bonds": it was rigidly hierarchical, with those at the bottom depend-ent on the patronage of landowners and officials rather than on one another. In the north small organisations such as guilds and credit associations generated "horizontal bonds," fostering a sense of mutual trust. Putnam stressed the "astonishing constancy" of the north-south divide: it survived the demise of the independent northern republics in the 17th century and the Risorgimento in the 19th century.

Putnam contested the prevailing view in the social sciences that civic virtue is "an atavism destined to disappear" with modernisation, which replaces small organisations that operate by custom with big ones that operate by rules. Instead, he said, even the biggest and most modern societies cannot function well if the local civic dimension is weak.

When Putnam brought his theory home to the US, it created a sensation. His article "Bowling Alone," published in January 1995, had a great impact. In its wake, Putnam was invited to Camp David to consult with Bill Clinton. His terminology has heavily influenced the past two state of the union addresses; he was even mentioned in the musings of Senator Bill Bradley about his disillusionment with politics.

The thesis of Bowling Alone is that "the vibrancy of American civil society"—the magic variable—"has notably declined over the past several decades." Putnam gets his title from the finding that between 1980 and 1993 league bowling declined by 40 per cent while the number of individual bowlers rose by 10 per cent. The rest of his evi-dence is less whimsical: voter turnout, church attendance and union membership are down. The percentage of people who trust the government and who attend community meetings has dropped. The leading indicator for Putnam—membership in voluntary associations —is down. Look at the Boy Scouts, the Lions, the Jaycees, the Masons, the Red Cross, the Federation of Women's Clubs: "Serious volunteering declined by roughly one sixth" from 1974 to 1989. For Putnam, the true import of these changes is that they predict a broader decline in economic vitality.

Earlier this year, Putnam stated his thesis more firmly, in an article in the *American Prospect* called "The Strange Disappearance of Civic America." He found that Americans who were born after the second world war are far less civic-minded than their elders; the reason is that they grew up after the advent of television, which "privatises our leisure time."

Bowling Alone struck a nerve in part because it provided a coherent theory to explain the dominant emotion in American politics: a feeling that the everyday quality of our society has deteriorated severely. It appeals to liberal politicians, who see in it the possibility of a rhetoric they can use to address an issue that has been owned by conservatives. Putnam's work also suggests the possibility of solving our problems through relatively low cost association-strengthening local initiatives that do not require higher taxes. This appeals to Democrats, who want to put forward a programme that is not vulnerable to anti-tax rhetoric, and to foundation executives, who want to believe that the limited grants they make can reap large social benefits.

There are, however, a few problems with his theory. For one thing, the Italian Putnam conflicts with the Bowling Alone Putnam. According to the Italian version, once civic virtue is in place, it is meant to be durable over the centuries; it cannot vanish in a generation as Bowling Alone suggests. Assuming the Italian Putnam is right, then the dire statistics in Bowling Alone may reflect merely a mutation rather than a disappearance of civic virtue. Perhaps civic virtue has found new outlets.

To test this idea I spent a couple of days telephoning around in search of examples of new associations. Putnam mentions several in

Bowling Alone, but dismisses them as replacements for the lost bowling leagues, either because they do not involve regular face to face contact (cyberspace forums; the 33m-member American Association of Retired Persons) or because they do not encourage people to build lasting ties (Alcoholics Anonymous). The most dramatic example I could find is US Youth Soccer, which has 2.4m members, up from 1.2m ten years ago and from 127,000 20 years ago. As a long-standing coach in this organisation, I can attest that it involves incessant meetings, telephone calls, and activities of a kind that create extensive civic links between people.

Another intriguing statistic is the number of restaurants in the US us, which has risen from 203,000 in 1972 to 368,000 in 1993. True, this probably means that fewer people are eating a family dinner at home. But from Putnam's perspective, that might be good news; it means that people who are eating out are expanding their civic associations.

The number of small businesses, too, has about doubled since 1970. These can be seen as both generators and results of civic virtue, because they involve so much personal contact and mutual trust. A small subset, community development corporations (which promote associations locally in the hope of a later economic pay-off), have grown from 500 to 2,200 over the past 20 years. Individual contributions to charity (still made by more than three quarters of Americans) rose from $16.2 billion in 1970 to $101.8 billion in 1990. Although church attendance is, as Putnam says, down, the Pentecostal denominations are booming. Membership in the PTA is also rising, although it is still far below its peak in 1962–63. Home ownership is high and steady, and, as Putnam admits in Bowling Alone, Americans move less frequently now than they did in the 1950s and 1960s.

Weighed against all this, the statistics in Bowling Alone are still impressive. But let us say for the sake of argument that Putnam's thesis that civic virtue is collapsing in the US is not true. What accounts for it being so widely accepted as gospel?

I have lived in five American cities: New Orleans, Cambridge, Washington, Austin, and Pelham, New York. The two that stand out in my memory as most deficient in the Putnam virtues—the places where people tend not to have elaborate hobbies and not to devote their time to neighbourhood meetings—are Cambridge and Washington. The reason is that these places are the big time. Work absorbs all the energy. It is what people talk about at social events. Community is defined functionally, not spatially: it is a professional peer group rather than a neighbourhood. Hired hands, from nannies to therapists, bear more of the civic virtue load than is typical.

To people living this kind of life, many of whom grew up in a bourgeois provincial environment and migrated to one of the capitals, the Bowling Alone theory makes sense. It is natural for people to assume that if their own life trajectories have been in the direction of reduced civic virtue, this is the result not of choices they have made, but of a widespread national trend.

Another reason for the appeal of Bowling Alone is that it challenges high-spending liberal social policy. Putnam himself wrote: "Classic liberal policy is designed to enhance the opportunities of individuals, but if social capital is important, this emphasis is partially misplaced. Instead we must focus on allowing space for religious groups and choral societies that may seem to have little to do with politics or economics."

A political challenge to Putnam's theory would run like this. There has been relatively little general decline in civic virtue. To the extent that the overall civic health of the nation did deteriorate, it was confined mainly to 1965–75—when, for example, crime and divorce rates rose rapidly. Instead, the overwhelming social and moral problem in the US is the disastrous condition of poor neighbourhoods, almost all of which are in big cities.

The model of a healthy country but with needy ghettos would suggest a programme much closer to the "liberal social policy" from which Putnam wants us to depart. Rather than assume, with Putnam, that such essential public goods as safety, decent housing and good education can be generated only from within a community, we could assume that they might be provided from without—by government. If quite near the ghettos are working class neighbourhoods (and not insuperably distant are suburbs) of varying ethnic character and strong civic virtue, then the individual opportunity model might be precisely the answer for ghetto residents: an opportunity, to move to a place that is part of the healthy American mainstream.

The difficulty with such a programme is that it is politically inconvenient. It would involve, by contemporary standards, too much action on the part of the government, with the benefits too skewed toward blacks. The idea of an entire US severely distressed in a way that is beyond the power of government to correct is more comforting.

A Tory communist • Ian Buruma

OCTOBER 2002

W as the omelette really worth cracking so many eggs? The number of deaths due to famines, mass murders and other man-made catastrophes under communist regimes is something between 85m and 100m. In Cambodia, almost the entire educated population was liquidated. Mao Zedong was responsible for about 30m deaths in the lunatic great leap forward alone. Stalin's gulag swallowed millions in its dark, frozen maw. And North Koreans are still dying of hunger.

To have remained a member of a communist party until the late 1980s, there must have been a residue of belief somewhere, deep down, that it might have been worth it, or at least would have been worth it, if things had not been so badly handled by the tyrants who ruled in the name of communism. Not many British intellectuals stuck it out for so long. Eric Hobsbawm, the eminent author of *Age of Extremes*, among other well-known history books, is one who did— not always as an active member, indeed for a long time as a sceptical one, but as a comrade none the less. In the *Age of Extremes*, he writes of the "unprecedented inhumanity" of Stalin's Russia and he now says that the communist project "has demonstrably failed and, as I now know, was bound to fail." But this makes his tenacity all the more puzzling.

In his latest book, a memoir entitled *Interesting Times: A Twentieth-Century Life*, Hobsbawm tries to explain why. Why he fell in line, in 1939, when Nazi Germany signed a non-aggression pact with the Soviet Union; or during the show trials in the late 1940s and early 1950s; and even after 1956, year of the Hungarian uprising. Words such as "background," "generation" and "anti-fascism" abound. But also "pride": a cussed refusal to give up on a course once embarked on with noble intent.

Whatever one's views on communism, Hobsbawm's memoir is a fascinating personal account of an ideal which attracted many people for the best of reasons, and provided an excuse for some of the most appalling crimes in the last century. Hobsbawm was, as he says in the preface of his book, "a participant observer," a historian as well as a political activist. He is a decent man who served a blood-soaked cause. Reading his book is an interesting, rewarding, but also, for me, frustrating experience. I wanted to know more. Too many questions remained incompletely answered. So I decided, in hope of further enlightenment, to visit the author at his north London house.

Hobsbawm appears a little weary of questions about communism. He has been asked them too often already. People like to hear a *mea culpa*. And that is where his pride kicks in. He wanted to know whether communism was all that interested me about his book. There are chapters, after all, about jazz, cottages in Wales, and travels in Latin America, but I had to admit I found the communism most compelling. Yes, he sighed, well, it was probably the hardest thing to understand. It was a generational thing. You had to "have been there."

"There," in Hobsbawm's case, was Berlin, 1932. Born in Alexandria, the son of an Austrian mother and a British father, both non-religious Jews, he spent his earliest years in Vienna, before going to a Gymnasium in Berlin. It was not a good time to be Jewish in Germany, even if you were protected by a British passport. The Weimar Republic was in tatters. Hitler would come to power a year later. SA men were already rounding up people for their torture chambers with impunity. Hobsbawm was spared their violent attentions, partly because he was "the Englishman" rather than "the Jew." None the less, as he writes in his book, he felt he was living on "the Titanic, and everyone knew it was hitting the iceberg." German nationalism held no appeal for an English schoolboy. Nor did Zionism. Social democracy was dead. Communism, he thought, was the only choice for someone like him.

Hobsbawm likes to see things in terms of time and place. In a different time or place, he probably would not have become a communist. But surrounded by Nazis in Berlin, he was in thrall to the promise of world communism. This is why, despite everything, he can write that he feels a "tenderness" for the memory and tradition of the USSR. To some people of his age it had once represented the hopes, not only of the Russians, but of mankind.

I asked whether his Jewish background had anything to do with his embrace of internationalism. After all, Karl Marx thought his communist dream would solve the Jewish problem. National and racial differences would disappear in the workers' paradise.

"No," he replied, that was not it, for he "never had any personal trouble with the Jewish problem. One was aware of being Jewish. How could one not be, in the circumstances?" His mother had taught him never to be ashamed of it. "Of course, we believed that what Marx said would happen. But that wasn't why I became a communist. I couldn't sympathise with nationalism, because it reserved for small groups what should have been kept for humanity. I had an 18th-century belief in humanity."

Humanity consists of groups, and groups are made up of individuals. One sentence in Hobsbawm's book had struck me as particularly revealing. Writing about himself in Berlin at the time of his communist initiation, Hobsbawm observed: "Human beings did not appear to interest him much, either singly or collectively; certainly much less than birds." Was this still true? "Well," he replied, "one likes certain peoples more than others: the Scots, the Italians, the Brazilians ... how could one not like them?" Yes, but what about individual people? "I don't really know what it means: to like individuals. Does it mean gossiping about them? I sometimes do that, I suppose."

He paused, then said: "I don't really like reading biographies." The point of writing his own appears to have troubled him. He asked me whether I thought there was any point in it. I said of course there was. But there is something impersonal about Hobsbawm's style, even as a memoirist. He has affection for individual people. His wife is mentioned many times. But no one is much described, apart from physical appearance. Character doesn't count. Ideas do. He told me that, although he loved France, because of the revolution, he didn't care much for the French. This seems rather typical.

Hobsbawm's style has the advantage of unsentimentality—even though he can be sentimental about collective entities, mere abstractions: the Vietnamese "had fought for us," against America. Did they really? But his approach also contains a rather chilling intellectual ruthlessness. We talked about Pol Pot—barely mentioned in the memoir—and Mao's carnage in China. Hobsbawm was never a Maoist. He described the murder of tens of millions as being "beyond cost-effectiveness." This struck me as an odd phrase. Later, when Hobsbawm was shown this text, he objected that the phrase had been "tongue in cheek." The Asian carnage, in any case, was not in the logic of communism. But the Soviet attempt to "liquidate whole classes probably was, in a primitive sort of way... We knew it was brutal in the Soviet Union. We had read Babel. We never believed it was a workers' paradise. But we believed it was better, and knew the costs were enormous. There were no solutions in the 20th century which did not imply catastrophes and suffering."

Hobsbawm went on to describe various popular movements in history, such as the extremely violent Dutch reformation in the 16th century, without which the 17th-century Dutch golden age would not have been what it was. "When you have a mass popular movement, you get a certain rebarbarisation, which is inevitable." Popular movements allow people to drive things to an extreme. For they are made up of common people, not intellectuals. I suggested to him that Pol Pot and his crew were intellectuals. Intellectuals often support and encourage violence. He repeated that he didn't really understand Pol Pot.

Hobsbawm had hoped that things would liberalise in the Soviet Union after the iron age of Stalin. "This might have happened, but it didn't." When did he realise this? The last straw appears to have been in 1968, with the end of the Prague spring. "We lost hope after 1968. Prague was a terrible shock. We didn't want to believe they would do such a thing."

But there had been earlier shocks that changed Hobsbawm from an activist believer in world revolution to a lapsed communist, as it were. In his book, Hobsbawm uses a peculiar phrase to describe Khrushchev's exposure of Stalin's crimes in 1956. He calls it a "brutally ruthless denunciation"—strong language for an unsentimental historian who could describe mass murder as not cost-effective, even in jest. But de-Stalinisation ripped open the communist church. And after 1956, when Soviet tanks rolled into Budapest, Hobsbawm "stopped being a communist who devoted his life to world revolution."

Why, then, did he stay in the party? It was partly a question of pride. He did not like to be like "those Frenchmen who go about beating their breasts. It had been part of one's life." He hates the way former believers become fierce anti-communists. He feels he owes a loyalty to his own past. It appeals to his British sense of tradition. He calls himself a "Tory communist." The loss of tradition pains him. It is one reason for his hatred of Margaret Thatcher: her populist attacks on traditional institutions. Speaking of his national loyalties, Hobsbawm says he "got to assimilate emotionally his *état civil*" as a British citizen, but "didn't like giving up my various identities. I remained loyal to my German cultural identity, and my Austrian identity, without taking them very seriously." Englishness lies in that last clause.

There was one other reason, however, for his loyalty to the communists. He remains convinced that the Soviet Union, however reprehensible, was "a necessary counterweight to the US." In this, Hobsbawm is not alone. Deep mistrust of the US is often all that remains of the left. Hobsbawm loves many things about America, especially New York and jazz music, and he has taught for many years at various American universities, but the US remains the enemy of everything he had once hoped for, the enemy of his faith. That is why he can still claim, as he does in his book, that he looks forward to "an American world empire ... with more fear and less enthusiasm than I look back on the record of the old British empire."

Even if one can easily agree that the current US administration does not inspire confidence, there is a problem with the necessary counterweight theory. He rightly points out that many regimes in the American camp during the cold war were nasty military dictatorships. But US support for them began to dwindle as the cold war neared its end. Hobsbawm mentioned the liberalisation of South Korea as an example of what he had hoped for in the Soviet bloc. But democracy came to South Korea (and Taiwan, the Philippines, Thailand, and other "client states") with US backing, precisely because the old communist counterweights were no longer seen as a threat.

I put this to Hobsbawm. He said something about South Korea proving the superiority of a planned economy, which had produced a liberal middle class. When I mentioned other new democracies in the American camp, he paused, and said: "You mean the Americans support elections. Is that necessarily a good thing?" Perhaps this is part of his traditionalism, but Hobsbawm—although he professes to be "deeply committed to a world governed in the interests of ordinary people and not elites"—is not a natural democrat. He seems to have a limited trust in what people will do when they decide their destinies through the ballot box. He mentions various countries where democracy didn't work. "Look at Turkey," he says. "If civilised values survive there, it is because the army protects them against democracy, which would vote for Islamic fundamentalism."

This fits with his other suggestion that the savagery of popular movements comes from the mobs rather than the intellectuals who lead them. It is as though he had an almost religious fear of the apocalypse without a disciplined church to save mankind from disaster. The October revolution represented a dream of universal equality and justice. But the trouble with the US, in Hobsbawm's words, is that "it has no project other than global hegemony and getting its presidents elected." Islamist terrorists, whatever else they represent, do have a project. It is a project Hobsbawm abhors, but he does not believe that "any rational person believes in that stuff about fighting terrorism. Iraq does not provide a serious danger."

To see the US, with all its faults and swagger, as a greater danger than revolutionary terrorist organisations, which regard mass murder as a legitimate means to their religious end, is to remain in thrall to a world view I find baffling. But then I am of a different generation. I have lived in less interesting times. I never saw the Brownshirts on the streets of Berlin. For a time, communism appeared to be the only counterweight. I can understand why a man would join because of that. But only a very conservative Tory communist would have stayed true to the faith ever since.

The science of eternity • Martin Rees

JANUARY 2002

Over the past few centuries, the earth has aged spectacularly. Its creation has been moved back from 6pm on Saturday, 22nd October, 4004 BC, as calculated by the 17th-century scholar and Archbishop of Armagh, James Ussher, to a time and date some 4.5 billion years earlier. The story of life has been stretched back almost as far, and the story of complex, multicellular life-forms—relative newcomers—has itself been almost a billion years in the making. As a result, the way we see the world has changed profoundly. Not only can we now have some sense of the millions of years it takes to raise and then level mountains, or to open and then close oceans, we also have the clearest evidence of humanity's *absence* throughout those ages.

If the earth's past has been stretched, what of its future? To those of Ussher's faith, the end of the world was a certainty and to some of his contemporaries history was already nearing its close. Sir Thomas Browne wrote, "the world itself seems in the wane. A greater part of Time is spun than is to come."

Current cosmology suggests a future that, if not infinite, dwarfs the past as much as the depths of time we now accept dwarf Ussher's exquisite estimates. What it cannot tell us, though, is whether these vast expanses of time will be filled with life, or as empty as the earth's first sterile seas. In the aeons that lie ahead, life could spread through the entire galaxy, even beyond it—and outlast it too. But life could also snuff itself out, leaving an eternity as empty as the space between the stars.

To begin at the beginning, we can, with some confidence, trace cosmic history back to its first few seconds, some 12 billion years ago. But in response to the fundamental question, "what happened before the beginning?" we cannot do much better than St Augustine in the 5th century, who sidestepped the issue by arguing that time itself was created with the universe. The origin of the "big bang" is, in some ways, as mysterious to us as it was to St Augustine. Cosmologists who study it are forced to jettison commonsense ideas, invoking extra spatial dimensions and postulating that space and time may have an inherently "grainy" structure on very tiny scales.

The sun—and the earth with it—came into being when the universe was approximately two thirds its current age. Minuscule though they may be in terms of their size, on a cosmic scale, they are thus of a respectable age. The sun will continue to shine for five billion years—longer than it has taken for our earth to evolve from a lump of molten rock to its present state. It will then swell up into a red giant, engulfing the inner planets and vaporising any life that remains on earth.

It is hard to say what life might remain on the earth at that point. The sun has been getting hotter since its birth and will continue to do so. This heating has been balanced on earth, to some extent, by trends that have tended to cool the planet; the most clear cut of which, over geological timescales, has been a long-term drop in carbon dioxide and a resultant weakening of the earth's natural greenhouse effect. This trend, however, cannot continue for long; carbon dioxide, once more plentiful in the atmosphere than oxygen, is now present at a mere 300 parts per million. Even a drop to zero would not cool the planet a great deal in the face of increased solar luminosity—but it would kill off the plants which rely on carbon dioxide as the raw material for their photosynthetic growth, and thus remove oxygen from the atmosphere.

Without the cushion provided by ever-lower carbon dioxide levels, over the next billion years the earth will start to feel the warming of the sun much more than it has in the past, and when the surface reaches about 50°C, the increased levels of water vapour will permit a new form of "runaway" greenhouse effect that will quickly raise the temperature high enough to boil the remaining oceans. Current estimates suggest that the biosphere cannot survive much beyond a billion years.

So by the time the sun finally licks the earth's face clean, life on earth will either be extinct, spread beyond its original planet or in a form impervious to extremes of temperature. Just as the universe is still young, so it seems that the emergence of intelligence and complexity is near its cosmic beginnings; we are far from the culmination of evolution. Intelligently controlled modifications could lead to faster and more dramatic changes than Darwinian natural selection allows. The future may lie in artefacts created by us and in some way descended from us, that develop via their own directed intelligence. Such entities might see the death of the sun as a minor or sentimental matter.

In the 1960s, Arthur C Clarke imagined the "Long Twilight" after the death of the sun and today's other hot stars as a realm at once majestic and slightly wistful. "It will be a history illuminated only by the reds and infrareds of dully glowing stars that would be almost invisible to our eyes; yet the sombre hues of that all-but-eternal universe may be full of colour and beauty to whatever strange beings have adapted to it. They will know that before them lie, not the ... billions of years that span the past lives of the stars, but years to be counted literally in trillions. They will have time enough, in those endless aeons, to attempt all things and to gather all knowledge. But for all that, they may envy us, basking in the bright afterglow of creation; for we knew the universe when it was young."

B ut even after the longest twilight, night will fall. There will come a time when the dimmest, slowest-burning stars are done. While academic cosmologists publish, month after month, hundreds of scientific papers discussing the ultra-early universe, they have written little about this long-range future. But it is an area ripe for speculation. I can claim to have made one of the first scientific contributions to "cosmic futurology" in a short 1968 paper entitled "The Collapse of the Universe: an Eschatological Study." Many cosmologists suspected then that the expansion that currently characterises our universe would cease and reverse itself. Galaxies would then fall towards each other, eventually crashing together into a "Big Crunch." I described how, as galaxies merged together in the countdown to the crunch, individual stars would accelerate to almost the speed of light (rather as the atoms speed up in a gas that is compressed). Eventually these stars would be destroyed as the blue-shifted radiation from other stars rushing towards them made the sky above them hotter than the fires within.

Currently, though, the big crunch is out of favour; more recent long-range cosmic forecasts have predicted that the expansion of the universe will continue for ever, with its contents becoming ever colder and more diffuse. Ten years after my paper, the Princeton theorist Freeman Dyson—who would not countenance the Big Crunch because it "gave him a feeling of claustrophobia"—made scientific eschatology more respectable in an influential article called "Time without End: Physics and Biology in an Open Universe," published in the austere scholarly journal *Reviews of Modern Physics*. "The study of the remote future," Dyson wrote, having noted that the handful of papers on the subject were written in an apologetic or jocular style, "still seems to be as disreputable today as the study of the remote past was 30 years ago." He set out to change the state of affairs with a rigorous study of the physics of the far future and the prospects for some sort of life persisting there.

Dyson charted the processes that would take place after the suns had burned out, and their timescales; the loss of planets from dead stars, the slow evaporation of galaxies, the decay of black holes (a process that takes 10^{60} years—that is one with 66 zeros behind it for a stellar-mass hole, and longer for a giant one) and the eventual transmutation of all remaining matter into iron. That last alchemical endgame is spun out for such a large number of years that to write it down would need as many zeros as there are atoms in all the galaxies we can see. That is how long you would have to wait before a giant quantum fluctuation caused an entire star to "tunnel" into a black hole. Throughout it all, Dyson imagined, life might persist in some form.

The universe's usable energy reserves are finite, and at first sight this might seem to be a basic restriction on everlasting life. But Dyson showed that this constraint was not fatal. Just as an infinite series can have a finite sum (for instance $1 + \frac{1}{2} + \frac{1}{4} + \ldots = 2$) so there is no limit to the amount of information processing that could be achieved with a finite expenditure of energy. And the nature of mathematics ensures that there could be infinite novelty generated in that infinite information processing. It might be an odd, stripped down sort of "life," a life abstracted to such an extent that only the most mathematical of minds could conceive it as life—but it would not have to be repetitive, and thus might not have to be dull. The rate at which the calculations were made would get slower and slower and enforced periods of hibernation longer and longer—as Woody Allen said, "eternity is very long, especially toward the end"—but life in some form could persist.

Recent developments in physics have modified Dyson's picture in two ways. First, we now suspect that atoms themselves live for "only" 10^{36} years—not for ever. In consequence, the cold remnants of stars and planets (and any complex entities made of atoms) will erode away as the atoms within them decay. Thoughts and memories would only survive beyond this stage if downloaded into circuits and magnetic fields in clouds of electrons and positrons—maybe something that would resemble the alien intelligence in *The Black Cloud*, the most imaginative of Fred Hoyle's science fiction novels of the 1950s.

Second, Dyson saw no limit to the scale of artefacts that could some day be constructed. He envisioned the observable universe getting ever vaster, as the expansion of space slowed down and galaxies whose light has not yet had time to reach us (galaxies further away in space than the big bang is in time) slowly came within range of possible communication and "networking," offering scope for ever larger cosmic construction projects. But within the past few years, cosmologists have discovered to their surprise that the expansion of the universe is not slowing down at all: some repulsive force or antigravity seems to be pushing galaxies apart at an accelerating rate. This means that, rather than more and more galaxies coming into contact with us, we will lose contact with most of the galaxies we can now see: these galaxies will accelerate towards the speed of light, eventually receding "over the horizon" into the unobservable. In the very distant future, our descendants (if any) would have lost contact with everything except the small group of galaxies that contains our own milky way (by then bereft of the starlight that makes it milky). There would therefore be a permanent limit on how large and complex anything can get. Some theorists suggest that this limit on the energy and complexity available would preclude infinite novelty and that eternity would become very dull.

The implications of accelerating expansion, though, need to be put in the context of the other uncertainties. First, we cannot be sure that the regions beyond our present horizon are like the parts of the universe we see, and this might influence future expansion. For another thing, there is a theoretical possibility that the nature of the universe, and the laws that hold sway in it, might be subject to radical and unexpected change. Very pure water can stay liquid below 0°C—a state known as supercooling—only to freeze in a flash when a snowflake falls on it. It has been suggested that our present "vacuum" —the fundamental stuff of space time—may also be "supercooled," and thus that some comparatively minor event could trigger a change to a new state of being, governed by quite different laws. There are occasional scares that this sort of catastrophe could be induced artificially by experiments that crash particles together with high energy. Those in charge of the Brookhaven national laboratory in the US were cautious enough to commission an expert assessment on whether any of their planned experiments could end the universe this way or trigger some other global catastrophe. (Another scare was that a new kind of atom called "strange matter" could be created in accelerators, which would by contagion gradually transform the entire earth into this new form—a scenario reminiscent of Kurt Vonnegut's *Ice Nine*, where the oceans are transformed into a new kind of ice with a high freezing point.) It is reassuring to note that "cosmic ray" particles, hurtling through space with far more energy than any terrestrial experiment can generate, have been hitting each other, on and off, for billions of years, without tearing the fabric of space or destroying the possibility of matter.

A hackneyed anecdote among astronomy lecturers describes a worried questioner asking: "how long did you say it would be before the sun burnt the earth to a crisp?" On receiving the answer, "five billion years," the questioner responds with relief: "thank God for that, I thought you said five million." What happens in far-future aeons may seem blazingly irrelevant to the practicalities of our lives. But I don't think it is. It is widely acknowledged that the Apollo programme's pictures of the island earth, its fragile beauty contrasted with the stark moonscape, changed the way we see ourselves in space —strengthening the collective ties that bind us to our environment. No new facts were added to the debate; just a new perspective. A new perspective on how we see ourselves in time might do something similar. (That is the hope of the Long Now Foundation, an organisation devoted to the construction of clocks and other instruments that can last thousands of years.)

Taking the truly cosmic long view, the view in which billions of years pass as hours, would require pictures of the earth, not from the neighbouring moon, but from light years away, from some far-off star. Within a few decades, new generations of space telescopes should provide the technology to take just such pictures—to produce images of the planets around other stars. Will they have biospheres? Will they harbour intelligent life? We know too little about how life began, and how it evolves, to be able to say whether alien intelligence is likely or not. The cosmos could already be teeming with life: if so, nothing that happens on earth would make much difference to life's long-range cosmic future. On the other hand, advanced life may be rare—so rare, perhaps, that it is unique to our earth. The emergence of intelligence may require such an improbable chain of events that it has not occurred anywhere else—not around even one of the trillion billion other stars within range of our telescopes. Claims that advanced life is widespread must confront the famous question first posed by the physicist Enrico Fermi: "why aren't the aliens here?" Why haven't they visited earth already, or at least manifested their existence in some way? This argument gains extra weight when we realise that some stars similar in many ways to our sun are billions of years older: if life were common, its emergence should have had a head start on planets around these ancient stars.

But if earth *is* the unique abode of intelligence, the fate of our planet could have an importance that is truly cosmic: it might conceivably be the difference between a near eternity filled with ever more complex and subtle forms of life and one filled with nothing but base matter. Yet this fate is finely balanced. One does not need to believe that the Brookhaven national laboratory is a threat to believe that technological civilisation carries risks that get greater with every century. The 20th century brought us the bomb; the 21st offers the more far-reaching threats of catastrophically replicating rogue nano-machines and engineered diseases. The latter are the biggest worry. Within a few years, thousands—even millions—of individuals may acquire the capability to make and disseminate weapons that could cause widespread epidemics. An organised network of al Qaida type terrorists would not be required: just one fanatic or weirdo with the mindset of those who now design computer viruses. In a few decades, such individuals may be able to trigger truly global catastrophes. Even if all nations applied a strict precautionary principle to dangerous procedures, the chances of effective worldwide enforcement are small. There is also, of course, the possibility of accidents in the most respectable of institutions.

Pessimism on these matters seems the rational stance. But technology also offers hope. Perhaps, by the end of the century, self-sustaining communities will have been established away from the earth—on the moon, on Mars, or freely floating in space. Although it will be little consolation to those on earth, life's long-term cosmic potential could thereafter not be quenched by any terrestrial catastrophe: life would have "tunnelled through" its era of maximum jeopardy. This is the best reason for prioritising programmes of manned, rather than unmanned, spaceflight. (New technologies may offer another option too: downloading our blueprint into inorganic memories that could be launched into space.)

The most crucial location in space and time (apart from the big bang itself) could be here and now. This new century, on this planet, may be a defining moment for the cosmos. Our actions could initiate the irreversible spread of life beyond the solar system. Or, in contrast, through malign intent, or through misadventure, 21st-century technology could jeopardise life's cosmic potential when its evolution has still barely begun.

Rereading Darwin • Matt Ridley

AUGUST/SEPTEMBER 2001

The first great ape to reach Britain and survive for any length of time was a chimpanzee called Tommy, who was exhibited in London Zoo in 1835 before he died of tuberculosis. He was replaced in 1837 by an orang-utan called Jenny. She died in 1839 but was replaced by another, also called Jenny.

These apes caused a small sensation. Queen Victoria, who saw the second Jenny, typified the reaction of horrified fascination. Jenny, she wrote, was "frightful, and painfully and disagreeably human." It was disconcerting that an animal could look and behave so like a human. It posed uncomfortable questions about the distinction between people and animals, reason and instinct.

Charles Darwin visited the first Jenny in early 1838, less than two years after returning from the voyage of the *Beagle*. A few weeks later, he wrote in his notebook, "Let man visit the ouran-outang in domestication … see its intelligence … Man in his arrogance thinks himself a great work … More humble and I believe true to consider him created from animals." This was 20 years before he unveiled the theory of natural selection. It was several months before he had his main insight into the struggle for existence after reading Malthus's essay on population.

To most people, Darwin is synonymous with animals and plants. To explain natural selection, he called on pigeons, Galapagos finches and orchids. While procrastinating over the publication of natural selection, he spent eight years studying barnacles. His last book is called, sensationally, *The Formation of Vegetable Mould Through the Action of Worms*. This was the epitome of an unworldly, reclusive naturalist.

The fact that he also dethroned man from his place atop the natural world by establishing the fact of evolution seems almost incidental to his natural history. In *The Origin of Species*, he famously confined himself to a single gnomic sentence about his own species: "Much light will be shed on the origin of man and his history." He left it to Thomas Huxley to argue with bishops about being descended from monkeys.

Or so goes the conventional wisdom. But far from being just a naturalist, Darwin was an obsessive observer of human beings. Instead of coming to overturn human exceptionalism via the study of animals, Darwin did almost the opposite. He started with human nature, concluded that it was different from animal nature only in degree, not in kind, and from there worked back to natural selection. His breakthrough owed as much to Hume and Wordsworth as to the finches and tortoises of the Galapagos islands.

This revolutionary claim is contained in a book published in May by Randal Keynes, Darwin's great-great grandson, called *Annie's Box*. A fine contribution to Darwiniana, it centres on his private life and the central tragedy of his experience—the death, at age ten, of his beloved daughter Annie, from consumption.

Though much praised, the book has suffered from an unusual degree of reviewer myopia. Most critics expected a revelation about the effect of Annie's death upon Darwin's thinking, perhaps reinforcing the bleak lesson taught by survival of the fittest. Though it is true that her death probably put the final nail in the coffin of Darwin's Christian faith (after it, he would walk his family to church, but not enter), for Keynes the story of Annie is different. He has tried to show how Darwin's experience of fatherhood fed into his thinking from the start. Keynes says that Darwin "learnt from his feelings for Annie about the lasting strength of the affections ... and the limits of human understanding."

In his relationship with Annie and his other children, Darwin emerges as anything but a typical Victorian. He was a warm and approachable father, who allowed the children to play roughly in his study. His approach to child-rearing was liberal and tolerant. Both his grandfathers had been admirers of Rousseau's dicta, that parents should be permissive and encouraging (not that Rousseau took his own advice: he insisted on his mistress sending all his children to an orphanage). Darwin's children were well treated. In his "memorial" to Annie, he writes: "her tender love was never weary of displaying itself by fondling and all other little acts of affection."

Keynes has recently put the real Annie's box on show in a special exhibition at Darwin's house in Kent. The box is a writing case with various family mementoes of Annie put away by her mother after her death and rediscovered by Keynes recently. This is part of a general refurbishment of Down House by English Heritage, which now includes a fascinating re-creation of the garden in which Darwin did so many experiments with pigeons, bees or plants. He grew no less than 54 varieties of gooseberry, for example. Plans are now afoot for a Charles Darwin centre for conferences on evolutionary theory.

There is probably no scientist for whom the sense of place is as strong as it was with Darwin. Having circumnavigated the world, he came to anchor in this little corner of Kent, so close to suburbia even then, but secluded in the hedges and banks of the North Downs. His every idea was tested and observed in some corner of this patch of land, fermented in his brain during "thinking walks" and written up in the cluttered study now restored to its original appearance. More relevant features remain of Darwin's milieu than of Newton's, Mendel's, Einstein's or Watson and Crick's. Down House is a scientific shrine of the finest authenticity.

And it is impossible to separate Darwin's science from his home life. Keynes shows they were all of a piece. He never "went to work." He enlisted the entire household into his inquiries. The children were made to track bees, their governess to count plants and the butler to boil the skeletons of pigeons. The children were not just lab assistants. They were also subjects. From their earliest moments they were under close observation. In his book *The Expression of the Emotions in Man and Animals*, he detailed the emergence of reflexes and habits in young children—his own. In *The Variation of Animals and Plants under Domestication*, he refers to a certain habit of twiddling the fingers when pleased that he had observed it in a boy, and how the boy's daughter had developed the same habit. The boy was himself; the girl his daughter Betty.

He also recalls repeating on the one-year-old Annie an experiment he had first done with the orang-utan Jenny: to see if each could recognise herself in the mirror. The evolution of the human mind must at least be possible, he argued, "for we daily see the faculties developing in every infant."

The question of human nature and whether it is an exception to brute nature was a central concern for Darwin from 1838. A few months after seeing orang-utan Jenny, Darwin found what he felt was an answer to the main obstacle to seeing human nature as derived from animal nature: human morality. His notebooks show that he had developed the idea that the notion of right and wrong might be rooted in a "social instinct" that had once contributed to survival. Conscience, he thought, might be "an hereditary compound passion" —though he also emphasised the role played by self-awareness and reflection. The reason we find it hard to analyse our moral motives might be because they were "originally mostly instinctive." These were very similar to thoughts expressed by Wordsworth in his *Lyrical Ballads*. They were also a far more radical heresy in the pious Victorian age than evolution itself.

Keynes's disinterment of this strand of Darwin's thinking is remarkable for three reasons. First, it shows how much putting man in his place in nature was at the beginning, not the end, of Darwin's evolutionary reasoning. Second, it reveals Darwin as a full-blown "evolutionary psychologist," ready to speculate about the evolutionary origins of complex human behaviour. Such speculation has flowered in the past decade much to the rage of conventional social scientists, who call it biological determinism. Third, it shows how little progress we have made. More than 160 years have passed since Darwin thought these thoughts about human exceptionalism, yet to write what he wrote would still get you condemned in most public prints.

Take this quotation from a pamphlet by Kenan Malik, "What is it to be human?" just published by the Institute of Ideas: "Humans are not like other animals ... we must distinguish between inert, mechanical nature and active, thinking man." More than a century after Darwin demonstrated that there is no hard distinction between nature and man, only differences of degree, Malik's appeal to human exceptionalism is still supported by most of the academy. It has been the presiding assumption of the followers of Durkheim, Freud, Boas, Piaget, Skinner and Foucault for 100 years: that there is a greater gulf between a person and a chimpanzee than there is between a chimpanzee and a slug.

Social scientists allowed Darwin his triumph over anatomy, but barred him from the mind. That was to remain determined exclusively by culture (that is, by other people's minds). Some scientists have even argued that Darwin himself did not intend his ideas to extend to psychology. But even a cursory reading of Darwin's later books, or his early notebooks, reveals otherwise.

Yet Darwin's foundations were hardly built upon in the 20th century. I wrote a book (*The Origins of Virtue*) on this theme, trying to demonstrate that the "good," pro-social human habits might just as plausibly have long evolutionary antecedents as the "bad," anti-social ones. I am embarrassed to find how much I failed to acknowledge Darwin's contributions to the argument. We say of a drunken yob, "he is behaving like an animal." We never say of somebody who initiates or reciprocates a kindness, that she is "behaving like an animal." Why not? There is just as much evidence for instinct in our good behaviour as in our bad. In any case, I was condemned by many social scientists for various heresies against environmental determinism.

There is a trap here for the unwary. To argue that human beings are no different from other animals is just as foolish as to argue that they are completely different. Humans *are* unique. They have language, written culture and opposable thumbs. But elephants are unique, too. They have trunks. So are goldfish. As Helena Cronin once wrote, "there is nothing unique about being unique." The trick in comparative biology is to find the similarities between species that speak of common descent or convergence, and to find the differences that speak of adaptation to particular ecological conditions or genetic accident.

This is no less true in behaviour than in anatomy. The male gorilla has a huge body, but tiny testicles; the male chimpanzee has by contrast a modest body and enormous testicles. The difference reflects the fact that competition between male gorillas happens before fertilisation (in fights over harems), while competition between male chimps takes place after fertilisation (as the sperm from several mates compete to reach the egg). This in turn has behavioural consequences: infanticide is common in gorillas when harems change hands because males are certain about paternity. It is rare in chimps because the issue of paternity is blurred. Why must we assume that the testicle size of the third African ape (ourselves) tells us nothing about *its* behaviour? We are, in fact, intermediate between chimp and gorilla, which is inconsistent with chimp promiscuity or gorilla polygyny, but consistent with a mostly monogamous mating system.

Darwin would have loved this data. It demonstrates the power of his neglected second great theory, sexual selection. And it makes clear the futility of drawing a hard line between man and animals. It is astonishing to realise that between Tommy's arrival at London Zoo in 1835 and Jane Goodall's studies in Tanzania beginning in 1960, we knew nothing of the complexity of chimpanzee social lives, in part because we assumed that we had a monopoly on complex, conscious behaviour. You still hear philosophers and neuroscientists talk of consciousness as if it were a purely human phenomenon, though anyone who has watched a dog dreaming knows otherwise.

Darwin drew no dividing lines through nature. Although he knew three natives of Tierra del Fuego who returned home on the *Beagle* after a spell in London (including a visit to court) and was "struck by how similar their minds were to ours," he was none the less shocked by his first sight of "wild" Fuegians. "They were naked and sent forth most hideous yells ... man in his most savage state ... the reflection at once rushed into my mind—such were our ancestors." If the three Fuegians on board had stepped so easily into civilisation, perhaps he was only a step away from sinking into savagery. Having seen the animal in himself, he was ready, as few Victorians were, to see orangutan Jenny as a cousin.

Towards the end of his life, Darwin was drawn back to human exceptionalism. But he began to worry that (in Keynes's words) "the human brain was not a perfect instrument for finding truths." This is a doubt that goes back to Hume, and Colin McGinn has recently coined the term "mysterian" for the belief that while there is nothing supernatural about consciousness, it may still be beyond the comprehension of the human mind.

Darwin's last book, *The Formation of Vegetable Mould Through the Action of Worms* contains the final irony. His point was to show how dramatically worms changed the appearance of the world by their churning of the earth, but he could not resist speculations on their "mental qualities." He brought worms into the house to test their reactions to the piano. This was a man who treated worms as sentient beings and children as experimental subjects. For 40 years he pursued the idea that humans were just another kind of organism wherever it would take him. Few since have had the courage to follow him.

Infantile leftist • Martin Wolf

JULY 2001

There, on the cover of *The Silent Takeover*, sits a young woman. She sprawls in an armchair, with a booted leg draped nonchalantly over one arm. The chair is placed, incongruously, on muddy ground by a small river. Thus do we meet the pundit as poseuse.

What is Noreena Hertz—an academic at the Judge Institute, Cambridge University—trying to tell us? The "silent takeover" began, she writes, with Margaret Thatcher in 1979. Global corporations were, apparently, invisible and uninfluential before then. But capitalism has now taken over the world. In the process it has destroyed democratic politics. "Governments' hands are tied and we are increasingly dependent on corporations." The result is an eroding tax base and crumbling public services, as "our elected representatives kowtow to business."

Hertz says she is *not* anti-capitalist, since "capitalism is clearly the best system for generating wealth." She *is* "unashamedly pro-people, pro-democracy and pro-justice." This, naturally, differentiates her from opponents who are unashamedly anti-people, anti-democracy and anti-justice. Her core worry is this: "as business has extended its role, it has come to define the public realm ... Governments, by not even acknowledging the takeover, risk shattering the implicit contract between state and citizen that lies at the heart of a democratic society, making the rejection of the ballot box and support for non-traditional forms of political expression increasingly attractive."

The new capitalist economy has, she claims, undermined the prosperity of the unskilled in advanced countries and increased job insecurity. It has failed to benefit the poor, as inequality has risen. By threatening to move abroad, companies have driven down taxes and regulatory standards. "The levying of taxes ... the most fundamental right of the nation state and a potential means of redressing inequality, is squeezed by corporate pressure ... The mindset is one of 'beggar thy neighbour.'"

Corporate interests dictate to government, which makes it impossible to pursue an ethical foreign policy. The WTO puts our health at risk. Our politics are sold to the highest bidder. Our media are monopolised. "Many people have simply lost their faith in politics."

Then, quite suddenly, we are told that the all-powerful corporation is not all-powerful, after all. Monsanto's campaign for GM food is crushed by media-fed hysteria. Shell abandons its plans to sink the Brent Spar platform in the Atlantic. Campaigns by shoppers force companies to change their ways. Evangelical entrepreneurs, such as George Soros, and the movement for corporate social responsibility emerge.

Yet corporate social responsibility is not enough, since "business will never place customer service, ethical trading and social investment above moneymaking whenever the two come into conflict." And protest, for all its attractions, "does not provide a long-term solution to the silent takeover," since the "majority risks being disempowered by the vocal minority." Protest must be seen, instead, as a catalyst for change. The proper aim is to "re-establish government as a democratic forum within which differing social needs are weighed, and all is not reducible to the corporation or the individual."

Hertz concludes that "to avoid permanent marginalisation in the decisions that shape our lives, now is time for action." To do what? "As citizens we must make it clear to government that unless politics focuses on people as well as business ... we will continue to scorn representative democracy, and choose to shop and protest rather than vote. Until the state reclaims us, we will not reclaim the state."

This, such as it is, is the argument. The question is not what is wrong with it, but what is right. Since space is limited, I will address just four aspects: the argument that corporations dominate the world; the thesis that taxes and regulations are in a race to the bottom; the notion that inward investment impoverishes the people of recipient countries; and, last, the idea that all we need is a revitalisation of democracy. This leaves out other issues: Hertz's superficial treatment of the impact of globalisation on inequality, her confusion between liberalism and mercantilism, and her misunderstanding of how the WTO works to name a few.

Do corporations dominate the world? To support this claim, Hertz cites an analysis which concludes that "51 of the 100 biggest economies of the world are now corporations. The sales of GM and Ford are greater than the GDP of the whole of sub-Saharan Africa." This is gross abuse of statistics. The study measures the size of companies by sales. But national economies are measured by GDP. Since GDP is a measure of value added, one must compare it with the value added of companies, which is the difference between the value of their sales and the cost of the inputs they purchase from suppliers. Last year the sales of GM were $185bn, the same as Denmark's GDP. But the *value added* of GM was only a fifth of its sales. So, this company's "economy" is not the world's 23rd largest but 55th, after Ukraine.

But the comparison between corporate and national economies is intrinsically absurd. They are as different as apples and artichokes. A corporation has to attract the labour and capital it employs from competitive markets. Its ability to survive depends on the returns it offers to those free to go elsewhere. Countries are governed by a coercive territorial power. States tax and regulate, companies buy and sell.

Moreover, the corporate sector has never been an omnipotent force for economic liberalism. It is divided, weak and intellectually lazy. Those desiring environmental or labour regulations have often overcome business resistance. Hertz gives several examples.

Have taxes been collapsing? No. Between 1980 and 1999, the average ratio of tax revenue to GDP in OECD countries rose by five percentage points. Between 1965 (the heyday of the Keynesianism Hertz admires) and 1999, that ratio *rose* from 26 to 37 per cent. The notion that the state is withering away is ludicrous.

Hertz refers to the difficulty Germany has had in sustaining its corporate taxes. What she does not state is that Germany has long had an exceptionally inefficient corporation tax. As a percentage of total taxation, corporate taxes in OECD countries *rose*, from 7.6 per cent in 1980 to 8.9 per cent in 1999. But Germany's fell from 5.5 per cent to 4.4 per cent. Contrast this with Britain, which is far more open to foreign direct investment, and so more vulnerable to the pressure

Hertz decries. In 1980, corporate taxes made up 8.4 per cent of British tax revenue rising to 11 per cent in 1998.

There is also huge variation in overall tax ratios. In 1999 it varied from less than 30 per cent of GDP in Australia, Japan and the US to 52 per cent in Sweden. Similarly, the share of corporate taxes in total revenue in 1998 varied from Germany's 4.4 per cent to Australia's 15 per cent. There is therefore no economic force preventing most internationally integrated market economies from raising taxes. The constraint is political. It is not beastly capitalism that prevents countries from raising the higher taxes Hertz wants, but the democracy she adores. After a big expansion in state spending in the past 50 years, voters have called a halt.

Much the same applies to regulation. Over the past two decades governments around the world have privatised many public enterprises. This was not done because of pressure from business, but because previous policies had been grossly inefficient. Yet environmental and safety regulations have generally increased. The story on labour regulation is more varied but Britain has just shown that a government wanting to increase labour market regulation finds it easy to do so.

There is no convincing evidence that capitalism is leading to a regulatory race to the bottom. Hertz states baldly that "'pollution havens' are created as environmentally unfriendly policies are allowed … and human rights are abused … all to attract foreign investment." But this statement is contradicted by the evidence cited in her own footnotes. In 1999, three quarters of all foreign direct investment went to high-income countries, not the countries with cheap labour and poor environmental standards.

What then of the impact of inward investment on poor countries? Foreign investors in developing countries virtually always offer higher wages and better conditions than those offered by local employers. Compared to conditions for many casual workers, employment in a foreign company is close to paradise. A recent study of Indonesia by the National Bureau of Economic Research in the US showed that inward direct investment raised wages not just in the foreign-owned plants, but in locally owned ones as well.

Pampered westerners shocked by the conditions experienced by workers in poor countries fail to compare these with domestic alternatives, rather than with what they themselves expect. But if people in poor countries are to enjoy the opportunities of those who live in rich ones, they must either be allowed to immigrate freely—precluded by the populist democracy Hertz desires—or be given the capital and know-how to raise their own output to western levels. Given the unwillingness of western voters—democracy again—to support higher transfers of aid to poor countries, the alternatives are private capital and know-how. This, in turn, must mean large-scale inward direct investment, as the majority of developing countries now recognise.

Finally, Hertz seems unaware of the vast literature on why unbridled democracy is dangerous. She talks of "we" the people as if that naïve collectivist notion was unproblematic. But we know that those who are willing to give their time and money to politics do not always have the aggregate interest at heart. Many voters are rationally ignorant about the issues confronting them, because the return on acquiring the knowledge is so small. The interesting question is not why do people fail to vote, but why *do* they vote, given the tiny probability that they will affect the outcome. And more important, we have no reason to suppose that those who run the state will necessarily be selfless servants of the public weal.

A book whose chief theme is the importance of subordinating the market to politics and corporations to politicians should have shown at least some awareness of these difficulties. It might then have offered a coherent view of the balance to be struck between the market and politics. Hertz provides, instead, the classic delusion of populism—the proposition that the interests of "the people" are self-evident and bound to be served by the state they are supposed to control.

Today's world is no utopia. The regulation of an integrating global economy, particularly of the financial sector, is a great challenge. Another is assisting unsuccessful developing countries to improve their performance. Yet another is how to secure protection of the global commons. But resolving such difficulties requires more effective international institutions, which will inevitably raise questions about political legitimacy.

This book adds about as much to these complex debates as do the idiots who throw stones at WTO meetings. It offers instead a simple-minded story of corporations that dominate politics, destroy the state's capacity to act and impoverish the poor. Against this it sets an equally naïve answer: to renew democracy. It is, alas, this very vacuity that will account for its appeal. It will permit the intellectually lazy and emotionally self-indulgent to believe they have the answers. That someone attached to one of the world's great universities should offer such shoddy work is depressing beyond words.

Climate change • Philip Ball

FEBRUARY 2000

The last year of the last millennium was its hottest. There was no global drought; no summer heatwave swept across the planet. Yet enough months were, quietly, that little bit above average to add up to a record breaker, for Britain at least. What conclusions should we draw? The most popular one is that this is the result of a human-induced greenhouse effect. That is almost certainly true, but the connection is not as obvious as it seems. Why scientists have been hedging their bets on the matter, when there is evidence of global warming by about half a degree centigrade over the past century, seems puzzling—until you appreciate the full complexity of the earth's climate.

Climate has no big idea. Evolution has Darwinian natural selection; cosmology has the big bang; genetics has DNA. Climate is just "one damned thing after another"; worse, it is lots of damned things at the same time. This makes for messy history. For example, it is not true that climate was steady and comfortable until we started pouring greenhouse gases into the atmosphere. Consider how global temperatures have fluctuated over the past 1m years: the graph looks like the jagged profile of the Dolomites. Focus in on the past millennium or even the past century and you see the same pattern: a series of peaks too fine to have been discernible in the million-year record.

We can make only one sweeping statement about the climate system: the average temperature of the earth's surface depends on a balance between how much heat it receives from the sun and how much it radiates back into space. Changes in global mean temperature are ultimately caused by changes in the amount of heat into or out of the planet.

The complexity arises from the fact that so many phenomena induce such changes. One is the greenhouse effect. The earth's atmosphere is roughly four fifths nitrogen and one fifth oxygen; but 1 per cent or so is made up of a mélange of other gaseous compounds, many in such small quantities that they were detected only over the past few decades. Most of this is argon, and the rest is primarily water vapour and carbon dioxide. Yet these tiny proportions exert a huge effect. Water vapour, carbon dioxide and other greenhouse gases such as methane absorb some of the heat radiated by the warm surface of the earth. So "greenhouse gases" retain some of the sun's energy which would otherwise be absorbed and then re-radiated to space. This warms up the lower atmosphere, and so surface temperatures rise.

Contrary to common belief, the greenhouse effect is not primarily human-made. There are natural sources of greenhouse gases. For example, carbon dioxide is generated by decomposition of plant matter, respiration of plants and animals, and volcanic emissions, while methane is produced by decomposition in air-free environments. These effects raise the temperature by about 35 degrees: most of the world would be below freezing if there was no natural greenhouse effect. But industry and agriculture add to the effect by producing significant amounts of greenhouse gases.

Another factor which influences the earth's heat is brightness. Clouds and ice sheets reflect sunlight and so act to cool the planet. Vegetation generally darkens dry ground and so reduces its reflectivity. The overall reflectivity of the earth is called its albedo. Both the greenhouse and the albedo effects are subject to feedbacks. For example, if the world cools and ice sheets grow larger, the albedo increases—more sunlight is reflected back into space—which induces further cooling. (The converse is also true.)

James Lovelock's Gaia hypothesis, advanced in the 1970s, suggested that the strongest influence on natural climate change comes from living systems, which display feedback loops which counteract any small changes, either cooling or warming. Lovelock and others proposed that albedo changes caused by clouds are regulated by marine algae which exude a sulphur-containing gas called DMS. This gas is converted in the atmosphere to sulphate, which is a component of the tiny salt-like particles on which water droplets condense to form clouds. If the earth warms up, they said, the algae are stimulated into producing more DMS, which results in the formation of more clouds, a decrease in the earth's albedo—and a compensatory cooling effect. By such means, say Gaia supporters, life acts as a kind of thermostat for the planet. There is no strong evidence that this hypothesis is true, although Lovelock's idea has had the effect of focusing more attention on the (undoubted) role that life does play in climate regulation.

The Gaia hypothesis looked as if it might be climate's big idea, but there is just too much else going on. The greenhouse effect might explain why this century was warmer than the last, but not why this summer was warmer than the previous one. On time scales of billions of years, the amount of heat received from the sun changes because its structure and composition as a star alters. (In about six billion years it will grow to fry and then to swallow the earth.) And the sun's heat output rises and falls with an 11-year pulse, accompanied by the proliferation of sunspots at each maximum. But the change is small, and it is not obvious how that could manifest itself as a big shift in climate.

This hasn't prevented some scientists from suggesting that all recent climate change can be explained by changes in solar activity. Certainly, a period of cold climate, from the 14th to the 18th century, coincided with episodes of lower-than-average sunspot counts. Such links have been trumpeted in the US by the Global Climate Coalition, an industry-funded body which opposes regulations on emission of greenhouse gases and seeks to find natural explanations for recent warming.

Looking back over longer time scales, we run into the pseudo-rhythmic cycle of the ice ages. The last ice age ended 11,000 years ago, having persisted for some 100,000 years. Before that occurred a warm period like today's, called an interglacial, which began at the end of the previous ice age about 140,000 years ago. And so it goes on—a succession of ice ages and interglacials repeating roughly every 100,000 years for the past half a million years.

During an ice age, the polar ice caps grow towards the equator. Water evaporated from the oceans falls on the ice as snow and is gradually compacted, under successive layers, until it forms new ice. This means that the oceans don't get the water back again as rain, and so they become shallower. Across the globe, sea levels plummet. At the height of the last ice age, some 18,000 years ago, the sea level was so low—on average about 120 metres below its present level—that Australia was connected to New Guinea by dry land, and Asia to Indonesia. The ice sheets in the northern hemisphere covered northern Germany and half of Britain, as well as most of southeast Asia and South America. The global mean temperature then was some six degrees lower than today. (Relatively small differences in the global mean can be accompanied by huge differences in regional environmental conditions.) And significantly, quantities of the greenhouse gases carbon dioxide and methane in the atmosphere were much reduced. This is consistent with a colder world; but what was cause and what was effect? Did a cold climate suppress the natural sources of these gases, or did some change in those sources trigger the cooling? This is a key question for scientists trying to understand what future changes in greenhouse gases have in store for us.

Dramatic climate shifts like the ice ages leave telltale signs. These were the catalyst for the revolution in understanding of climate which took place in the late 19th century. It all began with "erratic" rocks—boulders in mountain landscapes where they were not supposed to be.

Often the only known bedrock of the same type was miles away. What could have carried such boulders so far? The answer was clear to most geologists of the early 19th century: the biblical flood, which was believed to have rearranged the global landscape. But Swiss geologist Louis Agassiz revived the old idea of Scottish geologist James Hutton: that glaciers had borne the erratic rocks far afield before the ice melted.

Whereas it had long been assumed that the earth's climate had always been more or less as it is in modern times, geologists were now forced to conclude that in days past it had sometimes been much colder. What had caused these cold spells? The answer, it seemed, lay not in the workings of the earth's own climate, but in astronomy. In 1842 Joseph Alphonse Adhémar, a French mathematician, realised that a repeating cycle of ice ages might result from variations in the earth's axis of rotation. At present this axis stands at an angle of about 23.5 degrees relative to the plane of the earth's orbit around the sun. This tilt is responsible for the seasons: summer occurs in the hemisphere tilted towards the sun at that time. Adhémar knew that the earth actually wobbles around its axis, rather like a spinning gyroscope. This wobble is responsible for the precession of the equinoxes, and makes the apparent positions of the stars change slowly over many years. It takes 23,000 years to complete one wobble.

Another effect of the wobble is to make the length of the winters in the two hemispheres different. Adhémar proposed that ice ages might be triggered when the winters were longest—once every 11,000 years or so in each hemisphere. Adhémar succeeded in establishing the idea that periodic changes in the earth's orbit could trigger periodic changes in climate. But it was not until 1920 that a Serbian mathematician, Milutin Milankovitch, finally calculated the sums correctly. There are two other changes in the orbit which also affect the heat balance of the earth. First, the tilt angle itself changes—the earth tips back and forth—over a period of 40,000 years. Second, the shape of the elliptical orbit around the sun (called the eccentricity) alters on a 100,000-year time scale, becoming alternately longer or shorter. Milankovitch showed that a combination of these three oscillations will alter the amount of heat the earth receives over these time scales, and thus could trigger ice ages. Because the three rhythms are out of step, their combined effect is only semi-regular, and so ice ages of varying coldness are anticipated.

The predominant pulse of the glacials over the past 700,000 years has been on a 100,000-year scale, implying that changes in eccentricity have been the main driving force. Looking still further back in time, the rhythm of the ice ages changes to a beat of 40,000 years, suggesting that changes in the tilt angle were then more important.

How can we know about climate change over these huge stretches of time? We must dig. In the 19th century, James Croll, a Scottish scientist who had improved on Adhémar's astronomical theory of the ice ages, suggested that a record of past climate might be compiled by examining the remains of marine organisms in "the deep recesses of the ocean." The seas are full of microscopic creatures such as the plankton called forams, which construct elaborate shell-like skeletons for themselves from dissolved calcium carbonate, the stuff of chalk. When the forams die, their bodies settle to the sea bed, and the robust shells accumulate in the muddy sediment. Different species of foram live in waters of different temperatures, so if we can identify changes in the types of foram we may infer something about the changes in ocean temperature at that location when the sediment was deposited. In the 1920s, the German scientist Wolfgang Schott showed a progression in Atlantic sediments from warm-water species of forams in the upper layer, to cold-water species and then back to warm-water species lower down.

The development of radiocarbon dating meant that precise ages could be assigned to the different layers of sediment. This showed that the uppermost warm-water species disappeared about 11,000 years ago—just when, we now know, the switch between a glacial and an interglacial episode occurred. But these dead sea creatures have still more tales to tell. In the late 1940s, scientists discovered that the oxygen in the carbonate shells of cold-water forams is enriched in oxygen's heavier isotope, oxygen-18, relative to warm-water forams (which contain a higher proportion of the lighter oxygen-16). By measuring the oxygen-isotope ratios in sediments, we have a thermometer of the water temperature when the sediments were laid down.

In the 1950s, using this isotope method, the geologist Cesare Emiliani deduced that there had been seven ice ages over the past 300,000 years. In the 1970s, climate scientists initiated an international programme, called Climap, to map the climate record of the past 700 millennia from columns of sediment drilled from sea beds throughout the oceans. This record confirmed the broad features of Emiliani's work and showed that ice ages had recurred at intervals of roughly 100,000 years. Overall, the Climap record matched the pattern predicted by Milankovitch, and some scientists thought that the riddle of the ice ages was solved.

But it is not quite that simple. There seem to have been periods in the distant past when there was no cycle of ice ages at all. The Cretaceous period, 144m to 65m years ago, is thought to have been warmer than today, perhaps by as much as 60 degrees at the south pole. This warm spell may have persisted until about 30m years ago. Some scientists believe that, over time scales of millions of years, the slow movements of the continental plates may control global climate. For one thing, ice caps at the poles can form most readily if there are continents at the poles. Because of continental drift this has not always been the case—Antarctica may have been at the equator about 900m years ago, for instance. The cooling 30m years ago, meanwhile, might have been triggered by the collision of the Asian and Indian plates which rumpled up their edges to create the Himalayas. The formation of snow on this high ground increased the earth's albedo, and the increased "weathering" of the high rocks by rain would have had the effect of removing the greenhouse gas carbon dioxide from the atmosphere.

So Milankovitch cycles are not the only story in historic climate change. Further, the changes in earth's orbital characteristics provoke only very small changes in the amount of heat from the sun, and it is not clear that this is sufficient to trigger a switch in global climate—particularly on time scales as rapid as sometimes observed. Milankovitch's theory predicts gradual change but we often see abrupt shifts between glacials and interglacials.

Much of what we know about climate change now comes not from marine sediments but from the polar ice caps. The reason foram shells are enriched in oxygen-18 in times of cold climate is that this heavier isotope evaporates less readily from the seas. So when the world's water gets locked away in ice during glacial times, and the sea level sinks, there is proportionately more oxygen-18 in the seas—and correspondingly more oxygen-16 in the water of the polar ice sheets. By drilling cores out of these sheets—some almost five kilometres thick and 250,000 years old at the base—we can reconstruct a climate record over this period from isotope measurements. Better still, the ice is peppered with tiny bubbles which contain samples of the atmosphere from the time the ice was deposited as snow. This means that we can study how changes in the concentrations of greenhouse gases have varied with changes in climate, and deduce something about cause and effect.

In the early 1990s another dramatic discovery from ice-core climate records was that shifts in climate can be disconcertingly rapid. During some periods the temperature seems to have risen and fallen significantly over only a few decades. One fast switch happened as the world was emerging from the last ice age 11,000 years ago. It was warming gradually until, about 10,500 years ago, the world plunged back into ice-age conditions over a period perhaps as short as 50 years. The change was especially pronounced in the north Atlantic region. One explanation for this rapid cooling, called the Younger-Dryas event, involves ocean circulation.

The water in the oceans is constantly on the move. It doesn't simply slosh back and forth with the tides, but circulates steadily around the globe in huge currents. The surface currents, down to a depth of about 100 metres, are driven by the winds. But below this is a huge conveyor-like circulation of deep water which rises in the north Pacific, passes eastwards across the equator and around Africa, and travels north, to sink in the north Atlantic and make the return journey via the Southern Ocean. The Atlantic sinking happens because the water becomes colder; cold sea water is denser than warm sea water. The effect is accentuated by water freezing into ice at the poles: ice rejects salt, and the salt left behind in the water makes it denser. So the circulation of the oceans is driven by changes in heat and salt—the thermohaline circulation.

This conveyor belt carries warm water from the tropics towards the poles, and thus helps to redistribute heat across the planet. If it were to cease turning (or turn less vigorously) the high latitude regions such as northern Europe would be much colder. This may be what happened during the Younger-Dryas event. As the northern ice sheets melted at the end of the ice age, huge quantities of fresh water were added to the north Atlantic. This freshening reduced the density of the sea water and may have stopped it from sinking as it flowed northwards. That would have put a brake on the entire thermohaline circulation, depriving the north Atlantic region of heat and plunging it back into a short-lived ice age.

On time scales of decades the circulation of the oceans and atmosphere holds the key to climate. The tropics are warmer than the poles because they are struck squarely by the sun's rays; at the poles the rays arrive at an oblique angle and so the same amount of heat is distributed over a greater area. But, between them, atmospheric and ocean circulation constitute a worldwide heat distribution service which redresses some of this inequality.

What about the atmosphere? Air rises where it is warmed by heat radiated from the earth's surface; it sinks when it cools again and becomes denser. This is called convection. Crudely speaking, the earth is encircled by two bands of convective circulation in the tropics, in which warm air rises around the equator, moves outwards towards the respective poles, and then cools and sinks again at latitudes of 30°N and 30°S. The sinking air is then carried back towards the equator, where the circulations from the north and south converge in a region called the intertropical convergence zone. As the air rises and cools in this zone, the water vapour it contains, from evaporation of the equatorial oceans, condenses into droplets, creating towering cloud stacks which produce rain.

Interactions between the ocean and the atmosphere give rise to climatic phenomena such as El Niño and tropical hurricanes. El Niño events occur every two to ten years. It is still not known exactly how they arise; but their signature is a warming of surface water in the central and eastern equatorial Pacific Ocean. The effects of an El Niño event vary. Rainfall in central America, Brazil, Australia and Indonesia diminishes, causing drought, whereas rainfall is anomalously high in southeast Africa, Peru and Ecuador, bringing floods and landslides.

Predicting weather patterns—including freak events such as hurricanes—depends on our ability to simulate in computer models the interactions between the atmosphere and oceans. Predicting rainfall, for example, is a matter of estimating patterns of evaporation, convection, and transport of moist air. But even the best models cannot predict weather patterns for longer than about ten days ahead, because weather systems are intrinsically chaotic. Fluctuations too small to include (no matter how detailed you make your model) can turn out to have disproportionate consequences.

Nevertheless, climate trends on longer time scales can be predicted—because we are then asking broader questions. No one cares whether it will rain in Chelmsford 30 years from next Friday; but we do want to know whether northern Europe will be on average warmer, wetter, stormier, than at present. Different considerations come into play over different time scales: for example, predicting climate over the next century means that changes in the extent of the ice caps and mountain glaciers must be included in computer models. Ideally, these would also consider how ecosystems might respond to changes in temperature, rainfall and so on, and how this in turn affects the quantity of greenhouse gases released into or absorbed from the atmosphere by biological processes.

But this kind of climate modelling requires an understanding of feedback mechanisms which is at present only partial. We would like to believe that we now know all the main influences on climate over at least century-scale periods—but even that is by no means sure. This is why the predictions of future climate change over the 21st century made by the Intergovernmental Panel on Climate Change are uncertain. The world might warm by as little as 1.5 degrees, or by as much as 4 degrees. The mean sea level might rise by a foot or a yard. Legislating on climate change in the face of such unknowns is a tricky business—especially with vocal lobby groups eager to conflate uncertainty with ignorance. The current trend in formulating strategies on emissions of greenhouse gases seeks to include socio-economic factors and possible developments in future technologies as part of the climate models. But the fact is that the time scales of climate change are not those in which governments are accustomed to think, nor in which economists and technologists feel easy about making predictions. This is why it is vital to study the climates of times past, in order to see ahead more clearly.

Rights of apes • Peter Singer vs Kenan Malik
MAY 1999

4th April 1999

Dear Kenan,

I am told that you do not favour the idea of granting rights to great apes. The case for doing so seems to me so clear-cut that I am curious to learn why someone like you, who generally opposes the exploitation of the weak by the strong, is against it. Supporters of the Great Ape Project (GAP) are pressing the New Zealand parliament to extend three basic rights to our nearest relatives, the great apes: the right to life; the right to liberty; and the right not to be tortured.

Why am I prepared to restrict my campaign to the great apes? After all, the central thesis of my book, *Animal Liberation*, is that the principle which entitles us to regard all human beings as equal—the principle of equal consideration of interests—ought to be applied to all beings with interests. Because all beings capable of experiencing pleasure and pain have interests, this includes all mammals—indeed, all vertebrates, and many invertebrates too. I have not changed my views about extending this principle to all sentient beings, but I am attracted by the chance to extend basic rights beyond our own species right *now*. The great apes (chimpanzees, gorillas and orang-utans) are not only our closest relatives; they are also, more importantly, beings who possess many of the characteristics which we consider distinctive in our own species. They form close and lasting attachments to others; they show grief; they play; when taught sign language, they tell lies; they plan for the future; they form political coalitions; they reciprocate favours, and they become angry when someone for whom they have done a favour does not respond similarly. Their intellectual abilities have been compared with those of children between two and three years old, and their social bonds are stronger than we would expect from a child of that age. Why should we not recognise the basic rights of such beings, on the same basis as we include all members of our own species, irrespective of age or intellectual ability?

Such a step is not yet possible for all sentient beings. All over the world people are involved in raising and killing animals for food. The extension of rights to all sentient beings will remain politically impossible for a long time, no matter how strong the ethical arguments. By comparison, the step advocated by the GAP would not involve big changes in our daily lives. Yet to extend the idea of legally enforceable rights to members of another species would be a historic breakthrough. The GAP is not an appeal to save endangered animals, nor a plea for better treatment. It is a call to respect the rights of individual animals in the same way that we respect the rights of humans. It would mean a first breach in the species barrier which would, in time, make it easier to reach out to other non-humans.

It is true that no great ape can discuss philosophy, or reciprocate our recognition of their rights. But my argument for their rights is not based on the idea that they are our intellectual equals. If it were, we would have to deny these rights to many humans to whom we now grant them. For a typical great ape is the intellectual equal, or superior, of millions of young or disabled humans whose rights to life, liberty and freedom from torture we do recognise.

A right to liberty does not preclude confinement for a being's own safety, or the safety of others. These decisions should be made in the same way that we make decisions for humans who, because they are young or severely disabled, are unable to make decisions for themselves. We might, for example, appoint guardians for apes, to make decisions for them.

The crux is this: today, great apes are property which can be owned. They are not legal persons—unlike infants and the most brain-damaged humans—they are the closest things now existing to slaves. The US government's recommended cage size for a single adult chimpanzee is 5ft x 5ft x 7ft. Experiments on apes continue in several EU countries. Apes can also be used in zoos and circuses. It is time to put the slavery of the apes behind us. They need basic rights, enforceable by law.

Yours,

Peter Singer

7th April 1999

Dear Peter,

Two big issues divide us: your concept of rights and your belief in the mental abilities of apes. You argue that apes, like many other animals, should have rights because they are sentient and they suffer. But why should suffering be the basis on which we accord rights to apes? It is certainly not the basis on which we accord rights to humans. Humans possess rights by virtue of being rational agents.

I realise that many humans—children or the mentally handicapped—are not truly rational agents, yet we enact laws to protect such vulnerable groups. But to call these "rights" is a misnomer. They are protections which we use to ring-fence those incapable of bearing rights. The age of consent, for example, is a right for an adult, but a protection for a child.

A right requires us to make our own decisions. A protection requires us to make decisions on behalf of another. Indeed, many rights—for example, the right to vote—are denied to children, precisely because they cannot make rational decisions. It is plausible to argue that apes require protection; it is nonsense to say that they should have rights.

You insist that apes should have the "right to liberty." Do you believe that apes should be free to wander the streets? Or do you mean that apes should not be kept in cages? That may be a laudable aim, but it is not a "right to liberty." You say that "a right to liberty does not preclude confinement for a being's own safety" and that an ape might have a "guardian" to make its decisions. We seem to have followed Alice through the looking-glass here: apes have the right to liberty so long as they have a human to exercise it for them. The only consequence of extending to apes the "right to liberty" is to degrade its meaning for humans.

I agree that because animals are sentient, they have interests. I would not kick a dog in the same way as I would kick a ball. But it is wrong to assume that because animals have interests, they should be accorded rights. There is no logical link between interests and rights. And even where animals have interests, these are of a different order to those of humans. That is why I, like most people, consent to the use of animals—but not the mentally handicapped—in medical research.

You write that while all sentient beings should be accorded "equal consideration" you are attracted to the plan to extend rights initially to great apes, as they are not only our closest relatives but, "more important," beings who possess many human-like characteristics. But if, as you believe, all sentient beings should be accorded rights by virtue of their sentience, irrespective of their other characteristics, why should it be "more important" that apes supposedly show human-like capacities?

It is not clear whether apes do possess the capacities you attribute to them. What we see as purposive behaviour in animals is usually only adaptive strategies. One thing, however, is certain: whatever capacities apes may possess, language is not one of them. And it is language which has enabled humans to transform our relationship to our evolutionary heritage, to become aware of ourselves as rational agents—and to be bearers of rights.

Yours,

Kenan Malik

Dear Kenan,

If you are going to read what I write with so little care, we might as well stop now. You say that I attribute rights to animals on the basis of sentience, but where did I say that? In my last letter I link sentience to "the principle of equal consideration of interests." To give equal consideration to the interests of a being does not require attributing rights to it.

Rights have never been fundamental to my ethical scheme. I use the term as shorthand for the kind of protection that we give to all members of our species, not only to rational agents. All I want is that we protect apes in the same way that we protect vulnerable humans—that we show concern for their interests, reject the idea that they can be owned and, where they are at risk, we appoint guardians to protect their interests. Most people would express this by saying that children and the intellectually disabled have rights, but if you prefer not to use the term, I will drop it.

You ask if I believe apes should have the right to wander through the streets. No more than two-year-olds, or people with profound intellectual disabilities. They need to be looked after. And if someone should want to lock them up so that others can enjoy staring at them, then we need a law which allows a guardian to go to court on their behalf.

The other issue which you say divides us is the mental abilities of apes. But beyond your paean to our use of language, you don't offer evidence to contradict my claims. And since the GAP is supported by many scientists who have spent their lifetimes studying apes—Jane Goodall, Roger and Deborah Fouts, Adriaan Kortlandt—it would take a lot of evidence to shake my views on this. As for language, plenty of work has been done on the abilities of the apes to use sign language; but this is not crucial to my case, because young humans and humans with profound intellectual disabilities are no more capable of using language than apes. Given that you agree that these humans should have the protections they now enjoy, absence of language is not a reason for denying the same protections to apes.

Yours,

Peter Singer

Dear Peter,

I am sorry that you feel that I read your letter with insufficient care. You stated: "The extension of rights to all sentient beings will remain politically impossible for a long time, no matter how strong the ethical arguments." Therefore, you welcomed "the step advocated by the GAP." Surely this means that you believe all sentient beings should have rights, but feel that now is not an opportune moment to press for them.

I accept that when you refer to rights, you mean protections. This is not, however, a question of semantics. The conflation of rights and protections is one of the ways in which rights for humans are being degraded. But let us turn to what you rightly say is the heart of the matter: should apes be accorded the same protections as humans and, in particular, as children and the mentally disabled? I say no. Humans, actually or potentially, are moral beings. No animal is, not even an ape. Humans are moral beings because we live within a web of reciprocal rights and obligations created by our capacity for rational dialogue. We can distinguish between right and wrong, accept responsibility and apportion blame. Apes do not exist within such a community and it would be cruel to treat them as if they do. Your argument for according rights to apes does not depend upon them being able to reciprocate that recognition. But my argument as to why children and apes have different interests does depend on this distinction.

Children will normally grow up to be full members of the moral community. Most intellectually disabled people are sufficiently socialised to be members of the moral community. There are, certainly, a small number who are so disabled that they are denied a moral sense. (There, but for the grace of God, or an accident of nature, go you and I.) But children and the mentally handicapped are of the same kind as you and me: the kind whose normal instance is a moral being. Apes are not. It is not just that apes do not belong to a moral community. They do not have, never have had, and never will have, the potential to do so. This is important because our humanity derives not from our individual selves, but from our membership of the human collective.

You want apes to be treated as "legal persons." But this is to confuse moral and non-moral beings. Apes, like many animals, have distinct characters. But humans are individuals in a different sense: we are self-created beings who realise ourselves through our relations with other such beings.

I accept that we have a duty of care towards some animals. But care is an attitude which derives from human choices and therefore from our existence as moral agents. Our duty of care towards children is different because it is shaped not simply by our humanity, but by theirs, too. In time they will reciprocate, exercising a duty of care in a way no ape can.

I reject the idea that apes have the right to life, liberty and freedom from torture. I am happy to eat animals, cage them and use them in experiments. The right to life of millions of humans depends upon hunting and farming animals, and on medical advances which come from experimenting on them. The only consequence of according illusory "rights" to apes is to constrain the real rights of humans.
With best wishes,
Kenan Malik

14th April 1999

Dear Kenan
I am shocked by this bias in favour of your own kind. Go back 200 years and imagine that Wilberforce has asked you to join the fight against the slave trade. You reply: I will sign up when you show me that Africans are not Africans, but Europeans. It is wrong just to say: "If they are not my kind, I don't care about them." Africans are not Europeans, but are entitled to the same rights as Europeans. Apes are not humans, but are entitled to the same rights as those we grant to all humans—remembering that we grant these rights to humans who are no more capable of becoming part of a reciprocal moral arrangement than are apes. (There is actually evidence of moral reciprocity in

apes, see Frans de Waal's book *Chimpanzee Politics*.) You, like the European racist, are claiming that your own group is superior to all others. That is wrong.

You acknowledge that children and people with profound disabilities are not moral beings, but you now argue that children are "potential" moral beings, and that people with profound disabilities are "might have been" moral beings. Are you, then, against abortion? The first argument implies that abortion is wrong, because a foetus is as much a potential moral being as a newborn baby. And I can't take seriously your "there but for the grace of God go I" argument for giving protection to intellectually disabled people, but not to apes. "I" am not just a body, I am a being with a mind. If my parents had, at the time I was conceived, conceived a child with a genetic abnormality, that would not have been me, it would have been another human. Your resort to such a weak argument suggests that some prejudice against beings which are not "my kind" lies behind the distinction you are defending.

Yours,

Peter Singer

17th April 1999

Dear Peter,

Am I biased towards humans? Yes. What you deride as speciesism I celebrate as humanism, a tradition which, over centuries, has paved the way for scientific advance and social emancipation. The fact that you, like many intellectuals, feel uncomfortable with this tradition says more about the depth of anti-humanism than it does about the nature of rights.

You argue that it is wrong to say, "If they are not my kind, I don't care about them." Really? Human beings and vegetables are different kinds. Is it wrong to say that I care about my neighbour more than a cabbage? The problem is not discriminating between different kinds, but the basis on which we do so.

Your attempt to link my argument to that of racists is ignorant.

Central to racial science was the belief that there existed no real discontinuity between humans and animals; this allowed racists to claim that blacks were closer to apes than whites. If any argument echoes the racists, it is yours, with its failure to distinguish properly between humans and apes.

You believe that it is wrong to discriminate between humans and apes with respect to rights because apes have human-like capacities. As evidence you point to the work of primatologists such as Frans de Waal (who opposes ape rights). His research reveals the great complexity of ape social life. But it has not shown them capable of moral judgements.

Your other argument is that some humans are less rational and moral than many apes. But you miss my point that human rationality and morality derive from our existence as social beings—from our membership of humanity as a collective, something obviously denied to apes.

Finally, I do support abortion for the same reason that I oppose ape rights. I defend the real rights of women over the illusory rights of the foetus, just as I defend the real rights of humans over the illusory rights of apes.

With best wishes,

Kenan Malik

LIFE

"How can you be having a mid-life crisis?
You don't know how long you're going to live"

The last tiger • Ruth Padel

AUGUST / SEPTEMBER 2001

It is a late December afternoon in a hill-forest in Orissa, at about the spot on the map of India where, if the country were a revolver pointing south, you'd curl your finger above the trigger. Sitting well back from a river bank, among deckle-edged grass rising three feet above his head, is one of India's last tigers. One out of how many? It is hard to count tigers because of where and how they live. These days, you set photographic flashlights in the grass, you count faeces and pug marks. But the figures can be massaged like any others and in India tiger counts are politics as well as science. In 1900, when tigers were thick on the ground, the estimate was 100,000 Indian tigers in the wild, even after a century of manic tiger shooting. India was the greatest prize of empire, and the greatest prize yearned for by male servants of the empire was to shoot a tiger. In 1870, when the future king Edward VII shot one in Bihar, the whole race of Indian or Bengal tigers was rechristened the Royal Bengal tiger. And Indian royalty had to outdo the British. By the time he died, the Maharajah of Suguja had a tally of 1,150 tigers.

The London Zoological Society's Tiger Conference recently reckoned the Indian tiger population to be between 2,000 and 3,500. So this tiger on the bank is an important statistic. He has done his best to pass his genes on recently, but he's got to stick around. He has been away on a three-day mating spree, and is back now in the heart of his territory. Whatever neural flows and synapses take care of long-term planning in a tiger's brain are working full-time. He must repossess his patch, respray it. Male tigers spend hours patrolling their terrain, scent-marking trees and boulders, taking in what's up, who's where, what's died. But first a spot of short-term planning: food.

Tiger life is alternation. It is all long quiet followed by furious action. You fast and fast, then feast. On average, a tiger needs 15 pounds of meat a day. They can go without for several days, but when they have to find their own meals, they stuff themselves to balloon point. That average takes a lot of getting. Even in sleep, the animals that the tiger preys upon are always wary. They are made for running away, climbing, or fighting at bay with razor antlers and razor feet.

Hunting is the art of stillness. Tigers have great speed over short distances but are no good in a long chase. Once a tiger gets into a race, it has already lost. Cheetahs are light on their feet; they evolved their speed on open plains. Tigers are heavy-boned and heavy-muscled. They work through camouflage and cover: long grass, bushes, rocks. Geometry—the angle you come from—is everything. Head-on confrontation is no good; a tiger's job is to eat, not pick fights and get hurt. Hunts end with a few seconds of lightning and mayhem, but they depend on long, silent, trigonometric preparation. The 50 yards which a jungle-smart man will cover in two minutes, supposing himself quiet and invisible, will take a tiger 15 minutes. Rather than risk the crackle of a dead leaf, a tiger will very slowly crush it into dust with the pad of a gargantuan front paw.

Sensitivity is not always an advantage. Those pads, despite the strength of the claws they sheathe, are hopeless on a red-hot griddle fired by the midday sun. To foil him, deer will cross open ground at near-combustion point on heat-proof hooves to drink at the hottest time of day. The tiger cannot follow without blistering his feet, and a tiger with blistered feet will soon be no tiger at all. A tiger needs to be perfect.

Out of 20 tiger charges—all that powerful, beautiful bounding—19 fail. On every hunt the tiger weighs the maths, balancing the next meal against catastrophic injury. Which way is the wind blowing? How can you avoid being seen, not just by prey, but from above, by hundreds of grey langur monkeys, the eyes of the jungle, packing the trees with black judgemental faces and nothing to do but watch and yell.

Alarm calls are the jungle's lingua franca. Everyone wants to know when a predator is around, especially the largest, so a tiger will base his strategy on not letting any animal know where he is. Once you are pinpointed by alarms, or if you charge and miss, you have to give up and start over somewhere else, or you won't eat. It is a precarious way of life. Hunt for hunt, the tiger is the least successful of all cats.

He is watching the river bank from the grass. Animal shapes are appearing now by the reeds at the water's edge, through flexed stems and spiny stipules of wild madder. They are mostly in shade, but from time to time an ear or bony rump is lit by the horizontal rays of the sunset.

A tiger's eyes are less efficient than ours at gauging shapes, but adept as an alchemist's at weighing up movement. In low light, a tiger's vision is six times as good as ours. If you shone a torch at him his pupils would glow. A colour photo would bring them up fluorescent green. This is the tapetum: the reflective patch, a sequin in the centre of the retina. It maximises the concentration of dim light. Human eyes do not shine.

If we followed his gaze, we would see only dark shapes. They could be wild dog, or maybe wild boar; six or seven shapes, moving slowly, head down, head up, side by side, grazing (so not dog) and drinking. If we locked into the tiger's vision we would see four sambur does, two with fawns; a young stag and an older one.

Sambur love water. They spend hours up to their thighs in the shallows, drinking, ruminating, but all the time flicking up their heads and spreading wide spoon ears to catch any stir of grass. Their eyes have a tapetum too; the tiger has no advantage here. Sambur know they are the tiger's first-stop restaurant.

Some tigers are brilliant at hunting deer in water. A tiger at Ranthambhore National Park—the park rangers called him Genghis —did it all the time. He developed a hunt handwriting unlike any other tiger. He even had an imitator, an impressionable young tigress called Noon, but she never matched his style. Genghis would charge from cover, single out his victim, disappear under water and drag it out a few seconds later. Even the crocodiles were wary of him; one in five of his charges ended in a kill.

Our tiger, though, has never been watched or named. There are 23 official tiger reserves in India, but two-thirds of the country's tigers live outside them. This tiger was born on the fringe of Similipal National Park five years ago, one of three cubs. One of them, when six months old, was caught in a poachers' iron trap. The edges of reserves are full of people who know the forest and make money selling carcasses to people from the towns. This tigress watched her cub die in the trap before the poachers came—furious, with no one to be furious with. Then she moved her territory west; away, although she didn't know it, from the doubtful sanctity of the reserve.

Tigresses are passionate, dedicated, adoring mothers. It takes two years to train a tiger for its solitary life. There is much rubbing and pouncing and playing together, but the tigress's main job, apart from defending them, is teaching them to hunt and kill.

She does it in stages. first, she brings them, say, a dead monkey as an educational toy to quarrel over. Then a dead deer with the hide on, so they learn a new use for their growing teeth. Then she teaches them to stalk, wait, calculate, watch the vultures and langurs. Finally, the tertiary education: the angles of attack, the steel self-control and the killing grips. If you break cover a second too soon, you've lost. Even two-year-old tigers are not much good at killing on their own. It takes months of watching your children cock up your own long stalk, and dozens upon dozens of missed kills.

When this tiger's bereaved and agitated mother moved territory with two young cubs, she left the protection of their father, the one male who could be relied on never to harm them. In her confusion, she stepped into the territory of another male. An alien adult male tiger is the one big predator of tiger cubs. A tigress can see off a leopard or wild dogs, but with a male tiger she will have to stand up and fight.

She spent six months avoiding him. But lying in shade one afternoon, tail and chin laid over one cub, her spine relaxed against the other, she raised her head when three langurs started calling from the trees. Predator, large, close by, went the alarm. Unlike sambur, she couldn't melt away. She tracked the approach from the calls, waited a minute, disengaged herself from the cubs and stood up. Head down, crest arched like an Arab stallion, the male came into sight. He looked at her, at the cubs. She faced him from the grass and growled. The cubs fled up a tree.

Tiger confrontations happen in slow motion, in pure, sad stages. For a moment the two adults looked like one tiger gazing at its double in a mirror, bodies still but tails swinging slowly side to side The male looked up at the cubs, opened his mouth and roared. The tigress, lighter and skinnier, snarled and lashed out. From their tree the cubs watched her stand and swipe like a boxer, and the male rear up against her, heavier, and with a longer reach.

Twenty minutes later the tigress was lying on the grass again, this time on her side, flies dark round her nose, round the punctures over her ribs and her crushed front paws. The male reared up the tree, pulled down the lower cub, killed it expertly against the trunk, ate some, and walked off, leaving the head staring up at the sky: a cut-off tiger ruglet.

The tigress staggered into the shade. Two days later, she died. The lone cub, only a year old, came down from the tree and, against the odds, survived. He moved west again, away from the territory of the other male. He missed company, but shunned it. He taught himself to vanish into bushes, not to break cover too soon. He lived off peacocks, rodents, wild boar piglets, until he graduated to chital. At two, he killed his first sambur.

The forest he lives in now is surrounded, although he doesn't know it, by people whose treasured trade is tiger whiskers and whose favourite life-charm for hundreds of years has been a tiger's clavicle bone. The big money in tiger parts is made in the cities. Villagers get a few rupees in return for the carcasses.

In the four years since he lost his mother, this tiger has killed nearly 400 deer and evolved his own style. He is still there on the river bank,

working out the angle, watching the sambur through the vertical knit-
ting of the grass. Hunting is a game of deadly billiards, a question of
refraction and recoil. Which animal is in the best position for the
follow-up? Which line of approach will take him closest, unseen?
Where the cover fails, the tiger will have to use top speed, and the less
of that the better.

He begins his painstaking approach, low-slung between the whis-
pering grass-heads. As with cooking, the art is in the preparation.
That spectacular charge is just the final flourish, the parsley garnish.
The last seconds have an air of superstitious double checking. He
weaves his head in fractional advances and retreats, confirming his
assessment of distance.

Suddenly he breaks cover and bursts out, a steeplechaser on fire,
rocketing towards the drinking sambur. This tiger favours an oblique
angle, more from behind than from the side. He must try to knock
down large prey like this in the pell-mell of his weight at speed. When
he springs, he must try to get a hold with his teeth on the shoulder or
neck, and find a killing grip at once. He has two options. A nape grip
kills by crushing or displacing the vertebrae, and severing the spinal
cord. The smaller the animal, the easier it is. With a big animal the
tiger has to work by leverage and turn the beast's weight against itself.
The second option, the throttle grip, is the best bet with a large
quarry; it closes the windpipe and keeps you clear of backwards-
threshing antlers, although you can get tangled up with the feet. If a
tiger manages that grip at once, throttling can be a protracted but
curiously peaceful business: the deer's head thrown back like a wor-
shipper gazing at the sky, a thread of blood running down the
coffee-coloured neck. In a successful charge, victims die with scarcely
a mark on them except in the throat.

Killing must be precise, not frenzied. Those gothic teeth are very
sensitive. They find a killing spot by feel, like a burglar snicking a
skeleton key into the lock of a safe. Victorian hunters said that a tiger's
first act was to suck its victim's blood. This was a misreading of the
throttle grip. A tiger can no more suck than it can purr. A grown-up
tiger's mouth is made for dismembering and slicing.

For geometric reasons, this tiger has gone for the big stag. The other deer break and scatter, zig-zagging through the grass, white tails raised and flickering. White is the jungle's alarm colour; calls ring through the grass, and langurs echo them in the trees. If the tiger misses, he'll find no food for miles.

The stag has splashed through the shallows on to the bank, zig-zagging too. The tiger follows, his face a mask of concentration. Not ferocious; focused. The sinews of his long body contract and release as he bounds. The stripes, their ends forking over orange ribs and white belly, part and close as muscles bunch and stretch. Then he springs at the stag's throat, going for a throttle grip, but the old stag shifts at the last moment and the tiger's teeth take hold of the skin on the cheek.

The other deer circle a little way off, looking back, feet stamping, ears quivering. They know, once the charge is over, that there is no threat to them. A tiger depends on surprise and gets no second chance. The deer are spectators in a motionless stand-off.

A chital would have been smaller and lighter. One of the does, or a fawn, would be easier to handle. But this stag is heavy, twice the tiger's size and weight, his back scabbed with dried mud and old wounds. He stands, his cheek in the tiger's mouth, his antlers with heavy tines five feet apart. His head is lowered to tiger's-head height. The hair guarding the throat the tiger missed is spiky and ruffled. The tall legs are planted, pulling back, a few inches from the tiger. The tiger's rump is nearly on the ground, forelegs stubbed in earth like a labrador puppy playing tug-of-war with a child: two big animals, absolutely still, every cell in their bodies straining, eyeballs and toes less than a foot apart; a parody of love.

If these were two men, you'd see expressions on their faces. There are none here. The tiger's ears are laid back in hard-edged effort. He is using all his strength to pull the deer back towards him; the stag is using all his to resist. With a sudden, Promethean toss of the head, the sambur tears free of the tiger's teeth, leaving the side of his cheek hanging below his muzzle. Instantly the tiger leaps again and locks on to the back of the stag's neck.

The only sound is the puffing of each animal, and the occasional grunt. But whether tired from his first charge or weakened by three days of sex, the tiger's grip is not strong enough. Again the stag breaks free, bleeding from long, dragged claw-rips and tooth-punctures in back and neck as well as face. Through the glisten of blood, cobwebs of mucus hang from his black nose and mouth. He veers away.

The tiger works his weight under the belly and grabs a hind leg from inside, trying to break it. But he has miscalculated the angle and the stag's other hind leg threshes wildly in the air, then catches in the tiger's chest, scoring a deep gash there; then another in the left inner thigh, cutting nearly to the bone.

The tiger flinches, and the sambur wrenches free a third time. With a wild bunching of muscle he flounders to the river, staggers in and swims, his bleeding head holding his antlers up, across the shadowy water. He nearly goes under, but makes it to the further bank. He may die there, weeks later. The tiger watches from the bank, too tired to give chase.

Solitude is both the tiger's great strength and greatest weakness. He must be solitary, because of the country he has chosen—forest, ravines, thick bushes. In Africa, on the open plain, lions hunt together and feed together. If a lion is hurt, he can still eat while the injury heals. Tigers do not have that option. When this one licks his chest and back leg, antiseptic saliva will minimise infection. But to heal he needs to stay strong. This tiger hasn't eaten for three days. He had other things on his mind.

He backs off behind a fallen tree, and sits down. After a moment he bends his head to work his tongue round the welling red in his chest and leg. Even resting, he is working. He hears a faint rustle, like a hastily silenced witch's besom, in the bushes behind.

What do tigers like eating? Deer, pig, hare, monkey, peacock; even porcupine. But porcupines are high risk. They are slow, dumpy and easy to catch, but hard to kill and eat safely. They have 30,000 tweedy detachable quills and when they feel anxious they raise these, like hair lifting on skin when you are cold. They run backwards, bushy tails leading, and release the outer quills.

Jim Corbett, legendary hunter of man-eaters in the early years of the 20th century, who became the great champion of the Indian tiger, pulled hundreds of porcupine quills out of tigers he shot. The ones Corbett saw had lived for years with quills sometimes more than nine inches long, thick as pencils, embedded in their legs, in hard muscle, or wedged between bones. The Mohan Man-Eater lived above the Kosi valley in the Himalayas; he held the Almora District in a reign of terror for years. Yet he always moaned when he entered the village of Kartkanoula at night. That was how the villagers knew he was there. He must have moaned as he walked through jungle too, hunting would have been impossible. When Corbett shot him, he found no hair on the inner side of the left foreleg, and 25 punctures oozing yellow fluid. In the days when there were many tigers and fewer people, only wounds like this turned tigers into man-eaters. There are no antlers and hooves on a man gathering honey or a woman scything grass. No sense of smell; no running away. For an incapacitated tiger, people become the only prey.

Porcupines are rodents. They chew bark and herbs. That's their life. This one, in a slow fussy bustling nibble, is following a line of sweet thin root just under the surface of the soil.

Tigers attack porcupines from behind and on top. Leopards are just as keen on porcupine as tigers are, but they always catch them by the head. "Why tigers do not employ this safe and obvious method is a mystery to me," said Corbett, who admired tigers deeply and identified with them as a gentleman.

As the porcupine shuffles into his sights, the tiger, more slowly than usual because of his gashed back leg, gathers his hindquarters under him and charges.

The porcupine has a second to see what's coming, raise his quills, and run backwards. When the tiger springs, 50 quills shoot into him from his chest down to the inside of his right front leg. Twelve strike bone—the humerus, the tiger bone most treasured in Chinese medicine. One quill pierces his right paw.

He breaks his leap. The porcupine scuttles out from under, rattles into bushes, disappears.

The tiger is alone again. A very different tiger, with very different prospects, from the one he was an hour ago. He is in an unknown zone.

An animal's face is hard to read. Its body is what matters; a tiger's life story is physical. You tell its fortune from the way it walks. This one limps off, wobbly, into the bandaged shadow of the bushes.

He still needs to eat. He walks a little way, lies down carefully. The topaz eyes don't show the pain which human eyes would show. They have that concentrated, distant look eyes have when other senses, smell and hearing, are powerfully at work.

He hears no new sound. But among the wide palette of jungle-scents that he has tasted on the air every day of his life, there is a new one. He waits three minutes, then rises, takes two slow, silent limps forward and stares into the grainy dusk.

There is a dead goat in the clearing ahead.

The camping holiday • Carlo Gébler

JUNE 1998

It was July 1963, a Monday, and we were due to leave for our long promised camping holiday in Wales. We awoke early, my brother and I. He was six, I was eight. At that time we lived with our father. My mother had left the previous year.

My father's name was Ernest. He was an unhappy man, silent and angry. Luckily, we were seldom in each other's company because he worked at night and slept for most of the day. He preferred the night, he said, because he could work on restoring his beloved Railton motorcars (he had two) or write (he was an author and playwright) without interruption from his children.

He woke, usually, in the early afternoon. If it was a weekend we would bring him toast and Lapsang Souchong tea in bed. Weekdays he made his own and when we came back from school, he was usually at breakfast in the kitchen.

The three male Géblers ate together around 7pm. Then we would go to bed and he would go to work. In the morning he would always be asleep. On school days we would eat porridge and slip out, taking care to close the front door quietly; on weekends and holidays, we would sit and read until it was time to make his tea and toast. We were forbidden to leave the house or to invite friends in. If we broke the rules we got a verbal "dressing down" or a sharp blow with a pair of scissors behind the ear. I preferred a whack. The pain was less than the hurt of his words.

On this morning, because of the camping trip, we were quieter than usual. We made our breakfast in silence, washed up in silence, dried and put away in silence. Afterwards I went out into the garden and sat in one of the deckchairs that had come with us from Dublin to London. I took a book with me, *The Enchanted Wood* by Enid Blyton.

The sun rose and towards midday one of the upstairs windows at the back banged open.

"Karl," my father called. (That was my name then.)

I turned and saw him at an upstairs window, bald, dark-eyed, sallow-skinned.

"Camping's off," he shouted. "It's too late. You shouldn't have let me sleep in!"

When he wanted to wake up he usually left a red plastic toy fob-watch on the kitchen counter set to the time he wanted a knock. But this morning the fob hadn't been there on the counter and so I had assumed he was waking himself with his alarm clock. Apparently, I was wrong.

My father disappeared, shutting the window. I saw the back of our semi-detached suburban house, the veranda, and the brown vine that miraculously flourished under the glass. I looked at the grey wormy London earth of our flower beds and the fence sticky with creosote. I knew that I must not dwell on the news. If I got sad I would have an asthma attack, and then we'd never go on holiday.

So I bent my book open and threw myself into the world of Jo, Bessie and Fanny, the Faraway Tree, Saucepan Man, Moon-Face and Silky the elf.

The next day my father drove the black Railton round to the front. The car was a prewar, hand-built beauty and he loved it.

The camping gear was in the hall. I carried out a tent in a canvas bag, pegs rattling inside, a folded ground sheet spotted with grass stains, a Primus stove in an oily cardboard box. My father began to pack the boot, painfully slowly.

"Don't come near the car, you'll scratch the paint work … and don't touch the running board!" he shouted.

Eventually the packing was completed. I climbed carefully into the leathery interior and sat on the slippery rear seat beside my brother. My father got in. He checked the route plan. It was written on the back of an old envelope and clipped to the sun visor with a clothes peg. Then he started the engine.

We drove to a street of terraced houses in Raynes Park and stopped at a blue gate. This was the home of Kevin Francis, a school friend. I went to the door. Mrs Francis came out in a sari. They were Christian Indians. Kevin appeared with a holdall. This went in the boot. The running board was negotiated again and now we set off properly.

By teatime we were parked on a lay-by along the A40. The Primus was pumped but refusing to light. I produced the pocket camping stove I had bought from Millett's with my pocket money. My father put the kettle on, and a few minutes later he was sipping tea. I watched him carefully. He drained his mug and tossed the dregs away. Should I have produced my emergency stove? Did he think I was showing off? I tried to see if his eyes had gone small and dark and angry. But I saw nothing.

Our campsite was outside Abergavenny. It was a beautiful evening when my father nosed the Railton through the gate. I saw chestnut trees and a racing Welsh river.

There was a hut. A figure bounded out and hurried towards us, wearing sandals and a shirt covered with badges. I thought it was a boy scout, but in fact it was a man. He brought his creased old face to the driver's window, smiling, bespectacled.

"Hello," he said, pure Charles Hawtrey. My heart sank. Exactly the type my father loathed. "I'm William Whiteside," he said, "but just call me Willy, won't you."

My father paid for our pitch and we drove off. Willy, he told us, a few moments later, as we struggled with our tent poles, was the type who interfered with children. We were never to approach Willy, and if he offered us sweets, we were to report this at once.

"My uncle Willy has a ten foot willy," my brother murmured and we tittered.

I fell asleep that night to rushing Welsh water but when I woke it was to the sound of voices, guttural and angry.

I put my head through the tent flap and saw two women. They wore mini skirts and shoes with heels that sunk into the soft ground. They were from Birmingham. Their respective families had been feuding for years. They had arrived separately in the night, each having chosen the site without knowing the other would be there; they had woken to find one another and neither was now prepared to leave.

My father came out of his rather larger tent. He lit the Primus (having cleared the blockage with a needle the night before) and put on the kettle. It was Czechoslovakian, decorated with flowers and birds. When possible, he would always buy eastern European, in order to support socialism.

In the distance, the women stopped screaming and went their separate ways. I realised the feuding families were camped one on either side of us.

"Oh God," went my father, "the lumpenproletariat."

After breakfast, it was time to do "our business." My father believed that regular evacuation of the bowels was essential for mental and physical well-being, and conversely, that a constipated child was a poisoned child. He believed that all food must be masticated properly before swallowing (20 chews to every mouthful). This ensured stools that moved smoothly through the body. Processed foods and sugars were absolutely forbidden.

His ideas came from *The Culture of Abdomen*. I had sneaked a look at this book once or twice. It was filled with line drawings of the lower abdomen and passages (underlined by my father) which praised the Turkish squatter over our European crapper.

My father wasn't happy unless we went every day. Each evening before supper, he would smell our breath for signs of constipation. He would use liquid paraffin to get us moving. If nothing happened for three days, he would administer a hot water enema.

We washed our breakfast things in the peaty river. We pulled some lavatory paper off the roll and took off our plimsolls. There were no toilets on the site. We would have to cross the river and find a place in the bracken covered hill on the other side.

We set off, Kevin, my brother and myself. The water was cold, and fast moving. In the middle, Kevin dropped a plimsoll. It landed in the water and was swept away. On the bank my father shook his head.

We reached the far side and separated. I found a place and made a hole in the sandy ground and squatted down. I could hear Kevin hopping through the undergrowth in his single plimsoll.

When I finished I wiped myself. Then I buried everything and went back to the river and washed my hands.

We reassembled and crossed back over.

"Put something on your feet," father ordered Kevin.

"Can't," he whispered.

The plimsolls were all he had. He tried my spare shoes. Too big.

"How could you come camping and not bring another pair?" my father asked. "Are you an imbecile?"

Silence.

"I suppose," he said, looking at me, "as a stupid boy, it naturally follows you'd have a stupid friend like Kevin."

He was annoyed because now he would have to buy Kevin shoes.

"I'll go and try and find it," I offered.

"Don't be ridiculous," my father snorted. "It'll have washed out to sea by now."

I set off, and after a few minutes, I met a fisherman coming my way. He wore rubber waders and carried a rod like a rifle on his shoulder.

"Lost something?" he said. He must have guessed from my expression.

"Yes."

He swung the rod forward. The plimsoll hung from a feathered hook.

I thanked the angler and hurried off. I was happy. Perhaps my father would say, "Well done." But when I got back, war had started. The Birmingham families were down at the river's edge hurling rocks at each other.

Screams came from below. We were spectators at a medieval battle, I thought. I had read up on these secretly in my father's *Encyclopaedia Britannica*. He disapproved of all wars except those involving the Red Army.

A boy with a bleeding face scrambled over the bank and ran past.

"Why have I come?" my father muttered. "This is awful!"

Willy came and separated the warring parties. Adolescent boys and their fathers clambered up from the river and shuffled by. I saw thin men in wet clothes, blood in their hair, hard faces.

A little later, it began to rain. I watched thick, heavy spears of wet hurling themselves at the ground. Within minutes, sheets of water had covered the campsite and the swollen river started to roar.

We retreated into the bigger tent, the one where my father slept. My bored brother ran a toe idly along the canvas and water began to trickle through.

"I warned you not to touch it, you stupid boy," my father shouted. "You've ruined the waterproofing."

A saucepan went under the drips.

"That's it. I've had enough," he shouted. "You wanted this holiday, right, boys, you're welcome to it. I don't. There's plenty of food. There's fuel for the Primus. The pitch fees are paid. You can fend for yourselves."

He put his things in the Railton and went to a hotel in Abergavenny.

In the days that followed it went on raining and the warring factions went on fighting. Days and nights were punctuated by shouts and curses and screams of pain. The police came twice, and an ambulance once. We huddled in the tent and read—Enid Blyton and Richmal Crompton—and ate cold baked beans. One day, father brought us to the hotel and fed us. I had mushy peas and mashed potatoes with lamb fat in a dining room with an open fire and lots of horse brasses.

Then, one day, after lunch, the clouds cleared and the sun began to shine on the camp site. Everything began to steam and the river subsided from a roar to a chatter. Father came at teatime with his trout rods. A perfect summer evening was ahead of us. It was too good to be true—of course it was—and within minutes the families were back at war. This time they fought not by the river but on the camp site; and soon rocks were flying.

Father went off to get Willy. As soon as he disappeared into the hut, we saw our chance. Without thought or discussion, I watched while my brother picked up a boulder and hurled it at the side of the Railton. There was a thump as metal buckled and lovingly applied black cellulose paint came away in huge flakes.

We ran across the site and burst into the hut.

"Dad!" we piped. "You'd better come."

We led him back to the car with long faces and showed him the damage.

"The families," we explained and looked suitably frightened.

My father started walking in the direction of a knot of men who were fighting and then thought better of it and came back to us.

"Pack," he said, and within an hour we were on the way home.

England is a garden • John Keegan

NOVEMBER 1997

I wouldn't mind," I heard a woman's voice sobbing at my elbow, "If my own son had been killed I wouldn't mind so much if he could have lain here." Tears streamed down her kindly face. She clutched my elbow. "I wouldn't mind." There was a scent of roses and mown grass, the reflection of sunlight from white Portland stone, a gentle mediterranean breeze, the promise of heat to come. "I wouldn't mind."

We were two English people in a primal English setting: greensward, shrubs, flowering perennials, paved walks with saxifrage rooted in the cracks, low walls, statuary and masonry—an English enclosure far from England. "Remember, green is a colour," advised Gertrude Jekyll, inventor of the modern English garden; and here below the hillsides, arid after a long summer drought, green was a brilliant, almost overpowering colour.

The landscape beyond the garden was ageless, with that mediterranean quality which has captivated English travellers since they first began their journeys to rediscover, 300 years ago, the classical world their ancestors had done so much to overthrow. But the garden was timeless, belonging neither to the present nor the past, but to an arrested moment existing only in the English imagination. It is a moment suffused by classicism, inspired by the temperate wilderness, but transcending both; a moment when man's work comes into equilibrium with the beauty of nature and an ideal landscape is brought to perfection.

Where are these landscapes? Some are accidental tracts of the English countryside—an artificial creation 4,000 years old in parts—where contour and woodland combine with plough and pasture, hedge and wall, to form a vision the English call England. The English vision is particularly present in the Cotswolds west of Oxford, in the South Hams of Devonshire, in Thomas Hardy's Dorset, along the Welsh marches of Herefordshire and Shropshire, in Beatrix Potter country above the Cumbrian lakes, in the Kipling territory of remoter Kent and Sussex. Yet that vision is also present wherever population is sparse, rainfall heavy and agriculture intense, but with tracts of ancient forest land making a patchwork of settlement and emptiness, the familiar and the mysterious.

Many are not accidental at all, but the work of great landlords and the artists they employed to beautify what was already beautiful, in a manner quite alien to the environment. England is natural broadleaf forest land, with deep topsoil in which stone is hard to come by and the indigenous flowering plants are retiring and modest on colour. Without relentless human effort, cleared land reverts to scrub in a few seasons and to forest in a century. Despite the power of these natural forces, English landowners decided in the 17th century to create private landscapes which defy north European ecology and impose elements of Italian and French classicism. They began to build stone palaces in classical style, to lay out severely formal gardens on their doorsteps, and to reorder the more distant landscape into those idealised Italian ones painted by Claude Lorrain and Nicolas Poussin with which they filled their picture galleries. Near my house in Wiltshire, there is one of the greatest English ideal landscapes, the artificial lakeland garden of Stourhead. I often wonder whether the Hoare family, which created it, was not inspired by the southerly vista into Dorset, which typifies the vision of an accidentally perfect England. There are other such ideal landscapes at Blenheim and at Ditchley north of Oxford, at Stowe in Buckinghamshire, at Castle Howard in Yorkshire and at Chatsworth in Derbyshire. Every county offers dozens of less spectacular versions, and the English visit them in their millions, to commune with a central belief of their identity: that England is a garden, and that to be English is to be a gardener; that in life they are best at home in a garden; and that, in death, a garden is where they belong.

Few English people, of course, can hope to live at Stourhead or Stowe. Perhaps they really do not wish to inhabit such idealisations of nature. The English are homebodies, happy if in a fraction of an acre they can re-create some of the elements of that high style. They are helped to do so by the BBC's *Gardener's Question Time*, whose panel of experts instruct millions of radio listeners each week in the secrets of gardening by answering queries put by members of a local horticultural society. The popularity of *Gardener's Question Time*, which has been on the air now for 50 years, is a touchstone of the difference between English and American culture. The extremes of climate in the US, its highs and lows of fertility and aridity, rule out the viability of a programme based on uniform temperature and cultivability. More than that, however, *Gardener's Question Time* presumes that its listeners will have a lifetime to tend the same garden. It is a programme for a people who do not move, or move at most a few miles down the road, and it would therefore be untransplantable into the restless mobility of the US, whose people not only change states but coasts, with a frequency that seems reckless to the BBC's cosy stay-at-homes.

There is, alongside the great garden, an alternative English gardening tradition: the cottage plot, parish church of plantsmen and plantswomen. The great garden is formal and contrived, however artfully integrated into its natural surroundings, and its colour tones are modulated and subdued. The cottage garden, by contrast, is spontaneous and informal, full of colour with plants allowed to have their heads. The centre point of the great garden is the paved or gravelled walk running between trimmed topiary. That of the cottage garden is the herbaceous border and rambling rose. Both are equally English, though they have different origins. Towards the end of the 19th century a new generation of English garden designers succeeded in combining these traditions into what is now accepted as the classic English garden. Its layout draws on the 17th century fashion for formality, on the 18th century idealisation of nature and classical civilisation, and on a more recent enthusiasm for the vernacular. Some great gardens were adapted to accommodate the herbaceousness previously excluded as vulgar and unaristocratic, as at Arley Hall in Cheshire, where the beds date to 1846. Many others, the work of the newly rich, were radical reorganisations around old houses which had fallen into decay or houses which had been originally designed in the new fashion. Such houses were not necessarily large, but given spaciousness by a deliberate policy of extending the architecture of the building out into the surrounding walls, terraces, summerhouses and topiary hedges. The most sought-after designer of these new houses was the young architect Edwin Lutyens; and the most inventive designer of their gardens was the self-taught horticulturist Gertrude Jekyll. They often co-operated. Lutyens helped Jekyll with what is still one of the most influential of all English gardening books, *Gardens for Small Country Houses*, and the results of their collaboration can be seen at such places as Orchards, Surrey; Marsh Court and Amport House, in Hampshire; and Folly Farm, Berkshire.

Lutyens favoured low stone walls, paved walks, pergolas and pavilions in the stripped-down classical style. Jekyll encouraged the planting of dwarf roses, creeping ground cover, grey and silver border plants, azaleas, and climbers such as hydrangea and wisteria. Their purpose was to soften masonry with vegetation which liked support, to sharpen natural forms with architectural straight lines, and to relieve the greys and browns of stone and brick with blues, yellows and purples.

It was in exactly such surroundings that the tear-stained woman burst out about not minding if *her* son had been killed. I was not the least surprised by her reaction. I had heard it, in different versions, many times before in many parts of the world. This time we were in the Suda Bay British War Cemetery in Crete, where 1,571 servicemen are buried, mainly British, but including New Zealanders and Australians. Most were killed resisting the German invasion of 20th May 1941, a disaster for the German parachutists involved—2,000 died on the first day—but a strategic victory for Hitler, who secured the island despite the losses.

But we might have been in any one of the larger Commonwealth War Graves Commission's cemeteries anywhere in the world. The dead of the British Empire and Commonwealth of the two world wars are buried in 134 countries, from Algeria to Zimbabwe. The smallest cemetery is on Ocracoke Island, off North Carolina, with four graves. The largest is the Thiepval memorial in the département of the Somme, in France, where the bodies of 70,000 soldiers are buried and the names of those missing in the great battle of the first world war are commemorated. These are cemeteries proper, of which the commission maintains about 2,000 throughout the world. Besides these, the commission also cares for 23,000 individual graves or plots in non-military cemeteries. One such grave is in Kilmington churchyard, under my bedroom window: Private S Prince, Somerset Light Infantry, who died aged 22 on 5th May 1916—home on leave, I presume, from France just before the opening of the Battle of the

Somme. Every two years an official of the commission comes to scrub the headstone (one of over 1m identical headstones in the world), to cut the grass, tidy the surroundings, and ensure that Private Prince continues to repose in dignity.

There are, of course, many more dead than headstones. In every French cathedral a plaque, in French and English, reads: "To the glory of God and in memory of one million men of the British Empire who died in the great war and of whom the greater number rest in France." Of those killed in France, the bodies of nearly half could not be found or were unidentifiable, while most of the naval dead were lost at sea. There is a similar proportion of missing among the dead of the second world war. The commission commemorates the names of all of them—nearly 1.7m in number. Of these, 900,000 are identified servicemen and women lying in marked graves. There are over 700,000 monumental inscriptions to the missing, but 200,000 of those read "known unto God," because the remains recovered were unrecognisable. Some headstones record a casualty "known to be buried near this spot"; others bear two or more names of bodies too entangled to be buried separately.

How was this vast army of the dead to be decently interred? That was the question which confronted the British government soon after the first mass casualty lists were published in the national newspapers in 1915. The dead of Britain's earlier wars, frequent though those had been, were comparatively few in number. They had been buried near where they fell, marked by stones raised by their friends or regiments —if commemorated at all. It was a disposal accepted by the poor from which the bulk of the army's soldiers came. In civil life many of them might have gone to an unmarked pauper's grave in town or city. In the country a wooden cross, soon to decay, would have indicated their plot in the churchyard. In my village, a resident has calculated that 25,000 bodies have been buried in the churchyard since the Norman conquest, yet it contains only a few dozen stones—those of the wealthy, and none older than the 18th century.

By the beginning of the 20th century, however, the British people were better off. The funeral had become an important working-class ritual, and a marked headstone had become a symbol of respectability. For this reason it was unthinkable that the dead of a national army, dying in their tens of thousands for king, country and empire, should be left in hurried graves, marked by some makeshift cross nailed together by comrades. In the early months of the first world war soldiers dug graves in French or Belgian churchyards; but these rapidly filled up. The better off among the bereaved erected private memorials which most families could not afford; some repatriated the bodies. Both practices struck the wrong note in what the government represented—and the population endorsed—as a national war.

Very early on, therefore, Britain established what in retrospect are remarkable and nationally distinctive principles for the burial and commemoration of its war dead. First, there should be no private memorials, "on account of the difficulties of treating impartially the claims advanced by persons of different social standing." Second, there should be no repatriation of bodies, because of the common feeling that, as one officer put it, "in spite of all differences of rank, we were comrades, brothers dwelling together in unity." Third, officers and soldiers should be buried identically and together because, as Fabian Ware, founder of the War Graves Commission, wrote: "In 99 cases out of 100, officers will tell you that if they are killed they would wish to be among their men." The fourth, most important, principle was that each fallen soldier should be honoured individually; even in a war of mass slaughter, each should be represented as a hero in an epic of collective heroism.

These principles were to be greatly elaborated on and their implementation standardised in the years to come. That was the achievement of Fabian Ware, a modest man who deserves to be recognised as a major semiologist of British culture in the 20th century. Semiology was not, of course, his purpose; it was not a title he would have welcomed or even understood. But through him a particularly English (rather than British) language of symbols—some from nature, some from the mind or hand of man—has come to represent how the nation wished to be seen by itself and by other nations at the end of an ordeal that tested the roots of its culture and identity to destruction.

Some manifestation of this language of symbols can be found at sites all around the world; I can testify to its continuing power to move the emotions of those who come upon them. Wherever they are found— in places as far apart as Alabama, Israel, Pakistan and South Africa —the British are moved to tears, tears shed also by people who are not British at all. Fabian Ware, by instinct rather than artifice, created a great cultural artefact at which generations to come will wonder—as we wonder at the relics of Roman legions—long after Britain's world-wide power is only a memory for historians.

Ware had much help. In 1915, soon after his appointment, the French government passed a law deeding land for the cemeteries of foreign soldiers as a *sépulture perpétuelle*. It passed not without oppo-sition, for it was against the French tradition of storing the bones of the dead in ossuaries, a cheap way of burying remains *en masse* and of reusing burial plots. As a result, British war graves became the resting places of individuals in legal perpetuity. Ware also had assistance from several leading British architects, including Edwin Lutyens and Herbert Baker, who designed the Empire's great public buildings.

Rudyard Kipling's role in the design of the imperial war graves was a poignant one. John, his only son, was too myopic to meet the army's medical standards, but Kipling used his influence to secure him a commission in the Irish Guards. John was among the regiment's missing after the second Battle of Loos, in 1915. For several years Kip-ling and his American wife Carrie toured military hospitals in France seeking news of their son, but to no avail. In his grief, he wrote a short poem always quoted in his selected works:

My son was killed while laughing at some
jest, I would I knew
What it was, and it might serve me in a time
when jests are few.

The truth, never revealed to the parents, but discovered by a comrade from survivors of John Kipling's company, was that he was last seen crying in pain from a wound in the mouth. His body, lost for decades, has recently been identified by officials of the commission, and his headstone has been appropriately re-engraved.

Kipling conceived the inscriptions carved on the headstones and monumental sculptures of the commission's cemeteries. These monuments take three forms. One is a high columnar cross bearing a bronze sword known as the Cross of Sacrifice. The second is a monolith, the Stone of Remembrance, on which are carved words from Ecclesiasticus, adapted by Kipling: "Their name liveth for evermore." (They were adapted to avoid offending Hindus, many of whom died in the service of India's king-emperor.) The third is the standard headstone, two feet eight inches high, one foot three inches broad. It is cut from white Portland stone, engraved with the deceased's regimental badge—Private Prince's, below my bedroom window, shows the mural crown, slung bugle and battle honour "Jelalabad" of the Somerset Light Infantry—and a religious symbol. Today 1.5m bear the Christian cross; 65,000 the Muslim crescent; 100,000 the appropriate Sikh or Hindu symbol; 10,000 the Star of David; and 10,000 Buddhist or Confucian symbols. Each stone is also inscribed with the dead serviceman or servicewoman's number, name, decorations, regimental title, age, date and place of death; or as many details as could be ascertained when a body was disinterred for reburial. At the bottom of the stone relatives may place a personal inscription of up to 60 characters. These inscriptions are the exception rather than the rule—an indication of how heartfelt is popular acceptance of the guiding principle of uniformity of remembrance. They are often quite conventional—"Peace perfect peace," or "He died that others might live." Eccentric or distasteful inscriptions are not allowed. Occasionally, however, an extra tug of the heartstrings is given by an apt line of poetry or some quite artless phrase of lament, the labour of a young widow or a family struggling to express its love for a son and brother who will not return.

Kipling also struggled to find words that would dignify without mawkishness the grave of a body which could not be identified. He hit upon the phrase, "a soldier of the great war known unto God." Thus, unidentified burials of the second world war are inscribed "A Soldier

[Sailor/Airman] of the 1939–45 War Known Unto God." Altogether, 204,145 graves in the commission's care are now marked in this way.

None of this symbolism could be imposed until the missing dead were found and the makeshift cemeteries of the war reordered. Work began while the first world war was still in progress, but even at its end the condition of many burial places was deeply distressing to relatives who began to make their way to France and Belgium to find where lost ones lay. Too often the sites they discovered were patches of mud, bereft of vegetation or covered by weeds and grass. A scheme of order had to be devised. The task was entrusted to Frederic Kenyon, director of the British Museum. Within the principles of uniformity of commemoration and an individual grave for all recovered remains, he proposed that each cemetery should either "have the appearance of a small park or garden in no way recognisable as a cemetery," or that it "be marked by rows of headstones of a uniform height and width, the graves themselves being levelled to a flat surface and planted with turf and flowers." The rows of headstones would "carry on the military idea, giving the appearance as of a battalion on parade."

The second alternative was adopted; but the first idea was integrated with it. The commission cemeteries are unmistakably that; but they are also unmistakably parks or gardens in the classic English style. How did this come about? When the commission began to recruit maintenance staff, it decided for administrative reasons not to enlist locals but to commission British firms who would send their own staff abroad. The work was therefore begun not by French or Belgian labourers but by British gardeners, already experienced as horticulturists or later trained at the Royal Botanic Gardens at Kew. The style they brought with them was the one which Lutyens and Jekyll—she drew up plans for several cemeteries—taught in their seminal gardening book. By March 1921, 1,362 gardeners were employed. Many settled in France or Belgium, married local women, founded little English communities and introduced their sons into the commission's employment. These communities still exist and now have equivalents in Africa, southeast Asia, India and Pakistan, all trained in and carrying on the tradition of classic English country house gardening, in the desert and the tropics as well as in temperate northern Europe.

Other deeper literary influences were at work. The great war pro-voked in Britain—uniquely among combatant nations—a poetic response, much of it arcadian and pastoral. As Paul Fussell has noted in *The Great War and Modern Memory*: "Half the poems in the *Oxford Book of English Verse* are about flowers and a third seem to be about roses." He does not offer a similar count for first world war poetry, but the result might be the same. Certainly some of the most famous English poems are suffused with gardening themes.

The spectacle of the makeshift graves of the British in northern France inspired one of the most famous war poems, by the Canadian John McCrae, himself later killed in the war. It inspired the British custom of wearing a poppy on Remembrance Sunday:

> In Flanders fields the poppies blow
> Between the crosses, row on row
> That mark our place; and in the sky
> The larks, still bravely singing, fly
> Scarce heard amid the guns below.
>
> We are the Dead. Short days ago
> We lived, felt dawn, saw sunset glow,
> Loved and were loved, and now we lie
> In Flanders fields.

Those themes were also used by Rupert Brooke in the most famous of all English war poems, "The Soldier." I can still repeat it by heart from childhood memory, and feel that Brooke's idea of making "some corner of a foreign field" a place that would be "forever England" was a principal motivation, conscious or not, in making the war cemetery a pastoral, arcadian garden. This has been the result.

What has been the effect of this partly intentional, partly accidental effort to honour the hundreds of thousands of British and imperial war dead within the principles of individual, yet uniform, com-memoration? It is different from the French, who also buried their dead individually but under a cross, which creates a spiky and geometrical effect, lacking the mood of repose so immediately felt in British war cemeteries. It is certainly different from the Germans, whose dead lie in multiple or mass graves—such as that at Langemarck in Belgium, where 36,000 bodies of the young men killed in the first Battle of Ypres lie buried under a single giant slab—and whose cemeteries, heavy with evergreens and dark oaks, speak only of collective grief and national tragedy. It is also different from American cemeteries, in which the small size of the headstones, the paucity of inscribed personal detail, and, as at Arlington, the intermixture of large private memorials, often to generals or distinguished civilians, diminishes the sense both of uniformity and of the importance of the individual. Moreover, the absence of flowering plants and horticultural design brings a harshness quite at variance with the gardened serenity of the British equivalent.

The method of commemoration chosen by the British towards the end of their national tragedy of 1914–18 was immensely effective. It created a deep bond of unity between the bereaved and within the nation as a whole, and reached out to include the peoples of the Empire and Commonwealth. Its emotional touch was so sure that it extinguished—after a brief but intense controversy in 1919—all demand for repatriation. The dead of the second world war are buried in the same manner, and today the only demand met by the British government is that war widows should be assisted with travel costs when visiting their husbands' graves. Elderly women are now travelling as far as Burma and Malaysia on cemetery pilgrimages—usually returning consoled, if not positively inspired, by the beauty of the settings in which they find their husbands buried.

Often they find their husband's grave next to that of an Indian Muslim or a Burmese Buddhist, marked in the same way. That too has had, if not a unifying, at least a palliative effect. If the British parted with their imperial subjects on comparatively unacrimonious terms, that may be partly because they chose to make no distinction in the manner or the place where they buried those who fought the Empire's wars. Certainly it is remarkable that the rarest task of the War Graves Commission is the repair of desecration. War cemeteries in former colonial territory are hardly ever desecrated, even at times of outburst of nationalist rancour against the old imperial master.

Yet neither are graves desecrated in countries which were never part of the Empire or Commonwealth—former enemy countries such as Germany, or those which later went to war with Britain, such as Argentina or Iraq. Why should that be? To trample on the graves of an enemy is a universal if regrettable human instinct. One of the saddest places I have ever seen is the abandoned German war cemetery at Piontek in Poland, immaculately maintained until 1945, now a wilderness. Perhaps the immunity of British cemeteries is because Lutyens, Jekyll, Kipling, Ware and their army of gardeners succeeded in creating something symbolically more powerful than a site open to ritual desecration—a site of universally venerable sanctuary. There is a holiness in those cemeteries, both of the beauties of nature and of religion in all its forms, which defies hatred and brutishness; it speaks of the immortal, and touches eternity.

If foreigners are moved by those emanations, how much more the British themselves. When in 1920 they buried an unknown warrior in Westminster Abbey—the first of many unknown soldiers later buried by other countries—this inscription was chosen: "They buried him among the kings because he had done good towards God and towards His house." In burying their million and more warriors, known and unknown, in cemeteries evoking the country house gardens of the rich and propertied, the British in effect buried them, if not among kings, then among knights and lords. This decision ensured individual remembrance of the most humble, just as members of famous families are remembered in their ancestral plots—an evergreen and renewable remembrance, a celebration of pedigree and a testament of continual youth.

"I always feel young when I come here." The war widow who spoke was one of a party who had all lost their husbands in the Battle of Normandy 50 years before. None had remarried; time had taken its toll, but they returned each year to Bayeux to place flowers on the graves of men killed in their twenties, fighting to liberate Europe from Hitler in 1944. "I always feel young," she repeated, "just as if I was the same age as when I last saw him." She had grown very stout. It was difficult to picture the bride of the months before D-day. "Do stop, Betty," one of her friends interrupted, "or you'll make us all cry." It was I who was overcome with tears. The row of headstones of young soldiers of the East Yorkshire Regiment, the roses growing around the feet of their widows, the strange glow of happiness in the faces, were altogether too much for me. I was unable to speak—fortunately able to repress my impulse to embrace each in turn; to do so would have been an affront to our Englishness, to the fundamental Englishness of the place and the moment.

It was that same Englishness which overwhelmed my weeping companion in the Suda Bay cemetery on Crete. The tears I had shed in Normandy helped me to understand hers. Britain's war cemeteries create an aesthetic strong enough to prevail over the agony of grief. To see a child to the grave brings the harshest pain human sensibility can suffer. Yet to find a child—or a husband or a father—buried as a hero, among coevals and comrades all raised to heroic states by a symbolism central to one's own culture, is to experience the transcendence of pain through the keenest emotions of pride in family and nation. The garden is a metaphor for beauty, renewal and immortality to many peoples and many creeds. If this is indeed an age without heroes, seeking monuments which can touch every human heart, the ideal garden may be what is sought. It is some image of the 2,000 English gardens around the world which allows us to repeat each November on Remembrance Sunday, without false sentiment, some of the most famous verses inspired by the great war. Laurence Binyon's "For the Fallen (September 1914)" is an epitaph for heroes of any time or place:

> They shall grow not old, as we that
>   are left grow old:
> Age shall not weary them, nor
>   the years condemn.
> At the going down of the sun and
>   in the morning
> We will remember them.

Previous convictions • John Lloyd

NOVEMBER 1995

I have recently had one of the most important second thoughts of my life. I decided to stop hating my stepfather.

I had hated him for some 40 years. I had hated him for insinuating himself into the home where I was being brought up by my mother and grandparents: for his awkwardness and weakness in front of my mother; for his narrowness, his distrustfulness, for his greed and meanness, for the state of tension in which he held himself and all about him. I knew that he—a Pole—had been through Nazi invasion, Soviet prison camps, the war, postwar labour in coal mines and on road gangs. It made no difference.

I don't believe I resented him for marrying my mother but I hated him for failing to be a father to me. I carried a memory of him transforming the shabby little idyll of my first years, growing up in East Fife with my mother and grandparents, into a battleground of all against all. I had a version of my upbringing within me in which the stratagems, hypocrisies and treacheries to which I resorted in the family became second nature and were his doing. When I wasn't blaming or hating him, I would pity him—in an abstract and scornful way.

We had full cause of tension. Unable to be the master in his house because the house was my mother's and she was the mistress of it, he fell back on self-pity. Much of their life seemed like a grisly gavotte in which each would seek to manoeuvre himself or herself into a position of blamelessness. She was unable to conceive again, and had a hysterectomy. He had no stake in anything. Neither I nor, I think, my mother had any inkling of what that meant. He saw himself as bereft of the attributes of manhood. My mother thought she had given him everything. I thought they fucked me up—and unlike Philip Larkin's "mum and dad," I thought he had meant to. They divorced when they were in their early 70s, splitting the little property in Dundee so that they both lived in tiny flats. I scarcely saw him—although he loved my son.

My mother's death two years ago did nothing to dissolve this knot of hatred for my stepfather. Though we embraced at the funeral, we quarrelled furiously after it—I erupting in a roaring rage, tossing a table across the living room of his flat. Willy-nilly, in life she had put me into a position where to love her was to renounce him: yet her death seemed to change nothing.

Then, last year, a letter from him arrived for me in Moscow. It contained a wedding invitation. In his careful English he said he had met a woman—also Polish—and they were to get married. Would I come to Dundee for the ceremony?

I went. Walking up to the chapel I was as nervous as I had been for years. A pretty, middle-aged woman was standing on the steps with an older man, posing for a photographer. I stopped: she looked at me, and ran to kiss me warmly. She said—"You are John. I am your new step-stepmother."

My stepfather had struck it lucky in his 75th year. The wedding was delightful and happy. His new wife, in her 50s, was charming, intelligent—and comfortably off, following the death of her husband some years before. They were clearly very affectionate towards each other. He had some friends of his own. Life is not a modern film—it seems that it can have a happy ending.

And—it seems—I decided to stop hating him. I think that it was a decision—although one made easier, or perhaps possible, by the removal of the burden of him in my life. Where before I had only abstractly and hypocritically sympathised with him as an immigrant in a strange country, I could now really feel his difficulties, with neither impatience nor guilt.

I have indeed had second thoughts about him. The first thought, lasting decades, was of a man who could be no more than a repellent stranger with whom I was forced to live. The second thought is freer: I may or may not find in him a friend, but I no longer assume an enemy. My first was closed: it knew him in an absolute sense, because it defined him as existing only in relation to the harm and hurt done to me. My second sees a new man in him, capable of affection, warmth, dignity—in truth, traits which were there before, but which were buried by either him or me.

The grace of my step-stepmother was the intercession—above all her steady determination to cut through the hatreds which bound us, to create a new little "family" of three people with no blood tie, permitting a lifting of the grudge, a dissolving of the self-pity; stowing away the reflex of enmity and defensiveness which defined my step-father and me. I had to rethink him. I did it with the aid of bright primary concepts I had once found mawkish—or worse, religious: forgiveness and humility.

My stepfather was my first and longest hate. We came near to blows several times. I consciously delighted in his discomfiture. I lied to him and about him. I spoke ill of him to everyone and I thought myself right in doing so. Having new thoughts about him gave me hope that a Godless life can still have, if not meaning, then at least some moral content and even a moral victory over man's vileness.

Caviar thieves • Vanora Bennett

FEBRUARY 2001

On the shore of the Caspian Sea you can, if you know the right people, have a poacher's breakfast: a caviar sandwich. The poacher will hack a slice off a white loaf and smear it with freshly caught sturgeon roe. He might wave the inch-thick sandwich in your face, laughing through gold teeth. "How much would this cost in London ... Thousands! So go on, eat it. It's good for you. It's power food."

The caviar is ready before the fish stops flapping. My friend Sergei Bodagovsky was the grand master of caviar poachers. In 1982, he was accused in a Soviet court of stealing four tons of caviar. He had made an illegal profit of half a million roubles—the equivalent, in those days, of 430 years' wages.

Sergei keeps one grainy photograph of those times. There's sunlight in it, and a dark wild boy with a beaky nose, on a beach, grinning. He is wearing ragged cut-offs. He has a cigarette in his mouth. In one hand is a knife, in the other a huge sturgeon.

Today the swagger has gone. Sergei was 28 when he was arrested. His friend Rudolf was tried too and condemned to death: a bullet in the brain. Sergei got off lightly with a 15-year sentence. "When they read out the verdict," he told me when I met him, years later, "everyone in court gasped in horror."

We were in his sister's shabby flat in Makhachkala, the capital of Dagestan. Sergei is 46 now, careworn and fastidious, a little stooped, his voice filtered through bluish cigarette smoke. But the photo still made him grin. "Me, I'd been expecting execution," he said. "So I sighed with relief."

So much caviar, I said. Why had he taken the risk?

"Power and money," he said. "In those days, I thought money was everything."

Plenty of people still think that way in Dagestan. Life here is lived by the post-communist equation that money dishonestly acquired equals power. The legal economy is a shell. Regional cognac and carpet factories are at a standstill. But the streets are full of Mercedes, and a mysterious building boom has begun: fantasy mansions in the style of Walt Disney are springing up, with arched windows, jacuzzis, ten-foot-high garden walls and overwrought ironwork. No one yet knows who will move in. But everyone knows that a new elite is forming in the Soviet ruins.

Dagestan is a strip of land in Russia, east of Chechnya and west of the Caspian Sea. From there, illegally caught caviar is smuggled to the middle east and the west. The caviar trade is violent. When a building full of Russian border troops was blown up in 1996, killing 67 people, locals did not doubt that the attack was a warning from Dagestan's caviar gangs. Since then scarcely a month has gone by without some violent death: a drive-by shooting, or a car bomb. Most victims are innocents, though Said Amirov, the mayor of Makhachkala, lost the use of his legs in the first of a series of annual assassination attempts against him in 1992 (Dagestani wags call him "our Roosevelt").

Little of this appears in the local papers, so Makhachkala is full of rumours. Moscow newspapers report how the coast is overrun by gangs of poachers romantically known as "brotherhoods of the reeds." But in Makhachkala no one believes this. They think that it is their own ministers' trawlers harvesting as much caviar as they can carry.

The rules were different when Sergei started stealing caviar. In Soviet times, power didn't come from making money. The communist party had a rigid hierarchy; everyone knew their place. Those near the top got perks which were the cashless equivalent of wealth: cars, dachas and food parcels containing delicacies such as chocolate and two-ounce cans of caviar. Even the cans were graded. Blue was beluga sturgeon, red was osyotr, yellow was sevruga.

Sergei's family were nowhere near the top. His father mended telephones and his mother was a typesetter. Sergei went to technical college, not to university, and was convicted for brawling during military service. By his twenties he was married with two daughters to support.

He went to work for a fish factory in Astrakhan. It paid 100 roubles a month, enough for bread and sausage but not much more. He would steer his boat along the Caspian and up the Volga, picking up sturgeon caught by fishermen from collective farms. The fish was weighed and a fixed state price paid before the boat took the carcasses back to the factory.

Sergei loved the muscle and freedom of life on the water: sun-roughened skin, the click of bony sevruga snouts against metal as he hauled them on to the scales, and the wind that nearly knocked him down when he opened the throttle. He liked meals carved from the fish. He liked caviar breakfasts.

He spent the hot nights of his first summer on his bunk, reading. He listened to waves rippling, planks creaking—and rowing boats drawing alongside in the dark. "They were coming and going all night. It was all footsteps and whispers..." It was the fishermen returning to sell more fish and eggs, this time privately, illegally, and for much more money.

The next year, Sergei was promoted to inspector—or fish buyer. "At first, I never thought I'd steal," he says now. "But then I saw that everyone was at it. I didn't want to spend all my days in rags. I needed to feed the kids and dress properly."

In a way, he had no choice. An inspector had to be on good terms with the police, the fishermen and the mean, hard-drinking types from the slums around the fish farms. That meant bending the law, softening people up with drinks and bribes.

But Sergei also found that he liked stealing. He liked hurrying fishermen to close the deal over a vodka in the shadows. He'd buy half the fish privately, at ten times the state price, and give an official receipt for the other half. Everyone was happy. Then Sergei would stay up all night with his two-man crew, harvesting the caviar. They stored it in milk churns sunk underwater on lines, filling four churns a night.

At dawn, Sergei would sell the caviar. He'd chug out to the cruise liners sailing down the Volga with their banquets and bands. "Do you need caviar?" he would shout. He charged half the state price, but still made a big profit. "They always said yes. I could sell as much as my conscience let me," he says. "Everyone was at it, but no one sold as much as us. As Rudolf said: 'What's the difference, they'll shoot you whether you take one ton or five.' So we took five."

Rudolf, 16 years older than Sergei, was an exotic charmer. He'd been a chef; he'd been in a band; he gambled, danced, told wonderful stories, and could shoot straight at any target, even when drunk. Impulsive and flamboyant, he was the king of thieves.

Rudolf bought two houses, three cars, a gun and some tsarist roubles. Sergei left his wife; there was too much high living to be done. The Astrakhan elite were now their clients: the police and the politicians. Moscow was 1,000 miles north, and the politicos felt safe with their grimy new friends. Sergei and Rudolf went to their dachas. They shared jokes and women.

But one former colleague, a fisherman called Boris, felt left out and resentful. He informed on his ex-partners in a letter to Brezhnev's interior minister. To the terror of the town bosses, a commission came from Moscow to investigate.

Local politicians had everything to lose if they were named in Moscow as clients of the caviar thieves. They tiptoed away from the scandal, leaving Sergei and Rudolf—the outsiders—exposed.

Rudolf used to drop in to the police station as if it was home. "Everyone there was his friend, everyone ate his caviar. So when they said the police chief wanted to see him, he waltzed right in. 'Hi, guys, what's new?' he said. But they were too scared to answer. There were six strangers in the chief's office, with an arrest warrant and handcuffs."

The day they came for Sergei was warm, with a hot wind. Sergei was on his boat, with sweating fishermen lugging their fish towards it. He was in an evil temper. He knew what to expect. He had champagne on ice.

When the official black Volga cars drew up, and his ex-friends trotted nervously down the jetty in their suits, Sergei came out.

"Drink?" he asked. No one answered. No one dared to approach. He poured a glass. "Seryog, come with us," wheedled the men in suits. "What for? I'm going home, or perhaps I'll throw myself off right here into the depths."

Sergei smiles. "I kept them waiting for four hours ... I'd have stabbed them if I'd had a knife. I suddenly realised they weren't enforcing fair laws, only laws which protected them. They were legal criminals. And I didn't want to lose my freedom. I was 28, and I loved my robber's life. I wanted sea wind in my hair.

"But there was no choice. I gave myself up."

The case took two years to come to court. Sergei saw that he would be shot unless he co-operated. He gave up his hidden bank books and pleaded guilty.

But Rudolf refused. When the trial opened he looked defiantly at the prosecutor—a man named Nikolai Chishiyev, who'd been at his house more times than he could remember. Rudolf told the courtroom: "I will plead guilty only if the following people are put in the dock too." In the hush that followed he listed 40 of Astrakhan's most prominent bosses.

This was the most dangerous Soviet crime: exposing the hypocrisy of the authorities to public gaze. The judge ordered Rudolf's words to be struck out.

"They read out Rudolf's sentences for two hours," Sergei says. "It was 15 years for this, 14 years for that. Then they got to the last charge, and the sentence was *rasstrel*—execution.

"Rudolf didn't react. He'd been taking notes. He was still writing. A cop came up with handcuffs and barked his name. 'I'm listening,' Rudolf said. 'Handcuffs,' the cop said. Rudolf said calmly: 'Are you taking me to be shot right now?' He looked at the judge. No one expected this. People react differently to the death sentence, hysterics, fainting, whatever. But Rudolf embarrassed the judge, who muttered 'No.'

"'So wait while I finish,' Rudolf said. He went on writing. And when he'd finished, he went to the cells with his head held high."

The beach on which Sergei grew up runs from one end of Dagestan to the other, 300 miles of pale sand scarred by rusty metal and giant sewage pipes. Today's busy poachers don't mind the ugliness. They're pleased that day-trippers stay away.

They earn well. Umar, an ex-bank clerk, has seen his pay rise from $60 a month to $6,000. Magomed, a former engineer in a Soviet military factory, now earns $1,000 in two days, packing 150 pounds of stolen caviar into export jars. The boats are simple, but they track fish using computers. Magomed has gadgets galore: a machine for sealing the blue, red and yellow metal lids on to glass Russian jars, soldering equipment for silver cans labelled "Iranian caviar," a steriliser.

Umar's rule of thumb is that 100 pounds of fish should provide 15 pounds of caviar. He catches long-snouted sevruga weighing 30 pounds, and snub-nosed osyotr weighing up to 100 pounds. Rare beluga can weigh tons, but Umar says he's never caught one.

The local police can be bribed, says Umar. If the more aggressive Russian border guards approach, he dumps his catch back into the sea. Magomed tops off each load of the canned caviar he takes to Makhachkala in his truck with vegetables.

"Tell the truth and I won't punish you," said the last policeman to stop him. "What's under the onions?"

"Ah," Magomed replied, passing over $10. "At the bottom of my truck, all you'll find is bare boards."

Laughing, the policeman waved him on.

Sturgeon stocks today are one third what they were in the 1970s. Soviet programmes for replenishing them are long forgotten. The World Wide Fund for Nature says that beluga, the scarcest sturgeon, is "poised on the brink of extinction."

In prison, Sergei existed on discipline; press-ups before reveille, silent hours at the stinking workshop or a hot cell shared with 100 others. He divorced his wife. He borrowed journals from the prison library and became absorbed in the political changes happening in the new Russia.

The new politics offered self-justification. He learned to argue that his theft had been benign, a Robin Hood redistribution from party to people. He had paid more for caviar than the state offered, and sold for less than the state demanded. This was a crime under communism, but good business under capitalism. With hindsight, he cast himself as a "fighter" against an unjust regime.

He also started writing poetry. "I began to feel I had something to say. So I read less at night, but I wrote. I'd stay awake to be in that state when your body's relaxed but your brain's awake … you can catch thoughts. The lines just ran out. I'd write till five."

The poems changed everything. His sister passed the manuscripts to a local newspaper. It published them without knowing that the author was in jail.

Publication triggered a wave of interest. It was 1991, and Sergei's bitter verse perfectly matched the public mood on the eve of the Soviet collapse. Fan mail arrived in heaps. The national poet of Dagestan telephoned, demanding an introduction. When Sergei's sister confessed that the poems were written by her brother, eight years into a 15-year jail sentence, Sergei became a prisoner of conscience. Every scrap of his work, however raw and self-pitying, was published and praised.

A public campaign took off, led by a Moscow group working to release "economic criminals." The new president, Boris Yeltsin, signed his pardon in August 1992. Sergei didn't believe it when they woke him and told him to go to the governor. But by four o'clock that afternoon he was leaving prison with a second-hand suit and the train fare home.

No one told his family that he'd been released years early. When he walked into his mother's kitchen, on her 60th birthday, she fainted.

Soon after Sergei got out of jail, a married doctor called Lyuda was so entranced by his poems that she left her husband and three children to live with him. They married and had a baby son.

I first met them in July 1997, in an empty flat with a heap of suitcases against one wall. Lyuda and the baby were emigrating to the US. Sergei was staying behind. Because of his criminal record, the US embassy had refused him a visa.

Sergei was philosophical. Afterwards he moved across town to his sister's flat. His mother and sister share a pull-out bed in the television room. There is nothing in Sergei's room but a single bed, a tape recorder and Lyuda's letters from Houston.

Sergei is treated with exaggerated respect in Makhachkala, as someone who suffered unjustly and escaped by a miracle. He enjoys his reputation: back at the Smolensk Penitentiary, he says with a little smile, many prisoners have started writing poetry in the hope that they too will get their sentences cut.

But he is a monkish oddity in a place and time where money and power, the things he once wanted so much, are uppermost in people's minds. Sergei is no longer interested. He has published a book of prison verse, but he gives the copies away. He works at a local paper, but only as a typesetter. He dresses modestly. He often forgets to eat.

Mostly he sings. He's found his voice, and is recording an album of his poems set to music. He plans to name it after the last words of warders to prisoners: "Get your things and go."

He doesn't fish any more, although he still knows both how to gut a sturgeon and how to gentle one by stroking its head. He has eaten the rarest of delicacies, tsar's caviar, the pale eggs of albino sturgeon. He talks with love about the fish—their spring migrations down the Volga, the big beluga under the ice in February, the bream, wild carp, and the sevruga and osyotr sturgeon. And he talks with sorrow about the war on the sea today.

"Everyone's massacring the fish—ministers, lowlifes, Azerbaijanis in big boats. There's never been anything like this—people trawling in military boats in a sea so festooned with nets that the fish can't escape. Soon the fish will exist only in our memories."

In the evenings, when the wind blows, he sits in his white room playing his half-finished tape and trying to find a way to join his family.

Before leaving, I asked if he'd help me choose some good caviar. "Oh no," he said. "I never go near it any more. Every now and then I eat a very tiny bit of fish, so as not to lose the taste altogether. But caviar makes me sick to my soul."

Searching for mother • Richard Hoggart

MARCH 1999

The death certificate, when we finally acquired one a year or so ago, said that Adelaide (an error; her name was "Adeline") Emma Hoggart had died at the age of 46, and was buried on 17th February 1927. The cause of death was tuberculosis. She seems to have died on the 15th; the address given as her "abode" was "123 Beckett Street," which was and is the huge St James Infirmary in a grim part of north Leeds.

Two days from death to burial in the local churchyard—a quick procedure. A further 67 years passed before one of us even thought of enquiring about her whereabouts. Tom, the eldest of us three children, was by then recently dead. Tom was the only one of us who remembered the funeral, holding Molly and me by our hands, before we were rushed away to Grandma's on the other side of town, to working-class Hunslet.

Tom also vaguely remembered our father tossing him up and down. Father had died five or six years before our mother, but none of us knew his date of death. The three of us remembered our mother in the selective, highlighted way which memory imposes: gentle, soft-spoken, firm in controlling bad behaviour—and *down*, inescapably in low spirits. A consumptive combination. Her face had become heavily lined, of course. But the lines were ingrained, dark grey, from years of cold water washes. She could have boiled a kettle on the one gas ring but would not have felt able to afford it. She must have hated that.

What if neither of our parents had died? What sort of life would we all have had? What relationships? The Morels of *Sons and Lovers* always surface when I wonder about that: a more genteel mother; a father not of the rough working class but very much a working class NCO type. Tensions?

What had set firmly, before our mother died, was a typecasting of the three of us across the extended family: Tom quiet, serious, reliable, a model older brother; Molly rather frail and to be sheltered; me "a bit of a lad," which meant "something of a handful," but not ill-intentioned, not "a problem." These were the common family tags we carried until the generation ahead of us had died.

We never saw that bare little stone courtyard cottage in Potternewton again. The poverty-stricken widow and her kids had gone; it would revert to a landlord of whom we knew nothing. By the evening of that funeral day we reached our separate destinations: Molly and I to Hoggart relatives in Leeds; Tom to an aunt in Sheffield who had 11 children. A 12th "would not make much difference," but it was still a kindness. Our mother's relatives—the Longs from Liverpool, mid-middle-class shopkeepers and the like—made no offers.

Astonishing that, during all the years afterwards, not one of us asked for mother's death certificate so as to have details of where she was buried. Even more astonishing is that, as I have just now rediscovered, only ten years ago I wrote that I would not try to find out where she had died. "Probably St James," I said rather off-handedly. Now I find that almost inexplicable, even, perhaps, a matter for guilt; especially because the past has always been a preoccupation, insistently present to me, marked by the sense of decades passing like the chapters of a puzzling book turning over of their own accord. Why didn't one of us do something about finding out where the mother who had so suddenly left us had been put into the ground?

Going round and round the question since obtaining the death certificate, I can only conclude, though insecurely, that we were all suffering from what today would be called "trauma"; we were frozen within; lost.

It had been a very enclosed home since she had been widowed, striving to manage on £1 a week from the City Guardians (public assistance). I thought I had been the one who found her dying on the clip-rug in front of the fireplace. Molly seems to remember that she had. One of us had taken over the memory from the other, absorbed it and adopted it. But from the moment we turned away from the grave we had blotted it out, or let it sink, for all those decades. Why had we taken more than 60 years to feel able to make that connection—even then, prompted by one of Molly's daughters? I can find no satisfactory answer, only that fashionable excuse of "trauma," which is a fancy way of saying "shock."

Now that I had the death certificate, I determined to find the grave. This proved much more difficult than the first step—and a minor example of the ways of price-conscious, end-of-20th-century England. It was several weeks before the Records Office somewhere up in Yorkshire responded to the question: where in that graveyard, close to St James, is our mother buried? The staff couldn't easily say, because the records were not yet computerised. They could put someone to searching for the entry by hand, but I would have to pay that person by the hour. (One would have thought that an answer such as that would have stuck in the throat of the minor official who had to give it.)

I told the town clerk in Leeds that this response seemed not only dilatory but bureaucratically unfeeling. What if an old person living only on a pension had sought the information? The town clerk agreed and told the Records Office so; they reacted smartly. Well, smartly for them—in two or three more weeks. They said they had now discovered that no records had been kept of that particular cemetery. Perhaps the vicar of the church in question, St Michael's, had them.

The vicar was quick and helpful; he telephoned before eight on the morning he received my letter. He said that the city had taken over the graveyard some decades ago, when his church had been rebuilt a mile away; he had no records.

So that was why, with a friend, on a cold, grey and dank day, I sought out the graveyard in a Potternewton now tatty, run-down, drugs-and-prostitution-ridden. The front of the churchyard was almost hidden behind a facade of shops which mirrored the district; shops which knew the tastes and limits of their customers: mostly cut-price.

Inside, we found a desert, a desolation. There had been, near the front, a few fairly expensive graves—we used to play on some we called "potted meat," tan-coloured slabs. But the marble had long gone and only splinters remained. (Hardy's phlegmatic acceptance "Why should death rob life of fourpence?" as skilled urban theft.) The rest, for almost 100 yards back, were all broken flat stones and what once were uprights with inscriptions. A scatter of used syringes and used condoms; a few ragged trees wept over it all.

We looked as closely as we could but found no "Hoggart." Then my friend said what I had not the wit nor the wish to recognise. That area of dirty, damp and dog-shit-spattered earth, a few yards wide and long, up against the far back wall, would be where they put the paupers. No markers—not even a simple marker for each plot, recording which half-dozen had gone into one hole. (The casual blind cruelties some local authorities could commit!)

On that bitter day, I was not near tears, but suffused with grief and hoping for the way to a sort of expiation—at the thought of that family, the children dispersed, the mother buried, all within two days, and no record at all. Somewhere in that few square yards of mucky mud she lay, and had lain for more than six decades, and I was only now paying some sort of due. As I stood, there came to me, unexpected and unsought, the image of a skeletal figure, deep down but facing upward; still connected, still belonging; after all those years.

Sometime later I heard about what seemed to be called "penny plots": spare land near the hospital used for pauper burials by agreement with the local authority. I do not know if that story is true and, even if it were, it would seem not to apply to our mother because her death certificate places her clearly in St Michael's. It was marginally less shocking.

This belated search for our mother, as I went into full old age, was one—perhaps the main—impulse which set off my interest in writing a book on old age. Thinking it over now, I realise how strong a force the empty end of that search had been in making me try to think straighter about the mosaic of interests, of likings and dislikings, which year after year go towards composing what we call a character.

Modern manners • Jeremy Clarke

FEBRUARY 1999

Until fairly recently, every Devon village had a large, square police house, inhabited by a large, square policeman. There was also a vicarage containing a vicar, a primary school, a village store, a post office, a chapel and at least one pub. Our village also had its own blacksmith's shop and Women's Institute—both thriving until the second world war, when they were blown up by the US army, which had occupied the village prior to D-Day. (The Americans also trained heavy artillery on our parish church—an ugly, mid-Victorian edifice—but regrettably the damage was only superficial.)

Most of these old village institutions have gone forever. But "out with the old and in with the new" is what I say, and there are two new rural ubiquities which now, it seems to me, characterise British village life at the end of the millennium. One of these is the dazzlingly lit BP petrol station and convenience store—a God-send for out-of-hours cigarettes, porn mags and smoky bacon-flavoured Hula-Hoops. Our BP station is now the cultural centre of the district—it's quite trendy to be seen there—though many of us have yet to become accustomed to the startling green and yellow neon lights which blare out across an adjacent turnip field at night.

The other recent cultural phenomenon is the rise of the rural massage parlour. As recently as a year ago, if I felt like a "personal" massage, I'd have to drive all the way to Plymouth, about an hour away; a long way to travel for a J Arthur Rank, I admit. But today I can look in the back of the local *Free-Ads* paper and scan advertisements for massage parlours situated in nearby hamlets and villages. There is not (alas!) one in ours yet, but it can only be a question of time. If the recession in the local dairy farming and crab fishing industries gets any worse, and holidaymakers are deterred by another wet August, we'll all be on the game before long.

The weekly, southwest edition of *Free-Ads* is a remarkable publication. It is bright yellow, and printed on unusually porous paper. Old copies come in handy for cleaning windows. As well as being an emporium of second-hand items, many of them poignantly misspelled, it is also a noticeboard for personal messages, lonely hearts ads, new-age health fads, forthcoming events, council house exchanges, and flimsily disguised ads for prostitution of all kinds. It is the impoverished peninsula's equivalent of the internet. If ever the indigenous inhabitants were to rise up and commit genocide against the taller, more affluent incomers who have destroyed their culture without even noticing that there was one, the signal to begin would be given in the personal columns of the southwest *Free-Ads*.

Last week I called a lady whose advert offered "pampering" in "quiet, secluded surroundings" by a "busty, mature masseuse." I recognised the area code as that of a clutch of small villages situated on the edge of Dartmoor.

Was I calling for the first time, she asked. I was, I said; and she gave me a list of the things she was prepared to do, and for how much. She was cheerful and businesslike and called me "dear." The possibilities ranged from massage with hand relief (clothes on) to massage with "full intercourse" (clothes off) with every permutation in between, except, as far as I could tell, me massaging her. The massage and hand relief option was so cheap that I assumed it was a loss-leader.

It was late in the day, so I asked her what time she usually knocked off. "Oh, I don't like to be too late because I've got to be up early to milk the goats," she said. I wasn't sure whether this added to or detracted from my burgeoning fantasy, but I told her I'd be there as soon as possible for the half-hour massage with hand relief (clothes off). Her directions of how to get there filled the back of a Christmas card, and included a right turn at an old Celtic stone cross.

The place was an old farm at the end of a muddy track. I had to make a dash from the car to the front door to avoid a trio of hissing geese. She opened the door, shouted at the geese, then bared her teeth welcomingly at me. She was much younger than I had imagined. "Silly buggers," she said, and led me into the house. Passing the kitchen I saw an elderly man sitting at the table with his cap on, making a roll-up. He didn't look up as we passed.

She led me into a very warm room with a couch at one end and a bed at the other. A cat was asleep on the bed.

"Talcum powder or warm oil, love?" she said, taking off her shirt.

"Warm oil," I said. "Loads of it."

"How do you want the massage—hard, medium or soft?" she said.

"Take no prisoners," I said. "Hard as you like."

"Shall I put some music on?"

"Got any Gerry Rafferty?" I said.

She gave me quite a pounding. Then came the extras. Noting that Private Parts was reluctant to join in, she said, "You're allowed to touch if you like, you know." So I put my hands where her more rugged, goat-milking ones were and tried to coax some life into him.

"I mean touch *me*, not you, you idiot," she laughed.

Putting my foot down on the way home, I was back just in time for *EastEnders*.

Voodoo Chile • Paul Broks

JULY 2000

Monday afternoon. I am standing before 100 or so undergraduates in a cavernous lecture theatre at Birmingham University. Ten minutes to go and I am going to round off my lecture with a story. We can discuss it next week.

I scan the auditorium. The students are still listening attentively, pens at the ready. One in the front row, a pale girl, has a small tape recorder and reaches into her bag for a new cassette. A pigeon settles on the sill outside one of the high windows and, watching the pigeon, I forget momentarily what I was about to say. Then it comes back to me: Robert's story.

One day, in the foothills of his middle age, Robert took a look at himself in the mirror. He saw that life was running out and he was going nowhere. He was going stale: bored with his job, out of love with his wife, stifled by family life, disenchanted with himself. But what gripped him and shook him to the core of his being was the thought that he was literally going nowhere. The thought that, at the end of this dreary line of days, there was oblivion. It was time for a change, and changes there would be.

That same day on his way to work he stops at the newsagents, as usual, to buy a newspaper. He pays for the paper but on the way out he takes a chocolate bar from a shelf and slips it into his pocket. This little act of theft is curiously energising. His senses feel stripped and raw. He is engulfed by a feeling of elation and drives faster than he should. But instead of going to work, he travels 300-odd miles from Yorkshire to Cornwall where, by early evening, he finds himself sitting on a beach in the face of a warm sea breeze. Robert is profoundly happy. The sun sets, it grows dark and chilly, but there he stays all night, conceding to sleep only as the sun began to rise again. He returns home the next day with no explanation except the truth, and spends another sleepless night placating his distressed wife, who demands a more plausible version of events. What were you thinking of, she says. He says he's been thinking about everything and has put a few things straight.

Life reverts to routine for some weeks. Then, driving home from work on a Friday evening, he switches on the car radio and hears an interview with Julian Bream, the classical guitarist. At one point the interviewer asks Bream what he thinks of electrically amplified guitars. The electric bass is fine, he says, but otherwise he's not impressed. What does he think of Jimi Hendrix as a player? Robert detects a note of condescension in the interviewer's voice at the mention of Hendrix but thinks it's a good question, one he himself would have wanted to put. He waits for the reply. Don't let me down, Julian, he thinks. There is no let down. He was brilliant, says Bream, leaving the interviewer momentarily flummoxed. Robert gets another burst of energy like the one he had when he stole the chocolate bar. He turns the car round, heads back into town at speed and pulls up outside a musical instruments store. The shop is closing and the staff are cashing up. He tells them he must have a Fender Stratocaster, the guitar Hendrix played. They oblige. He buys an amplifier to go with it and a book containing note-by-note transcriptions of Hendrix songs. This comes to nearly £700. But Robert, says his wife when he gets home, you can't play the guitar. He says he is going to learn.

But that night all elation has drained away. He lies awake until the early hours in a state of agitation, tormented by thoughts of annihilation, of fading into nothingness. He is close to panic. It's coming, it's coming. Changes there would have to be. The next day, out of nowhere, he announces to his wife that their marriage is over, and he leaves her, the house, the children and his new guitar, never to return. He goes back to Cornwall, where he finds a bar job, grows his hair, cultivates a tanned and weathered look, and becomes, in effect, someone else.

Two years later, living alone in a threadbare bed-sit in the suburbs of a northern city, he can scarcely recollect any of the Cornish interlude. There are fragments of memory, images from someone else's memory almost, but they don't cohere—a blue lampshade, a rainy, windy night somewhere, the shiny stainless steel surfaces of a hotel kitchen, a woman (Jackie? Jenny?), a fist fight, the sea. In fact, he is finding it hard to pull together his thoughts from one minute to the next.

He feels nauseous and experiences a strange, feathery sensation rising from the pit of his stomach to his gullet. Looking into the bathroom mirror, the reflected face seems empty, drained of any meaning—almost the absence of a reflection. He stands there for a while, staring, then turns on the washbasin tap, turns it off, turns it on again, turns it off, turns it on, before crashing to the floor. His limbs stiffen briefly then jerk fiercely for several minutes and a spreading patch of urine darkens his trouser leg. He sleeps.

It is Robert's third seizure this week. The next happens in a supermarket and, afterwards, he's taken to hospital. The doctors are concerned that, despite recovering from the fit, he has remained for days inert and disoriented. They investigate and find on the MRI scan a large mass just behind the eyes in the orbitofrontal region of the brain, extending back into the anterior temporal area. It turns out to be a meningioma. This is a tumour, intrinsically benign, which has invaded the outer coverings of the brain. It has been growing for several years, distorting the frontal lobes of Robert's brain in the process, so that the very person he felt himself to be was being pulled out of shape. Post-surgically, tumour excised, he asks his nurses most days: when are my children coming? Can I go home now?

My lecture seems to have gone well enough. These neurogothic tales generally do. "Robert's story" is an embellished account of a real case. I have tinkered with some of the biographical information and, of course, the patient's name, but the clinical details are faithful. This man really did leave his family on an impulse, following several episodes of uncharacteristically eccentric behaviour, including acts of petty theft and spontaneous trips to seaside towns. He really did spend sums of money he could ill afford on luxury goods like musical instruments (which he could not play) and expensive clothes (which he might, or might not, subsequently wear). He was a Jimi Hendrix fan, too. A large, iconic image of the great man stared from his bedroom wall at the rehab unit. That, at least, remained constant in his life. Whether or not he stood looking into the mirror in the way I describe,

I have no idea. I threw that in. Perhaps, somewhere, I had in mind the image of Jekyll standing before the mirror as he watches his transformation into Hyde, and then, at the end, perhaps it was Dracula, bereft of soul, bereft of reflection. I don't know. It's only just occurred to me. After the operation he really did expect to return to his family, unaware that they had long since moved on.

That slow tumour: when did it take root? How long had it been growing, heaving its bulk into his frontal lobes, insidiously recalibrating his personality? A meningioma like Robert's can take years to develop. The brain can accommodate, up to a point, a slow-growing mass without betraying significant clinical signs. It depends on the rate of growth and where it is located. Some people grow old and die, never knowing that for years they were harbouring a benign brain tumour. I once saw a man in his seventies, admitted to hospital after a stroke, who turned out to have a tumour the size of an orange nestling in the parietal lobe of his brain. God knows how long it had been there, but it had nothing to do with the stroke and, apparently, wasn't giving him any trouble.

Perhaps Robert would have left his wife and children anyway. Perhaps he was restless and bored, or depressed. A mid-life crisis. Could it be that the tumour just hastened the process or even had nothing at all to do with his impulsive decision to pack his bags and go? Maybe. We can't rule this out, but I think not. Impairments of social judgement, impulsive behaviour and the rest are a typical consequence of damage to the frontal lobes. Unlike the man with the stroke, Robert's tumour was causing him trouble. He developed epilepsy. But suppose he hadn't? Would there have been any grounds for saying that his behaviour was, in itself, pathological? Not necessarily. You would say it was a mid-life crisis.

Despite my undisguised haste to draw my lecture to a close there are several questions from the students. Some are theoretical, but mostly they are about the story, as a story. Fair enough. Have you ever considered all this from a Christian perspective, the pale girl at the front asks as, finally, I gather my notes. No, not really, I say a little briskly, but I have a train to catch, perhaps we can discuss it next week? Then she asks: but what happened to Robert, in the end? He became profoundly depressed, I reply. I spare her the information that after being discharged from his rehab hospital, there were two botched suicide attempts before he eventually succeeded in killing himself. Third time lucky. I have this image of Robert hanging himself with Hendrix playing *Voodoo Chile* in the background: "I don't need you no more in this world/I'll meet you on the next one/Don't be late." As far as I know it did not happen that way.

My train is delayed. A two-hour journey becomes three, and I have a couple of beers. I think about the pale girl. She seemed genuinely distressed by the story and I regret not allowing her more time. But when finally I get home, I feel deeply content to be there, immersed in my family. Secure, immutable, invulnerable, immortal. As Robert once felt, perhaps.

Danish porridge • Sally Laird

JULY 2003

I suffer from an illness called erysipelas. It attacks once or twice a year: I get a high fever, then a fiery red patch starts spreading down my leg. These days I know what to do. As soon as my teeth start chattering, I set off for Grenaa Centralsygehus (central hospital). The drive, down country lanes, takes about half an hour. If the hospital isn't too busy, I will be wheeled within an hour into one of the medical wards on the ground floor. There I will spend the next week hooked up to a penicillin drip, until the fever subsides and the doctors declare I am ready to go home.

My home for the past ten years has been in Ebeltoft, a small town on the east coast of Jutland, but I come from London. It is a peculiar experience for a foreigner to spend a week in a Danish country hospital. The first time I stayed in Grenaa, I experienced its most innocent procedures as an assault on my person. I resented being identified by my social security number instead of my name, and being made to wear underwear stamped Aarhus Amt (county). I did not like having a thermometer poked up my arse and I wanted curtains around my bed, like we have in England. I felt as if my body had been nationalised by the Danish state, which was now free to display it, or insert things into it, just as it wished. And I refused point blank to eat *øllebrød* for breakfast. It's a porridge made from rye bread (featured in the film *Babette's Feast*) and seemed to me to have the colour and consistency of fresh liquid manure.

But an odd thing happened to me on my most recent visit to Grenaa. When I entered the main doors, I saw a handwritten notice was stuck to the glass: "Long Live Grenaa Centralsygehus!" I felt an unexpected pang. In an economy measure by Aarhus Amt, Grenaa is soon to be "amalgamated" with Randers hospital 60 miles away. Most of its own wards will be scrapped. Perhaps this would be my last visit to the hospital. I found myself hoping that I would stay in one of the wards I liked best, with the tall windows overlooking the trees. I realised then that the hospital had ceased to be a strange Danish institution; it had become my "local." Now that its days were numbered, I felt like writing an elegy for a country hospital—a *klagesang* for Grenaa Sygehus.

The hospital was built in 1922, and many of its patients are about the same age. Some are townspeople who once worked at the port, in the fisheries, or at the now defunct textile factory. Others come from *opland*: from the villages and farms up and down the coast and in the rolling countryside behind. They are people like my friend's father, Gerhard Nielsen, who lived all his life on the farm at Kobbergaard, south of Grenaa, and is now buried in the village churchyard at Dråby. Grenaa was the capital of Gerhard's world. Randers would have seemed to him a strange place to be cared for or to die.

On my first visit to the hospital I shared a room with an old lady, roughly Gerhard's age, who had lost all track of time and place. She thought she was at home in the 1930s. Father was at work all day at the tanning factory, while Fru Hansen herself—she must have had a different name then—had just finished *realskole*, and was embarking on a typing course. Her brothers Sven and Erik, who had something to do with the sea, were thought to be somewhere about the house—possibly hiding under my bed. Fru Hansen also had a little sister called Aase, and it soon transpired that Aase was, in fact, me.

I didn't mind being Aase. In a way, I was touched that Fru Hansen considered me up to the part. It made no difference to her that I was English, or that we were decades apart in age. We spent hours poring over the television listings in *Se og Hør* (a popular weekly), where, Fru Hansen believed, we would eventually find the phone numbers of our dead relatives.

I only got truly fed up with her when she tried to climb into bed with me, or stole my dressing gown.

"Look here, Fru Hansen, this is my dressing gown and that one's yours, OK? The reason they look so similar is that they belong to the hospital. You are in hospital, Fru Hansen," I rubbed it in unkindly.

"Am I?" she asked, gazing about her in bewilderment. Then her face cleared: "What about you, Aase?" she asked shrewdly. "Are you in hospital too?"

We don't talk much in the wards about who we are or what we've done in life. Now and then, when I sense that my Danish sounds particularly idiotic, I feel tempted to tell my wardmates, and the doctors and nurses, that I am really a woman of education and accomplishment. I speak Russian; I play Beethoven sonatas; my name has appeared in print. Under the circumstances, though, none of this seems to count for much. Instead we talk about the weather and what's for lunch; about our lungs and hearts and legs; about our children, grandchildren, great grandchildren. Sometimes we watch the news on television, but—whether from indifference, or for fear of offending one another—we don't discuss out loud what we think of George W Bush or lesbian motherhood.

It was a different matter, though, when we heard that Queen Margrethe was in hospital having an operation. Suddenly the ward became quite animated. We speculated on how many rooms the Queen and her retinue occupied, and whether Her Majesty was allowed to smoke in bed. Obviously she did not wear her tiara in hospital, but did she have to wear an official nightie? Although we did not say so, I think we were all imagining the Queen's naked back and the surgeon's knife going in. There was nothing disrespectful in these musings. On the contrary, we felt great empathy for the Queen in her pain—all the more so because she lay revealed as a "poor, bare, forked animal" just like us.

There is something restful—even self-affirming—about discarding one's customary identity for a while. Perhaps the Queen also feels this. To be in hospital is akin to attending a jury or going to church. You are there in your capacity as a human being, or as one of God's creatures and, in the right mood, you can feel a special kind of pride in this.

"On a scale of one to ten, how would you rate your pain?" When I was first asked this question, I tried conscientiously to measure my suffering against that of torture victims, or people with legs blown off by mines and in these terms I thought it ranked very low: one, perhaps two at the most. Later, I understood a more subjective measure was intended: how close was I to screaming? I upped my score to seven, even eight, and thus entered the morphine zone.

Morphine acts upon one somewhat like love: it induces a paradisical sense of benevolence. I looked at the doctor—how clever and handsome. The nurse—a saint. As for the curtains in the window, they called up a special tenderness. What thoughtful person had chosen this gentle fabric with its cheering, sunny stripes? After the morphine wore off, the fate of the curtains began to trouble me. What would happen to them when they closed the hospital? All these things about me—the trolley with the vases, the candle holders on the windowsills—were the result of thought and investment. Were they going to throw them all away?

We patients keep farmers' hours. They wake us soon after 5am, as if to milk the cows. Breakfast follows two hours later. The *stuegang*—the doctors' rounds, focal point of the day—takes place mid-morning, by which time the patients should be washed, combed and in their beds. Lunch is at 11.30am; later, we're supposed to take a nap. Around 2pm, the trolley arrives with coffee and cake, and we get the first round of visitors. Dinner is at 5.30pm; then the evening guests, a little snack around 8pm, and lights out at 10pm.

It is, in many ways, an ideal regime. There is plenty of time to read, listen to music, or just look at the sky. At the same time, there is always, even at night, a sense of help at hand, a distant bustle, the chink of things on trolleys. You learn to recognise the different sounds approaching: the women in green with their needles, straps and tubes; the cleaning ladies with feather dusters; the welcome rattle of the telephone on wheels. And then come the unexpected friends, people you haven't seen for months. No matter how stressed their own lives may be, they shower attention on you, they bring chocolates and flowers, and you do not have to cook for them.

Meanwhile, you are being cooked for. To women patients especially, this means a great deal. Some patients have only the vaguest notion of what their treatment consists of; what gives them the sense of being cared for is the nursing—the washing, the wheeling, and above all the food. The dishes are homely and consoling. We get vegetable soups, *skipperlabskovs* (skipper's stew), *risengrød* (rice pudding), *havregrød* (oatmeal) and of course *øllebrød*.

In the slow death of the hospital, it is said that the kitchen will be the first organ to go. I am shocked by this news. I know how quickly, once the cooking has stopped, a house turns sour, loveless, dead.

One day I was taken down to the radiology department for a scan of my heart. I lay on my side on the examination couch, facing a computer screen and while the radiologist slid his cold instrument over me, leaving a trail of jelly round my breast, I watched my heart on the screen. There, lodged in its chambers, sat what looked like a small grey homunculus, a creature out of Gogol, obsessively rocking back and forth as if striking, over and over, the same one letter on his typewriter. Who was this ardent, faithful clerk, and what letter had he been practising these 46 years? The room he inhabited looked dingy and cobwebbed, full of strange, clinging fibres like seaweed on an old wreck, but I was amazed by the vigour and precision of his movement: boom—swish! boom—swish! boom—swish! he went. I felt privileged to have been offered this glimpse of my heart. If everyone could see the astonishing machinery inside them, might they begin to treat it more kindly, as they treat the engines of their boats or blades of their drills?

The regime here is liberal. The lady opposite me, who is suffering from pneumonia, alternates between sessions on the oxygen machine and visits to what I call the gas chamber—the sitting room for smokers. It operates as a public *memento mori*. Here sit the skeletal and obese, the slumped figures in wheelchairs, the shuffling spectres clutching their drips. Through the corridor windows it is hard to tell whether the patients inside are laughing uproariously at the television, or bent double from coughing. A notice enjoins us to keep the door closed so none of the smoke can escape.

Once, I overheard a doctor suggesting to my wardmate that she might try giving up. "It's my only comfort," she told him. They left it at that. There is a great solicitude in the way the nurses prepare patients for the gas chamber, propping a pillow behind their backs, and placing their coffee and pack of cigarettes neatly on the table of the wheelchair.

When my daughter comes to visit, she usually keeps her jacket on. I have noticed this in the other teenage visitors. They are still at the immortal stage of development, where it is inconceivable that they should ever run aground like us, or indeed belong to the same species. So they sit at the edge of the big family groups, examining their nails in strenuous denial.

Sometimes the grown-up sons look uncomfortable too, standing hunched at the end of their mothers' beds. It falls to the daughters-in-law to keep up the conversation. When the group is large—two or three generations seated round the bed on a Sunday afternoon—the talk may stray to inappropriate themes, like the *flæskesteg* (roast pork) that the family has just had for lunch. The patient, talked over, looks exhausted. But later on she enjoys regaling us with who was who, and how they are all related.

Especially touching are the withered old husbands, many as frail as the wives they have come to see. Most live nearby; it is hard to imagine them making the journey to Randers. Some bring little gifts—a magazine, tangerines—but don't know what to do with them; it has never been their lot to arrange things on tables, in cupboards. So they lay these offerings on the bedspread, as if on a grave; and then sit speechlessly holding their wives' hands.

The information that 30 nurses and assistants were quitting the hospital was on the local evening news. We heard it in the lull after dinner. None of us made any comment, but a peculiar silence ensued. Then there was a slow gathering of sounds. The old man in the ward next to ours, who grunted monotonously all day, seemed to be banging his head against a wall. I heard footsteps running far off, and something crashing to the floor. Nobody came our way, apart from a demented old lady who had lost her shoes.

I registered then that I had skipped one dose of penicillin today. Perhaps this was it. The staff were giving up. Surreptitiously they would put on their coats, turn off the lights, and softly lock the doors behind them. It would be up to us, the more mobile patients, to take charge. I stayed with this vision for an hour or two, while my wardmates fell into their customary snores. Then, just a little later than usual, came the rattle of the trolley down the corridor: tea, coffee, and cheese sandwiches for supper. "*Du forkæler os*" (you spoil us), I meant to say to the nurse, but it came out wrong. "*Du kvæler os*" (you strangle us), I said. She nodded and smiled as she always did.

I was discharged the next day. In the late morning, still wearing my hospital stigmata—the hole in my hand for the drip, the Aarhus Amt knickers—I went for a walk through the woods to the river that gives the town its name. It was a mild morning; men were fishing from the towpath. On the other side of the river was the main road, then the meadows stretching away. Behind me stood the stricken hospital, with its 400 employees, its 35,000 cases a year, its chapel, kitchen, files, systems, scanners, test tubes, curtains.

"I hope we won't be seeing you here again," said the nurse kindly when I shook her hand.

And I don't suppose they will.

Notes on contributors

Philip Ball is a science writer and consultant editor for *Nature*.

Vanora Bennett is an author living and working in London.

Paul Broks is a clinical neuropsychologist and the author of *Into the Silent Land*.

Bartle Bull has written about the middle east for a variety of publications. His next book, *The Tree of the Knowledge of Good and Evil*, is about Iraq.

Ian Buruma is a writer and professor at Bard College, New York.

Ben Cheever is a novelist and is writing a book to be called *Strides*.

Amy Chua is professor of law at Yale University and author of *World on Fire: How Exporting Free Market Democracy Breeds Ethnic Hatred and Global Instability*.

Jeremy Clarke is a columnist for the *Spectator*.

Matthew Collings is a writer and artist.

Philip Collins is currently chief speechwriter to Tony Blair.

Robert Cooper is a European diplomat working for Javier Solana. At the time of original publication he was a foreign affairs adviser to Tony Blair.

Mark Cousins is the author of *The Story of Film*. His last documentary was *Cinema Iran* for Channel 4.

Michael Elliott is the editor of *Time International*, based in Hong Kong and London.

Julian Evans has reported from Europe on literary subjects for more than a decade. He is writing a biography of Norman Lewis.

James Fergusson is a former foreign correspondent and author of *Kandahar Cockney*.

Carlo Gébler is a writer and occasional director of documentary films. His recent books include *The Siege of Derry: A history* and *The Bull Raid*.

Ernest Gellner was a theorist of modernity and nationalism, a philosopher and a social anthropologist. He died in 1995.

David Herman writes a regular column on television for *Prospect*, and has produced a number of programmes over the last two decades, including BBC2's *The Late Show*.

Christopher Hitchens is a columnist for *Vanity Fair*, a visiting professor at the New School in New York, and author of *Thomas Jefferson: Author of America*.

Peter Hitchens is a columnist for the *Mail on Sunday* and author of *The Abolition of Britain*.

Richard Hoggart is a writer and academic, and author of *The Uses of Literacy*.

Pervez Hoodbhoy is professor of nuclear and high-energy physics at Quaid-e-Azam University, Islamabad, where he has taught for three decades.

Michael Ignatieff is professor of human rights policy, Kennedy School of Government, Harvard University.

Richard Jenkyns is professor of the classical tradition, University of Oxford, and fellow of Lady Margaret Hall.

John Keegan is a military historian. He has been defence editor of the *Telegraph* since 1986.

Dan Kuper is a writer who supplements his income by working for London Underground.

Sally Laird is a writer and translator from Russian and Danish, and author of *Voices of Russian Literature*.

Nicholas Lemann is dean of the Graduate School of Journalism at Columbia University, an author, and a staff writer for the *New Yorker*.

Anatol Lieven is a senior research fellow at the New America Foundation in Washington DC. His latest book is *America Right or Wrong: An Anatomy of American Nationalism*.

Michael Lind is senior fellow at the New America Foundation in Washington DC and the author of *What Lincoln Believed*.

John Lloyd edits the *FT Magazine* and was a correspondent in eastern Europe and Russia for the *Financial Times*.

Kenan Malik is a writer and broadcaster. He is the author of *The Meaning of Race* and *Man, Beast and Zombie*.

Sarfraz Manzoor is a writer, broadcaster and documentary filmmaker.

Andrew Marr is a political journalist, and the BBC's former political editor.

Rowan Moore is director of the Architecture Foundation.

Andrew Moravcsik is professor of politics and director of the European Union programme at Princeton University. His most recent book is *Europe without Illusions*.

Geoff Mulgan is director of the Young Foundation. He was previously head of policy and director of the strategy unit in the prime minister's office.

John O'Sullivan is editor at large of the *National Review*.

Ruth Padel is a poet and writer and chair of the UK Poetry Society. Her most recent book is *Tigers in Red Weather*.

Melanie Phillips is a columnist for the *Daily Mail*. She also writes a regular diary at www.melaniephillips.com.

Martin Rees is professor of cosmology and astrophysics, and master of Trinity College at Cambridge University. His books include *Our Cosmic Habitat* and *Our Final Century*.

Jens Reich was co-founder of the citizens' movement that in 1989 contributed to the collapse of East German communism. He is now emeritus professor at Berlin's Humboldt University.

Matt Ridley is the author of *Genome* and *Nature via Nurture*.

Malise Ruthven has lectured widely on religion and politics. His books include *A Fury for God: the Islamist attack on America*, *Islam in the World*, and *Fundamentalism: the search for meaning*.

Brian Sewell is an art critic and columnist.

Peter Singer is professor of bioethics at Princeton University. His books include *Animal Liberation, Practical Ethics* and *One World*.

Robert Skidelsky is professor of political economy at the University of Warwick and chairman of the Centre for Global Studies. His books include *The World after Communism* and a biography of John Maynard Keynes.

Wendell Steavenson is a writer. She is the author of *Stories I Stole*.

Polly Toynbee is a social and political commentator at the *Guardian*.

Geoffrey Wheatcroft is a journalist and author. His most recent book is *The Strange Death of Tory England*.

Alison Wolf is professor of public sector management at King's College London and author of *Does Education Matter? Myths about Education and Economic Growth*.

Martin Wolf is associate editor and chief economics commentator at the *Financial Times*.